# EVERY MARINE

## 1968 Vietnam
## A Battle for Go Noi Island

By Robert A. Simonsen

Illustrations and Maps by Doug Anderson

HERITAGE BOOKS
2008

# HERITAGE BOOKS
*AN IMPRINT OF HERITAGE BOOKS, INC.*

**Books, CDs, and more—Worldwide**

For our listing of thousands of titles see our website at
www.HeritageBooks.com

Published 2008 by
HERITAGE BOOKS, INC.
Publishing Division
100 Railroad Ave. #104
Westminster, Maryland 21157

Copyright © 2004 Robert A. Simonsen

All rights reserved. No part of this book may be reproduced or transmitted in any form or by any means, electronic or mechanical, including photocopying, recording or by any information storage and retrieval system without written permission from the author, except for the inclusion of brief quotations in a review.

International Standard Book Numbers
Paperbound: 978-0-7884-3351-1
Clothbound: 978-0-7884-7652-5

There is an old Marine Corps saying, that
*'EVERY MARINE is a basic rifleman.'*
This is their story.

**DEDICATION**

This book is dedicated to <u>EVERY</u> <u>MARINE</u> who has ever worn the uniform and to combat veterans of all wars, especially to those who paid the ultimate sacrifice.

And, to the memory of Pat Jones, a special supporter of Vietnam veterans and Marines.

## TABLE OF CONTENTS

PAGE

LIST OF ILLUSTRATIONS AND MAPS . . . . . . . . . . vii

FOREWORD . . . . . . . . . . . . . . . . . . . . . . . . . . . xi

I.  GENESIS

    1. Beginning history . . . . . . . . . . . . . . . . . . 3

    2. Orders for Vietnam . . . . . . . . . . . . . . . . . 7

    3. Going over . . . . . . . . . . . . . . . . . . . . . . 35

    4. Arriving in the Nam . . . . . . . . . . . . . . . 51

    5. Patrolling the rocket belt . . . . . . . . . . . . 61

II. ARMAGEDDON

    1. Go Noi Island 1968 . . . . . . . . . . . . . . . 133

    2. Operation Allen Brook (phase I) . . . . . . 137

    3. Operation Allen Brook (phase II) . . . . . 349

    4. Overview of Operation Allen Brook . . . 379

III. EXODUS

    1. Leaving 3/27 . . . . . . . . . . . . . . . . . . . . 387

    2. Return to the USA . . . . . . . . . . . . . . . . 397

## TABLE OF CONTENTS (cont'd)

    3.    Concluding history . . . . . . . . . . . . . . 407

APPENDIX

    Honor Roll . . . . . . . . . . . . . . . . . . . . . . . . . 413

    Roll Call - 2003 . . . . . . . . . . . . . . . . . . . . . . 417

    Unit and Individual Citations . . . . . . . . . . . . . 421

    Abbreviations . . . . . . . . . . . . . . . . . . . . . . . 461

    Sources . . . . . . . . . . . . . . . . . . . . . . . . . . . 467

    Name Index . . . . . . . . . . . . . . . . . . . . . . . . 471

Every Marine-vii

## LIST OF ILLUSTRATIONS AND MAPS

**Description**                                                           **Page**

★ Marine Units and Sizes in 1968. . . . . . . . . . . xiv

★ Forming Up, Moving Out-February 1968. . . . . . 6

★ From the U.S. to S.E. Asia-February 1968 . . . . . 36

★ 3rd Battalion, 27th Marines In Relation to the Indochina Theater-1968 . . . . . . . . . . . . . 52

★ Cau Ha, Home Base 3/27-February thru August 1968. . . . . . . . . . . . . . . . . . . . . . . . . 53

★ 3/27 Tactical Area of Responsibility . . . . . . . . . 65

★ "Sniper-One Shot, One Kill!" . . . . . . . . . . . . . . 71

★ Tu Cau Bridge Compound . . . . . . . . . . . . . . . 80

★ Leprosarium Colony . . . . . . . . . . . . . . . . . . . 82

★ Go Noi Island . . . . . . . . . . . . . . . . . . . . . . . 134

★ Go Noi Island, India Company Movements-13 to 17 May, 1968 . . . . . . . . . . . . . . . . . . . 142

★ "CPL Robert Simonsen, WIA." . . . . . . . . . . . . 161

★ "Lucky Helmet." . . . . . . . . . . . . . . . . . . . . . 164

★ NVA Ambush of India Company-17 May 1968   180

## List of Illustrations and Maps (continued)

- ★ "PFC Robert Burke, Medal of Honor." ...... 196
- ★ "Hot LZ." ........................... 205
- ★ Go Noi Island, 3/27 Movements-
  17 to 28 May 1968. ................... 219
- ★ "LT COL Tullis Woodham, Jr., Silver Star." .. 250
- ★ "CAPT Anderson, Heat Casualty." ......... 253
- ★ "Mute Testimony." .................... 256
- ★ "L/CPL Gary Much, Silver Star." .......... 260
- ★ Go Noi Island, 3/27 Movements into Le Bac (1)-
  24 May, 1968. ....................... 280
- ★ Battle of Le Bac (1), Company M Box Ambush-
  1300 hours, 24 May, 1968. .............. 297
- ★ "CPL Richard Buchanan-Navy Cross." ....... 299
- ★ Battle of Le Bac (1), Company M Box Ambush-
  1300 thru 1630, 24 May, 1968 ........... 301
- ★ "Grenade!" .......................... 321
- ★ Company I Engagement Pulling Off
  Go Noi Island-28 May, 1968. ............ 333
- ★ Go Noi Island, 3/27 Activities-16-31 July, 1968. 351

List of Illustrations and Maps (continued)

★    Unit and Individual Citations. . . . . . . . . . . . . 421

Note: All illustrations and maps were prepared by Doug Anderson based on information, sketches and hand drawn maps provided by the following former 3/27 Marines: Bill Jung, Bob Simonsen, Richard Buchanan, Dale Camp, Allen Ciezki, Garland Sisco, Ray Fisher, Bill Prish and Steve Easton.

## FOREWORD

To Marines stationed in the southern I Corps region of Vietnam in the late 1960's, news of an upcoming operation in the Go Noi Island sector always brought fear and anticipation of an upcoming battle. Everyone knew that the enemy was sure to be met and that it would be on his own turf.

The 'Island' was located 15 miles south of Da Nang, five miles east of An Hoa, and just north of the Que Son Mountains which the North Vietnamese Army (NVA) used as an infiltration route from Laos. Although not truly an island, its 7,000 acres were surrounded by rivers, streams, and roads. It had traditionally served as a staging area for NVA units building up for future attacks against the Da Nang area. In May of 1968, three VC battalions and a fresh, untested, NVA regiment just in from the North had found its way to the 'Island.'

In early May 1968, the Marine Corps began Operation Allen Brook in the Go Noi Island sector, under control of the 7th Marines. By mid May, the operational control switched to the 27th Marines. The 27th Marines were much like the newly arrived NVA regiment. They had just arrived from the States in February in response to the Tet offensive. Raw Marines with little or no combat experience were mixed with just a handful of veteran NCO's and Officers with previous Vietnam tours under their belts. The 3rd Battalion (3/27) was the leading element of the Regiment. Nearly 3/4 of this battalion had non-infantry MOS's (military occupations.) These Marines were taken from every possible place at Camp Pendleton, California (cooks, engineers, truck drivers, mechanics, etc.) to form up the battalion in a rapid response to the Tet build-up. The author was one of these Marines, himself taken from the engineering ranks where he had served as a construction surveyor. These Marines would soon prove the old Marine Corps saying that, '<u>EVERY MARINE</u> is a basic rifleman.'

In two short weeks in May, 3/27 earned two Meritorious Unit Citations, a Presidential Unit Citation, and its members received a Medal of Honor, two Navy Crosses, 13 Silver Stars, and numerous Bronze Stars for bravery. They suffered 72 deaths and countless wounds while inflicting great losses upon the enemy.

The battles for Go Noi Island would be fought time and time again by many units. Operation Allen Brook would be followed by operations Meade River (December 1968) and Pipestone Canyon (May 1969.) Operation Allen Brook was representative of all of these battles and serves as a tribute to all Vietnam Marines.

The book takes the reader from 3/27's formation at Camp Pendleton to the battlefields of Vietnam where they slowly honed their war skills before joining the battle on Go Noi Island. It is told in a oral history format. Events and feelings are described by the individual Marines who fought their war in their own words. The use of * * * separates incidents and locations to minimize reader confusion.

Marines, who joined up in the years of 1966 to 1970, knew fairly well that they were going to war in Vietnam. The reasons may have varied but these young men were, for the most part, ready for the ultimate experience of their lives.

Receiving input from several non-military readers on an initial draft, it was determined that their most common problem was an inability to distinguish and understand the different military units and sizes. Therefore information is provided up front which hopefully will lend itself to a better understanding and easier reading. Use it as a quick reference. The appendix also contains a glossary of abbreviated terms and other useful information. Feel free to glance over it prior to your reading.

In 1968, a Marine Corps infantry battalion consisted of approximately 1100 men. It was made up of four letter rifle companies (225 Marines each) and a Headquarters and Services Company, which included staff and support personnel. The Marine Corps has undergone some organizational revisions since 1968 and it should be noted that this description represents the Vietnam era Marine infantry battalion.

Each infantry regiment in the Marine Corps had three infantry battalions. The 1st infantry battalion of a regiment had companies designated as companies A,B,C and D. The 2nd battalion had companies E,F,G and H and the 3rd battalion had companies I,K,L and M.

Therefore one would find a company 'I' in the 3rd Battalion 5th Marine Regiment, the 3rd Battalion 7th Marine Regiment and the 3rd Battalion 27th Marine Regiment.

The organizational term 'regiment' in the Marine Corps is generally replaced with the term 'Marines' such as the 3rd Battalion 27th Marines.

The chart at the end of this section breaks down one battalion (3/27) in the 27th Marines and should help the reader to better understand its structure and size. It should be noted that the numbers on the chart are the designated table of organization (T/O) strengths. In reality, there were usually fewer men. For instance, a typical rifle squad would probably have 8 and not 15 Marines. This was due to the constant attrition of men caused by wounds, illness, transfers, R and R (Rest and Recreation vacations) and normal rotations back to the United States, coupled with an insufficient influx of new men.

# Marine Units and Sizes in 1968

## Regiment
(Known as "Marines")
Consists of three Battalions

### Battalion- 1,100 men
Four Letter Rifle Companies plus a
Headquarters & Services Company

### Company- 225 men
Three Letter Rifle Platoons
and a Weapons Platoon,
plus a Headquarters Section.

### Rifle Platoon- 45 men
Three Squads- (14 men each)

### Squad- 14 men
Three Fire Teams

## 27th Marines
*Each Battalion - 5 Companies*

**1st Battalion**
**1/27**
**(1,100 men)**
Co A
Co B
Co C
Co D
H & S Co

**3rd Battalion**
**3/27**
**(1,100 men)**

| Co I | Co K | Co L | Co M | H & S Co |
|---|---|---|---|---|
| India Company (225 men) | Kilo Company (225 men) | Lima Company (225 men) | Mike Company (225 men) | (200 men) |

### Each Company - 4 Platoons plus a HQ Section

| Rifle Platoon (45 men) | Rifle Platoon (45 men) | Rifle Platoon (45 men) | Weapons Platoon | HQ Section |
|---|---|---|---|---|

**Each Platoon consisted of**
- Platoon C.O.
- Platoon Sgt.
- "Right Guide"
- 3 Rifle Squads

*From H&S Co:*
- Radio Man
- 2 corpsmen

**2nd Battalion**
**2/27**
**(1,100 men)**
Co E
Co F
Co G
Co H
H & S Co

**Rifle Squad**
- Squad Leader
- Grenadier
- Three Fire Teams - each consisted of one automatic rifleman and up to 3 riflemen)

**Weapons Platoon**
- Machine Gun Teams
- Rocket Teams
- 60 mm mortars

The writing of this history has been a catharsis for 35 plus years of internal dwelling on the author's own personal ultimate lifetime experience.

Semper Fidelis,
Robert Simonsen
Former Sergeant (E-5)
Co I, 3/27

## ACKNOWLEDGMENTS

Special thanks goes to all who contributed information for this book, especially to those who went out of their way to provide in depth input and editing. You know who you are and I greatly appreciate your efforts. Singling out specific individuals is hard to do since scores of Marines spent their valuable time in helping to put this book together, but I cannot ignore the extra contributions of Andrew Boyko, Bill Jung, Rich Buchanan, and Colonel Tullis Woodham Jr. (Retired.)

The Marine Corps Historical Center also provided a great deal of important information for which I will forever be thankful.

Also, I would like to thank my wife and son who supported me through this writing project, my typists: Sheri Torelli, Cindy Frasco, and Ginny Wright, and finally, Doug Anderson who provided the graphics for the sketches and maps.

# PART I
# GENESIS

# 1. BEGINNING HISTORY

The 27th Marine Regiment was born out of World War II on 10 January 1944. It was formed at Camp Pendleton, California as part of the 5th Marine Division. In August of that year, the Regiment relocated to Camp Tarawa in the territory of Hawaii.

In January 1945, the 27th Marines received its first combat assignment; the invasion of Iwo Jima. The seizure of Iwo Jima was considered vital to the American war effort as it was approximately 750 miles from the Japanese Islands. American authorities felt that the island would provide the United States with an excellent base from which fighter planes could protect and escort B-29's on their raids.

The invasion of Iwo Jima began on 19 February 1945. The 27th Marines stormed ashore at 0900 in its designated area of Beaches Red 1 and Red 2. The Regiment was initially assigned the mission of helping to cut off and isolate Mount Suribachi from the rest of the island. As the Marines pushed inland, resistance by the Japanese became more determined. Once Mount Suribachi was isolated, the Regiment was ordered to move north to join with other units in continuing the attack on the main enemy defenses.

Rugged terrain, heavy enemy fire and well placed mines all combined at times to hold the attacking Marines to a standstill. They repeatedly met the Japanese in hard close combat.

On 16 March, Iwo Jima was declared secure, although some resistance continued for about another two months. The severity of the fighting left 566 killed and 1703 wounded in the 27th Marines alone. Four Marines from the Regiment earned the Medal of Honor (the Nation's highest award for valor.)

In April 1945, the 27th Marines again found itself back at Camp Tarawa where it started to reform and prepare for the invasion of Japan.

The capitulation of the Japanese canceled the plans for

the invasion and on 16 September, the Regiment sailed for Japan and occupation duty. Returning to the United States on 20 December, the 27th Marines was deactivated at Camp Pendleton on 10 January 1946.

Due to the intensification of the American effort in the Vietnam war, the 27th Marines was again activated at Camp Pendleton on 1 June 1966. The Regiment embarked on a training program that was oriented towards operations in Vietnam. The primary goal was to bring the Regiment up to a high state of combat readiness. Not until the end of 1967, however, was this end accomplished. Personnel shortages and a high turnover of officers and men plagued the Regiment from its reactivation date.

On 10 November 1966, 3/27 was reactivated at Camp Pendleton's Camp Margarita. The Battalion commenced an extensive combat training cycle, and participated in several training operations including Operations Alligator Hide (May 1967) and Blue Lotus (August/November 1967.)

During 1967, 3/27 experienced a continuous fluctuation of personnel. Throughout the year, the unit continued to receive equipment and progressed its training to form a combat ready Battalion. On 5 January 1968, Lt Col Tullis J. Woodham, Jr. assumed command of 3/27. Colonel Adolph G. Schwenk took over as the Regimental Commanding Officer (CO) on 23 January 1968.

**LT COL TULLIS WOODHAM, JR. - 3/27 BATTALION CO: When I reported in to the 5th Marine Division, I was ordered to San Mateo to take a battalion in the 28th Marines. Unfortunately my home was in Vista which was about as far away as you could get from San Mateo and a long drive back and forth daily. Lt Col Pierre Reisner, the Division G-1, suggested I take the position as assistant G-1 of the Division which could lead to a probable later assignment to an infantry regiment. I**

did, and six months later when 3/27 became available, I assumed its command at Camp Margarita.

# Forming Up - Moving Out - February, 1968

## 2. ORDERS FOR VIETNAM

The now infamous Tet Offensive, beginning on 30 January, 1968, resulted in attacks throughout the entire South Vietnam Republic. Militarily speaking, the United States forces, although caught off guard, were able to defeat the enemy at all places of engagements. President Lyndon Johnson, however, was especially concerned about the siege that was going on at Khe Sanh and the lengthy battle for the City of Hue, both in the northern I Corps. He started giving signals through General Earle G. Wheeler, the Chairman for the Joint Chiefs of Staff, that additional troops might be made available for deployment if they were asked for.

General William Westmoreland, the Commander of U.S. forces in Vietnam, was slightly puzzled. From the very beginning of the siege of Khe Sanh and through the initial days of the Tet Offensive, he had repeatedly reassured Washington that the situation was well in hand and that troops were not immediately needed. Westmoreland, along with the Joint Chiefs, now sensed an opportunity to get more men and perhaps the removal of constraints on military operations. At first, Westmoreland laid out a request for long range troop requirements for the upcoming year. However, this initial request didn't seem to have the urgency that Washington wanted, so on 12 February, 1968, he sent another request. This time he described both a great opportunity and heightened risk in asking for 525,000 troops including an emergency augmentation of 10,500 troops immediately. This request was approved. The 27th Marine Regiment and a brigade of the 82nd Airborne Division were selected for this emergency action.

**LT COL TULLIS WOODHAM, JR. -3/27 BATTALION CO: I was home sick that Monday with the flu. Col Schwenk (Col Adolph Schwenk - 27th Regimental Commanding Officer) called to see if he could come over that night. You don't turn down a Regimental CO, so I**

changed out of my pajamas and was ready when he arrived. He got quickly to the point; we had received orders for an immediate deployment to Vietnam. I had a "miraculous" recovery and was able to report to work the next morning.

One of the many things that made this Battalion rather different was that a majority of our Staff NCOs (Non Commissioned Officers) and our Officers had already served in Vietnam, many within the last year. This experience later on was to serve our Battalion in Vietnam immeasurably.

We had superb Officers and NCOs. Captain Ernie Fitzgerald, our S-3, would later be a Major and our Executive Officer (XO.) He would not receive near enough credit for the great job he did on Allen Brook. The Company Commanders were great. Captains Miles Keefe and Blake Thomas with Mike, John Ernest over in Lima, and of course Captains James Pinnick and Tom Ralph in India. Julian Parrish was our Adjutant who later took over India when it was necessary. Billy C. Steed, who retired as a Colonel, was in just about every company we had. Jim Kent in Kilo was outstanding. Sgt Major Snyder, Gunny Martin who was in the S-3 shop, Gunny Delacerna and Lt Roy Casteel with the 81's were super. You cannot believe the talent and wealth of experience that these Marines gave to our Battalion.

**SGT GARY HARLAN - Co I:** The Marine Corps had a regulation that enlisted men were entitled to one year Stateside before being subject to orders back to the Nam. So as to minimize my chances of returning, I extended my overseas duty 6 months, volunteering for MP (Military Police) duty in Iwakuni, Japan. My thinking was that when I finally got home in May 1967, I wouldn't be eligible for the Nam until May of 1968, and by then I would only have 4 months remaining in my enlistment, and surely, even the Crotch (slang for Marine Corps) wouldn't send me over with a lousy 4 months to go, would they?

I never gave them a chance to. Three months before that deadline, following the Tet Offensive, 3/27 was mobilized for the Nam. A list was posted by the company clerk, with two columns. One side was labeled DEPLOYABLE the other NON-DEPLOYABLE. Like most of the corporals in the platoon, I was a non-deployable. But Leroy and Dawson weren't, and neither was Sgt Haugen or Sgt Lee. They were being sent back to the Nam.

Had I not become so tight with those guys, there never would have been a choice. But despite the fact that I had only been with them 5 months, they were like brothers. Leroy and his wife had just had their first baby in December, and we were all there to meet his father when he came down. We were like a family. Haugen had loaned me his VW to visit a girl in San Diego, and then there was Sgt Lee. We had argued every chance we got; about the war, about religion, about anything. Leroy and I were the perfect pair for him; I'd piss him off while Leroy made him laugh.

I didn't feel like signing a waiver, waiving my right to one year Stateside, but I sure as hell didn't want to abandon Sgt Lee, Leroy, Tom Haugen, and Steve Dawson. So I told the company clerk that should my name appear in the deployable column, I wouldn't say a word. He saw to it that I became a deployable.

A couple of days before we flew over to the combat zone, we picked up our platoon commander, Marcus Fieblekorn, straight from OCS (Officer Candidate School.) The Lieutenant demonstrated his intelligence right off the bat by informing us that until he knew the ropes, he would rely heavily on the experience of the NCOs who had been there.

We picked up the rest of the platoon as well; mostly PFCs with MOSs (Military Occupation Specialties) unrelated to the infantry such as cook, water pump engineer, motor t, and the like. It was pretty grim at first, but I will be the first to admit that those guys with off-the-wall MOSs ended up making fine grunts.

Sergeant Gary Harlan wasn't the only 3/27 Marine to sign a waiver to go back to Vietnam. These special men would not take the easy way out. They simply could not leave their friends. It's hard to explain Marine camaraderie, but that's what makes the Corps so special.

**CPL MARLIN 'JACK' JACKSON-FORWARD OBSERVER (FO) FOR 105 FOX BATTERY ASSIGNED TO Co M:** I had been assigned to Mike Company for a couple of months and had made several friends, both in the artillery and infantry. I was in Vietnam in 1966-67, but my tour was shortened due to a death in the family and other family problems. I was sent home on a hardship leave. When 3/27 received orders for Nam, I assumed I would be going with them but my name did not appear on the deployable list. I asked the 'old man' why I wasn't included and he said that my record files stated that I wasn't to be sent overseas because I was still considered a hardship case. He said that the only way for me to ship out with the company was to sign a waiver. I didn't know what to do so I talked it over with my parents and my dad told me to do what I thought was best. I couldn't let my friends leave without me, so I signed the waiver.

**SGT GEORGE HIGHT - H & S Co:** Sgt Jerry Kline was a hell of a friend. He signed a waiver to go with us when he had only been back for just 5 months.

**SGT HIAHWAHNAH RICHARD NEAL - Co L:** We were out in the field on a Tuesday and we were brought back into Camp Margarita. I thought they were bringing us in just for breakfast because we left our 782 gear in the field. The First Sergeant had orders for many of the guys and asked the rest of us to waive our overseas control date and return to Nam. I did and left my 18 year old wife and son.

**SGT RICHARD PELKY - Co M:** I was with Mike Company when orders for Nam came. Initially, I was told to go to the 28th Marines because my overseas control date made me undeployable. I told the Executive Officer (XO) that I wanted to go with my men, so he had me sign a waiver to stay with 3/27.

**SGT JON PAHL - H & S Co:** I was in the 81mm Mortar Platoon with 3/27 after I returned from Nam with 2/4. One night, after quite a few beers at the 'slop chute,' the officer of the day came through the barracks and woke everyone up. We all thought it was probably a drug check or something, but we soon learned that we were Vietnam bound.
Non-combat Marines started flooding in from all over. There were cooks, office pogues and truck drivers. We had a whole battalion filled with these replacements. At first, I couldn't believe it. I mean, what could I do? I just had to go along with this one. I signed a return waiver and jumped on board.
I soon became impressed with the 'can do' attitude and the fact that so many good and qualified NCO's were going back like I was.

Staff Sgt Frank Cortez (Co I / Co M) had already been to Nam twice, but as soon as he got back in December, 1967, he started trying to get back again. Headquarters Marine Corps ignored his requests and his CO sent him to the battalion's 'shrink,' who thought wanting to go back into combat was a death wish.

**STAFF SGT FRANK CORTEZ - Co I:** On the 15th of February while I was having breakfast at the 15 Area Staff Club, my roomie who worked nights at the Communication Center, sat down to have breakfast with me. He asked if I had heard that a regiment was being put together down in 33 Area for immediate deployment to Vietnam. I am sure he understands that I didn't mean to be rude by not finishing breakfast with him. I did say thanks as I shook his hand and ran out the door.

**CPL RAUL FONSECA - Co I:** I was a grunt with the 28th Marines stationed at San Mateo, Camp Pendleton. I was prepared for Nam, knowing that my orders could come at any time. When I joined up with the 27th Marines, the situation was mass confusion at first. We were constantly told to go from one place to another. No one seemed to know what was going on. Eventually, I was assigned to India and things settled down.

**CAPT E. MILES KEEFE, JR. - Co M CO:** I arrived at Camp Pendleton after spending 2 years in Guantanamo Bay, Cuba. After getting orders for 3/27, I was assigned to Mike Company as the Commanding Officer. I was given five boot 2nd Lieutenants for platoon commanders. I think I only had three or four Marines who had infantry experience. The entire situation was scary.

**CPL BILL BACH - Co K:** I had returned from my first tour in Nam in October 1966 and was assigned as a rifle instructor with the Range Platoon at Camp Pendleton. I came to work one morning and the First Sergeant told me I was going over again with 3/27. I was in shock. I definitely did not want to go back to Nam.

    1ST LT BILLY C. STEED - H & S Co: I was a First Lieutenant and had received orders to go back to Vietnam for my second tour. I had been assigned as a CO of a transplacement company at Camp Pendleton in January 1968. One morning, I'm not quite sure of the date, I received a call from the training adjutant that all infantry officers were supposed to report to the 27th Marine Regiment, which was headquartered in Camp Margarita on Camp Pendleton.

    We had heard on the radio that President Johnson wanted to send another Marine regiment and I think an airborne brigade or something to Vietnam. When I received the call from the adjutant, it was about 7 in the morning and I immediately went back to headquarters, which was about 20 miles away. He just said I was one of the ones picked to be assigned to the 27th Marines. I wasn't really surprised, because I knew that they were going to need infantry officers and just build a regiment from scratch.

    I made it back to headquarters about 9 o'clock and got orders and went out to Camp Margarita, which was about four or five miles away. I reported in to the Regimental XO and he said, I'm going to assign you to 2/27 and they're leaving in two hours. I said, well, I could leave in two hours, but some of my gear is still down in San Diego and I'll have to call my wife and tell her to bring the gear up. So he said, well, in that case I'll assign you to 3/27, who were going to leave about six hours down the road.

**L/CPL LONNIE MILLER - Co K:** I was married on 3 February and returned to Camp Pendleton around 8 February. I spent my last dime on an apartment in Oceanside. I was totally broke! One week later, they had a recall and off to Nam we went! I felt I was dipped in shit.

**LT COL TULLIS WOODHAM, JR. - 3/27 BATTALION CO:** Once 3/27 was ordered to Vietnam, about 800 Marines who were not eligible to return to Nam were transferred out of the Battalion and nearly 950 or so were ordered in to bring the Battalion up to strength. 2/27 had priority in the Division and received most of the infantry MOSs. When our turn came, there was not many left so we were saddled with what people thought was a problem. Well, the Marine Corps has always had the slogan 'Every Marine is a rifleman.' I guess this is what started the 'cooks, bakers and candlestick makers' situation that we found ourselves in. We were forced to take Marines from the engineers, tanks, artillery, communications, cooks and you name it. And so, they filled out our Battalion.

First Lt James Kent (Co K) had returned from a first tour in Vietnam in September, 1966. He was assigned the task of organizing an NCO Leadership School for the 5th Division. Kent geared the school for all military specialties, but stressed the importance of being a basic infantryman. Most of the emphasis for the Corporal's two week school was put on small unit leader's reactions to leadership problems. As the 27th Marines were being formed with Marines with various MOSs from all over the 5th Marine Division, Kent was able to observe the practical results of the work he put into the school.

**1ST LT JAMES KENT - Co K:** That's how we

knew the course was effective. Nearly all Corporals in the 3rd Battalion had attended the NCO school. When we moved out they assumed positions of leadership. They moved right in with no trouble at all.

      **CPL GARLAND SISCO, JR. - Co K:** I was stationed with Co A, 13th Engineering Battalion. At the time, I was in NCO Leadership school at Los Flores. I could not believe I was going back to Nam. After all, President Johnson said he would not escalate the war. I then remembered that I'd always been told we were a 'force in readiness' and 'every Marine was a basic rifleman first.' I knew it would be different this time and much more traumatic.

      **L/CPL STEVE EASTON - Co I:** My MOS was 1391, which was Bulk Fuel. I had been in the Corps for eighteen months and only had six more months to complete my two year enlistment. When I received orders for 3/27 and Nam, I was concerned that I would not get out when my remaining six months were up.

      **CPL BILL JUNG - Co K:** I had been stationed with the 13th Engineering Battalion for a year by that February 14th night. It wasn't too long before a clerk passed the word that volunteers were needed to go. Soon there was a group of us down at the company office turning in our names.

      Around 1930 of that night, three names were called. I was one and another was my old friend, Bob Simonsen. They only gave us two hours, so I had to hurry.

      We were to go up with all our gear, so I made up my pack and readied all my equipment. Then there was the task of packing seabags. One was to go with me. The other I gave to a girlfriend of a buddy, both who were out in the parking lot. She said she would ship it home to my folks. Her boyfriend would eventually go over too. They didn't know it then, but she could sense it. Women are funny about that.

While I packed, many members of the platoon helped me, gave advice, or threw jokes around. Ours was a tight knit bunch. When one went, all felt it. They were not only worried about me, but also about themselves. It seemed that more could go now, and this was right. Almost all of those watching were shipped to the 27th Marines the following morning. A good share of them would be wounded in the following weeks, some killed.

A friend in a nearby rack gave me a Catholic prayer for good luck. He said that it would protect me or warn me of death. The fellow was very sincere, so I gratefully accepted the piece of paper. I would carry it on me for the next few years.

He should have given one to his bunkie too. The bunkie was a big burly Marine. He would be dead in a few weeks. Serving with the 1st Battalion of the 27th Marines, a bullet would catch him between the eyes while his company fought near Hue City. I would learn this the following May.

With my gear all ready, I walked over to the armory to get a bayonet and some more rifle magazines. Another short walk took me to the aid station where I was given some shots.

It was two hours since I had started, and I was ready. With my rifle and orders in hand, I said goodbye to my friends. Throwing my pack and seabag in the back of a waiting truck with Simonsen and another Marine named Pokrzywa, I hopped in the cab and rode north through the night to Camp Margarita. Another part of my life was left behind.

Around 2300 that night we were dropped off by the

3rd Battalion's messhall. For it being so late, the camp was in utter confusion. People and vehicles were going every which way. We were told to report in at the messhall.

 We walked up to a desk in the huge room. Behind it was a burly Lieutenant named Kent. He looked at us, then our orders. I was assigned to Co K of the 3rd Battalion. My friend Simonsen went to Co I. After giving directions, Kent sent us on our way.

 Dragging my load through the confusion that was to go on for the next three days I found Co K's office and reported in. After waiting a few minutes, I was ushered into the back office. Sitting behind a desk was the same burly lieutenant that I had talked to in the messhall. Lieutenant Kent was our company XO, a former enlisted man who had come up through the ranks. A Korean veteran, he had a mean look. He wasn't the type that I'd cross up.

 The Lieutenant asked me what part of the company I wanted to be in. Since math was one of my better traits, I figured mortars would be just right for me. The Lieutenant had different ideas though. Since I was a corporal, he assigned me to the third squad of the third rifle platoon, saying that they needed NCO's there.

 With that information and a barracks number, I went off into the night. Being around midnight, the camp was quieter now as I walked among the rows of low concrete buildings. Mine finally stretched before me. I went into a bay with gear strewn and piled about. A good deal of snoring came from the darkness. Finding a rack, I locked up my rifle and threw my gear on the mattress. The day had done me in so I went to the head to shave and shower. A boot Marine told me the company was a good outfit, but very under-strengthened and being filled by men such as I. Every one was sleeping anywhere they wanted to for the night, so the morning should prove interesting.

Once the whiskers and dirt were off, I dressed again and crawled up on the bare mattress. The California night was a cool one, so I put on my field jacket and just lay there thinking.

My wish had come true. I was on my way to Indochina, but not as a surveyor. Instead I would go as a rifleman, which seemed much more glorious to me. In the months ahead I would learn differently. On that night this didn't enter my mind though. Instead I wondered what would lie ahead. It scared me. With that feeling, I went to sleep.

L/CPL DAVID STEFFENSEN - Co K: When we got the word, they secured us from leaving Camp Pendleton, told us to pack, but didn't really tell us exactly where we were going.

PFC DALE CAMP - Co I: I had just gotten out of Schools Battalion and was assigned to H&S Co, 5th Tanks, as an auto mechanic. It was a Friday, just after work when I got my orders for Nam. I had always wanted to be a grunt when I joined so I was excited to get my wish. When I arrived at Camp Margarita, it looked like something out of World War II. Marines were going in every direction. Lights were set up and trucks and forklifts were hauling equipment around. Marine families were sitting in cars talking and crying with their men. There was electricity in the air.

HM MIKE LUTZ - Co I Corpsman: The first time I can remember hearing much about Vietnam was in Social Studies class as Mr. Swider tried to teach us about current events. I'll always remember his saying, "And by next year some of you people in this room will be there." Some of us more studious students smiled and winked at each other while thinking "what in the hell is this asshole talking about?"

Somehow, I did join the Navy after high school and in boot camp I requested my MOS to be a draftsman which had been my major in school. When I received my orders, it was for hospital corps school in San Diego, California! After graduation, it was on the bus to Camp Pendleton for a month of Fleet Marine training. This month of almost 'boy scout' activity was soon to become an every day harsh reality.

Eventually, I ended up with India Company, 3/27 in January 1968. In mid February, the word came suddenly that we were going over and 'play time' was now over.

**SGT WES LOVE - Co K:** I was a combat engineer with the 13th Engineering Battalion when I got my orders. I only had four months left on a four year enlistment. When I got to Camp Margarita I finally had a chance to call home and tell everyone I was going to Vietnam. Mom yawned and said "OK, I'll see you when you get back, but did you have to call me at two o'clock in the morning?"

**L/CPL ROBERT SIMONSEN - Co I:** I was stationed with the 13th Engineers, assigned to a surveying and drafting section on that cool February 14 evening. I remember I had just returned to the barracks from chow when the Duty NCO came around shouting that the Division needed 3 immediate volunteers to join up with the 27th as riflemen. My first chance at Vietnam had finally arrived after a year and a half in the service. My body felt as if thousands of needles were being pressed against my skin. My pulse went up drastically. I could almost hear it thumping aloud even though the barracks was now filled with shouting and excitement. About twenty of us volunteered and we were told that our battalion Executive Officer would make his choice within an hour. Somehow I knew that I was going to be selected. I started to pack my sea bag and even managed to write my sister a letter during the wait. My body had now numbed. Several of my friends came over to me and told me how crazy I was for volunteering for combat duty. I knew they were probably right, but I just shut it out of my mind. I really had no choice. I had to go to Vietnam. I was obsessed with just the thought of it. It seemed like hours had passed but finally the Duty NCO read the three names off with mine included. I shouted for joy even as my mind had now become engrossed with doubting thoughts. Had I done right? Would I be killed or maimed? How would I react in a combat situation? Could I kill a man? There was no time to contemplate these questions. I had to finish packing and get several shots from the corpsman before taking off by jeep to go to Camp Margarita where 3/27 was forming up.

  The three of us were quickly assigned to a company. I was sent to India Company of the 3rd Battalion. It was past 2300 that night when I reported in to the proper barracks. I was told to pick out an empty rack and try to get some sleep. I stumbled through the darkness and after some difficulty, found an upper rack with no one on it.

  So, there I was, one minute a construction surveyor and the next minute a rifleman, only three days away from Vietnam. I couldn't sleep, but this I expected. I finally had time to think and evaluate what was happening to me. The first thing I did was to become scared. I started realizing what might happen to me and if I would freeze in a combat situation. My body broke out in a cold sweat, and I started to itch all over due to a rash reaction which was from the results of the six shots I had received earlier in the evening. I thought about the political aspect of why we were even in Vietnam. Although my views have since changed, at the time I honestly believed that the U.S. should be in Vietnam supporting the South Vietnamese and stopping the spread of communism throughout Southeast Asia. I felt as if I would be welcomed by the Vietnamese as a hero trying to help save their country. I also had ideas that when or if I returned to the U.S. that I would be treated with honor and respect for helping to stop the communistic threat of world domination. Little did I know then just how wrong I was to be.

I was not alone in my sleepless night. I heard other Marines tossing and turning in their racks. I wondered if their thoughts were similar to mine. The silence was broken by three very boisterous drunken Marines. They sung the Marine Corps Hymn several times and shouted to everyone just how brave they were going to be in Vietnam. Someone finally quieted them down.

I started to wonder just how my parents and sister would react when I told them I was going to Vietnam as an infantryman. I decided that I would call my sister and then have her tell my mother. I knew Mom would cry and I really didn't know how I could possibly calm her down. I heard someone vomiting in the bathroom. I thought it was probably one of the three drunks or perhaps just someone who had become so scared and confused that he had become sick. My stomach started to hurt and consequently I developed a case of diarrhea which would last the next two days.

Through all of this, believe it or not, I was still glad that I was Vietnam bound. I looked forward to the trip and to the new challenges and experiences which lay ahead. I just started dozing when the lights went on.

L/CPL CHUCK 'BIG SPENCE' SPENCER - Co L: I was an Automotive Mechanic stationed with Motor

Transport, 5th Service Battalion at Camp Pendleton. While I was on mess duty, I was told to report to our 1st Sergeant. He said "Pack your shit, you're going to Nam." I was very excited. I had wanted to go to Nam as a grunt ever since I joined the Corps.

L/CPL THOMAS FULEKY - Scout/Sniper, H & S Co: At the time of the call up of the 27th Marines, I was TAD from the HQ sniper platoon working with the range platoon. I was stationed at Camp Margarita so I didn't have far to go back to Regiment headquarters during our activation. While on TAD (temporary assigned duty) I was stationed with former brig rats, short timers, Marines who had just returned from Viet Nam and Marines who just got out of the hospital from their wounds. Having only nine months left in the crotch I fit right in with this group. I got back to the sniper platoon and started packing two seabags. One for storage and the other with items that I needed for Viet Nam.

I remember the blockade that was set up to keep everyone in place, and also the long lines trying to make phone calls. There were Marines trying to sell their cars and we had to get that dreaded GG shot in the ass. We also went to the mess hall to make out wills. Being 20 years old it all seemed like a bad dream.

L/CPL TIM 'MAD DOG' DAVIS - Co I: I was a truck driver with Motor Transport stationed at Camp Pendleton. We had just got back from a run on a Friday night and the CO told us all to meet in the barracks at 1800. We were all told we were going to Nam. We were shocked and numb. We had no choice, we were drafted to go to Vietnam. I felt very lonely.

PFC CLOVIS ACOSTA - Co L: I was a truck

driver with 13th Motor Transport at Camp Pendleton. I remember it was a Friday afternoon when MP's pulled my truck over and told me I had been transferred into the grunts! Friday, I was a truck driver. Saturday, I was a grunt being issued my rifle and '782' gear. Sunday, I was off to El Toro to fly out to Nam.

SGT ANDREW BOYKO - Co I: Early February, 1968, I was a Sergeant assigned to Supply Company, 5th Service Battalion, 5th Marine Division, at Camp Pendleton, California. I turned twenty-one years of age the month before and had already served one complete tour in Vietnam from August, 1965 to September, 1966. Having approximately 8 months left in the Marines, I was simply biding my time until my discharge date.

At the time, I lived off base in Oceanside, California and drove to work in a tan '62 Chevy Nova. I did, however, have a rack and wall locker assigned to me in a two-story wooden barrack. My bunk was on the second story at one end of the squad bay separated from the rest of the racks by wall lockers and a blanket which I used as a door. Non-commissioned officers were allowed this type of privacy while the rest of the enlisted men were assigned to an open squad bay with two-tier racks lined up and down both sides.

One morning I came into the barracks to change from civilian clothes into my uniform for work. When I walked into the squad bay, I observed that the doors were open on a number of the wall lockers. I became angry, thinking some of these dumb troops left their lockers open. Didn't they know how easily their belongings could get stolen! And then I would have the responsibility of filling out all of the stolen item reports for them. I walked down the squad bay slamming the doors shut as I went; suddenly I realized the lockers sounded hollow. I backed up, and when I opened the lockers, sure enough, they were empty. In an attempt to find out what was going on, I went downstairs to talk with the officer in the duty NCO office. He informed me that there was a big build up and my men were being sent to Vietnam.

I chuckled out loud and said, "Poor bastards. I've already been there, and I'm too short to make another full tour." With that, I went on to my job and at the end of the day, I got into my car and drove back to Oceanside.

About 4:00 AM the next morning, I was awakened by a telephone call from the duty NCO, who announced, "Sarge, you've got to come back to the base right now and start checking out. You're going to Vietnam!"

"What? You're full of shit!" I said. "I've already been to Vietnam. They told me you're allowed two years stateside duty after a tour in combat before being sent back over. I haven't been in the states two years yet! And besides, I'm too short to go back to Nam. I get out in 8 months." A tour of duty in Vietnam was 13 months.

But the duty NCO insisted, "I've got your orders right here on my desk. You're going!"

Because I was becoming upset, I decided to get dressed and drive in to the base to argue in person my position that I couldn't be expected to go back to Vietnam. I asked to see the officer in charge and tried to explain my dilemma that I had already served in Vietnam and my time was too short to go again. He informed me that this was a national emergency and I had no choice in the matter. My checkout papers were there. I had no alternative and began to check out. This meant getting my pay records, medical and dental records, turning in sheets and blankets and preparing to leave the outfit.

I returned to the barracks by about noon and was ordered to put my gear on the truck going to Camp Margarita, an outlying camp within Camp Pendleton.

"What gear?" I said, "I haven't even packed! All my gear is in Oceanside."

"Well Sarge, you'd better get home and get your gear and meet us at Camp Margarita."

I got on the phone and called my mother, who worked at Deutch Company in Oceanside and told her I was going back to Vietnam. Offering to meet me at home and help get my belongings together, she soon arrived at the house with tears in her eyes and helped me pack my things. I was literally just stuffing clothes and anything else I might need into my seabag. After kissing her goodbye, I drove to Camp Margarita.

Upon arrival, I was assigned to India Company, 3rd Battalion, 27th Marines.

A formation was called, and roll call taken to see if everyone was there. We were then placed on a one hour standby, which meant about every hour they would hold a formation to see if we were all there. No one was allowed to leave the base.

After dark, three friends and I managed to get hold of a bottle of Seagram 7. We sat in my car passing the bottle around thinking, "This may be our last night in the States. Even if we get caught, what can they do, shave our heads and send us to Vietnam?" Or, if they arrested us for drinking on base, we'd miss the trip to Nam altogether. The only thing that worried me was what to do with my car because I wasn't allowed to leave the base to drive it home, and I was afraid that if I left the car for 8 months or a year, it would either get stripped for parts, stolen, or impounded by the provost marshal for being abandoned. Anyway you looked at it, my car wouldn't be there if, or when, I got back.

We passed the bottle around and tried to come up with a solution to the problem. As I lifted the bottle for another sip, I caught sight of two girls parked in the car next to mine. Jokingly, I asked if they wanted to join us for a drink, and they said, "Yes."

So, we sat the girls between us, one in the front and the other in the back and continued passing the bottle around. The girl sitting next to me was Donna, and she came by with her friend to see her brother off. As we talked, I mentioned that I had no way to get my car home and, to my surprise, one of them volunteered to drive it off base for me. "Wow! This is great," I thought. I gave them the address to my mom's place and asked if they would deliver the car there for me, and they agreed. Finishing off the bottle, I gave them the keys and kissed them good-bye.

About an hour later, a few of my buddies started harassing me that I had been taken in and that the girls probably drove the car down to Mexico and were living it up on the money they made from selling it. My friends kept it up to the point that I called home just to see if they had delivered the car as they had promised. Sure enough, they were there having a nice talk with my Mom. What a relief that was!

The next morning we were put on 15 minute alert, which meant that every 15 minutes there would be a roll call to check that everyone was there. By about 10:00 AM, the girls came back, handed me a ten dollar bill and said it was from my Mom in case I needed anything before going overseas. I was so happy to see them that I kissed and hugged them both for delivering the car and bringing me the money. I was broke! Just about that time another formation was called. I told them we were having these little musters all morning.

"Now don't go away, I'll be back in a few minutes."

Then I ran off, through the barracks and onto the parade ground where the formation was held.

After roll call we were ordered to put our gear on

the trucks and board them. We were leaving! As the trucks roared off, I thought, "I didn't even get to say goodbye to the girls and now we're leaving. What will they think?"

**L/CPL ALLEN CIEZKI - Co I:** After reporting in from the 13th Motors where I was a truck mechanic, I was assigned to India Company. An office pogue at the company office, told me I was going to the 3rd Squad. I told him there was a mistake. I was a mechanic! He took my service record, stamped 0311 infantry on it and handed it back to me.

During the 96 hours after the departure notification on 13 February all personnel and essential equipment were prepared to be air lifted. The short notification did cause some considerable problems. Of the greatest magnitude was the transfer of 800 non-deployable and the joining of 950 deployable men. During this time all companies conducted extensive familiarization for both old and new personnel with all weapons organic to the Battalion.

**LT COL TULLIS WOODHAM, JR. - 3/27 BATTALION CO:** While 2/27 was receiving priority of equipment and men, and were mounting out a day or two ahead of us, I took the opportunity to go to the G3 at the Base. With the Division's blessing, we fired all of our crew served weapons around the clock. The Base made ranges available and Division supplied all the ammunition we needed for weapons familiarization. I felt it absolutely imperative that our people learned to use those weapons that they were going to shoot when they got over there.

**CPL BILL JUNG - Co K:** At reveille I woke to the sight of new faces and the feel of a new unit. In the following half year I would serve this unit and fight along side of my new comrades. At that time though, I had no idea of what lay ahead.

The camp was still one of confusion as men poured in from all the other Division units. Long lines of these replacements were outside the messhall. As I went by one, I noticed about a dozen of my friends from the 13th Engineers, the same ones who had said good-bye the night before. We were all in it now. Most were assigned to one of the two rifle battalions while others went to regimental headquarters. Many were assigned to my third Battalion.

One of these was my old friend 'Doc.' His real name was Devitt, but he was given the nickname because his father was a neurosurgeon. Doc was a rebel from Mississippi, and I a yank, but this was the only place we differed. Meeting each other at Fort Belvoir, Virginia, we became inseparable friends as we went through the surveying course together. Many a time we could be seen drunk in Washington D.C. Not only did we have a common background, we two even looked somewhat alike. NCOs were always getting us mixed up.

Both of us had been sent to the 5th Marine Division. Doc was standing Corporal of the Guard at the 13th Engineers the night before when I left.

We bumped into each other outside of the messhall. He had already been sent to the 3rd Battalion's Co K. After telling him of my platoon, I hoped that by some chance we would end up together. Doc did better than that. He not only ended up in my platoon, but also in my squad. It was a streak of luck for us both.

My squad leader sent me to the Battalion supply to draw more gear. Walking through the throngs of troops, I found a building bustling with activity. It was the supply building, and before long I came out piled with a flak jacket, another poncho, a poncho liner, a sleeping bag, and a pair of jungle boots. I stumbled along under the load and wondered why I had a damn sleeping bag if we were going to Vietnam. The situation in Korea was bad at the time. It made one wonder.

After getting rid of this new issue, I joined another line to get some green skivvies. A man couldn't wear white ones in Vietnam. I was lucky enough to get some before they ran out.

With that I went back to the barracks where everyone was remaking their packs. We had to get all our gear ready quickly. No one knew when we were to leave. Rumors of all kinds were flying about.

In the evening I did the inevitable and called my folks to break the news. They weren't very happy, but my parents knew it would have happened eventually. My Mother didn't cry over the phone. This surprised me. I knew she was gentle, but it would take more time before I realized her inner strength.

Another night went by without any further word about our departure.

**L/CPL ROBERT SIMONSEN - Co I:** The day was very busy. We packed, received equipment, had medical check-ups and got to know just who was who. I was placed in the first squad of the first platoon in India Company. There were fourteen men in our squad. Three had been to Vietnam previously, and the rest of us were a mixed bunch consisting of various military experience, very little of which was infantry training. The day went by quickly. I was tired from the running around from place to place and therefore I had no trouble sleeping that night.

**SGT RICHARD NEAL - Co L:** We received all new troops from around the base, most of them non-infantrymen. Only four knew anything about a machine gun. On the plane over, we gave a crash course on assembly and disassembly, parts and nomenclature of the M-60 machine gun.

L/CPL ALLEN CIEZKI - Co I: I reported to 3rd squad, first platoon and someone handed me an M-79. He said, "You are the grenadier for 3rd squad!" I looked at another Marine and said I don't know the first thing about the M-79. This guy said, "Fine, I'll take it if you don't want it."

CPL BILL JUNG - Co K: By morning we were starting to look like a unit. Our platoon and the company as a whole were just about up to strength. The trouble was, not many of the men were riflemen or machine gunners by trade. Our company, like the entire regiment, was made up of Marines of many different job specialties. The ranks of the 3/27, now becoming known as the Bastard Battalion, were filled with men drawn from Division support units. The rifle companies were filled with bakers, clerks, mechanics, supply men, engineers, and every other job under the sun. Our company had 31 various job specialties. All Marines are basically riflemen and are trained as such, but if you're a communications man or truck driver, you never receive the intensive training that a regular rifleman gets.

Our 3rd squad was a typical example. The squad leader, Sergeant Blazer, was a Vietnam veteran and a rifleman. Thank God for that! He would see us through until our feet were wet. Then there was Sergeant Grupa, a Vietnam veteran but an ordnance man. Our grenadier was Chief, a friendly but ugly looking Indian. He too had been to Indochina. Then there were the rest of us. Doc and I were surveyors. Mendez, Leytem, and Murphy, a big quiet farm boy, were all riflemen, but boots and inexperienced. Henry, a soul brother, was a heavy equipment operator. Benoit, a former jeweler, made his fame in the Corps as a truck driver. We also had Lowery, Webber, a bulk fuel man, and Wingard, an amtrac mechanic.

This was the story of the 27th Marines. Our platoon even had a Marine Corps disk jockey. The lieutenant in charge of our platoon was a motor transport officer. Co K's commander was an amphibious track vehicle (amtrac) officer. With a mixture of such people who had just met each other, the Regiment was being sent overseas. Time and experience would pull the unit into a good outfit, but that would be many dead and wounded men later.

Later in the morning we boarded vehicles and rode to range 116. All of us had M-14 rifles that we brought from our old units. Soon we were lined up behind the firing points. Every man was to shoot for his battle sights. We were at a range of 300 meters. When my turn came I laid down in the dirt. I remembered what my sights had been set for in the 300 meter firing the previous April, and then set the same on again. The rifle cracked and I had a bullseye. Another round gone and one more bullseye. After the third bullseye, they threw me off the line. I felt good knowing that my rifle was such a beauty.

The air was full of racket as the rest of the Battalion fired. Then the canyon of range 116 was again quiet. We jammed into the trucks and went back to camp. At least we were getting some training as a unit before the real thing.

In the afternoon and evening we had long classes on mines, booby traps, and mapping. Luckily our platoon had a number of experienced veterans. We green ones took it all in. There was no time to fool around.

Of course we had to go to the aid station for some

more shots. Marines are always happy about that. As the day ended though, our platoon was up to strength, around 45 men with the corpsmen and our lieutenant. Everyone knew that time was at a premium, so we listened to all instructions, followed all orders quickly, and did our best to get to know one another. We all worked together.

Sergeant Blazer gave me a quick but valuable lesson. When he gave me an order and I asked why, Blazer gave me a cold stare, and then questioned me as to if I would ask "Why" in Vietnam. I answered no and learned the point. Doc just gave me a look as if to say, "You asked for it." One never questions why in combat. I never asked why of Blazer again.

Rumors again had it that we were to leave that night. Nothing happened though. Our restless platoon slept off and on.

1ST LT BILLY C. STEED - H & S Co: I received orders to go to 3/27 and reported in where I was assigned as the XO of H & S Company. Of course you try to find out who's in the Battalion and what kind of experience they've got. I was happy to find out by looking at the roster in the adjutant's shop, that they had some former enlisted guys as equal to myself as far as commissioning; Julian Parrish and Roy Casteel. Things were hectic. They had sealed off the base and a number of dependents were trying to get in. As I was assigned to H & S Company, I received numerous telephone calls directly from congressmen concerned about some of their constituents, wanting to get them out of going to Vietnam. That happens all the time; some mother calls a congressman and the congressman calls the Marine Corps. I said nope, he's not getting out. He's going to Vietnam. Obviously you couldn't tell them too much, because the whole operation was supposed to have been classified.

Finally I called my wife. She brought the rest of my field gear up. By that evening, we had headed toward El Toro to get on airplanes to fly out. I was a plane commander for my group on a C-141 and I had the Battalion Executive Officer with me and mostly cats and dogs left over from H & S Company. One of my concerns after looking at some of the rosters was the number of Marines who were assigned to our infantry Battalion with no infantry types based on their MOS. You always hear the story, which was later confirmed, that everybody is basically a rifleman. We had mechanics doing an infantryman's job, but again you had scattered throughout the Battalion some enlisted guys who had been there before and volunteered to go back. I think that's one of the reasons the Battalion did so well when it got to Vietnam.

**CAPT JOHN ERNEST - Co L CO:** We found ourselves in a very undesirable position. We lacked training and coordination as a fighting unit. None of the Company Commanders even knew each other. I wished they could have delayed us for two or three weeks and allowed us to train on Okinawa before going to Vietnam.

Another problem we had was twofold; the reduction of the deployment status from two years of stateside duty to one year and the non-infantry MOS Marines. Although most accepted their orders for Vietnam, every company had a handful of complainers. Several Marines formally requested that their status be changed and even parents and Congressmen got involved. Eventually, most of these men were weeded out of the Battalion.

**L/CPL ROBERT SIMONSEN - Co I:** The next day we received a couple of indoctrination lectures on Vietnam and made final preparations for our departure on the following day. I tried calling my sister but no one was home. I made friends with the two Navy corpsmen assigned to our platoon and helped them pack their field transport packs. We were going overseas with full combat gear, so we had quite a bit to do to get everything ready in time. Everyone test fired his M-14 rifle so that the sights could be adjusted for what was considered to be the average combat firing distance. My squad started to get to know one another. It appeared as if we would get along very well together. Lights went out early that night, but most of us sat around talking for a couple of hours. Several bottles of booze were passed from one man to another. One by one we went to our racks and either slept or just stared at the ceiling. I laid on my rack fully clothed that night. I thought about the next 13 months which lay ahead. How many of my fellow squad members would be killed? How hot was it going to be? Where would I go on R&R? I experienced a great deal of excitement in my thoughts, yet I still believed myself to be completely at ease. I had no fear of the unknown that was before me. Tomorrow would start a new phase in my life. I was now confident that I would meet and conquer anything put against me. In a few days I would be put to the test of man against man. The loser would be killed or maimed. The winner would win nothing except another sunrise. I don't know how long I had slept, but at 0230 in the morning we woke up and started to get ready. Excitement was present everywhere. We were no longer going to play games, everything from now on would be for keeps. Mistakes could mean death.

## 3. GOING OVER

**L/CPL ROBERT SIMONSEN - Co I:** Silence filled the air as we boarded buses which would take us to the El Toro Marine Air Station. There was a long wait for the planes to arrive, so we either slept in one of the hangers or played cards. Buses took us over to the mess hall for breakfast later on at around 0630. Our squad got together for a few minutes and talked over what was before us and what we should do under certain combat situations. Finally, the planes taxied up to our area and we prepared to get on board. I was now tremendously excited. We all looked across the El Toro base for it was to be our last look at the mainland U.S. for over a year. For some, it would be their last view ever. We all got aboard and sat three abreast with our equipment at our feet. It was extremely crowded to say the least. The engines started up, and after what seemed to be a long wait, the planes took off and headed for the Pacific. For the first time in several days I felt extremely calm. It seemed ironic that here I was headed for war, yet I was finally at peace with myself. I closed my eyes and swiftly fell asleep.

After the command group and other leading elements had departed, President Johnson flew to El Toro to send off the rest of the Battalion. He would later write that the visits with these brave men were among the most personally painful meetings of his Presidency.

**S/SGT FRANK CORTEZ - Co I:** We hung around 33 Area and later on El Toro for what seemed weeks (actually two days) waiting to sky-out. The problem was that LBJ could not make up his mind whether to send us to help out in the areas that had been hard hit by the Tet Offensive a week or so earlier, or send us to Korea as an Assault Force due to the USS Pueblo being captured by

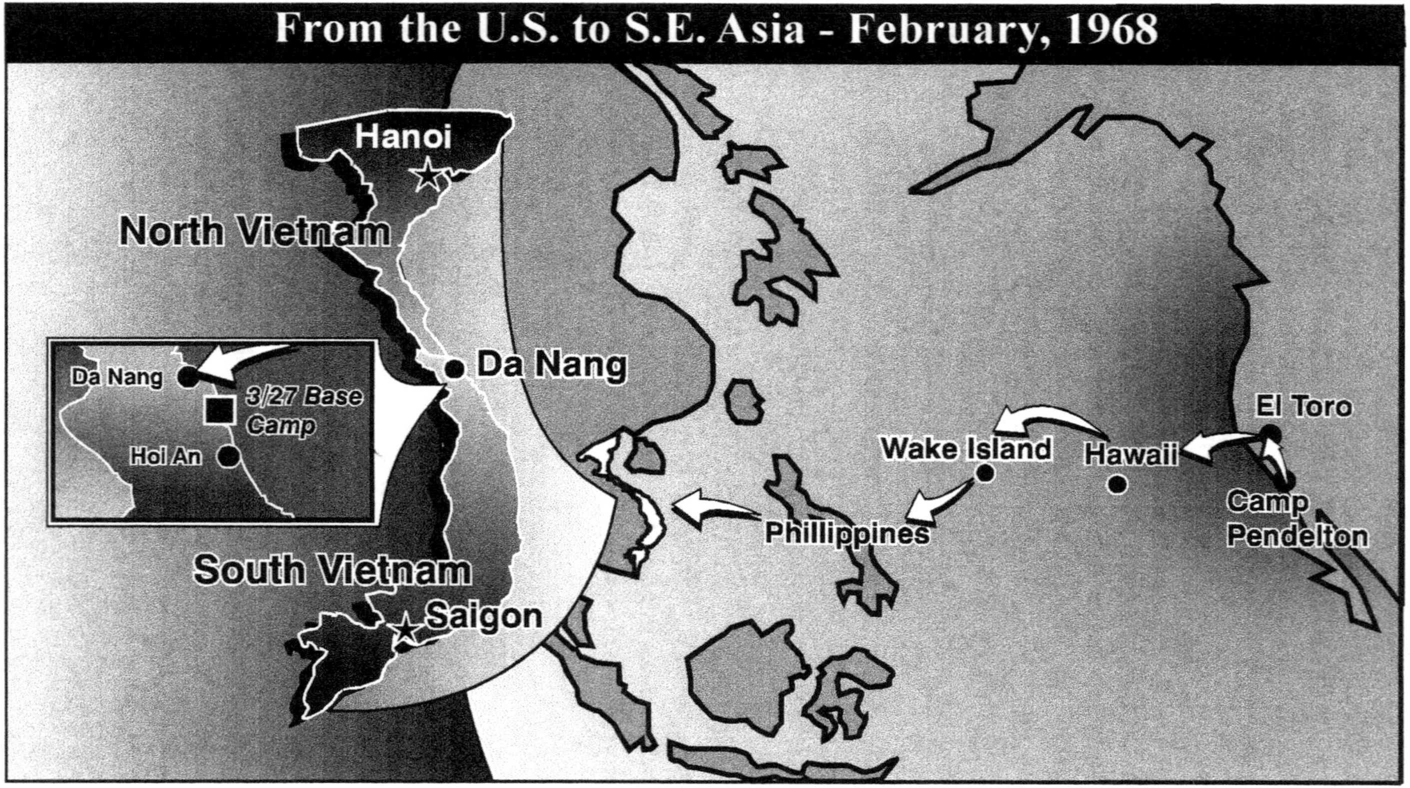
From the U.S. to S.E. Asia - February, 1968
Hanoi
North Vietnam
Da Nang
Da Nang
3/27 Base
Camp
Hoi An
South Vietnam
Saigon
Phillippines
Wake Island
Hawaii
El Toro
Camp
Pendelton

North Koreans three weeks earlier on 23 January.

Finally, after a lot of fanfare, television cameras and the President kissing his boys good-bye, we left on a long flight to Da Nang.

SGT GARY HARLAN - Co I: On February 18, 1968, we were loaded up in the 6x's (trucks) heading for El Toro, when suddenly the convoy turns around and we are heading back to the barracks at Pendleton. Once we got back inside the Lieutenant informs us that the reason we returned was because we had just been told that the President was going to send us off later in the day.

"If that son-of-a-bitch Johnson tries to shake my hand, I'll refuse!" I declared to no one in particular.

"Now don't make a scene, Sgt Harlan," the Lieutenant warns, in a semi-serious manner.

"What are they going to do, sir, send me to Vietnam?" The new troops were so green they hadn't heard this old line a hundred times like the rest of us, so I got a pretty good laugh out of it.

After standing in formation for hours waiting on His Highness, Air Force One finally showed up, the local Marine Band hailed his ass, and he was at the podium.

"If those Marines in Khe Sanh were here," he drawled, "and you were there, you know they would want to go over there and help you out." Yeah, sure they would.

Then came time for him to inspect the troops, and naturally he had to stop in front of me.

"Good to see you," he said, offering his hand. "God bless you and keep you." I shook his hand, mostly because we were heading for the bush, and I was already operating in the superstitious mode, in which you get into, in the bush. When the President tells you God bless you and keep you, it just might be bad luck to blow him off, who knows?

CPL BILL JUNG - Co K: In the morning Co K went to the field to practice assault tactics in the nearby hills. We worked hard and listened to all Blazer said. There just wasn't enough time! We needed more! At least we were starting to feel like a unit, and this showed when we marched down the trail back to camp.

Camp Margarita was still a madhouse. Women and kids were crying as they said good-bye to their men. For many, this was a final farewell, forever.

Rumors flew around about the other battalions. Many had the 2nd Battalion wiped out before they even left the States. Everyone speculated about where we were going. Khe Sanh was the most popular guess.

In the afternoon the word was final, saddle up your gear and move. We trudged across the parade ground, piled our seabags, and boarded olive drab buses with the rest of our combat gear.

Dusk was settling as our Battalion traveled along the freeway going north. Everyone had his own thoughts. Some thoughts were the same though. When would we see the United States again? Would I ever? Sure, I would. It's always the other guy who gets zapped. The ride was a quiet one.

The sky was black when we entered the Marine Air Base at El Toro, south of Los Angeles. Quickly we unloaded off the buses near a large hanger and formed up. Not long after our company was in the hangar, a huge one. We piled our gear here and there and began to pass the time, talking and kidding, all of us tense and eager to be on our way.

A fat staff sergeant came over and gathered us together. He lectured us on being so carefree and told us to be more serious. We thought he was an ass at the time.

What did he expect? We were young and anxious. None of us knew what lay ahead.

In time I learned the fat man was a good decent fellow. Three months later a bullet would get him in the side. Two months after that one of our own grenades would almost kill him. But on the night of the 17th, I was still a youth, a young Marine full of fire and vigor. Time would change that.

We lay on the cement for some time wondering when we'd leave. Finally we learned why we were delayed. It seems that President Johnson was going to say good-bye. He had already seen the Vietnam bound Army 82nd Airborne off, now it was our turn.

A large part of the hangar was roped off, and then the circus began. Newsmen and photographers crowded up on to a large platform. The El Toro band appeared. Formations of El Toro Marines marched up and took their places. Many spectators appeared. A speaker's platform with the President's seal was placed in front of us.

Finally a few hundred of us formed into a large formation in the roped off area. We had weapons and full combat gear, all ready to go. Only the planes were needed. People gawked at us and flashbulbs popped while movie cameras whirred. It was like being in a zoo. The affair made me madder than hell.

Eventually the President's plane landed and taxied up close behind the throng. The band struck up 'Hail to the Chief' and we were called to attention. The speaker's stand was forward of me, and since I was only in the third rank, I could see well without moving my eyes.

The President walked down an open way and took his place behind the stand. He gave us a patriotic speech, but as a Marine who was finally waking up to the idea that he could be dead in a few days, I thought the speech was a bunch of bullshit. Johnson could afford to talk like that.

He wasn't coming with us.

When his talk was ended, Johnson, accompanied by the Assistant Commandant of the Marine Corps, Lieutenant General Walt, and the Sergeant Major of the Marine Corps, inspected our ranks. They walked up and down them, stopping to talk to some men. When they passed me, I couldn't help but notice how big the President was. He looked very old and tired though. I felt some sympathy for the man. He must have had a lot of weight on his shoulders, looking at these men and wondering how many would die.

Johnson stopped to talk to the Marine on my right. Then Walt halted in front of me, and the Sergeant Major stopped by Doc on my left. Walt asked me if I was ready, and I answered yes, for even though I couldn't buy all of that speech, Corporal Jung was a proud Marine and believed in the war. Besides, I respected Walt, as all the enlisted men did. Walt gave me one of his big famous smiles and moved on with the President.

After the inspection, they boarded the plane and left. The newsmen departed and the spectators disappeared. Soon those of us going to war were alone again. If the President hadn't come, no one would probably have shown up.

Soon Air Force transport jets were out on the blackness of the runway. We formed up, answered the roll call, and walked out to the huge concrete platform.

As we marched, we all took one last look at the land we wouldn't see for some time. Each had his own thoughts when we entered the huge C-141 Starlifter. 90 of us crowded on the jet at 0145 on the morning of 18 February. Packed in tight, the doors closed behind us. All was quiet except for the whine of the engines. Before long we felt ourselves airborne and on our way, and in the dim light, each man said good-bye to the past and wondered what lay ahead.

**SGT ANDREW BOYKO - Co I:** The convoy left Camp Pendleton and headed north to El Toro Marine Air Base. When we disembarked the trucks, we formed up on the flight line between two large hangers and stood around in formation. As I looked around, I noticed what I believe were Marine snipers on top of both hangers.

I asked around, "What's going on?"

Someone said, "The President is coming."

I chuckled in disbelief and responded, "Sure."

A little while later we were called to attention, and sure enough, President Johnson stepped up to a platform, gave some kind of pep talk, then started walking up and down the ranks shaking hands with some of the Marines. As he walked back and forth, he moved up my rank from my left. I was pushed out of the way by the base photographer, who was standing behind me hoping to snap a picture as he passed by.

Noticing the President coming toward me, I quickly got back into rank and stood at attention. To my surprise, he stopped in front of me and extended his hand. My rifle was slung on my right shoulder, and I was holding the sling with my right hand. I grabbed the sling with my other hand so that I could shake his hand with my right hand. I remember that he had a firm grip and he said something to me like, "God be with you, and come home safely soon." As he walked away, I stood there dumbfounded. I had just shaken the hand of the President of the United States.

We were then told, "At Ease," which meant that everyone could stand around and talk for a while. Some of the men walked up to me and asked, "Gee, how did it feel to shake the President's hand?"

Another guy walked up and said, "Why the hell

didn't you cold cock the S.O.B.? He's sending you back for the second time. You've been there already. You don't need to go back." I just chuckled and brushed them off, you know, with a grain of salt.

Before long, we were instructed to board the aircraft and off we went. I don't know how many hours we were in the air but, at that point, time was irrelevant. We landed on Wake Island just long enough to get fuel, pack up and fly off again.

The 27th Marines were airlifted to Vietnam at the end of just a forty-eight hour notice and became the first regiment to fly from the United States directly into combat. In actuality, 1/27 was stationed in Hawaii and traveled by ship to Vietnam.

The first elements of 3/27, including the command group, left El Toro Marine Corps Air Station on the afternoon of the 17th. Within eighty hours after departure of the first element, all Battalion personnel had departed CONUS (Continental United States.)

**L/CPL TIM DAVIS - Co I:** We were all jammed in the plane along with jeeps and other equipment. There were no seats and every Marine was passing gas. I had very few friends on the plane. My whole Motor Pool was split up.

**L/CPL STEVE EASTON - Co I:** We stopped in the middle of the night in Hawaii to refuel. We were allowed to get off the jet and went into a deserted airport terminal. As I was walking back to our plane, I slid my hand along a counter and came across a card. I picked it up and found it to be a Geneva Convention Card that belonged to my best friend back in Bulk Fuel, Russell Trentham. I couldn't believe it! Later in Nam, I was in the back of a truck in a long truck convoy when we came across a stalled truck pulled off on the side of the road. As we approached this truck, someone yells my name out. Sure enough, it was Russell Trentham. I yelled back that I had his Geneva Convention Card. Over the next few months, I saw him in our Battalion area two or three times.

**PFC DALE CAMP - Co I:** I think it was great that we carried all of our weapons and gear with us on the plane. It really added to the feeling of urgency. I sat in the very back of the plane and the officers had all of their gear stacked on, under and around me. I don't think they would have done that after spending time together in the bush. It was a great equalizer. Wake Island was very eerie when we landed at night. We walked down to the beach and looked at an old WWII bunker and a war memorial to Marines.

**SGT ANDREW BOYKO - Co I:** Our next stop was in the Philippines at Clark Air Base. I remember when we disembarked we were told that the aircraft had problems and we would have to stay on the ground until it could be repaired.

Just then an officer came out and announced, "Okay, those of you who want to go clean up, shave, shower or rest, get in this line over here and we will take you to a set of barracks where you'll have time to do whatever you want. But, on the other hand, those of you who want to go out on the town and have a few drinks before the aircraft takes off, get into this line." Only one Marine walked over to the clean-up line. The rest of the guys went to the drinking line. Realizing he was in the minority, the guy in the clean-up line shrugged his shoulders, walked over and joined the rest of us.

We boarded a bus which hauled us into Angeles

City, a nearby town. Arriving at the local bar, we went in, sat down and ordered a few beers. We soon realized that if you ordered one beer at a time, you would have a long wait before you got the second beer. "The hell with this," we said and decided the best thing to do was to order by the case, so we ordered a case of beer and started drinking. We figured since this was our last day in a civilized nation anyway, what the hell, we might as well enjoy it. At some point, word was passed to get back on the bus. The aircraft was repaired and we were headed back to the air base. Unable to finish the case of beer at the bar, we thought why not take it with us and finish drinking it on the bus. Suddenly, as our bladders began filling up, it occurred to us that none of us had stopped to go to the bathroom. So what do you do on a bus going back to the base when you have to go? Well, someone came up with the idea, "Let's try going back into the bottles." Have you ever tried urinating into a bottle on a moving bus? Well, I have and I can tell you from first-hand experience that it is physically impossible. In desperation, not knowing what else to do, we opened the windows on the bus, stuck out our dicks, and there we went right as the bus traveled through the middle of the Philippines. I'll bet that was a weird sight for the locals of that town, but by then, we didn't care. Within a couple of days we could be dead, so why not live life to the fullest and worry about the consequences later. We finished the beers back at the base before we were told to board the plane.

After what seemed like many long hours, we landed in Da Nang. From there, we boarded trucks which took us past Marble Mountain to Cau Hau, somewhere south of Da Nang.

**CPL MARLIN JACKSON - Co M:** When we landed on the Philippines, our plane had trouble. We actually ended up landing sideways! It was quite scary. We arrived in Da Nang under a rocket attack. The heat, smells and explosions all told me that I was back in Vietnam!

L/CPL MARK SMITH- Co I: Our plane started to develop trouble prior to landing at Clark Air Force Base in the Philippines. At first, they told us it might be a few days before we could leave. But after just a couple of hours, we were on our way again. It was about midnight when we landed in Nam. It was very hot and humid. I remember seeing tracers over the mountain ranges.

1ST LT BILLY C. STEED - H & S Co: We landed on Kedina in Okinawa, in Guam and at Clark Air Force Base. On the plane, you couldn't talk because most people were trying to get some rest. I slept on and off. I was trying to sort out who we had on the rosters. Accountability of the people was a main concern. When we were about 30 minutes out of Danang, we found out we were going to land at the Da Nang airfield. The crew chief came on the intercom and said they were receiving rocket fire on the airfield. That was routine at certain times, although this was daylight. You normally get them close to evening. We passed out ammunition and the Air Force got all excited about passing out ammunition aboard the plane, but we went ahead and did that so a Marine could have some self-protection when he came out. When we landed, the rockets stopped firing and we were congregated in the holding area and eventually were picked up by a truck. It was a typical Vietnam smell and it was hot and humid. People were running around from the rocket fire and we also had people who were rotating out of Vietnam who were attempting to get on the plane, so we had to vacate as rapidly and as orderly as possible. There wasn't any great danger other than indirect fire. It was late afternoon. By the time we got to the place where we slept that night, it was dark.

L/CPL ART RIORDAN - Co L: We landed in Honolulu for fuel and were back in the air headed for Guam. When we landed in Guam, Dave Thompson and I decided we needed haircuts. As we exited the C-141 the 'Top' was there counting heads. As we boarded the bus to take us to the Air Force Mess, he counted heads. As we entered the Mess Hall, he counted heads. As we entered the bus for the trip back to the Air Field, he counted heads. Dave and I saw a small strip mall near the Mess Hall so we ate quick and went to get our hair cut. I was watching through the window of the barber shop as the troops formed up for the bus ride back to the airport. When I saw the bus appear, my barber had just finished. I turned around to Dave's chair and I saw he was getting a shampoo and massage. What the hell! We ran like hell but missed the bus. I was wondering if they still put you in front of a firing squad if you were AWOL on a troup movement into combat. Something I will never forget was a Marine, washing his 1955 Chevy Convertible, on that tiny Island. He gave us a ride to the airport terminal where we ran through it only to find a pair of locked and chained doors. Adjacent to the terminal was the Crash Crew hanger. They gave us a ride in a fire truck to the opposite side of the C-141 to where they were boarding. Dave and I ducked under the fuselage and slid into the back of the line. The 'Top' looked confused in his counting as his numbers now came out correct. As he neared us it became apparent who had been missing, Dave still had shampoo in his hair. Dave and I still get a chuckle out of Guam.

CPL BILL JUNG - Co K: All of us soon realized

that besides having a long flight ahead of us, we also were going to have a very uncomfortable one. The jet was cramped to begin with, and the so-called seats didn't help any. The seats consisted of webbing woven together and then connected to pipes. They formed rows that resembled long benches and ran parallel to the side of the jet. The two rows of men in the middle had their backs together. There were also no windows. It was like riding in a flying shed. C-141's were transports anyway, so we couldn't expect much better.

Not only were we elbow to elbow, we were also sitting with all our gear, packs, helmets, and cartridge belts under our legs and rifles between the knees. No way at all to stretch, lay down, or move about.

Doc was next to me. We talked awhile and shared our thoughts, but like all the other men, we soon put our heads on our chests and drifted off. The last few days had been long ones.

Early in the morning we landed at Hawaii. It felt good to stretch for awhile and get some fresh air. Our stay wasn't long, only two hours, but at least we were able to say that we had been there. Before we could get very attached to the place, our bunch was loaded up and the flight west began again. The next stop would be Wake Island.

During this leg of the trip, we crossed the International Date Line. There were no games though. Everyone was too busy with his own thoughts or else sleeping. There were only a few low conversations.

As we neared Wake, I wondered how the pilot could find it. Being a history buff, I knew a little about the place. It was only a small speck in the vastness of the Pacific. When we did find it, I wondered how a big jet like ours could land on just a small atoll. One bad pass and we probably would end up in the ocean.

We mud Marines didn't have anything to worry about. The Air Force landed us perfectly on this postage stamp. Climbing down into the hot sun, all we could see was sand, a flat nothing, and a small terminal. My mind wandered to the fight Marines had made here in December of 1941. I hoped that my courage could be the same.

Again our stay was short, enough time to mail some post cards and that was it. Soon we were again crammed together like sardines and heading toward the Philippines. Being nervous, and scared too, not many of us talked. We followed the tips of our veterans and got as much sleep as possible.

A few hours later and our C-141 landed at Clark Field in the Philippines. Stretching and blinking from the dimness of our flying shed, we stepped down into a hot humid day. Sweaty and dirty with a day's growth of beard, we began to drip with more sweat from the humidity.

With our cartridge belts on, our group boarded buses and headed across the base to get some chow. God and all his friends knew we were hungry.

Unloading quickly, we filed into a messhall that was a beauty to us. Big, new, clean, with tables that had cloths and plates, it was a far cry from the barn-like slop holes we ate in at Pendleton, with their wooden tables and benches, and men clanging tin trays.

The Air Force personnel stared at our ragged bunch, probably wondering what hole we crawled out of. Soon we were shoveling down a good hot meal that had to be taken advantage of. None of us figured that we'd again eat in such luxury for some time. All of us wondered at how good these men had it. I would learn that even in Vietnam the Air Force lived in better conditions than did Marines in their tinderbox World War II barracks back at Camp Pendleton.

With our stomachs bulging, we loaded the busses and rode back to the field. Clark looked fine to us, but we were eager to get on our way, to see what was ahead.

A short while later we were again in the air. Our next stop would be Da Nang, South Vietnam. This time no one slept.

Each man kept to his own thoughts on the last leg of our journey. Some minds would wonder to a distant past, others to thoughts of people thousands of miles to the east. Many thought of the future. As we neared Da Nang, everyone thought of only the present. Heavy fighting had been going on in Vietnam for weeks. Our jet could land on a peaceful runway or arrive in time for a rocket attack.

As the big jet made its descent, all was ready, packs, helmets; all our gear was on. There was only a deathly silence to be heard, that and the scream of the jet engines. Faces just stared into nowhere.

The transport landed and began to taxi. We were lucky, all was quiet, so far. The doors opened to the Vietnam blackness; it was night.

Quickly we unloaded and fell into formation. The big air base was busy, its lights shining near and around us. Far into the night on the horizon, flares were burning, and further to the south, one could hear the rumble of artillery.

Trucks were waiting for us, along with ammunition. While the company climbed aboard the vehicles, a few of us loaded the ammunition on. With that done, our convoy of two-2 ton trucks rode off into the night, through the base gate, toward blackness.

## 4. ARRIVING IN THE NAM

**LT COL TULLIS WOODHAM, JR. - 3/27 BATTALION CO:** During the airlift to Vietnam, I received VIP treatment along the way. Landing both in Hawaii and Wake Island, a staff car was sent out and I received special briefings. I thoroughly expected the same treatment when we arrived in Da Nang. When the jet's cargo doors opened, Sgt Major Snyder said "Colonel, I'll go out and find us a staff car." A little bit later after we had formed up the Battalion, a big engineer dump truck shows up with the Sgt Major. He tells me that this is our transportation to the Division CP. To compound the situation, the driver didn't even know the way to the CP!

Most of the Battalion Staff proceeded to the 1st Marine Division CP at Hill 327. I, along with Captain Fitzgerald, was briefed by the Division G-3, Colonel Paul Graham. It consisted principally of an overview of our TAOR and the current tactical situation.

While the Division briefing was being conducted, the remainder of the Battalion that had arrived was being formed up for movement to our eventual area of responsibility south of Marble Mountain.

**SGT RICHARD PELKY - Co M:** The only significant things I remember on the trip overseas was stopping at Hawaii and not being allowed off the plane. When we landed on Wake Island, we got off and walked up a small hill where we saw a monument to the Marines from WWII. Upon arriving in Nam, I remember being very disturbed at seeing the Vietnamese Popular Forces (PF) armed on our air base. The next unsettling thing was the children asking for a 'cig moke.' Hell, they couldn't have been but ten or eleven years old.

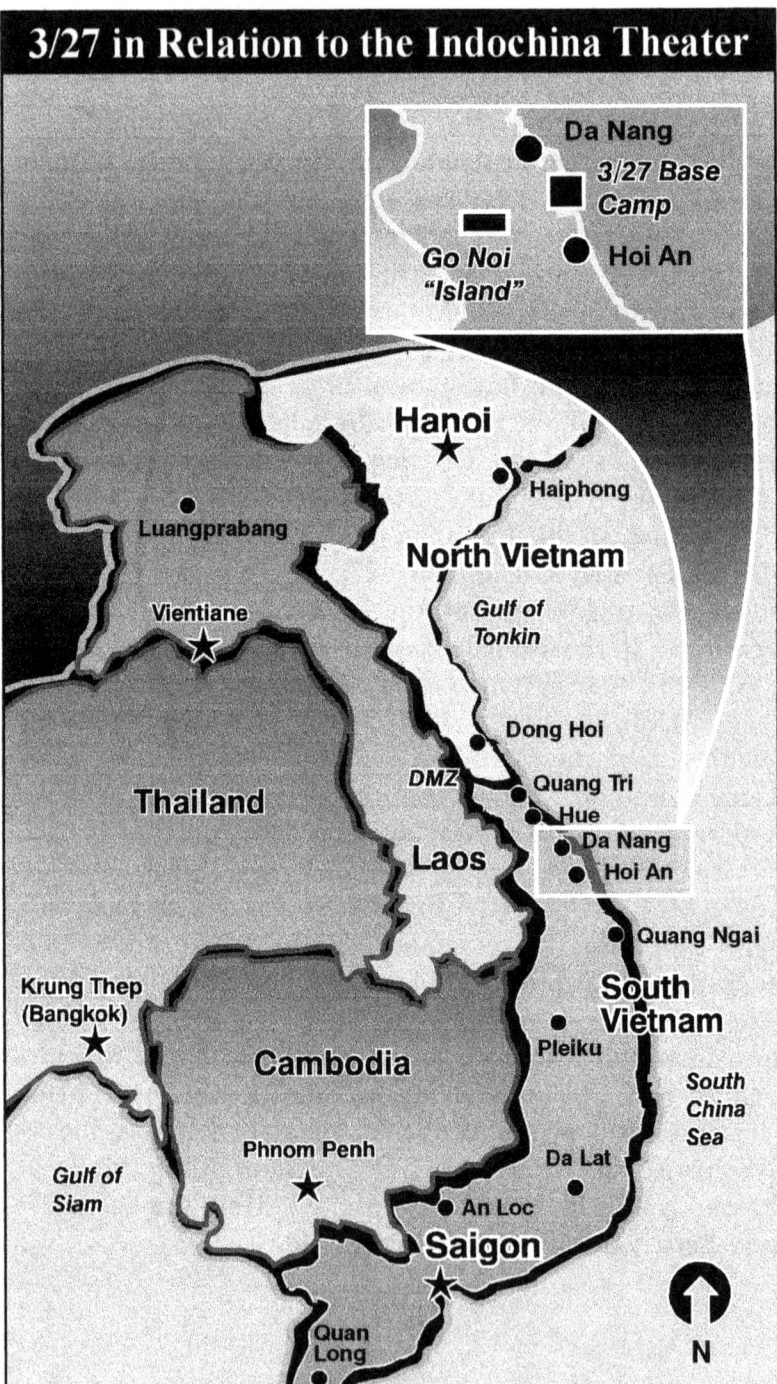

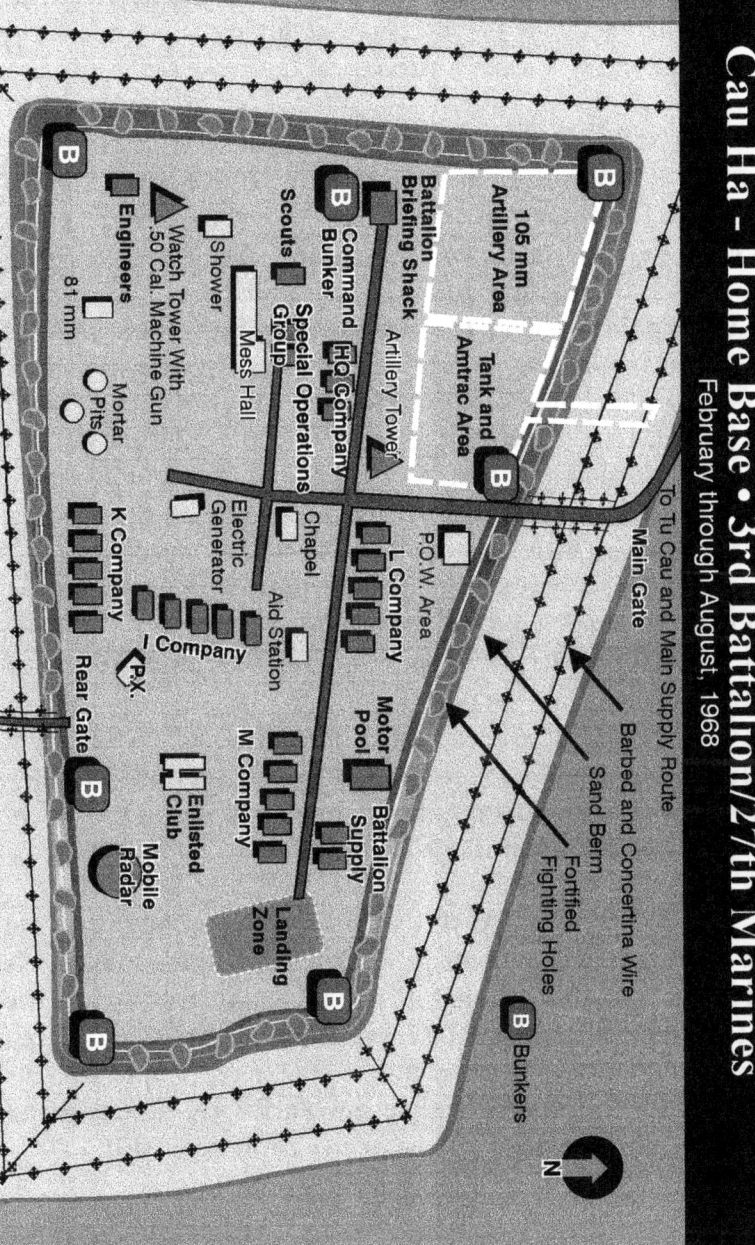

L/CPL TIM DAVIS - Co I: When we arrived in Da Nang it was very quiet. It was wet and foggy. It didn't seem like a war zone. Then came the smells and music. When the truck in front of us got hit on the way to the camp, we knew we were there.

L/CPL THOMAS FULEKY - Scout/Sniper- H & S Co: Upon descending in the Republic of Vietnam, I started getting a little nervous. I was sure the rounds were going to come screaming through the plane. We departed from the C-141 and loaded into a 2½ ton truck and had our M-14 rifles pointing over the sides. With our empty rifles we drove out to Regiment HQ and were assigned a hooch.

Nothing much happened in the first month. I went on patrol, LP, guard duty and in March, Cpl Ted Sambas and I went to sniper school in Da Nang. The school lasted for one week and we competed with other sniper teams from throughout Vietnam. I really loved the school.

Before I was assigned to 3$^{rd}$ Battalion, I got to meet a lot of Marines from 1/27 who would later on go to Hue. They came back with some horror stories when they rotated back.

The end of March I was assigned to the 3$^{rd}$ Battalion scout/sniper platoon. My squad leader was Sgt Rodney Brown who was mustanger who had dropped out of OCS. He was one of the most brilliant Marines I'd ever met.

PFC DALE CAMP - Co I: My first thoughts as we left the plane was how beautiful the mountains looked. It was very hot and humid. We loaded into trucks but the Sgt Major wouldn't let us leave until we got some ammo for our rifles. On the way out of Da Nang, people gave us the thumbs up sign. Then we saw an F-4 jet fighter going down in smoke and we knew we were in deep shit.

**PFC CLOVIS ACOSTA - Co L:** When the C-141 landed in Da Nang, we didn't know what to expect. We thought we might have to fight our way out of the plane. As the plane rolled to a stop, we zipped up our flack jackets and prepared to run for cover. The back door opened up and we began to run for our lives only to find one of the largest and safest airports in the world. Everyone was walking around in tee shirts and not carrying any weapons. We were very surprised and felt kind of stupid. It was very hot and everything smelled bad.

**HM MIKE LUTZ - Co I:** The flight over was long. I remember my heart started to race as we flew into Da Nang. We landed around 7:00 in the morning. The jagged mountains to the north had heavy fog rolling over them. I pictured it as the lower half of the mouth of hell, with smoke coming out of it.

**L/CPL CHUCK SPENCER - Co L:** When we arrived in Nam, I was somewhat nervous. I didn't know if the camp fires I saw on Hill 327 were ours or theirs. I just hoped that I wouldn't let my buddies down when we went into combat.

**1ST LT BILLY C. STEED - H & S Co:** I got about an hour or two of sleep. We got up the next day and we were transported down south of Marble Mountain. It was better known then as Booby Trap Alley because there had been so many units in and out of there and there hadn't been continuous patrolling of the area. The Viet Cong and some of NVA had planted numerous booby traps throughout the area. It was just a little triangle. We went there by trucks and of course you had to sweep for mines. The trip took a couple hours. We started digging the people in and getting the camp set up. They already had sea huts and some pretty good bunkers there.

We started patrolling and defending the base. Almost every night we'd get mainly mortar and some sniping fire and occasionally we'd get some big rockets. I recall one night we got about 10 of them and one of them hit right on top of our command post COC. Fortunately, it was dug in and reinforced enough so that people only got sand down their backs. There were some minor injuries throughout the camp, but mainly people were in their foxholes, so there were just minimal casualties. They did destroy some of the sea huts and some minor equipment. We stayed down there from February through April doing routine patrols.

We also manned Tu Cau bridge to keep it open because that was one of the main MSRs (main supply route.) We took numerous casualties from booby traps, everything from hand grenades to 250-pound bombs. A lot of them were command detonated. That was one of the hardest things to defend against. You were very cautious when you went on patrols. The point man was basically a guy looking for booby traps and the next guy was normally the scout. We had numerous fire fights down there but most of the casualties in those days were from booby traps. I remember one night, since I was kind of the camp security headquarters commandant, we had a platoon of tanks with us and they were getting mortar and rifle fire from a tree line. The Battalion Commander directed that I take a force out and try to flush out the enemy that was firing at us. It was about 0200 and you had people riding on tanks and amtracs and with the noise you couldn't hear where the fire was coming from, but you could hear it when it struck the side of the tanks. We finally flushed them out, killed a few of the enemy by just overpowering them, running a sweep around them. They were probably squad-sized, maybe platoon-sized. I had about 30 men, some of the reactionary force we kept on a 24-hour alert around the camp to do just that sort of thing. We set up numerous patrols from the companies every night to keep the enemy from infiltrating and going north and around the airfield at Marble Mountain and the big airfield at Da Nang. It was one of the corridors that they used and that was one of our primary missions. We'd do search and clear missions through the little villages around our command post location.

**CPL RAUL FONSECA - Co I:** The trip on the jet was like you were in a sardine can. There were only a few windows, but I guess it was better than going over by ship. When we arrived in Nam and the jet doors opened, I remember smelling the death smell.

**CPL GARLAND SISCO - Co K:** When I arrived in Nam, I woke up to the realization that I could get killed in this country. I was mad at the Corps and thought, how could they do this to a bunch of Viet vets. I was nervous about the whole situation, but growing up, I had always thought of being a combat Marine. Now, indeed, it would come to fruition. I had many other feelings, too difficult to explain in words.

**SGT RICHARD NEAL - Co L:** I felt great when we arrived in country! We relieved my old outfit, 2/3 in the sand near Marble Mountain. Boy, were they ever surprised to see me after only four months.

Not all 3/27 Marines went overseas with the unit in February. Many would join later and act as replacements for wounded, killed or transferred Marines.

PFC THOMAS BARLETTA - Co I: I arrived in Nam about 8 May 1968, and upon exiting the plane, wondered what I had gotten myself into. It was like the movie PLATOON, with people filling sandbags and the air base being rocketed. I remember some Marine asking me what unit I was assigned to, and after responding 3/27, I was told "Good luck, you're going to need it."

PFC TOM HANSON - Co I: I was elated, of course, when I received orders for Nam. Where else did a boot Marine want to go? We flew on a commercial jet and everyone was laughing and kidding around with the stewardesses. It was a great party all the way to Okinawa. A few days later, we flew to Da Nang and no one was laughing any more.

HM3 (Hospital Corpsman 3rd Class) DAVID 'DOC' WATSON - H&S Co (assigned to Co M): When we arrived, I couldn't believe the heat, humidity, dust, noise, confusion, babble and squalor of the place. I was apprehensive, to say the least, as were the other corpsmen. We had already heard of our Corps School classmates who had been killed or wounded.

Although my training was excellent, combat first aid is something that has to be experienced. I wasn't sure if I could physically keep up with the Marines (I did) but I was confident that I would remember what I was taught. When the 'caps' were popping, I wasn't sure what I would do. A joke at Corps School was, "How do you tell a good corpsman from a bad one? A good one gets shot by the enemy and a bad one gets shot by the Marines." I was 22 and didn't know if I would ever make 23.

After processing in at H&S Co, I was sent to the Battalion Aid Station. I weighed in at 230 pounds and they all laughed. "You'll get rid of that." Six weeks later,

I weighed 155 pounds.

I was sent over to the supply tent to draw my gear. I took everything they had and put it together the best way I could. When I got back to Mike Company, Sgt Ronald Campora said, "Doc, you got to get rid of that extra gear. Uncle Ho could hear you in Hanoi." He helped pare everything down to a reasonable level.

I carried the usual flak jacket, helmet, 4 canteens, pack, E-tool, K-Bar knife, .45 with magazines and a spare box of rounds, towel, insect repellent, and extra pair of glasses, albumin for blood replacement, two bottles of IV fluids and a Unit-1 medical bag. This bag contained bandages, antiseptic, minor surgery kit, splint, Copper sulfate crystals for WP (white phosphorus) burns, morphine, aspirin, salt tablets and some other drugs. After a few patrols, I also carried 6 to 8 grenades, a mortar round and a link of M-60 ammo.

PFC Larry Frye (Co M) didn't join up with 3/27 until April. He was happy to be going to Nam. It's the reason he joined the Marines. He flew over on a Pan Am 707 with flight attendants which, at the time, seemed strange to him. It was like going on a vacation instead of going to war.

**PFC LARRY FRYE - Co M:** I stepped off the plane at Da Nang and noticed the heat and smell. I saw lots of combat aircraft coming and going. I joined Mike Company at Tu Cau Bridge. The men all looked filthy and hard as nails. I thought I must have really looked green, but they took me in and treated me well. Everyone was cleaning their weapons and getting ready to go out on a patrol. Within a half an hour, we were told to saddle up and I was on my first patrol. No contact was made and I guess I was disappointed. I had expected fire fights all the time.

**2ND LT JOSEPH RENAGHAN - Co L:** My orders out of the Basic Officers Training at Quantico, VA, were to Vietnam. Enroute, I visited Lt Col Woodham who lived in Vista, CA and was commanding the 3rd Bn, 27th Marines at Camp Pendleton. Colonel Woodham had been the Marine Officer Instructor at the University of Oklahoma where I was a Marine Option Student with the NROTC.

My wife and I had supper at Colonel Woodham's quarters on the weekend of 12 February, prior to my departure overseas. He informed me that he would probably see me in Vietnam sometime later that summer as he was tentatively slated for orders there.

About ten days later, upon arrival in Vietnam, I was assigned to an infantry regiment south of Da Nang and placed in an Officers replacement pool awaiting assignment to an infantry battalion. The Regimental Adjutant phoned the squad tent I was in shortly after my arrival and told me to report to the Regimental Commander's hut. I couldn't believe it when, upon reporting, I opened the door and saw Lt Col Woodham with a big grin upon his face asking me why it took so long to get to Vietnam. I was then assigned to 3/27 and Lima Company.

## 5. PATROLLING THE ROCKET BELT

Upon arrival in Vietnam on 18 February, the Battalion was placed under the OpCon (Operational Control) of the 1st Marine Division and integrated with elements of the 2nd Battalion, 3rd Marine Regiment (2/3.) Within 48 hours after arriving, these integrated elements were conducting operations in the field. On 27 February, 3/27 assumed total responsibility for the TAOR (Tactical Area of Responsibility) vacated by 2/3.

Most of February's daytime activities were search and destroy type operations, on both a company and platoon level. Night activities consisted of patrols and ambushes conducted by squad size units, with saturation patrolling in the rocket belt.

By the end of February, the Battalion's first combat losses were 14 wounded, one of whom would later die. All casualties were caused by surprise firing devices (booby traps.)

3/27 operated in a 25 mile square area beginning about five miles south of Da Nang and extending southward and inland along the Gulf of Tonkin, under the 1st Marine Division. The Battalion would serve as a blocking force to stop any attempted enemy penetration of Da Nang and would conduct both day and night missions into a portion of the enemy rocket belt.

Sniper fire, occasional rockets and surprise firing devices would be the main problems encountered by 3/27 Marines. The booby traps and mines would turn up just about anywhere. Grenades, mortars and dud artillery shells could be easily rigged with trip wires. Much of the Battalion's area was covered with sand and thus it was very easy to conceal the booby traps.

**LT COL TULLIS WOODHAM, JR. - 3/27 BATTALION CO: Our main mission was rocket belt suppression in the area south of Marble Mountain. We were to prevent the NVA or VC from firing rockets into Da Nang, the air field and hospital. We were also there for**

blocking positions because it was an historical route of invasion from the south into Da Nang.

We rotated companies from the Command Post, to the Tu Cau area, Riviera area, Desert area and back to the Command Post. Our system worked quite well in helping us carry out our mission.

*   *   *

**STAFF SGT FRANK CORTEZ - Co I:** I have never seen a battalion so happy to be relieved as 2/3 was. They were working with seven and eight men squads and the platoon that we relieved at the bridge was being honchoed by a young corporal not even 21 years of age. It didn't take us very long to figure out why they were happy to boogie. Charlie had been by and had left his calling cards all over the area. In my three years in-country, I had never seen that many booby traps in so small an area.

India Company was completely up to T/O, meaning full strength, which to me was a novelty. To have sergeants as squad leaders and corporals as fire team leaders was unheard of and we even had grenadiers. With the other outfits I had been with, the squad leaders carried the M-79's and most fire teams consisted of three men, all of this due to constant personnel shortages. Since I had arrived at the last minute at Camp Pendleton's 33 area I had bumped Sergeant Lee into the Platoon's Guide Position. I am sure he didn't mind. I don't think I ever saw the sergeant in an angry mood, and I am sure no one in the platoon would have liked to.

It was clear that the enemy main force had moved out of the area, apparently to heal it's wounds. The small band that was in the area, however, was doing a fine job of maintaining exploding devices and installing new ones. Every morning a mine sweeping detail would clear the dirt road between Highway 1 and our base camp and just about every day a vehicle would get disabled. I had always thought and taught my troops that it was impossible to booby trap a sand dune, but surprise, the local 'slopes' had figured it out. One of my squad leaders damn near got his right leg blown off not more than half a click (500 meters) away from the gate of our compound. Ironically, we were supplying the Stars and Stripes Newspapers that they needed to cover their booby traps with.

After about five or six weeks of trying to get something solid going with Mr. Charles and with very little luck, my platoon drew duty providing security for the POW (Prisoner of War) Compound up by Marble Mountain. It was choice duty, as we slept all day and the troops manned defensive positions at night. The choice part was that we got to eat three square meals a day at the Seabees messhall, and these guys had steak and lobster at least once a week.

\* \* \*

**SGT RAY ALLISON - Co I:** We were on a company size operation near Tu Cau Bridge in the area we would later call Booby Trap Alley. My squad was ordered to search the river bank for caves. One of my men who was providing flank security on top of the bank stepped on a booby trap. I was evacuating him back to the company perimeter. I had him in a fireman's carry. Maddux (Pfc Roy R. Maddux) came running up to assist me as I was coming up to the perimeter. I was yelling at him to slow down and to watch for booby traps, when he hit one. Shrapnel got me, two more of my men and the Marine I was carrying. We were all medivaced.

Maddux got a piece of shrapnel in his heart cavity and he died a few hours later. He was our Battalion's first

KIA. The Marine that I was evacuating was shipped to Japan and then to the United States. I think the other two and myself eventually returned to duty.

\* \* \*

SGT GARY HARLAN Co I: The area we were assigned to was the same place I had left in 1966, the Quang Nam province, with the Battalion area located near Marble Mountain. The area had grown uglier and much deadlier since my first tour. The booby traps were more sophisticated and more plentiful. The disparity between America's official explanation of our presence in Vietnam and the image of a hostile and victimized peasantry was more glaring than ever.

But the why was no longer a relevant question for me, because I was responsible for an oversized squad of mostly inexperienced men. The only relevant question was how; how to keep as many alive as possible. From the moment that I chose to be deployable, I plugged back into the same survival program that I was committed to in 1966. From that moment on, political discussions were suspended, and the moral implications of our intervention in Vietnam didn't concern me a bit. All that concerned me was survival, and in that environment, personal and group survival was intimately connected to the goal of killing the enemy.

\* \* \*

CAPT E. MILES KEEFE, JR. - Co M CO: We were on our third rotation after arriving in country. We had been at the command base first, then moved to the Riviera area and were now in the Tu Cau sector. We were patrolling near An Luu, which was located in the north-

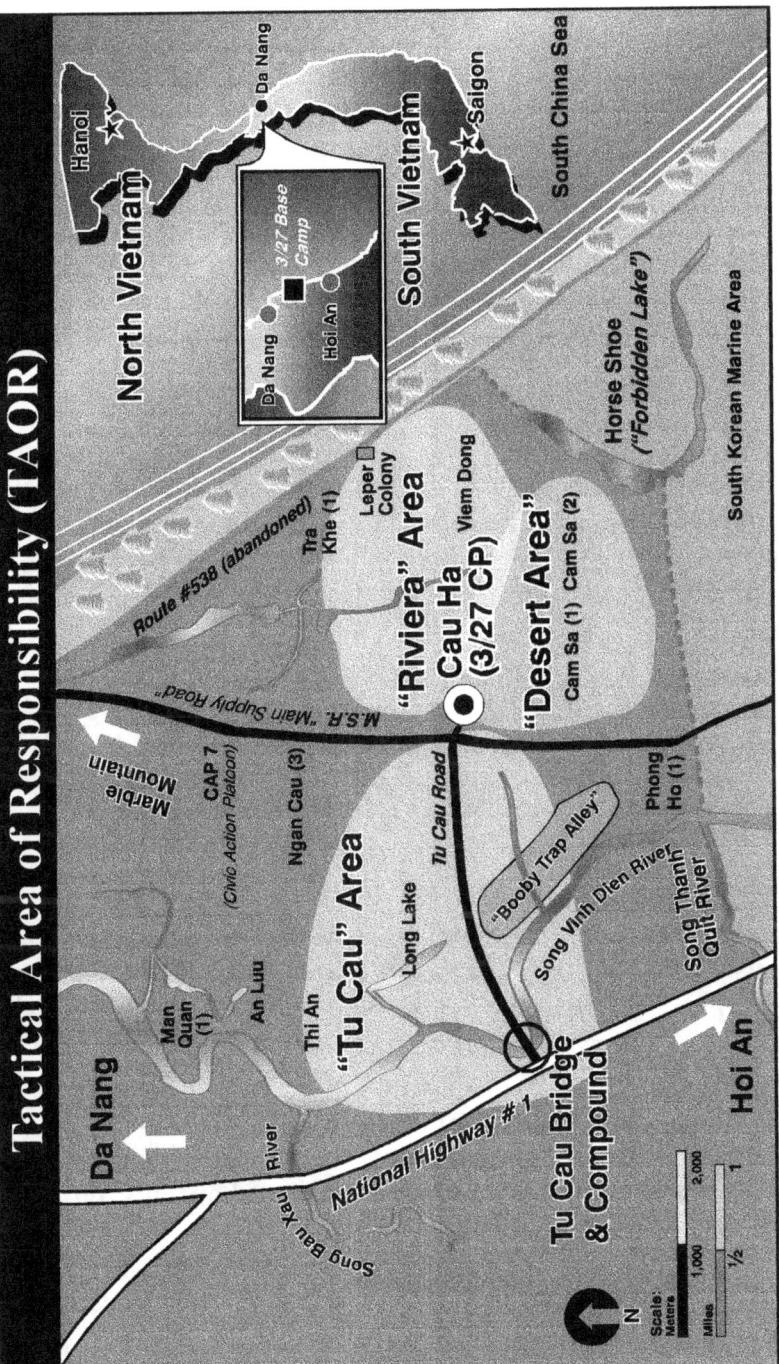

west section of our TAOR when we came under fire. Approximately fifty rounds, in short 4 or 5 round automatic bursts, were fired at us. I was laying down when it felt like a baseball bat hit me in the leg. A small caliber round struck me and made a fairly nice through-and-through hole. I was evacuated to the NSA Hospital where I spent about a month. I had the dubious distinction of being the first 3/27 officer wounded.

\* \* \*

PFC Gary May, Co K, had recently returned to his unit after being wounded by a grenade. While serving as pointman for a squad patrol, May was seriously wounded by an enemy explosive device. Disregarding his own wounds, he displayed outstanding courage as he directed the efforts of his fellow Marines, offering words of encouragement. May would later be awarded a Bronze Star for this action and his overall skill and performance while serving with 3/27.

\* \* \*

**SGT JON PAHL - H & S Co:** On my first tour, I was in the S-4 section and worked as a scout. I liked the bush and became very proficient with the map and compass. Being in the 81mm Platoon, I felt that I was well suited as a forward observer and that's the assignment that I got. I reported to India Company and was disappointed at first. There were some good NCO's, a couple of green officers and the troops were just typical Marines. My experience with 2/4 made me worry about my current assignment.

Slowly, India started to improve. That necessary combat edge, needed to survive the 'deep doodoo,' finally materialized. When Captain Ralph took over, the outfit changed overnight and his leadership brought everyone together.

**HM MIKE LUTZ - Co I:** Although they wear flak jackets and helmets, corpsmen are still squids! Grunts always went out of their way to protect them and dole out special treatment. I almost never dug. "Doc, wanna be in our hole tonight?" "Hey, Doc, I got peaches, want 'em?" 1st Platoon had one guy (Cpl Tex Massey) who didn't follow this program. If you were in his hole you dug your share. You also stood your hours on watch. Benny (Paul Benesch, the other squid) and I soon learned to stay away from him.

\* \* \*

**CPL GARLAND SISCO - Co K:** We were on a search and destroy mission right after we got to Nam. There was a big mound, a pagoda and a tree line to our front. We were walking on line and we were told to stay off all trails. Well, Pfc Ronnie Cureton, a former chaplain's assistant, walked up on the trail and stepped on a booby trap. He was seriously wounded and medivaced to Japan where he died of his wounds.

\* \* \*

**L/CPL LEROY R. DRIFFILL - Co K:** I will never forget our first night in the new battalion area, they put us up in a hooch near the berm, and I remember waking up that night to a very familiar odor, tear gas! Screaming out gas, gas, to my fellow Marines, we all scrambled from the hooch. Shoot. I even forgot my weapon. Just knowing the enemy was attacking, and me without my weapon, was quite upsetting. This turned out to be a practical joke, or a welcome to the new area from the battalion of Marines (2/3) we were replacing. It wasn't too funny to us at the time, but I will never forget it, nor would I ever forget my weapon in the future.

**SGT WES LOVE - Co K:** I remember we just arrived in country and were standing in line at the armory drawing ammo when we got our first incoming. I couldn't believe that we were getting ammo in the middle of a fire fight. Later that night some clown from the outfit we were replacing threw a CS grenade into our tent and hollered "Incoming, welcome to Vietnam."

\* \* \*

**PFC TOM HANSON - Co I:** When I first arrived at the Battalion CP I was assigned to India Company, but they were out in the field for the next few days. I was issued a rifle and 782 gear but no ammunition. After a day or two I had to make my first trip to the 'shitter.' It was night and I took my rifle and went to the facility. Propping my rifle by my side, I dropped my trousers, sat down, and proceeded to go about my business. The thought occurred to me, "It would be just my luck that we'd get hit right now." Sure enough, there's a 'Whump' somewhere in the compound. The lights went out and the recoilless rifles start blasting away on the perimeter. There was a great deal of commotion and people were flying out of their tents. I cleaned myself up as quickly as possible and bolted out the door. There I was, holding my trousers up with one hand and an empty rifle in the other, frantically running around in the dark looking for a bunker. I thought, "Boy, if the folks at home could see me now. What a hero!"

\* \* \*

3/27 Battalion scouts and Regimental snipers were out on a familiarization patrol shortly after the Battalion arrived in their new area. The patrol leader was Sgt Rodney H. Brown (H&S Co).

**SGT RODNEY BROWN - H&S Co: I honestly didn't think there would be any VC in the area where the patrol was going but our point man spotted at least a squad of VC to our front.**

The guerrillas were eating and sleeping in an open area, visible to the Marines. Cpl T.A. Sambas, a sniper, fired one round and killed a VC 500 meters away. He fired again and another VC fell wounded. Brown directed mortar fire into the tree line as he maneuvered his squad of Marines on line and had them sweep across the open area, a shallow lake and rice paddy, towards the enemy positions.

**SGT RODNEY BROWN - H&S Co: By the time we made it to the tree line the VC had all dispersed but the point man quickly spotted where they had moved to. Artillery fire was called in on the VC's new position and again they fled. We started moving out in the general direction of where we had last seen them. At the end of the tree line we spotted them again. This time they were out in the open.
The scouts quickly deployed and opened with rifle fire. Three VC were killed as they attempted to flee. Two others surrendered. One of the slain VC was an intelligence officer. A diary found on his body indicated he had recently returned from intensive training in Hanoi. Other documents captured included detailed maps of allied military installations in the Da Nang area.**

L/CPL THOMAS FULEKY - Scout/Sniper, H & S Co: In Tra Kha we set up in a tree line overlooking a rice paddy. To our front about 500-600 meters was the start of another tree line. It was my turn to be a spotter and Cpl Sambas carried the Remington 700 when I spotted a VC walk out of the tree line to relieve himself. Cpl Sambas took careful aim and squeezed off a round and dropped him. We saw more movement so we called in artillery. They told us to keep our heads down because they wanted to try something new. The rounds went flying over our heads and before they hit the target area, they exploded, sending little bombetts flying all over hell. It just shredded all the trees and jungle and most important four more VC. We started crossing the rice paddy to sweep the area, when 4-5 more started sprinting away from us. We ran after them and opened up with our M16's killing four more. I've never been more excited in my life. One of the VC was carrying a pack loaded with explosives when we shot him and he exploded. Another one was an NVA officer with detailed maps of our battalion compound. I think he came down to take over the local group of Viet Cong. We were searching the other VC when more opened up on us. I used one of the dead VC for a shield. It started to get dark and a group of amtracks came in from the South China Sea to pick us up. The next day reporters from the Stars and Stripes and Leatherneck magazines interviewed us. We also had our belongings moved out of a tent and into a hooch across from the mess hall. We had Kit Carson scouts staying with us and going on patrol. Just a few weeks before, we were trying to kill them and now they were sharing our living quarters with us!

When we first arrived in country our platoon commander, a $2^{nd}$ Lt in charge of the sniper platoon, told us that the first sniper team to record a kill would receive $100.00 and 3 days R&R at China Beach. I got the R&R

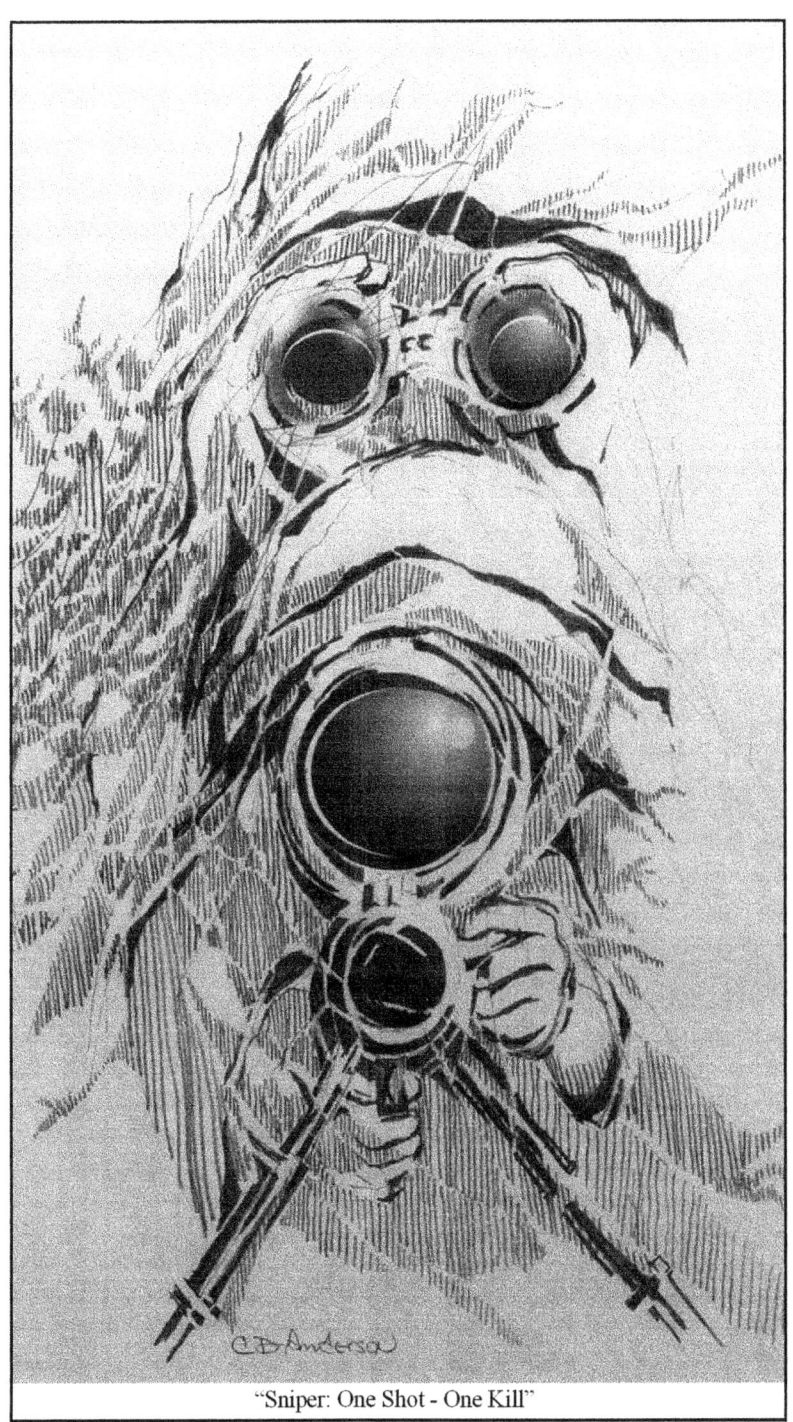
"Sniper: One Shot - One Kill"

but never saw the hundred bucks. I think that Lt got transferred before we got any money.

\* \* \*

CAPT E. MILES KEEFE, JR. - 3/27 S-3: Sgt Brown was one hell of a Marine. I don't know how he made it out of Vietnam alive. He went out in two or three men killing teams almost every night.

\* \* \*

L/CPL THOMAS FULEKY - Scout/Sniper, H & S Co: I missed the patrol that Sgt Brown and our point man Rico were on when they got wounded. They were patrolling Tra Kha when they were ambushed. I could hear the firefight from the battalion CP and I could pick out the AK47's from the M-16's. Rico got shot in the knee and Sgt Brown through the shoulder. I got to the hospital to see Brown and he was sitting around holding on to his IV when he said we got to get out of here. So we walked out, him carrying his IV and we climbed over the side of a 2 ton truck and got a ride to Freedom Hill where we had a few beers at the Thunderbird Club. They just don't make them like Sgt Brown anymore.

\* \* \*

LT COL TULLIS WOODHAM, JR. - 3/27 BATTALION CO: We used to run drills in the CP area. These reaction drills were used to simulate a fictitious enemy attack. Captain Bob Anderson (we called him Andy or Snoopy) was the Headquarters CO and he was responsible for making sure that everybody went to the right places after the gongs went off. He reported back to me as to the status of our reaction forces. All attached and supporting units, as well as 3/27 personnel in the CP, proceeded directly to assigned fox holes, crew served weapon's positions and firing slots around the perimeter.

\* \* \*

**SGT RICHARD NEAL - Co L:** We were on a patrol to show the new people how to make a night march. Myself and a few of the other 'old salts' were at the rear of the column when all at once, we heard a new Marine shout, "Come back, come back. I'm suppose to tie in with you. Come back here. Hey wait. Son-of-a-bitch, it's a gook!" As it turned out, a VC had joined our formation and was moving right along with the column, for who knows how long.

\* \* \*

**LT COL TULLIS WOODHAM, JR. - 3/27 BATTALION CO:** The Division soon became aware of our wealth of talent (Multiple MOSs) that we had and began to siphon off some of our people to send to other outfits.

**SGT ANDREW BOYKO - Co I:** When we finally arrived, they asked, "Is anyone a demolition man or has anyone had any demolition experience?"

I volunteered, "Yes. On my first tour in Vietnam, I used to blow up things and I have experience in demolition work. I'm an ammunition technician by profession."

"Great, we need a demo man. Here's a couple pounds of TNT, some time fuses and some blasting caps and you'll be our demo man. Anytime we need to blow anything, get rid of booby traps or whatever, you're it."

Every Marine-74

    I was given so much explosive that I couldn't handle it all at once, so I started passing it around my squad and told each man to carry a couple of pounds of TNT. I tried to logically rationalize where the safest place would be to store the time fuses and blasting caps. I figured out that if I put the blasting caps in the front of my flak jacket in my shirt pocket and I took a round or experienced any kind of shock like a concussion grenade exploding next to me, the blasting caps would detonate causing damage to my body, namely my chest and heart area. I didn't want to be killed by my own blasting caps. I decided to tape them into a piece of rubber that I wore around my helmet. If anything happened, my helmet would fly off and any kind of explosion couldn't do me any harm. I felt that the helmet had enough steel and cover for protection not to wound me seriously should the blasting caps detonate. I might get some shrapnel on my forehead, but I didn't think I could be killed. Anyway, with that in mind I felt the best place to carry the blasting caps was on my helmet.
    I was issued a demolition man's kit which contained the explosive, time fuse and blasting caps. Normally there is also a crimping device that crimps the blasting caps onto the time fuse preventing the blasting cap from falling off while it's being burned or knocked around. This process secures the blasting cap to the time fuse. Anyway, when I received my kit, it didn't have a crimping tool, so I asked around and said, "Well, gee, how am I going to crimp the blasting cap to the time fuse."
    Their response was, "I don't know. It's up to you. You're the demolitions man. Fake it. Do something. Improvise."
    I found that by biting down with my teeth on the end of the blasting cap, I could secure it to the time fuse. There is about two inches of free play which is non explosive on the blasting cap. If you pinch or bite too close

to the explosive head, it will detonate. But, if you bite at the other end, it is merely a hollow tube and that's the way I used to tighten my blasting caps onto the time fuse before inserting it into the TNT and blowing charges later.

Subsequently, they supplied me with C-4 which is a plastic explosive, but initially I was given half pound blocks of TNT, a rectangular shaped object which is detonated by inserting the blasting caps.

Sgt Boyko was later transferred to 1/27 where they needed his expertise as an ammo tech.

\* \* \*

During March, the Battalion's first full month of combat operations in Vietnam, direct contact with the enemy was light and sporadic. However, the enemy by the use of landmine warfare and sniper fire inflicted a large number of casualties. Approximately 10% of the Battalion's strength was wounded during March due to surprise firing devices. To counteract this, a school on landmine warfare was conducted by Division at the CP (Command Post.) Twenty-one men were also sent to the Division Landmine Warfare School in Da Nang.

Total casualties for March included 136 wounded (WIA) and 6 killed (KIA.)

**LT COL TULLIS WOODHAM, JR. - 3/27 BATTALION CO:** We received so many casualties from booby traps that eventually the Division began to question whether or not we had the knowledge or ability to spot or detect these types of devices. They were criticizing the Battalion for the large number of casualties that we received. They ignored, I believe, the fact that we had quite a few engineers and more people who were land mine and booby trap oriented than any other battalion in the Division. Saigon sent an Army Major up to investigate the reason for our large number of casualties and his final report vindicated our Battalion. In his opinion, our patrolling area had a higher percentage of saturation of booby traps than any other sector in the history of land warfare.

We received several replacements from areas such as Khe Sahn and they invariably asked for a transfer back after patrolling our booby trapped area.

\* \* \*

The entire Battalion was also issued the M-16 A1 rifle. All Marines test fired their new weapons and obtained their battle sight setting.

**LT COL TULLIS WOODHAM, JR. - 3/27 BATTALION CO:** For some time after our arrival we still had the M-14 as our principal weapon. We were the only infantry battalion in Vietnam to still be armed with it. For a number of reasons, the M-16 had received bad press and troops were reluctant to use it when given the option of the M-16 versus the M-14. As a matter of fact, one of the biggest problems we had the first several weeks in Vietnam was keeping members of 2/3 (with whom we were integrated and sharing spaces) from procuring 'stray' M-14's from careless 3/27 Marines.

When we finally were issued M-16's, I directed all Officers and Staff NCO's to carry the M-16 as their T/O weapon. This continued for several weeks until some confidence was instilled in our troops. Subsequently, the Officers and Staff NCO's reverted to the use of their assigned T/O weapon, the .45 pistol. Various modifications, over too long a period of time, did rectify the majority of

M-16 malfunction problems.

**L/CPL ROBERT SIMONSEN - Co I:** We were very worried about getting the M-16's. It was common knowledge that Marines had problems with this rifle previously. Despite its weight, we knew the M-14 to be a good and tough rifle, and we didn't want to give it up. My fears would prove true, when in May during my first major fire fight with the NVA, my M-16 jammed up.

**SGT ANDREW BOYKO - Co I:** It seemed like we were in Nam only a couple of weeks when word came down that we were going to turn in our M-14 rifles and get the new M-16's to replace it. The M-14, a semi-automatic rifle weighing 11 pounds fully loaded, was considered a good, hard hitting, reliable weapon. The M-16 could either fire semi-automatic or automatic and weighed about 7½ pounds. One full magazine of the M-14 weighed about the same as several M-16 magazines.

After getting the M-16's, we went to the west end of the compound to zero in for battle sights on the 900 inch range. We heard rumors of how bad the weapon was jamming and that many guys were killed because the rifle had malfunctioned. Those rumors became reality when I was test firing the rifle. The magazines were made of aluminum and sometimes the lips would spread out so that when the bolt came forward it would pick up two rounds and try to force them both into the chamber. To prevent this, we were told to load only eighteen rounds in our twenty round magazines. The other problem was that the empty case wouldn't always extract from the chamber. The bolt would pick up another round and drive it into the back of the empty case stuck in the barrel.

With all of these problems, we were more afraid of the rifle than the enemy. We wondered who in their right mind would manufacture such an inadequate weapon and just whose side was he on! We were warned that the M-16 had to be constantly cleaned and pampered. Hell, we were in combat, not a dress parade!

The best thing about the M-16 was that it had three open fingers for a flash suppressor. This was the greatest C-Ration wire cutter we ever had. You just stuck the flash suppressor over the wires on a case of C-Rations and turned the rifle. The wires would pop open very easily.

**SGT WES LOVE - Co K:** We called it a Mattel toy because the toy company made the arm guards that ran along the barrel. There was no ring around the flash suppressor. You couldn't put more than 18 rounds in the 20 round magazine because the lips would bend up and you would have 2 to 3 rounds headed for the chamber at the same time. This piece of shit was no match for my M-14, the last lock, stock and barrel weapon they made.

**L/CPL LONNIE MILLER - Co K:** The first man (I can't remember what his name was) that I saw killed was by another Marine shortly after they issued us the M-16's. He was cleaning his weapon with a round chambered. POW! Jerry Graymire, our Corpsman, did well but freaked out when he realized the guy was dead.

\* \* \*

The general routine of the four rifle companies was to operate on a twelve day cycle, nine days in the field and three days in garrison. The nine field days were spent rotating in three strategic areas; Tu Cau area, the Desert area, and the Riviera area.

The Tu Cau sector was primarily flat, with small villages, tree lines, streams, and scattered sandy areas. The western border was the Vinh Dien River, while the eastern edge was formed by the MSR Road. The southern border was the Tu Cau Road which connected the CP with the Tu Cau Bridge adjacent to Highway 1.

One platoon was always stationed at the bridge. This was considered good duty since swimming in the river was permitted.

**SGT ANDY BOYKO - Co I: At the river on Tu Cau Bridge, life was a little easier. You stayed in one spot and protected the bridge from being hit. You could wash up in the river and catch up on writing letters home. At night, it was a free fire zone. If a log floated toward the bridge, you were allowed to shoot at it, and every so often we'd throw a grenade or dynamite into the water in case Charlie was trying to sneak up underwater.**

To the north was an ARVN compound where occasional joint patrols were conducted. CAP-7, a combined action platoon site, was situated along the MSR Road. Some platoons would base their operations from this strategic position.

The Riviera area was located between the MSR Road on the west and the ocean to the east. To head towards the ocean from the CP, rice paddies and streams had to be crossed. It was nearly impossible to escape from getting wet when traveling to the Riviera. There was nothing worse than being wet and patrolling in the sand.

**L/CPL LEROY R. DRIFFILL - Co K: The Rivera was the first area our platoon went on patrol. I'll never forget the big rice paddy, and the first time I had to cross it. The soft mud would be sucked in the air vents in our jungle boots. I remember thinking how uncomfortable that felt, and how I cussed those boots. I eventually found out what make them so special, as they dried out in about two**

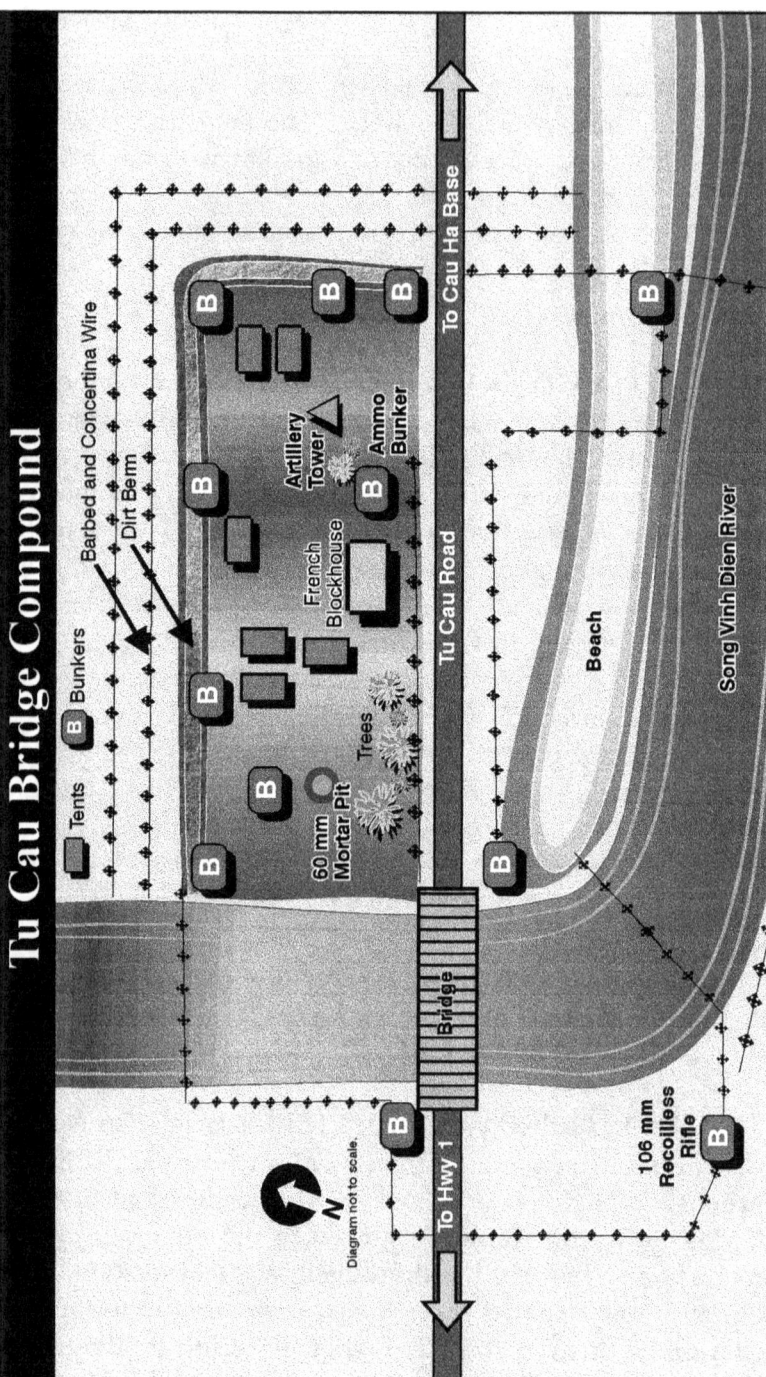

hours. Wearing our issued boxer shorts would eat me alive. My legs would be raw from them. One of the veterans, who had been here before, told me a little secret. "Don't wear any underwear." I found this to work although I did feel a bit strange.

Once there, small rolling sand dunes and isolated villages awaited the Marines. This, like all of the TAOR, was VC territory. Along the beach, pine trees swayed in the ocean breezes. At night, these trees would cast eerie shadows which more than once fooled many Marines.
One unique feature in this area was a leper colony, which was established fairly close to the ocean.

**CAPT E. MILES KEEFE, JR. - Co M CO:** Mike Company's first time in the field was spent in the Riviera area. We actually went inside the leper colony and didn't find anything, but we did notice that no one looked sick. The men all appeared to be very strong and we suspected that they were, in fact, Viet Cong. There was nothing that we would do about it.

**PFC DALE CAMP - Co I:** One night we were out on a squad size ambush near the leper colony. We had always suspected that it was a haven for VC. Later, in the evening, we spotted almost 40 VC coming out of the front gate. We were too small of a force to attack them and they headed off, away from our position. We called it in on the radio, but I don't know if anything every happened.

**PFC LARRY FRYE - Co M:** While assigned to 2/1, who replaced 3/27 in September, we flushed out a large NVA force in the leper colony by surrounding and starving them out.

# Leprosarium Colony

South China Sea

N

Supervisor's Quarters

Compound- 400 M X 600 M

The Desert area, to the south of the Cau Ha Base, consisted of dry rice paddies, sand dunes, cemeteries, and scattered jungle terrain. Very few people lived in the area which was thoroughly saturated with surprise firing devices. The southern boundary was protected by the South Korean Marines.

The most dangerous place, nicknamed 'Booby Trap Alley,' covered an area several hundred meters wide, south of Tu Cau Road and along the Vinh Dien River. Numerous casualties, including many lost limbs, occurred in this death trap.

**L/CPL LEROY R. DRIFFILL - Co K:** On one patrol into Booby Trap Alley, we had entered the area along the river, and patrolled along a tree line with fourteen Marines. Around halfway down the tree line, one of the points stepped on a mine. We set up a perimeter and awaited a medivac. The medivac chopper picked up the Marine and had just gotten out of sight when another Marine stepped on a mine. As we reached the end of the tree line area, another mine was set off and another Marine went down. We began to set up another perimeter, and it wasn't but a short few minutes when a Marine set off another mine! This Marine had a LAW (light anti-tank weapon) strapped across his back and the LAW exploded on his back. This wounded a total of five more Marines and killed the Marine who had carried the LAW. After medivacs had removed the remaining wounded, we radioed back and the patrol was canceled. We returned to the Tu Cau Bridge by another route. This one patrol had killed one and wounded eight Marines. I think we would have rather faced a battalion of hard core NVA at times, than to enter this area, and fight the mines.

Companies would sometimes operate as an entire unit for daytime sweeps or blocking forces but usually they would break down into platoons. The platoons would conduct daytime platoon or squad patrols and would establish night time PPB's (Platoon Patrol Bases.) From these bases, night squad size patrols and ambushes were sent out. Usually the perimeter lines would be manned by two squads in two or three man foxholes, while one squad would always be out on patrol for about four hours. As one squad would return, another squad would leave. This insured that the Battalion's Rocket Belt Area was thoroughly saturated by patrolling Marines. Cau Ha base command post was situated in the sand just to the east of the intersection of the Tu Cau and MSR roads. H & S Company and the reserve rifle company which could be deployed as a situation dictated were always present, along with other supporting units such as tanks and amtracs.

The perimeter was a sand berm with strings of barbed wire placed in front. Claymore mines, along with other devices, were strategically positioned to hamper enemy penetrations.

Sand and log bunkers and fighting holes were spaced throughout the perimeter and were continuously manned at night. There was one main gate and a narrow rear gate which was utilized for patrols headed out for the Riviera area.

The base had a mess hall, a landing zone for helicopters, shower facilities, small post exchange, a chapel, motor pool and artillery and 81mm (millimeters) mortar sites.

The rifle companies had their own billeting area and company headquarters. When the Marines were in the rear, they slept on canvas cots in South East Asia huts (wooden sided, tin roofed buildings.) Bunkers, in case of rocket or mortar attacks, were situated nearby.

The three days spent at the Battalion's base gave the Marines a chance to shower, get clean clothes, have a few hot meals, cold beers and maybe even catch a movie. It wasn't, however, three days off. Patrols and ambushes were continuously conducted out of the CP and the base perimeter had to be guarded.

**SGT ANDY BOYKO - Co I:** One day back at the base, I was assigned to guard duty for the night. I got a corner bunker of the perimeter off from the barb wire fence. I was to share the hole with an M-60 machine gunner. I had the new M-16 rifle and we were provided with a starlight scope to view the area. A starlight scope doesn't generate any light but gathers light from the stars and produces a green hue when you look through it. Everything, even in the darkest night, can be seen through this scope. We'd take turns guarding and sleeping; one hour awake on guard, one hour of sleep, etc.

At around 0100, I scanned the barbed wire perimeter in front of my bunker and thought I saw movement. I continued to look at the area and saw three men crawling into the wire. I woke up the machine gunner to verify the sighting and called the Sergeant of the Guard on the field phone. He arrived with, I think, the Corporal of the Guard. The four of us checked our sighting and verified it was probably VC trying to get through our lines. We each looked again through the starlight scope to get a fix on the men in the wire, then we all took aim where we though they were.

On command from the Sergeant of the Guard, we opened up into the area where we spotted the men. As we were shooting, the shell casings of the guy who was next to me were ejecting and bouncing off my helmet. It was extremely irritating, but I kept firing until we emptied our clips. At that point we ceased fire and looked through the scope at the area we had just shot up. At first, all you could see was dust. But when the dust settled, we saw forms on the ground, but they weren't moving! We settled back down into the bunker and laughed that those guys wouldn't be trying that again. We were told to wait until morning before doing anything, so we settled back down to our 50/50 watch (1 man guarding, 1 man sleeping) and waited until dawn.

    In the morning we got a couple of men together to get the bodies. But a strange thing happened. We couldn't see them before we left our perimeter. We went ahead to where we had shot them the night before and, to our surprise, the bodies were gone. We found blood, but no bodies. Someone must have dragged them off just before dawn.

    **L/CPL ART RIORDAN - Co L:** We manned the perimeter/berm at the CP whenever we were back from patrol. I don't know of any grunt who did not resent the fact that after spending anywhere from 3 days to over a week on patrol, when we returned to Cau Ha we manned the bunkers at night.

    I knew the Sgt-of-the-Guard, and he suggested I take the tower. We had two 80/85 foot towers in our compound which were attained by climbing a wooden ladder. The tower was about 12 feet by 12 feet and was roofed. The walls were sand bagged to about 3 feet. In the center was a swivel mounted .50 caliber machine gun and at its base was a 360 degree compass with a radio next to it.

    When I arrived three other Marines were already there. They asked me if I wanted to take the first watch so I could go back to my hooch and get a good nights sleep. The 'little red flag' inside my head should have gone up but I was too exhausted from a week long patrol, naturally I jumped at the offer. One by one they left the tower after asking me if it was okay to write a letter before lights out, do laundry etc., etc. I was sitting alone listening to the radio when the disc jockey, Chris Noel, came on and said in her familiar voice, "Hi I Corp, it is now 5 minutes to eight p.m." The 'little red flag' come to life this time. I started scrambling around looking for my helmet, flack jacket and M-16. We received harassment rounds into the compound at 8 p.m. You could almost set your watch to it. This time I found out what they were aiming at. Wood was splintering above my head and the walls and roof were getting hit. I jumped up and spun the .50 cal. around and pumped about 8 rounds before it jammed. Unbeknownst to me, if the gun tower opened up, it gave the berm permission to fire. Everything let loose and from where I was, 80 feet in the air, I thought we were getting into a fire fight with a large force. The ladder started shaking and I knew someone was climbing up. I had my M-16 aiming at the hatchway. He made it clear who he was before he came to the top rung. It was the FO and he was chuckling. He seemed impressed that the dinks were getting better as he put his fingers through the new holes. I didn't find this too amusing as I climbed down the ladder.

Sleep, food, water and mail were the basic needs of the field grunts. The body and soul required them all, but they were not always available in the desired amount.

If you ask any of the 3/27 Marines, sleep is one issue which they didn't take lightly. On a typical day, they probably averaged only four to five hours of sleep. Usually, they would get a 1-2 hour rest in the afternoon. Then at night, they would get 3-4 hours in two or three shifts of 1 to 2 hours at a time. It was difficult to stay awake during ambushes or watches. Each man learned to play mind games to stay alert. It was amazing what the body could do with so little sleep, coupled with the heavy exertion of patrolling during the day and evening.

It was interesting to observe new replacements. For the

first two or three days they were extremely scared and would stay awake the entire night. They were sure a VC was behind every tree. By the third night, they were totally exhausted and it was nearly impossible to wake them up. Eventually, the body adjusted to the conditions and most Marines would be able to conquer their fatigue.

**SGT ANDY BOYKO - Co I:** After long periods of time in the field, men started feeling exhaustion from constant walking, short periods of sleep, and the stress of combat. In fact, your priorities change the longer you are in the field. One example of this was an afternoon chow break during a patrol. Our platoon normally ate twice a day, once around 10:00 a.m. and again at about 4:00 p.m. This was a particularly long, hard-going day. It was hot when the platoon spread out at the base of a tree line surrounding a rice paddy. Exhausted, we pulled out our C-Rations and sat down quietly to eat our meal.

Just about the time everyone started eating, a sniper opened fire. The whole platoon, except for two men, simply slid down behind the rice paddy dike and continued to eat. A rifleman and the M-79 Grenadier got up and went after the sniper but the rest of us just continued eating. We were not about to be bothered by such a 'trifle' distraction. We viewed him as we would a pesky gnat or fly, and our meal was far more important to us than that sniper or getting shot.

The basic food consumed by the Marines were C-Rations. These boxed meals (twelve different kinds) consisted of a canned meat dish, crackers and a dessert. Toilet paper, cigarettes, coffee or cocoa mix, and a heat tab were included in all the boxes.

When there was time and it was safe, the grunts heated their meals with the heat tabs or C-4 (plastic explosive) which burned quite well. The meals varied in taste; some good and some terrible. Everyone had their likes and dislikes. The favorite was canned fruit and pound cake, while ham and lima beans was despised the most.

**L/CPL ART RIORDAN - Co L: When we arrived in Vietnam, our main staple was boxed C-rations. They were not exciting to the palate, and when you read the fine print you realized why. They were boxed in 1945! Chicken noodle became my mainstay to life support. Ham and lima beans were thrown to the Vietnamese kids begging along the streets, who generally threw them back. We did find a 'FNG' (fucking new guy) who liked eating them, and at first I thought him weird until I found I could trade Ham and Limas for anything he had. The main problem I had with the C-rats other than the taste was the Chicklets. A friend of mine's father was a VIP with the Chicklet company and we use to see the Yankee Games in the Chicklet box seats. I liked Chicklets. The problem was getting them from the cellophane sealed package to your mouth with out getting sand on them. I tried everything and anything to get them into my mouth with out chewing on a piece of sand. I was convinced the Nazi's infiltrated the Chicklet company and were dumping beach sand into the Chicklet mix. Not until three months later when we got the 1963 C-rats did I realize that we were in a country that you ate sand with your meals. Between the sand and red clay, everything crunched when you chewed.**

Usually, the Marines would be resupplied with food and water, every one to two days. The resupply would arrive mainly by amtrac and occasionally by helicopter. If there was no fresh water, then streams, wells or even bomb crater or rice paddy water was utilized. Water purification tablets containing iodine were sometimes used in the tainted water.

Mail usually came out with the food and ammo resupply. Along with the mail, 'care packages' from home were prized items. Canned fruit, cookies, Kool-Aid to help kill the taste of bad water, all helped to raise the spirits. Another valuable item was hot sauce which helped mask the flavor of some of the worst meals.

\* \* \*

**HM MIKE LUTZ - Co I:** Booby traps were the real mind fuck. People were seriously maimed by them, but rarely KIA. You always wondered when it would be your turn. The worst feeling for a corpsman was to have an explosion up on the point and hear the call of "corpsman up." My biggest fear was to get up to a wounded Marine and not know what to do. It was always on your mind.

\* \* \*

**SGT RICHARD PELKY - Co M:** One night we were on patrol out of Tu Cau when my sniper using a night scope, spotted men walking across a paddy dike. We all opened up with a field of fire. It turned out to be our second squad who was on the wrong side of the MSR road. Fortunately, no one was hurt but it was a very close call judging from the conversations I had with the other squad leader the next morning.

\* \* \*

**SGT WES LOVE - Co K:** We were on a patrol and came across a deserted village. There was a water hole, like a artesian well, with water flush to the surface. We figured the VC would possibly hide in the water and use reeds to breathe through. L/Cpl Dillard 'Sweet Pete'

Peterson said he was going to drop a grenade into the water hole. Two seconds later - BOOM! My first reaction was to holler, "Fire in the hole, fire in the hole, Dammit!" I ran over to see Sweet Pete on his back with several wounds. I yanked my own tee shirt off and tried to wrap his forehead with it, while yelling for a medivac. The corpsman walked over and said "Forget it Sarge, he's gone!" I watched him try to gasp for breath for just a few seconds and then he died.

I picked up my rifle, walked over to a small berm and started to peel off everything, my pack, bandoleers and flak jacket right down to bare skin. I broke out in a cold sweat thinking about what had just happened. The corpsman walked over and asked if I was all right. I said I was. We saddled up and moved on out after the medivac.

I figured the grenade Peterson had used had been tampered with by having some of its time fuse removed. After this incident, I initiated a safety practice of always checking out all grenades and other explosive devices for potential problems.

\* \* \*

**CPL GARLAND SISCO - Co K:** We were out on a night ambush along the river up stream from Tu Cau Bridge. One of our helicopters put a huge light right on top of us. As the squad leader, I just knew that we were going to be killed. I had everyone lay perfectly still and finally the chopper left us. We were all pretty shaken from the incident.

\* \* \*

**L/CPL ART RIORDAN - Co L:** We were sent by

truck to Anomo Bridge which is just north of Danang on Highway 1. Foxtrot of 2/7 was out on an Operation and we hoped they took their time coming back. The Bridge was located in paradise, it spanned a river that dumped into the South China Sea which was less than an 1/8 of a mile away. Our only function was to guard the bridge which held 3 positions, two facing the river and one facing the sea. We shot at anything that floated towards the bridge ( in case the enemy was using sticks for breathing tubes ) and dropped a 1/2 pound block of TNT off the bridge every 5 minutes (in case the enemy had swimmers underwater.) Other than that we ran patrols up the river and into the 'Banana Grove.' We had a gun tower and under that a plywood mess hall with tables. We lived in a tent that had cots. There was a two-holer that was screened in. We could swim in the river or sea. It was an in-country R and R, until March 29th. That day we took a direct hit from a 500 pound bomb which was purportedly dropped from a crippled Marine fighter, that was trying to land at Danang air base. I somehow remember a propeller aircraft flying overhead just before the bomb hit.

    The gun tower took a direct hit as well as the mess hall which was right below it. I believe we lost two gunners and it wounded seven men, in the mess hall, who were being briefed for a patrol.

    My squad took over the patrol. Everyone was a little edgy. L/Cpl Dave Thompson volunteered to take point. Pfc Clovis Acosta was second and I was third man in the patrol. We didn't get a hundred yards out of the wire when there was a large flash and explosion. All I saw was an outline of Acosta as he was blown backwards and I could not see Thompson. The Corpsman went to work on Acosta and we were trying to locate Dave Thompson who was somewhere out front. Not until the CP fired a flare did we see Thompson laying still about 30 feet in front of us.

As soon as the flare subsided Dave crawled back to our position.

Clovis Acosta lost an eye and Dave Thompson still carries shrapnel in his back. I believe it was our squad leader, Sgt Najenski who carried Acosta back to the road. Although Acosta's head was wrapped in bandages he would not let go of his M-16. He was one tough Marine.

Funny things happen in the midst of disasters. L/Cpl Dante Gusti was walking past our CP when the bomb hit. An FNG was in the screened in two-holer. The explosion blew the roof and wall of the shitter and lit the new guys pants, which were around his ankles, on fire. Gus who is about 5'7", put the fire out and carried the new guy, who Gus said was over 6 feet to the river and dropped him in. He then picked him up again and carried him over to the CP where they were setting up a triage. Gus carried him quite a distance and when they were about 10 feet from the CP the new guy says, "you can put me down," and calmly walks away as if nothing happened. Gus was pissed.

I had acquired a metal mess tray and had it hanging in the tent above my cot. The tent and cots were peppered with holes and so was my mess tray. Now I was pissed.

Because we had lost 2 KIA and 7 WIA, the Army, who was just up the road, sent us some replacements for the night. Our position was on the north side of the bridge and a little ways into the bush. Since we were told that the NVA might launch an attack I had gotten 3 LAW rockets and set them up near my position. They sent over two huge Army guys to help with our line. My adrenaline was winding down and I was exhausted so I asked the Army guys if they would take first watch. I dug a fighting hole right behind them and was trying to get some shut eye when I saw one of these guys lighting a cigarette and talking loud to the other one. I jumped out of my hole and explained to these guys that I would blow their heads off if they lit another cigarette and didn't shut up. Now I couldn't sleep, my adrenaline was back up. Somehow I nodded off and at first light I woke with a start, knowing I had slept through my watch. I looked up and saw that the Army men were wide awake, looking forward and not saying a word. I apologized for not believing them. They both shook my hand and said, "It was great working with you Marines." Go figure.

     PFC CLOVIS ACOSTA - Co L: I was wounded on March 29 by a booby trap. The last person I saw as I was being loaded onto the helicopter was Bill Gostlin. He gave me a hug and said, "Congratulations for getting a one way ticket out." I had mixed feelings. I felt guilty about leaving my friends, happy to get out of there and scared beyond belief. Even though the wounds were serious, I felt that I wouldn't be sent home. I only hoped for a 2 or 3 week rest before being sent back to the bush. I was so scared that I got constipated at NSA Hospital in Da Nang and didn't go to the bathroom for 2 weeks. Finally, my problem was corrected at the 249th Army Hospital in Japan.

     L/CPL ART RIORDAN - Co L: On Guard Duty, stateside, you can expect an NCO to make his rounds, checking to see if the Guard is alert and responsive. In combat sometimes it is not a wise idea. In a three-man position we were suppose to have two men 'up' and one man 'down.' That was the rule. Not many abided. Shut eye was at a premium. One 'up' two 'down' was the norm.
     We had an NCO who was constantly sneaking up on our positions to ensure they were manned properly. This is not healthy. You expect the VC to be in stealth mode, not your own people. When a man is alert, he is usually a bit edgy. Combine this with an automatic weapon and a finger

close to the trigger and it is not wise to startle him. The men were pissed. If they accidently 'waxed' the NCO, they were in trouble. If the NCO successfully infiltrated their position, they were in trouble. This had to stop.

Our position was located next to an Army Tank. Every night they would come through our position in order to set up claymore mines in front of their tank. To save the NCO's life and us from getting in trouble, we decided to let him sneak up on a hand illumination grenade. I set up a hand lume at the only entrance to our position from behind, and placed a trip wire across it. When the Army tankers came to put out their claymores, I told them to step over the trip wire connected to the hand lume. They took one look and decided not to set up their mines that night. I know I had told their TC ( tank commander) what we were doing. They probably never handled a grenade after boot camp. Actually there is little difference between a fragment and an illumination grenade except for a rim at the base. In reflection, the tankers must have called our CP and alerted the NCO because he was whistling and making one hell of a racket and the man couldn't whistle. We went through the procedures and he announced who he was and didn't move an inch. It was obvious he knew the trip wire was nearby.

The next morning I told one of the tankers I wanted to see their TC. They told me he went to Da Nang. I suspect he stayed in his tank for the next three days that we manned that position.

* * *

**CPL BILL GOSTLIN - Co L:** Four guys in my squad were killed on 5 May (Cpl Paul Evans, Pfc Rodney Melton, Pfc Louis Nelson and Pfc Wallace Shane.) The war ended for me on 9 May while another squad member was killed (L/Cpl Nelson Swanker.) The last 'salt' made it until the 12th of July when he too was killed (L/Cpl Gerald Hetrick.)

Cpl Bill Gostlin lost his leg and was medivaced to Guam and then on to the Philadelphia Naval Hospital. He spent most of his hospital time with his Co I friend, Tim Davis.

\* \* \*

**L/CPL THOMAS FULEKY** - Scout/Sniper - H & S Co: I also worked with L Co and had the honor of patrolling with L/Cpl Gerald Hetrick, a fellow Marine from Michigan. As scouts we were very careful of our movement, never taking the same trail twice. When we did, that's when we got into trouble. At about 1600 we finally took a break when we received a call on the radio to saddle-up on the double. Hetrick's squad was about 500 meters away and they had just set off a booby trap. By the time we got there, L/Cpl Hetrick had already called in his own emergency medivac. I don't think he made it to the hospital before he died.

\* \* \*

**L/CPL BOB NEILSON** - Co I: I was point man on a patrol on 7 May. I stepped on a mine and my right leg was blown off right away. I never lost consciousness.
My best friend was Jan 'Mitch' Mitchner. He and I would eventually hang out together for almost a year after he got out of the service. He died of bone marrow cancer in the late 1980's.

\* \* \*

**SGT DENNY CHRISTY - Co I:** On the morning of April 23rd our platoon sized tank/infantry operation was making a sweep through booby trap alley south of Tu Cau bridge, along the river bank in the sand dunes. Being in third squad, we were on the right flank. The month before, on March 23, we got hit in the same area. We were in column this time and we sustained one killed and four wounded on the tanks. We were on the third tank back and we didn't take any injuries at all. We were in sandy soil, more like sand dunes, basically. I left half the squad on the tank and the rest of us were in the tank tracks because the area was heavily booby trapped. About 1130 we took a chow break, and the tanks were about 30 yards ahead of us in staggered formation. Then all of a sudden there were three quick shots, and I felt like bumblebees got hold of me and I hit the ground like a ton of bricks, bleeding pretty good on the right forearm. It ripped a pretty good hole. Basically it was three shots and from that point on I was conscious, but I was laying out in the middle of this sand pit. I had seen a waterhole up ahead of me a little ways and I got up quickly and moved towards it, grasping my arm and trying to stop the bleeding. I remember I drank 2 quarts of water real quick. The corpsman came by, I think it was Doc Stewart, a white football type of character, and he gave me a shot of morphine. Apparently that put me into a state of suspended animation. It didn't take long for the choppers to come. I walked to the chopper, got on, looked back at the guys and the next thing I knew I was in Da Nang. I got off the chopper, but nobody was there to greet me. I walked into the medivac hospital and there were 2 corpsman sitting on the gurney b-s'ing. I said "I've just been shot." The old boy said, "Oh, okay. Get up and sit on the gurney here." Shit, before I knew it they cut every inch of the clothing off my body, threw me into a shower and threw half a gallon of disinfectant on me and away we went to the operating room.

L/CPL TIM DAVIS - Co I: The saddest day for our squad was when Denny Christy was hit and medivaced. He was the first in our squad to be wounded. I couldn't help to remember back when Don Compton came back from the club at midnight and told Christy that he was "Going to kick his ass." Don is 5'6" and Denny was 6'4". Christy won!

\* \* \*

L/CPL CHARLES SWAGERTY - Co M: We became closely familiar with the term 'booby traps.' Like a lot of Marines, I'm now offended by that terminology and it's implication that the unfortunate souls who set one off were 'boobs,' or idiots. But at the time it was the words we used to describe a myriad of devices used to blow us up and away. And if we could be honest with ourselves, we *were* magnificently ignorant about them when we arrived. Unfortunately, the crash course we got upon arrival came at the sacrifice of dozens of limbs, and the lives of friends and comrades. Some replacements literally did not last a day. Ken Noonan, who was blown up in April by what we believe was a command detonated mine and would spend a year in the hospital in the states, told me at the 30 year reunion of going to meet a replacement that had come in the night before. It was too late. The boy never made it a day, dead by land mine. God, we lost an incredible amount of men to booby traps.

\* \* \*

L/CPL CHRISTOPHER STERLING - Co K: We

were running a patrol out of Tu Cau bridge into the sandy area. That morning I think I had found 3 booby traps and disabled them. Two of them were probably duds, nothing would have happened anyhow, so I thought I was kind of cool. I was a combat engineer, so I was used to dealing with demolitions, booby traps and shit. I hated working around the sandy area because you couldn't see the booby traps. Basically we thought we were getting lucky because they sent out a tank to bring us back. We got on the tank and probably went about 30 feet when we were hit by either an RPG (rocket propelled grenade) or more than likely we hit an anti-tank mine. It got 6 of us at that one time. At the time, there were only 14 of us left in the platoon and it got 6 of us in that one shot.

Sgt Caesar Watkins and myself got it the worst I think. Basically we were sitting with our legs over the tank treads on the mud guard above it and it blew through the tread and actually what I got was rubber shrapnel from the tank tread. I was lucky it wasn't the metal, it would have taken my leg off. I remember jumping off the tank and running. The corpsman tackled me and said "You're hit." That's the first I knew of it. I heard this ringing in my ears because I was right over the blast. The shrapnel, about the size of a quarter, went in below my knee and came out the top. I got some shit on my right foot. I got a compound fracture on my first metatarsal (one of the joints past the toe more towards the base of the foot.) It was pulverized and sticking out the skin a little, even though the boot was still intact. I didn't think anything was wrong with the boot, it's just like the blast effect or maybe some shrapnel hit the bottom of the boot and shattered my foot. I had some other scars on my lower leg that I didn't pay much attention to. By the time I saw my leg later on it was already in a cast.

That was five weeks into my time in country. I'd

gone into Vietnam on February 21 and got zapped on March 28. The next day, the remaining 8 guys in the platoon all got it at the ARVN compound; 2 killed and all the rest wounded. So five weeks and one day in country there was nobody left in the platoon. I knew I had the million dollar wound when the corpsman tackled me and told me I was hit. I knew I wasn't going back. It was such a relief.

* * *

L/CPL MARK SMITH - Co I: Thompson told me to get the radio out and exchange it. I asked him how I was supposed to do that and he told me to ride in the back of the tank. 3 tanks went out and I was on the 3rd tank facing back the way we had come. We came up the Main Supply Route (MSR) where the Tu Cau bridge turns off. We turned off. I could feel the tank going up over the top of the rice paddy and all of a sudden I heard shooting up front. Well, I got up in a position to jump so I could see what's going on, when something hit me. I just felt myself going up in the air and going back down. I came back down and the first thing I see was my first index finger bleeding. I said to myself, "I got my second purple heart." Then I started seeing all of my other wounds. I was injured in my back and most of my leg was off. It was all from shrapnel. One piece broke my wrist, another broke my thumb, one broke my back and paralyzed my left leg. To this day I don't know what caused the explosion. The only way to find out is to interview somebody who was there with me. The only thing I know, there was an explosion, a lot of small arms fire and that quick, it was over. You know, it was what the VC do; that quick and they were out of the woodwork. These guys were playing cat and mouse tonight and I got to be the mouse. The first guy I seen laying on the tank when I rolled over was looking at me, and he said to me, "Hey, what the hell did you do?" I said, "I don't know, tell me what I did." There were four of them trying to get me out. It was such a thing, you want to scream and yell and carry on, but you get so thirsty and everything else. You want to drink a lot of water. Then they got me off and took me back to Battalion; stabilized me at the time and then sent me over to the hospital. It was the Naval Hospital in Da Nang. I stayed in Da Nang, then got shipped to Yokohama, Japan to the 109th Army Hospital. I stayed there for about three weeks and from there I got shipped to the Naval hospital in Philadelphia. I was discharged when I got out of the hospital.

I got hit on the 24th of June at 1300 on a Sunday. It was the nicest day. You figured, what's going to happen on a day like today!

\* \* \*

**SGT EDWARD BENAVIDEZ - Co M:** Sometime early in the morning on April 11, some kind of insect bit my ear and it was sore as hell. We moved out at 0630 and got close to a village about an hour later. LT Guhl, our platoon leader, found a 60mm booby trap by almost stepping on it. He called for demo men to blow it up in place. A few minutes later, as he was stepping back, he hit another booby trap. He lost both legs and was in bad shape. Sgt Hein and I took over and called for a medivac. While setting up landing zone security, Pfc Miller also stepped on a mine. He lost both legs too, but he died after about five minutes.

**L/CPL CHARLES SWAGERTY - Co M:** I was the only grunt in my squad, but someone decided I was just the guy to be a rocket man. That lasted until just after Lt Guhl got blown up. I was a rocket team leader at the time. When the Lt stepped on the mine, someone yelled for guns and rockets up. I ran up front, and the corpsman who was attending Lt Guhl told me to come and help him. As I started walking to them, another giant explosion went up behind me. It was a member of my rocket team, Pfc Miller, running the same path I'd taken, but not stepping in the tracks I'd made. He died, and became one of many Marines I've periodically agonized over for the last thirty years; confused, wondering why the inches that saved us or ended our lives were always on my side. I've always thought Guhl was a brave soul. While I was walking ever so carefully across that sand to aid the corpsman, Guhl was chastising me, saying, "Slow down, Goddammit, Marine, be careful." There he was, blown all to shit, worrying about me stepping on a mine. I recall holding a handkerchief soaked in water to his lips, trying to comfort and reassure him until the medivac arrived. I was sure he wouldn't make it, and for 30 years I thought he was dead. I learned at the 3/27 30th Reunion that what was left of him, made it home.

2nd LT ALFRED GUHL - 1st Platoon Leader, Co M: My nicknames were Crazy Al and Grub. I lost my left leg above the knee and my right at the hip. I thought the other man on the medivac chopper with me was William McAdams, an outstanding Marine. I was very concerned why the crew leader wasn't chatting with him too. I was told the next day that McAdams was KIA and not WIA. Years would pass before I learned that it was really Miller and not McAdams who was killed.

SGT EDWARD BENAVIDEZ - Co M: After the medivac, we went back to the Battalion CP. In the afternoon, Sgt Hein and I went to the 1st MED BN in Da Nang to identify Pfc Miller. Afterwards back at the area, I went to the club. I needed a beer after today. Tomorrow we were going to sweep the same area!

**2ND LT ALFRED GUHL - Co M:** Sgt Benavidez was an excellent squad leader who really knew his stuff.

The most pride I take in anything I did in the 'crotch' was being the platoon leader of Mike One. Serving with my men was very special. They were good Marines, whether they were in Mike One or the attached rocket and gun squads. I never cease to brag about my guys. How lucky I was.

\* \* \*

**HM3 DAVID 'DOC' WATSON - Co M:** The Marines seemed to accept me but I knew I would have to be 'blooded' before I wasn't considered a FNG (fucking new guy.) On one patrol near the leper colony, the point man stepped on a booby trap and was blown out of his boots. As I ran to treat him, I tripped a booby trap and took a blast in the butt. As the M-60 man was setting up security for the medivac, he too, tripped a booby trap in a tree line. The point man died in the hospital in Da Nang, the M-60 man was temporarily blinded and for several years after I was married, my wife picked shrapnel out of my butt and upper legs.

\* \* \*

**L/CPL EDWIN VELEZ - Co M:** The first time I went out on patrol we were ambushed just a couple of minutes outside of the compound. Our point man was hit and when I asked Sgt Roy Watkins, our platoon sergeant, how he was, he said that he was dead. I cried.

* * *

**GY/SGT FRANK CORTEZ - Co M:** About the middle of April we made contact with some VC stragglers who apparently were headed for the Go Noi area. We inflicted some casualties but we lost one of our boys with a direct shot to the heart. We kept working the area for the next couple of weeks and on one of our company size sweeps a large explosive device laid waste to three troopers, S/Sgt Rosenfelt, and myself. Rosie and I were the more seriously hurt. So much for my theory that there is safety in numbers. At least it didn't work that way in the Tu Cau area or the rest of Nam for that matter. It was April 30th 1968. I was to spend the next six months in three different hospitals being put back together. After four or five major reconstructive stomach surgeries I was sent back to duty.

* * *

**CPL BILL BACH - Co K:** In May, I was on a squad size patrol/ambush, out of the Battalion CP. We had no contact and we were on our way back to the CP. When we were within 500 meters of the base, we took 5 or 6 incoming mortar rounds. They must have been waiting for us to return. I was wounded and since it was my third purple heart, I was evacuated back to the States.

* * *

**2$^{ND}$ LT ALFRED GUHL - Co M:** 2$^{nd}$ Lt Bob Tuttle, replaced me as Platoon Leader of Mike One. Bob was one helluva guy! He was a Navy Academy graduate in the class of 1967.

**SGT EDWARD BENAVIDEZ - Co M**: On April 12 at 0400 we got up and got ready to move out. M company was blocking while L company was sweeping. We got into position about 0700. L company swept right through us, but nothing much was found. We all got back about noon. We got a new platoon leader from K company to replace Lt Guhl. His name was Lt Tuttle. The rest of the day was spent cleaning up. In the evening two squads went out on patrol. 2nd squad and the CP stayed behind. I went to the club and later to the movie. We had a meeting with our new Platoon leader. I didn't know how he would be in the field yet. Only time would tell.

**L/CPL THOMAS FULEKY - Scout/Snipers - H & S Co**: Most of my time was spent on patrol with the scouts, but on occasions my sniper team would be sent out with a line company. We were on patrol with Mike about 2 miles outside of our CP with their new Platoon Commander, Lt Tuttle. He was a tall muscular man. A patrol brought in a suspected Viet Cong and Lt Tuttle had his shirt off, carving away with his k-bar, a native melon, when the dink saw him. Needless to say he was getting a little nervous. Just then the Viet Cong started walking mortars in on us. No one was hit. A few days later I was to find out that Lt Tuttle had stepped on a landmine killing him instantly.

**SGT EDWARD BENAVIDEZ - Co M**: On May 8, at about 0730, we left in the same direction that we had come from the day before. Just before the paddy we set in as sort of a half-ass blocking force for some South Vietnamese troops. While waiting for word to move out, Sgt Richards stepped on a mine. He was hurt pretty bad. We hailed a medivac and I almost got hit by the chopper when it came in! About 1030 we got the word to move out. I suggested crossing the paddy instead of using the trail, but the Lt was in a hurry. I was in the rear when I heard a loud explosion. Lt Tuttle had set off a booby trap 105. Lt Tuttle was KIA and Diaz and Morrison were WIA. Morrison lost an arm. I took over and called in a medivac.

\* \* \*

The Marines would learn where and how to walk in their booby trapped infested area. One should always stay off trails and paddy dikes, avoid openings in tree lines, and walk in the foot steps of the person in front of you. Look for anything unusual. Always take extra precautions in every movement you made. Point men would use thin branches to probe for trips wires. Village gates would be pulled open with the use of ropes. The enemy and the Marines would constantly try to second guess each other. The VC knew the Marines liked to spend the night on high ground, so these areas were always potential booby trap and sniper areas. Mistakes were constantly made. You were tired and hot and figured it wasn't your day to get hit so you got careless. Or, maybe your CO was pushing you to speed up to get to an objective on time. The constant influx of new men who needed training on booby traps also added to the burden. Even though the senior men were skilled in booby trap detection, it was impossible to enforce each individual's movements. Skill and luck played a big part in every day survival. There probably isn't one 3/27 Marine who didn't have one or more close calls in dealing with booby traps.

**CPL RAUL FONSECA - Co I: We were ordered to sweep right through booby trap alley. I told the Lieutenant that it was crazy to do this and that we would**

lose men. I took the point on the left flank through a sandy area. I told my people to follow me and jumped off a dike and into the sand. I traveled about four steps and froze. I felt something on the bottom of my feet and told everyone to get the hell away from me. When they were clear, I leaped off of a bouncing betty booby trap and was wounded. I am still on 40% disability.

\* \* \*

**L/CPL DALE CAMP - Co I:** I was walking flank security for the company which was in a column with tanks down in the valley next to the sand dunes. As I walked along the ridge of the dunes I saw a well used trail. At the base of the trail I discovered a trip wire in the sand. As I brushed the sand away my leg slipped into a hole. The wire had been a decoy. I knew that I was dead. When my butt hit the ground and nothing happened, I began to think I might get lucky. I jumped up and ran for a low spot in the dunes. As you can imagine, I was pretty freaked out. When I tried to yell down to the column, I couldn't speak. My frantic waving finally attracted their attention and one of the guys came up. I was still afraid to go near the booby trap but he did and was shocked to find that it was a 105mm artillery round. We tried to blow it with grenades, but it wouldn't explode. I am sure that I know the same fear all others had as their feet fell through those holes. As I would continue to do all through my time in the bush, I beat the odds.

\* \* \*

**L/CPL ART RIORDAN - Co L:** We were on a day patrol when the point man stopped dead in his tracks. He told everyone not to move. Directly in front of him was a slightly uncovered booby trap. This particular booby trap consisted of a chicom (Chinese Communist) grenade placed in a small hole with the trip wire across the top. The VC would then use discarded cardboard, which had been used as the case wrap for c-rations, to place on top of the hole. They would then put sand or dirt on top of the cardboard for concealment. Wind must have blown the sand away from one edge of the cardboard and the point man spotted it. We were going to back track from where we came. As I looked down to find my previous boot prints I remembered I had a satchel (10 pounds) of C-4 plastic explosives, hanging from my shoulder. Without moving an inch, the C-4, was gingerly passed back towards the end of the patrol. The booby trap was blown 'in place' and we continued our patrol. One Marine, protecting his groin with one hand, started doing a funny dance with one foot forward. He announced that he was a human mine detector and chicoms would only blow a toe off but it can get you a ride 'home.' We laughed hysterically. I have always wondered if he was half serious.

*  *  *

Another lucky Marine was L/Cpl Chuck Spencer (Co L). Not only did he escape death once, but twice in extremely close calls.

**L/CPL CHUCK SPENCER - Co L:** I was standing guard in the Battalion area. I had my M-16 sitting on my boot while I was leaning on the rifle barrel. A sniper shot the pistol grip right off of my rifle. I brought the grip home.

Another time, I was walking point along the river during the daytime. I was carrying my rifle at high port arms and the next thing I knew it felt like several hammers were hitting me in the chest and I went down. I knew I had been shot in the chest several times and was dying. I laid there for a minute while the firefight was going on. I said a prayer that I still remember, "Dear God, please forgive me for everything I've ever done wrong, as I know I'm about to die!"

I started feeling for the wounds and couldn't find any. I didn't see any blood. Looking at my rifle, I discovered the handguards and stock had taken all the hits. I tried to roll to cover right and left, but they boxed me in with bullets. I got mad and thought "If you're going to die, die like a Marine, go down fighting and take some of them with you." I really did think that! I picked up my rifle, stuck it out and pulled the trigger. It worked! I started burning up magazines. Like a dummy, I put my hands around the barrel and blistered them good. We got a base of fire set up and I dove for the river. The gooks broke and ran.

Bill Dahl, my squad leader, and Del Westover never forgot the look on my face when we got back to the platoon base camp. My eyes were as big as saucers and all I could say was "Those goddamn gooks tried to kill me."

\* \* \*

Two unique ways to counter effect the large number of surprise firing devices found in the Battalion's TAOR (Tactical Area of Responsibility) and to hurt the enemy using his own methods were both the ideas of Capt E. Miles Keefe, Jr., who in June 1968 would become the S-3 Operations Officer. The first one was to set up a 'Rat Patrol,' and the second was to establish a Special Operations Group (SOG.)

There were two main roads leading out of 3/27's Cau Ha base. One was the 5 mile MSR road leading north to Da Nang and the other a 3 mile road leading to Tu Cau Bridge next to Highway 1. These roads were constantly mined; and casualties and damaged vehicles were common occurrences. Capt Keefe established a Rat Patrol by having jeeps with mounted M-60 machine guns constantly patrol these roads, thus denying the VC and NVA the opportunity to set up their mines. Three men per jeep and two jeeps per road made up the Rat Patrol teams. The teams were rotated amongst the companies that provided security for the roads.

From Capt Keefe, the idea of a special unit to be used at night against the enemy went to the Battalion Commander. Next, Lt Col Woodham discussed the formation of the SOG unit with Sgt Major Snyder and decided how it could be best used to the Battalion's advantage.

The SOG unit was made up of a group of 14 volunteers from the different companies in the Battalion to operate at night in the enemy's home territory. The team members were all interviewed for the job by the Battalion Sgt Major, a former 12 year Marine Reconnaissance veteran. Sgt Major Snyder made sure all of the men worked quietly at night and were skilled at booby trap detection.

The 14 man unit would leave the CP at dark and would be given a grid area of free fire. No other units would be allowed into their assigned territory. Once at their designated area, the unit would split into three four man teams, each given a sector to patrol. Each team carried a starlite night vision scope. The VC would quickly learn that they didn't control the night when the SOG group was out.

\* \* \*

As a whole, whenever the Marines could make friends with the villagers, they did so. It was very difficult, however, especially when it was assumed that most of the area belonged to the VC at night. Children were always begging for food and cigarettes, but in actuality, they were serving as the eyes and ears of the local VC. As soon as a patrol left a base camp, the kids would start up a chorus of shouting to warn the VC. They would also often be seen playing around the CP appearing harmless. Later, a Marine patrol would likely find a booby trap left by these 'harmless children.' Regardless of the negligible impact, many Marines did make an effort to be friendly.

\* \* \*

**L/CPL MARK SMITH - Co I:** We spent the day in a hamlet outside of the CP and I became fairly friendly with one family. When it was time for chow I said my goodbyes, but the interpreter said the family wanted me to eat with them. We had a nice meal of rice, a green weed of some type and raw fish heads.

\* \* \*

**CPL ROBERT SIMONSEN - Co I:** There was this old papasan who lived on the outskirts of booby trap alley. He was very nice to us and every time we came across his hut we gave him food and cigarettes. He constantly warned us that 'beaucoup' VC and booby traps awaited us to the south. He may have been a VC himself, but we all liked him anyway.

\* \* \*

**L/CPL ART RIORDAN - Co L:** We were sweeping through a village, on a search and destroy, when I spotted a papa-san squatting on a hooch step. It appeared he was eating rice from a gourd that was full to the top. Something didn't look right. As I neared I noticed the rice was moving. He was brushing a bowl full of flies with his chop sticks in order to eat a few grains of rice in the bottom of the gourd. Americans are used to eating white rice. Theirs is brown and black rice. To me it looked like dead flies and fly feces. I was disgusted and drop kicked the gourd from his hands. Later I thought, this is their culture-not mine.

    We were checking civilian ID's on a well used path. When Vietnamese wait for anything they squat. A woman, three back in line was squatting. She was smiling at me with blackened 'beetle nut' teeth. Something didn't look right. I realized she was relieving herself right in the middle of the path. It wasn't easy adjusting to their culture.

    I was in Danang near hill 327 and I needed a haircut so I found a Vietnamese barber shop. When I entered, I noticed rifles standing in a rifle rack. They belonged to Army Soldiers who were already getting hair cuts. I kept my M-16 with me and placed it between my legs when I sat for my 'high and tight.' When the barber was done cutting, he grabbed the back of my head with one hand and my chin with the other. I thought he was going to break my neck. I flew out off the seat and had my M-16 (which always had a round in the chamber) aimed at his mouth. He dropped to his knees and was shaking. One of the soldiers started laughing and said he was only going to crack my neck. I said, "Oh yeah, I'll blow his ------- brains out." The soldier realizing I was new to this, and dead serious, said, "No don't, he is only going to relax you and it feels great." I sat back down and put my M-16 across my lap. I told the barber to go ahead. With shaking hands he cracked my neck. I felt as if someone lifted a 100 pounds off my back. This time it was the barber who got a taste of cultural shock.

\* \* \*

**LT COL TULLIS WOODHAM, JR. - 3/27 BATTALION CO:** The Battalion did a pretty good job of winning over the local people by means of medical, food and other civic action programs. On one occasion, villagers came in to tip us off about 50 Viet Cong (VC) who were planning an attack.

\* \* \*

Humor has always found itself in wars. Perhaps it was escapism from the brutal reality of everyday life or it was just simply that when you put young men together, they will find a way to have fun despite any circumstances. Laughter and crying could always be heard amongst the 3/27 Marines.

**HM MIKE LUTZ - Co I:** Early one morning out in the Rivera, we awoke, had some C-Rats and we began saddling up to move out. Mitch (Cpl Jan Mitchner) stood up, opened his flak jacket, looked up at the sky and said, "God, if I don't die today, you got no balls."

Everyone gave Mitch plenty of space for sometime after that.

\* \* \*

**HM3 DAVID 'DOC' WATSON - Co M:** When I got back from a patrol with WIA's, I would get debriefed by the Sgt Major (Sgt Major Robert Snyder.) He was a typical Sgt Major, tough and demanding on the outside and concerned about his Marines on the inside. He always wanted to know what we could have done better. After debriefing, I would get resupplied, clean my .45, get a shower and read my mail. Then I would shoot the breeze with the Marines. I always laughed to see Marines cleaning their weapons and intently watching 'Combat' on

## AFVNTV (Armed Forces Vietnam Television.)

\* \* \*

**L/CPL ALLEN CIEZKI - Co I:** We were out in the sand dunes with tanks. One of the tanks ran right over 'Senator Mudflap's' foot, never even hurting him because the sand gave way. It was funny because he used to say how tough he was because he had been run over by a tank.

One of the tanks turned over an unexploded 105 round, standing it straight in the air. Dale Camp and I were told to blow it up. As Camp laid a stick of C-4 against the round, it fell over and rolled about a foot. I looked at Camp, his eyes were closed and he didn't move. After a few seconds, he looked back at me, rolled his eyes and shook his head. He then placed the C-4 again and tiptoed away. We blew the round and joined the rest of the platoon.

\* \* \*

**PFC CLOVIS ACOSTA - Co L:** Everyone in my squad had non-infantry MOSs and we really didn't know what was going on. For the first two weeks we set up claymore mines backwards. Finally a 'real' grunt told us we were doing it wrong!

One night we dug in on a side of a hill near a ville. We had settled in and I began eating my boned chicken, when I started smelling something very bad. The smell was so over powering that I couldn't even eat my meal. The next day we discovered we had camped right in the middle of the community shitter for the ville. I never could eat boned chicken again.

**L/CPL ART RIORDAN - Co. L:** Pfc Acosta and I

were fighting hole buddies on this particular patrol. The usual patrol consisted of 'digging in' around sunset and then moving out after dark, to another position, where we dug in for the night. This daily ritual was accomplished, not to keep us in the habit of digging holes, but was done in case the enemy saw us setting up for the night and had their mortars zeroed in on us. On this night the second dig was near a cemetery. In Vietnam, Buddhists are mounded above ground and Christians are buried below ground. We were in a Christian cemetery. Acosta and myself thought a headstone would give us added protection in the event of an attack. It was Acosta's turn to dig first and I would dig second. He got about 3 to 4 feet into the ground when he jumped out and said, "There is a grave down there." We looked at the headstone again, and thought the grave should be on the other side. We were both too tired to dig another hole so we put some earth back on the grave. Acosta got the 'willies' and did not go in the fighting hole. He tucked in behind the headstone and the hole for the rest of the night. I figured there was nothing inside the hole that was going to kill me but outside the fighting hole was a different story.

* * *

L/CPL ALLAN CIEZKI - Co. I: I wasn't too worried until my squad leader, an ex-supply sergeant, asked me if I could help him learn how to read a compass! Fortunately, he was transferred out after a week or so.

* * *

HM MIKE LUTZ - Co I: When we were in country early on, our patrols just outside the battalion area would sometimes involve medically treating people from the nearby ville. We went there the first 1 to 2 weeks in country. "Doc, see what you can do for these gooks, okay?" They lined up like sick call, young and old with various problems. I had absolutely no idea what I was doing. Babies with weird skin rashes, old people with willy peter burns on them. In my unit one there was several tubes of some kind of white cream.

Whatya got? Burns, leprosy, tumors, eczema, sunburn? I don't fuckin' know. Every gook in line got an application of some magic white cream. They went away happy, but I doubt if we helped anyone.

* * *

L/CPL ART RIORDAN - Co L: I had been out in the bush for a couple of months before I was volunteered by 'Machine Gun' Butler to go to DaNang. We were either going to identify a body, going to the hospital or both. Charlie and I had about a weeks growth of beard, red clay dust all over us and I am sure did not smell all that pleasant. We had on our helmets and flack jackets. Charlie had a thirty round belt of ammo wrapped around his M-60 and I had my M-16 with 10 mags and grenades. I felt totally out of place. People were walking around in Bermuda shorts, not carrying weapons and acting as if they were at a resort. I thought the war was over and they neglected to tell us. We boarded a military bus and sat towards the back. Everyone on the bus would sneak a peek at us but were afraid to make eye contact. When new passengers boarded they were joking and carrying on until they saw us, then they became quiet and sat towards the front of the bus. Our own people were more afraid of us than the dinks.

We went to the PX at Hill 327. Our PX cards had

a big X across the area set aside for liquor. Marines were not allowed booze! I thought alcohol should be placed under Sundries. I was 23 years old, in combat and not allowed to drink. I found a young Air Force kid and told him in no uncertain terms that if he ever wanted to see his Mommy again he best come out the back of the PX with a bottle of Scotch in his hand and he did. I came to a basic conclusion there were a hell of a lot more non-combatants than 'grunts.'

\* \* \*

**LT COL TULLIS WOODHAM, JR. - 3/27 BATTALION CO:** One day, Capt Anderson came to me and said he had an 'in' with the Sea Bees to our north. He said they would be willing to trade us lights for our perimeter for eight or ten K-Bar knives. I told him fine, but I didn't want to know about it!

\* \* \*

**PFC TOM HANSON - Co I:** We were out in the field somewhere and we had rendezvoused with some M-48 tanks to set up for the night. We had dug our holes but the Lieutenant was digging a work of art. The sides were perfectly straight up and down and the corners were perfectly square. A tank close to us wanted to fire a canister round to clear the brush to their front but the Lieutenant said, "No, wait, I'm not done."

Eventually, when the hole was completed to his satisfaction, the Lieutenant got in, stretched out his legs, covered his ears and said, "Okay, now you can fire."

The tank let loose, the ground shook violently, and the Lieutenant's hole collapsed in on him. There he sat with his hands over his ears, buried up to his chin. His only comment was a soft, "shit." When we got done laughing, we dug him out.

\* \* \*

**L/CPL ART RIORDAN - Co L:** On any patrol, the point man directs his attention to the ground, always alert for booby traps and trip wires. To this day, I instantly stop when anything brushes against my shoe or ankle. The second man in the patrol is watching directly in front of and above the point man. He tends to watch the trees.

We were on a night patrol. There was a full moon which was so bright it seemed like an endless dusk. As our patrol moved into a dense area the second Marine whispered, "Don't move." We looked up and with the full moon as a background there was the largest spider I have ever seen. It was in a huge web and almost directly above the point man. Someone grabbed a large stick and knocked it to the ground. There was a lot of whispering, "What the hell are you doing?" "Why did ya do that, asshole?" Everyone was pissed. Not wanting to fire our weapons and give away our position, we gave the area a wide berth.

I look back and chuckle to myself. Here was an overly armed Marine patrol that could probably take over a medium-sized city, and one extremely large spider kept us at bay.

\* \* \*

**PFC MEL THANE - Co L:** On June 1, I was promoted to Lance Corporal and was on a night patrol from the Tu Cau bridge. In the morning when my squad returned to the PPB at Tu Cau bridge I was told to report to Lt Renaghan ASAP. I was all pissed off because I thought that I was going to have to go on another patrol and everyone in my squad was exhausted from the night's outing. I reported to Renaghan and Sgt Belser (I believe he was there) and Joe Renaghan asked me what I was doing the next day. I looked at him in bewilderment. He then asked me if I would like to go on a three day R and R at China Beach. I figured this was some sort of trick question and asked him to repeat himself. Evidently there was one R and R freebie available and Renaghan picked me. Great I thought, no patrols, a shower and some sleep. Hey when do I leave? I was told to report to the company driver and Gunny Hoagland the next morning at Tu Cau bridge and await transportation back to the Battalion Area with them. I met the driver and Hoagland, climbed back into the jeep and off we went. Now you remember that we were in the 'booby trap capital of the world' then and nobody used the road without a mine sweep. Well, we were halfway down the road when we saw these Marines on foot coming towards us. I noticed they had flank support and immediately realized that this was the mine sweep. Now when I had climbed into the jeep the Gunny offered both the driver and myself a swig of whatever he was drinking. The Gunny had been drinking quite heavily and when we approached the mine sweep he ordered the driver to stop. He climbed out of the jeep quite slowly and ambled over to the Marine in charge of the mine sweep and asked them, "How the hell are you guys doing?" They kept staring at us in silence. The Gunny then waved his bottle of booze across the sky and said, "You Marines can go back to the Battalion Area because I just swept the fucking road." The driver and I were just about ready to crap our pants. I remembered thinking that I would be safer on R and R than on duty with my platoon. Well, that wasn't necessarily the case when you were in the company of Gunny Hoagland.

**CAPT JOHN ERNEST - CO, Co L:** Gunny Hoagland knew more about weapons than anyone I had ever met in the Marine Corps, but he did like his booze!

\* \* \*

**HM MIKE LUTZ - Co I:** I remember one rare night back at the battalion area and we were just sitting around 'shooting the shit.' The conversation eventually got around on how in the fuck we ended up in Vietnam. PFC Robert 'Bobby' Burke told us the story of a wild Friday night that involved cars and excessive malt beverages. As he awoke early Saturday morning groggy with a splitting headache in the local jail, there was an impressive looking dude with a crew cut and an outstanding blue uniform looking in at him.

"Son, I can get you out of here," the Marine recruiter told him.

I don't know if this was a true story or not, but it had us all rolling around with laughter.

\* \* \*

The battle for the rocket belt was neither won or lost. The VC inflicted numerous casualties, mainly through surprise firing devices and snipers. The body count in 3/27's operational area definitely favored the communists. 3/27's mission, however, was to suppress enemy rockets from penetrating the strategic city of Da Nang and its important airfield and to block large enemy force movements. Regardless of the injuries incurred, 3/27 professionally fulfilled its task. No matter the odds of being wounded or killed, 3/27 Marines constantly patrolled, swept and ambushed its TAOR. The enemy was restricted to small operations and never mounted a large scaled attack against Da Nang, the Cau

Ha command base or any other 3/27 field base camp.

If the Marines had stopped their patrol saturation in order to reduce casualties, then surely one could state the VC won and that they had complete control of this vital area. Such was not the case while 3/27 operated from February through September 1968. The unit relieving 3/27 had its command base attacked and penetrated and the Tu Cau bridge was blown up.

The VC were not the only ones inflicting casualties. 3/27 also had several successes in hurting the enemy on its home turf.

\* \* \*

**SGT GARY HARLAN - Co I: I don't recall who discovered the tunnel cleverly dug into the bank, but I said I'd do the flashlight and .45 routine. Haugen got a rope and tied it to my ankle. The tunnel began at a roughly 45-degree angle and then abruptly turned back in. The moment I spotted the two figures in black, I put a round in the chest of the one sitting closest to me. I didn't get an opportunity to get the second because Haugen jerked my ass out of there the second he heard the explosion.**

**Without prior discussion or ceremony, I just told Haugen to get back, and I crawled back in just far enough to toss a grenade inside. When the smoke and dust cleared enough to see, I started pulling out the contents, which included a couple of rifles and their identification. One of them, the one I killed with the .45, was a young woman.**

**For me, it was a grand and glorious moment. It had only been days since we lost Loyd Kinsworthy, a twenty-year old Lance Corporal in Leroy's fire team, who we could always count on to do the job. This was payback time, and all the Marines standing on top the riverbank looking down as they watched me drag out things from the**

tunnel, were digging it. All but Sgt Lee, that is. When I thought I was going to drag out a corpse when I found a bare foot to pull, I was surprised to discover that all I pulled out was the foot attached to the ankle, severed by the grenade.

Twenty-six years later, Gary Harlan would return to Vietnam on a personal visit. While there, he was fortunate to meet with Le Van Tra, the former VC commander of the village forces near the Tu Cau Bridge. Both Tra and his mother were awarded numerous medals for heroism while conducting guerilla operations in the Booby Trap Alley area. Tra actually recovered and buried the two VC killed by Harlan in the tunnel incident. The man was a propaganda specialist while the woman was a member of the political team.

\* \* \*

Corporal John Hazelwood was leading a patrol and ambush of 12 Marines from Co I one late evening. As they set up their ambush, one of the men heard a clanking sound of metal on metal. Minutes later, a group of VC fired off rockets towards the Da Nang airfield.

**CPL JOHN HAZELWOOD - Co I: As soon as the rockets were launched and we spotted the enemy position, we were on our way. When we got to the area, the VC had already fled.**

Since artillery began pounding away at the rocket blast, only moments after the attack began, the VC launched only six rockets before they were driven away.

Hazelwood and his squad set up a perimeter to keep the enemy away from the remaining seven rockets. The light weight rocket launchers were carried away by the enemy, but the rockets, weighing more than 100 pounds each, were abandoned.

An hour after the Marines seized the enemy position, four VC tried to regain it. When they got within 25 meters of the Marines, they opened up with AK-47 assault rifles.

**CPL JOHN HAZELWOOD - Co I: It couldn't have lasted more than three minutes with our M-16's and a M-60 machine gun firing. It wasn't long before they turned back and ran again.**

Although Hazelwood saw one drop to the ground, a later search revealed only empty cartridge cases and blood trails. The squad claimed credit for the most rockets captured at one time by the 27th Marines.

\* \* \*

**CPL BILL BACH - Co K: We were on a platoon size patrol out of the Battalion CP. We were in a column and a large command detonated booby trap went off in the middle of our group. One Marine lost his legs and a few others received minor wounds.**

**Normally, that would be the end of the incident and we wouldn't find the elusive enemy. This time, however, my fire team was on high ground and we saw three NVA sprinting away through the rice paddies. We chased after them, firing our weapons as we went. We managed to kill all three. One was an officer who carried a 9 mm pistol.**

\* \* \*

**PFC JAMES SHAW - Co M: As we were crossing a rice paddy we spotted two VC at the end of the hedgerow to our front.**

The squad of Marines fired and hit one in the leg. Moments later, however, the VC got up and tried to escape to the other side of the barrier. As L/Cpl John Hayes ran towards the enemy, Shaw circled around the hedgerow from the other side in order to trap the VC. The other VC found a fighting hole and jumped in it for cover. Shaw found him and his AK-47 assault rifle as he emerged from the hole. The wounded VC got away.

**CPL RICHARD BUCHANAN - Co M:** Shaw ran the gook down, pushed him down on his back, put his boot on his throat and pointed the M-16 between his eyes. By this time the fight in him was gone.

**PFC FRANK NEIHART - Co L:** That night the VC was interrogated rather roughly at the CP. He finally agreed to show the Marines a supply of weapons and ammo. The next morning, he was dressed up like a Marine, given a helmet and put on point.

The VC detainee led Marines of Co L to a village 2000 meters north of the Battalion Command Post. He pointed out two gardens and one grave site. The Marines began to dig.

**PFC FRANK NEIHART - Co L:** Word came down to saddle up for patrol, but to take empty packs because we were going to recover enemy munitions.
I saw the prisoner and he was bruised and battered, with a bandage on his head. The graveyard was maybe 4 or 5 clicks from our rear. When we got there, a perimeter was set up around it.
Two burial urns were uncovered. One had 20 or 30 mortar round in it and the other had about 100 anti-personnel mines. The mines were about 6" x 6" x 3".
We lined up to go back to our rear. Everyone lined

up to carry them back. Each riflemen ended up carrying 3 or 4 mines.

Everybody was pissed because these mines were the ones that had been tearing 3/27 up; one Marine at a time.

The only way that bastard made it back to the rear was because he stayed close to Lt Colpas and the radioman. No accidental shots were fired.

**2ND LT GARY COLPAS - Co L:** There was no way anyone could've found it without knowing exactly where it was.

The enemy cache was the largest discovered since the Battalion arrived in Vietnam. Both Hayes and Shaw earned an in-country R&R as a reward for their effort.

\* \* \*

**L/CPL ART RIORDAN - Co L:** We were moving forward through a small notch. On our right was a small hill (where we should have had a flank.) There was this tremendous explosion that shook the ground and almost knocked us off our feet. We crept up the hill and found the remains of two NVA. We found their packs which were hi-tech compared to ours and their mess kits were more useful than what we used. The air smelled strongly of cordite and it had a peculiar metallic taste. We estimated that the NVA were trying to booby trap an unexploded 250 pound bomb. Sgt Najenski (Ski) found a third pack. We figured the third NVA was setting the booby trap when it exploded and he 'vaporized.' I realized what the metallic taste was and didn't stop spitting for the rest of the day.

After mentally debriefing the experience we had in Viet Nam, especially the area that we worked in, I have come to a conclusion that ordnance lacked in quality control. We lost many excellent Marines to unexploded ordnance that was used as booby traps by the NVA and VC. This includes, short fused hand grenades, dud 3.5 rockets, 105 and 155 artillery and a variety of aircraft deployed bombs. If the military is going to use ground troops in the future, they had better get a strong grip on the manufacturers of the above ordnances. I would think that any Marine grunt who served in Viet Nam would love the job of Quality Control; they knew the consequences.

\* \* \*

L/CPL DALE CAMP - Co I: On a night patrol, we set up an ambush. As we got into position, we heard snoring behind us in a bamboo grove. We moved away and sent two grunts back to the grove. They opened up on the snoring area and we had one dead VC and one captured VC recruiter.

CPL ROBERT SIMONSEN - Co I: When we pulled the two VC out of the bushes the one kept saying, "No VC, Joe, No VC." We said, "Yeah right!" He had a picture of Ho Chi Minh in his wallet and they had several grenades amongst them. We blindfolded the live one and half carried/dragged the dead one back to our PPB (Platoon Patrol Base.) The next day we took the two over to the MSR road where a jeep picked them up. We couldn't believe that the one had survived. Probably forty rounds were shot into the bushes and the dead VC took almost all of the bullets. When we picked him up, his entire brains fell out the back of his head. The other VC didn't even have a scratch!

\* \* \*

**L/CPL CHARLES SWAGERTY - Co M:** I recall, after setting up our perimeter for one night, an enemy patrol stumbled into our lines about 0200. A pretty good fire fight ensued. In the morning we found three dead within five meters of the lines, clad in the stereotypical black pajamas. All were obviously (previously) healthy, well built and sporting fresh haircuts. One of the three had to be six feet tall. A sergeant said he was Chinese. I didn't know about that, but it sure got my attention.

\* \* \*

**L/CPL LEROY R. DRIFFILL - Co K:** One incident that I recall in the Rivera was a patrol where we came up from behind a small island to the west of the large rice paddy. It seemed that every time we went to cross the paddy, I would see around five people running from this area of this island. Always in black pajamas but with no weapons. As we moved up into this area on this patrol, the point man stepped on a land mine. We set up a defense and one Marine noticed personnel moving on this island carrying weapons. Myself and four other Marines crossed a small ditch with about three feet of water. I got hung up in barbwire which ripped my pants and cut my leg (not too badly) while chasing the enemy. One of the Marines I was with extended a law and fired. It hit high in the tree on the island and got an air burst effect. The enemy soldiers then ran out into the rice paddy to evade us. We ran up to the island and saw three enemy each running with weapons. I tried to run across the narrow dike with the machine gun but fell off into water up to my chest. I crawled out, stood up on the dike, and fired a burst at the one enemy soldier in an opening. I fell off the dike at least four times from the recoil of the gun each time I fired. The soldier finally went down. A grunt reached him and, with his k-bar, finished him off by repeatedly driving his knife into him. We had been taking a lot of casualties and the frustration of the killing and wounding of our brothers was demonstrated in our aggressive behavior on that day. I remember that Battalion wanted to know who had killed a NVA soldier with a k-bar. We laughed about what had happened. The point man that stepped on the concussion mine broke both his legs, but it didn't break the skin. I was amazed from the size of the explosion. The enemy KIA's were three, one being a doctor, and all being NVA regulars.

* * *

**SGT JON PAHL - H & S Co:** I was in the tower at Tu Cau Bridge with my FO team when we observed heavy air strikes, arty and lots of enemy green tracers about 10-15 clicks south of our position. It was my experience that when the NVA engaged during daylight, it was a very dangerous situation. I knew the battle was on a place called Go Noi Island. I had been there previously on my first tour during Operation Stone. I had an eerie premonition that we would soon join in on this battle.

**L/CPL LEROY R. DRIFFILL - Co K:** We received word while out in the field in early May that we would be going on an operation. This news was greeted with mixed emotion. I can recall all of the guys like me who had never been on an operation were kind of excited, as we were going to finally get to fight the enemy face to face, and not fight these damn booby traps. The Marines who had been there before knew what the operations were like. I remember telling Sgt O'Connor with excitement in my voice that we were going on an operation. I still remember that look on his face, which said, "Are you stupid or something?" He had spent time on operations and knew what we would face, and soon enough we all would know.

# PART II
# ARMAGEDDON

# 1. GO NOI ISLAND 1968

Go Noi Island is located in the Dien Ban District, Quang Nam Province, I Corps, Republic of Vietnam. It is approximately fifteen miles south of Da Nang, west of Hoi An City and five miles east of An Hoa. Although it is not truly an island, it is surrounded by rivers, streams and roads. To the south is a large mountain range (Que Son mountains) which is used as a North Vietnamese Army (NVA) infiltration route from Laos.

Go Noi Island generally consists of low lying flat land broken up by several deep banked streams, canals and ditches. There are numerous small settlements usually surrounded by thick hedges, shrub growths and bamboo thickets. In between the populated areas of thick growth are low dry wash areas which vary from bare dunes to heavy elephant grass as tall as a standing man. In near proximity to the populated areas are numerous closely spaced grave mounds. In some areas, particularly west of the railroad line, there are rice paddies separated by earthen dams of one to two feet.

The soil consistency throughout is rich, loose, sandy and loamy. During May, 1968, the soil was firm enough to provide good cross-country tracked vehicle mobility. Foot movement is slowed by dense shrub growth, loose sand, high elephant grass and steep soft stream banks.

The area is devoid of prominent terrain features from which long range observation can be accomplished or which can be used to fix locations on the ground. However, many of the areas of thick growth are positioned in such a manner as to dominate the intervening open areas thereby giving the defenders excellent fields of fire.

Natural cover in the area is almost non-existent, but it has been honey-combed with tunnels, caves and bunkers. All indigenous personnel live in bunkers with 2 to 3 feet thick walls. Often such bunkers will be built underneath the roof of what appears from afar as a normal straw hut or brick house.

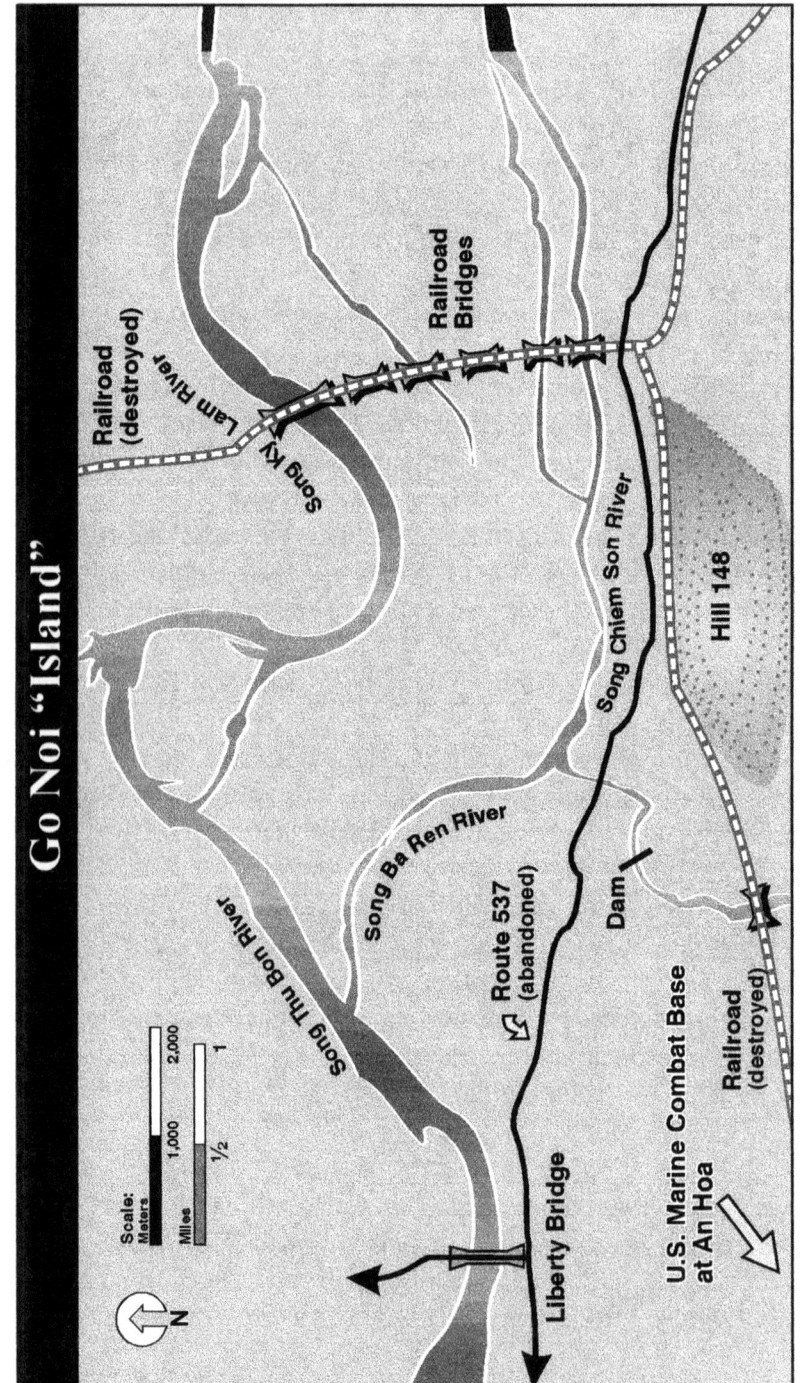

The thick growth and high stands of elephant grass which characterize the area provide excellent concealment against observation from ground or air. However, because of the frequent open areas which must be traversed, movement of any significant distance during daylight hours can be readily observed from the air.

During May, 1968, the average daily temperature was well above 100 degrees farenheit and the humidity exceeded 80%. A variable wind was usually less than five knots. The temperature and humidity in the area of operations was continually higher than that in the surrounding area. The heat factor necessitated severe restriction of troop movement which was usually limited to early morning or late afternoon hours. Towards the end of May, rains became frequent, mostly in the early or late afternoon. These were mostly intermittent and did not significantly affect cross country movement. In July, torrential rains would arrive and would affect normal operations.

Although the civilian population is considered sparse, they are all strongly VC oriented. Most of the men of military age are active Viet Cong.

Traditionally, Go Noi Island served as a staging area for NVA units building up for attacks against the Da Nang area.

In May, 1968, the 36th Regiment of the 308th NVA Division and elements of three VC Battalions (R-20, V-25 and the T-3 Sappers) had found their way onto the Island. Ralliers who had operated in the area reported that Go Noi contained a sizeable hospital complex and was used extensively as a training site. The overall control of enemy forces in the Go Noi Island area was exercised by the Quang Da Zone Headquarters known as Group 44.

These NVA forces were well trained and equipped. Their field packs were stocked with medical supplies, munitions and gas masks. Their uniforms were immaculate and neatly pressed.  The men were young (18-25 years old) and had fresh haircuts.

The NVA possessed great fire power.  They had rockets, crew served automatic weapons and mortars.  They would fire as many as 60 mortar rounds in a single salvo.  The standard weapon carried was the AK-47 assault rifle.  They had Polish rifle grenades and the new RPG-7 rocket launchers.  Their supply lines and leaders were excellent.

When not surprised, the NVA wanted to pick the time and place of their engagements.  Usually, they liked to utilize a general pattern of contact which served them well time after time.  Friendly forces would approach a tree line from across an open field.  The lead elements of the friendly forces would enter the tree line and would be taken under fire and pinned down.  The follow-up elements would then be fired upon as they attempted to move forward across the open ground to assist those units already in contact.  The ranges were always under 150 meters and in many cases, less than 50 meters.  The enemy would not disengage but would continue contact at close ranges, thus denying the friendly units from using supporting arms (mortars, artillery or air power.)  Therefore, many NVA casualties were caused by small arms fire.  Close in fighting was common.  It can be said that the enemy died hard!  The NVA tactics were never wholly successful.  Eventually the Marines would be able to disengage, and the deadly rain of fire from the sky would begin.

## 2. OPERATION ALLEN BROOK (PHASE 1)

### BUILD-UP / PRE 13 MAY

By late April 1968, through reconnaissance observations and limited engagements, it was determined that the enemy had fed in an equivalent of an NVA Division in the area south of Da Nang.

Major General Donn Robertson, the 1st Marine Division Commanding General, now decided to change his tactics for the defense of Da Nang. Up to this time, the defense consisted of heavily patrolling the rocket belt extending in a semi-circle around Da Nang. With additional available troops (the 27th Marine Regiment had arrived in Vietnam in February,) it was decided to fan out in deeper reaching, more mobile operations which would keep the NVA forces away from doing damage to the Da Nang area.

On 4 May, Operation Allen Brook began under control of the 7th Marines, commanded by Col Reverdy M. Hall. The first unit committed was the 2nd Battalion, 7th Marines (2/7). The battalion went in on the western edge of Go Noi Island and attacked eastward towards the railway. Reconnaissance teams had earlier reported several sightings of enemy troop movements of groups with as many as sixty to eighty NVA criss-crossing the Island. Prior to the initiation of the operations, no allied force had been in the western end of the Island for about one year.

The first large contact was made on 7 May when some Marine tanks reversed direction returning to refuel. A fight followed, resulting in 30 NVA killed. The tanks then changed direction again and made a second contact, killing another 12 enemy soldiers.

On 8 May, while fighting was still going on, 3/27 was notified of their pending participation in Operation Allen Brook and the general location of Go Noi Island.

Every Marine-138

**LT COLONEL TULLIS WOODHAM, JR. - 3/27 BATTALION CO:** After months of griping to the Regimental Commander that 3/27 hadn't gone off on any kind of campaign (Hue or Khe Sahn,) we were alerted to prepare for Operation Allen Brook. Colonel Schwenk (later Lt Gen Adolph G. Schwenk) was a fine Regimental Commander. He finally told me he didn't want to send his best Battalion off just any where. He was saving us for something when the time and need was special. I was desperate to get us out of booby trap alley and patrolling the rocket belt.

On 9 May, 2/7 ran into a large enemy force in the vicinity of the ruined railroad bridge over the Ky Lam River near Xuan Dai. During a hot fight, 80 NVA were killed.

On 11 May, 3/27 Commanding Officer (Lt Colonel Tullis J. Woodham, Jr.), his S-3 (Major E.T. Fitzgerald) and Air and Artillery Liaison Officers, flew visual reconnaissance flights over the Island. They landed near the mobile command post of 2/7, where they were briefed by the 2/7 Commander (Lt Colonel Charles E. Mueller.)

Original plans called for 3/27 to enter Go Noi Island as part of a task force consisting of elements from the 7th Marines and the Army of the Republic of Vietnam (ARVN.) Several days prior to the planned coordinated venture with the 7th Marine forces, the concept was modified. The plan now was for 3/27 to eventually operate west of the railway bisecting the Island without the 7th Marines while the ARVN forces were to sweep the area east of the railway towards Highway 1 and Hoi An. The basic reason for the planned withdrawal of the 7th Marines from the Go Noi sector was that III MAF believed another NVA buildup was occurring in the western Quang Tin Province near the Laotian border. III MAF instructed Major General Robertson to institute an attack into this valley region, located west of Da Nang. This 7th Marine

Every Marine-139

operation would be known as Mameluke Thrust. 3/27's mission was to seek, close with, and destroy the NVA and VC forces within the Go Noi area in order to preempt enemy attack efforts against Da Nang.

**LT COLONEL TULLIS WOODHAM, JR. - 3/27 BATTALION CO:** When I got the word that 3/27 would be operating in the Western half of Go Noi alone, I was apprehensive that we might be walking into more than we might want to handle. I had heard that a similar venture by one of our Marine infantry battalions, not too long before we arrived, had resulted in a lot less than was desired. They were virtually run off the Island. I did not want to see 3/27 experience the same fate.

On 13 May, India Company 3/27, with a section from 81mm mortars, would be attached to 2/7 and act as 3/27's leading element.

**CPL ROBERT SIMONSEN - Co I:** A long talked about rumor of a big operation was finally materializing. We were told to get our gear ready for the next day (13 May.) We made light marching packs, drew ammo, and then stored our extra gear. My Company, India, was to be the first company landed, with the rest of the Battalion to follow at a later date. That night we were sent out on a PPB (Platoon Patrol Base) and no one could believe it. They couldn't even give us one good night's sleep before the operation!

**HM MIKE LUTZ - Co I:** When word came down that we were going to Happy Valley for what was going to be called Operation Allen Brook, my good friend Melvin 'Mud Flap' Cox reassured me there would be no booby traps. Then he added, "but big operations were where you got all of your KIAs." Thanks a lot!

**LT COLONEL TULLIS WOODHAM, JR. - 3/27 BATTALION CO:** I thought very highly of all of my companies. The strengths of the companies varied from time to time, dependent on officer and NCO strengths, as well as other obvious factors. I chose Co I to go out first because, at the time, it had its act together. They had been the first to hurt the enemy in our area and were under the able leadership of Capt Tom Ralph. Ralph had been a student of mine at the Officers Training School at Quantico when he was a 2nd Lieutenant. I thought a lot of him.

<u>13 MAY</u>

Activity was very brisk in the Co I area sector of the Battalion CP in the early morning hours of 13 May. The Commanding Officer of Co I (Capt Thomas Henry Ralph, Jr.) was busy briefing and organizing his men for the helicopter air lift to the Go Noi area.

**CPL ROBERT SIMONSEN - Co I:** We arrived back from the PPB at 0400, slept for two hours, and then went to chow. I barely had food on my mess kit when someone came in and told everyone in India to leave and get their gear on. We then headed over to the Landing Zone (LZ) and shortly, the first bunch left in four helicopters. Several of us huddled near Capt Ralph for news of the landing. About fifteen minutes passed and finally we heard over the radio that the landing area was safe. There had been no enemy resistance. I can still remember Capt Ralph saying "Happiness is a secure LZ."

Co I was heli-lifted to Hill 148 in the Que Son

Mountains, just to the south of, and overlooking Go Noi Island. Once landed, the platoons were dispersed around the crest of the hill and began digging fox holes. The ground was hard and progress was very slow. There was no shade and the temperature was extremely hot. Water was a premium and there would be no resupply of food or water that day.

**L/CPL DALE CAMP - Co I:** I was on the first chopper to land on the mountain. While we were flying out, someone noticed that the windows in our chopper had all been knocked out. The crew chief said that was because grunts were always knocking them out so they could shoot back. As you can understand that didn't make us feel too good. Then we noticed that there were bullet holes all through the chopper and that really freaked us out. I was scared shitless and kept trying to remember what to do when we got there. We finally got over the hill and spiraled down to the LZ. The chopper was tipped over to my side and I could see the hill all the way down. The chopper hit the LZ and we ran out the back and set up some security. It all happened very fast and it took a few seconds to realize that we weren't taking any incoming. That was quite a relief. All the others came in and nothing happened.

The next few hours were spent digging in. The top of that hill was hard as hell. It was the toughest place we ever dug in. I worked and worked and when it was almost deep enough I hit some Willie Peter and it started to heat up and smoke. I was so pissed. I wasn't about to start over again so I just covered it up and crawled in. While we were waiting, we started noticing NVA down in the valley. There were a lot of them just walking around, so we called in some fire missions on them.

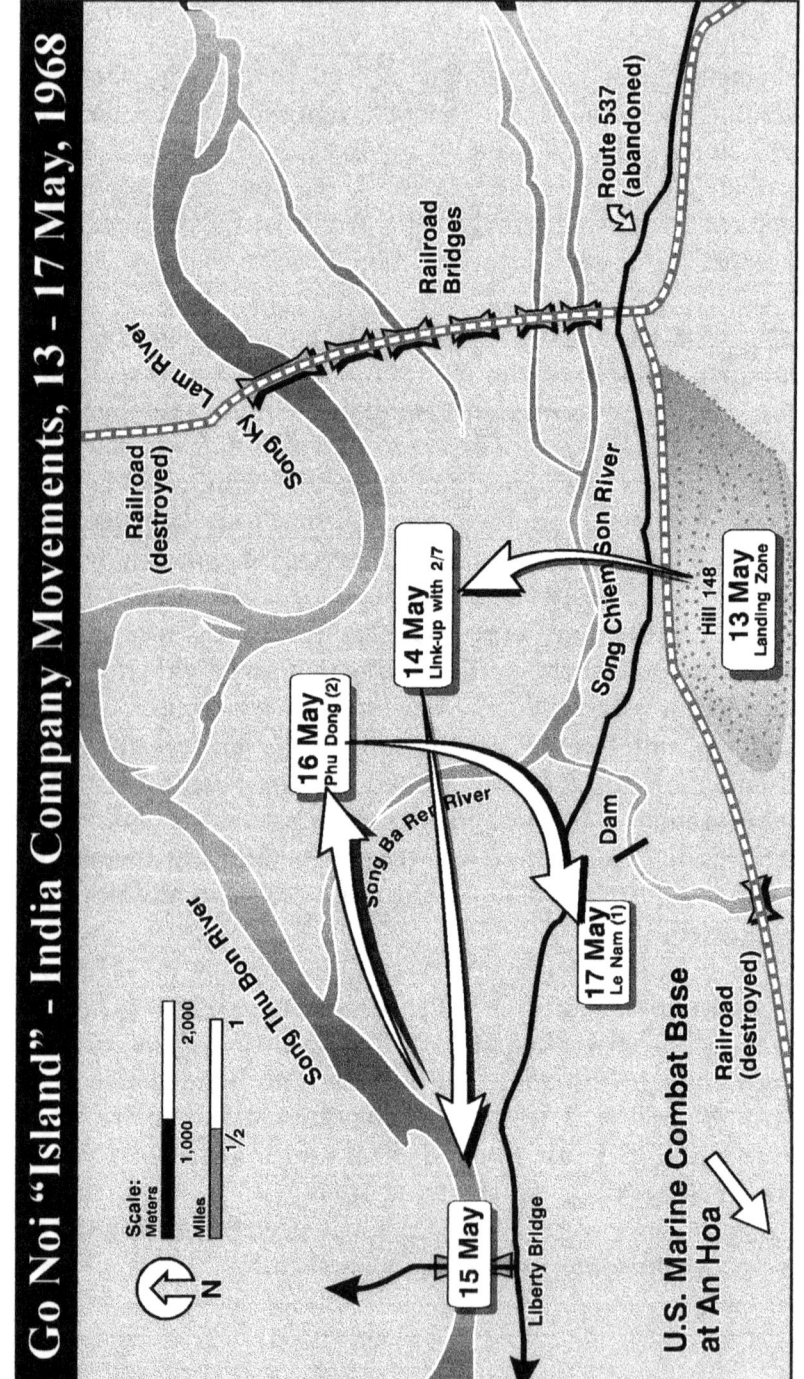

**CPL FRED STUEBE - 81 MORTARS - H&S CO:** I was a squad leader with 81's. We were attached to India and landed on Hill 148 on the last choppers in. We all had a very uneasy feeling of things yet to come.

**PFC TOM HANSON - Co I:** We waddled on to the CH-46's loaded down with rifles, extra ammo, grenades, food, assorted personal gear, ammunition for crew-served weapons, and other equipment. After a short flight we landed on top of a hill, and spread out down along a ridge. My squad, headed by Sgt Phillips, was stationed along a level spot on the ridge approximately 200 meters from the top. We began to dig in; my fire team leader L/Cpl Steve Easton and Pfc Bob Bauer in one hole and L/Cpl Tim Davis, our grenadier, and I in another. Someone had apparently been on that hill before because there were piles and platforms of old sandbags lying about. Tim and I stripped to trousers and boots and dug down about two feet when we hit a layer of solid rock. Captain Ralph, our company commander, happened to be there and when he saw our predicament he advised us to take old sandbags from a platform about 30 feet away and pile them around our hole.

We had made several trips back and forth, all the while Tim was singing a Hank Williams song.

I started to walk back to our hole and after a few steps I stopped and considered dropping one of the sandbags I had because it was about to fall apart. Tim walked past me going the other way, and I again started walking back to our hole, when a tremendous explosion behind me blew me to the ground. The thing I remember most was that it was so *loud!* I thought we were getting mortared. Somebody behind me was moaning, obviously in pain. My back was stinging, and unsure if or how badly I might be wounded, considered just staying down, but then I jumped up and dashed to my hole. Diving in, I threw on my flak jacket and helmet.

Unhesitatingly, Doc Price, our corpsman, was running to the wounded man, despite everyone yelling, "Get down, Doc!" He began ministering to the casualty, and after a short while, we realized that we weren't being mortared and that someone had tripped a mine. Gathering around, we saw that the wounded man was Tim. One leg had been completely severed at the knee and the other was only connected by a few sinews. Without a doubt that one would go too.

One of the Chinooks returned as a medivac and Tim was lifted aboard. As it lifted off I remembered the words to the song Tim had been singing: "My hair's still curly, my eyes are still blue. Why don't you love me like you used to do?" I knew Tim had a beautiful girlfriend back home and I prayed that the answer wouldn't be, "Because your legs are gone."

As the medivac helicopter headed for Da Nang, L/Cpl Davis, feeling a leg near his head, asked the black door gunner "Who else had been wounded?" The gunner told him that he was the only one and that the leg he felt was his own severed leg. Asking if he felt it could be re-attached, the gunner said "No man." He then told the gunner to kick it out of the helicopter and said, "That should feed a family of six!"

\*   \*   \*

**L/CPL TIM DAVIS - Co I:** I was sent to the hospital in Guam where my friend from Lima Company, Bill Gostlin, was a roommate along with several other 3/27 wounded Marines. I have never forgotten my head nurse in Guam, a Miss K (Sandy Kirkpatrick Holmes.) She refused to help me when I first fell out of my wheelchair.

I yelled and threatened to report her. Finally, after an hour, I was able to get back into my wheelchair. Miss K came back and started a hand clapping which spread throughout the ward. She told me I was a Marine and taught me to take care of myself even without my legs. She turned my life around. On June 13, I was transported back to the Philadelphia Naval Hospital. I wouldn't leave the hospital until October.

Upon leaving the hospital, Tim Davis would marry his high school sweetheart. Twenty-five years later, just prior to his 25th wedding anniversary, Davis and several other former 3/27 Marines including Bill Gostlin and Mark Smith met in Washington, D.C. for the dedication of the Vietnam Women's Memorial. While there, due to his persistence, he was able to locate Miss K, his former nurse in Guam. He arranged a meeting and met her with an arm full of roses. Bill Gostlin presented her with his purple heart and said, "The guys on the 'wall' would want her to have it."

\* \* \*

Several sightings of NVA troop movements on Go Noi Island were made throughout the day. The enemy seemed to be moving at will with no fear of discovery.

**SGT JON PAHL - H & S Co:** We observed a fight between the 7th Marines and the NVA right below the hill. The NVA broke and ran out into the open ground. We had this area on preplotted arty concentrations. As we called for Battery 3 to "fire for effect, shoot when ready," the ground soon started to be torn up all around the NVA. We then had to "check fire" as A4 Skyhawks came on station. They dropped CBU's (cluster bomb units) and nearly five acres of Vietnam were saturated with explosions. We stared in disbelief at the destruction. There wasn't any movement left.

* * *

**CPL ROBERT SIMONSEN - Co I:** At around 1500 we prepared to leave the hill. Our squad started up the top to pick up more equipment. Our squad leader (Cpl Steven D. Zucroff) led the way with L/Cpl Jack Watson and myself close behind. The rest of the squad followed. Just before reaching the top, Watson and I stopped to rest and the next thing I knew I was blown to the ground by another large explosion. Cpl Zucroff and another Marine were both killed outright. Watson broke an ear drum. We were both covered with dried blood and bone fragments. It was one of the worst sights that I had ever seen as we carried the bodies in ponchos to the evacuation point.

**CPL JOE THOMAS - Co I:** It was late afternoon and we were getting ready to move off the top. I saw a Marine who was kicking at a sandbag and then I noticed Sgt Black storming up the hill. I knew he was getting ready to chew out this Marine when 'BOOM!' The Marine kicking the sandbags had hit a booby trap and both he and another were killed. I picked up a piece of shrapnel in my knee. It was my third Purple Heart but nothing too serious. Some of the guys told the Captain that it was my third heart and he had me evacuated to the NSA hospital along with the two KIA's (killed in action.)

**L/CPL DALE CAMP - Co I:** Cpl Zucroff was the new squad leader for 1st squad. He came over to my hole and the guys came over and we got to know him a little. He had already done a tour but came right back because he hated the bullshit back in the states. He showed us photos of his wife and two girls. He told me that in a few minutes we would be going down into the valley and that I would be walking point for the company. A lot of things went through my head. The main thing was fear of what we would find down there. When it came time to head for the trail, Zucroff said to go in order of our fighting holes and we would line up when we got over there. This meant that I was a few Marines back in line instead of being in front. As we moved across the top of the hill there was a huge explosion and I was knocked on my face. As I lay there big pieces of earth and rocks were coming down on us. I thought it had been a mortar and anticipated another. When it didn't come and the rocks quit falling I looked up. There right in front of my face was the top pallet of someone's mouth. The teeth were still in it and it was burned and smoking. That was just too much for my mind, and I blanked that scene out for many years. Sometime in the 70s while thinking about Nam for the millionth time it all came back to me. I wonder how many other things are still hidden inside there? Marines started yelling and I realized that Zucroff was gone. We were all yelling his name and we couldn't understand where he was. Then we found out that he and another Marine had been blown clear off the top of the hill. What was left of him was 50 feet or more down the side of the hill. Two Marines went down that slippery slope with a poncho to get him. As they struggled to get back up the slope, Zucroff's bones ripped out the poncho and he fell through it. The exhausted and demoralized Marines gave up and crawled to the top. Lt Stephen Thompson turned to me and asked if I would help him retrieve Zucroff. We slid down there and put him on a poncho. His clothes were gone, his face was gone, his arms and legs were gone, and he was split wide open from his crotch to his sternum. The only way we knew it was him was that he was balding and had red hair. Thompson and I also struggled with the body and hill. When we finally made the top we must have looked pretty grim cause Doc Lutz asked me if I was OK.

Because of delays in evacuating the bodies we spent the night on the mountain and the NVA pestered us with mortars.

**PFC TOM HANSON - Co I:** I moved in with Bauer and Easton, but after a few hours the word was passed to saddle up again, we were moving off the hill. We were waiting to move out when a tremendous explosion erupted on the top of the hill. A huge splash of smoke went across the sky, people were running down the hill, and debris was raining down. The carrying handle of an M-16 landed at my feet. A larger object rose out of the smoke, sailed lazily through the air, and landed on the side of the hill. It was only then, that although it had no arms or a head, I realized what it was. "Look," I said, "It's a body!" "No, don't look," Steve Easton said, and we turned about and faced away from the scene.

Because night was approaching, we were ordered to stand down, it being deemed too dangerous to try and move off the hill in the dark. We were, of course, bitter. At least two men had been killed, Tim Davis, if he lived, had lost his legs, and other casualties had been incurred in a place where there weren't supposed to be any booby traps.

We saw a human finger on the edge of our hole and we thought it was part of Davis. We figured that it was blown off when he was reaching down for a sand bag prior to the explosion. Twenty years later we found out it wasn't Davis' finger, so it must have been from the second explosion on top of the hill.

Every Marine-149

Plans were now changed and it was decided that Co I would stay on the hill until the next day. There was little talking that night as everyone was pretty well shaken by the earlier incident. Despite their exhaustion, the Marines did not sleep well.

**CPL RAUL FONSECA - Co I:** We were sniped at that night but we were told not to return fire because we would be revealing our positions.

**HM MIKE LUTZ - Co I:** In the darkness there was a pretty good fire fight going on down in the valley. The comedian I shared a hole with that night couldn't help but break my balls. There were red, green and white tracers flying and richochetting back and forth. "Looks like Christmas down there Doc. It'll probably be us tomorrow night!"

As 13 May ended, Company I prepared to enter Go Noi Island and their disastrous fate. It is ironic to mention that on this day, the Paris Peace talks had also started thousands of miles away.

<u>14 MAY</u>

**CPL RAUL FONSECA - Co I:** At daybreak, two C-130's flew over the Island and dropped cluster bombs (pineapple shaped) below the hill.

Co I awoke to a blistering hot day. They hiked down the hill and entered Go Noi Island for the first time. The going was extremely difficult under the boiling sun. Streams and wells helped to replenish water, but the heat still took its toll on the Marines. The grunts helped one another by taking turns carrying the heavy weight of extra M-60 and M-79 ammunition.

**PFC TOM HANSON Co I:** In the morning we moved off the hill. The large explosion the day before had been triggered by members of a mortar section and their unexploded rounds were scattered about the hilltop. EOD (Explosive Ordnance Disposal) people gathered them up, and with cries of "Fire in the hole," one last explosion rocked the hill.

**HM MIKE LUTZ - Co I:** One of my most vivid memories was on the morning of the 14th as we were almost at the bottom of Hill 148. Hanging right there on a bush was Zucroff's helmet camo. His helmet and liner were nowhere to be seen. Facing out at us was his grafitti, "Vietnam, Never Again." I believe it was God playing one of his little mind games with us. I pointed at it as we passed but I don't know if anyone else saw it.

**L/CPL DALE CAMP - Co I:** On the morning of the 14th we left hill 148 on a steep trail down the north side of the hill. This trail was very rough and grunts had to help each other down many sections. As we reached the valley we passed a small stream and filled our canteens with the best water I ever found in the bush. That was the last good thing that happened while we were on Go Noi. Down in the valley we marched for a while on a dirt road. This road was in very good shape and I have always wondered if the NVA used any trucks there. There were trenches and bunkers everywhere and we saw some that had used American made decking for reinforcement. This was the perforated metal decking we used for LZ's and such. Seeing all this gave everyone the creeps. You could tell that this place belonged to the NVA. This was their home turf. It was very hot that day and many Marines were dropping out. The officers kept pushing everyone, but some guys, like the 81 mortar crews were carrying too much weight. We all tried to help each other. Later in the day, word came down the line that Golf 2/7 was trying to catch the NVA, and we would be a blocking force for them. Although we were exhausted, we ran quite a ways and started digging fighting holes in a dry river bed. Later we were ordered to move to the top of the bank and dig in again. Now we were exhausted and pissed. As we should have expected, the NVA gave us the slip. We finally met up with Golf Company and moved to a nighttime position. Because this was an extended operation, we all carried extra gear. I remember carrying a 50 round belt of M-60 ammo, a 60mm mortar round, extra ammo and canteens, 6 grenades and all my regular gear. I carried an M-14 the whole time I was in the bush.

For the second day in a row we got no resupply. The 7th Marines were supposed to handle this, so we were pissed off at them. While watching the 7th Marines get their C-Rations, I decided I'd had enough of this bullshit. I told another India Company grunt that we should go get in line with Golf Company and steal some C-Rations for us. So that's what we did. We got 4 cases and went back to the India Company area. No one even noticed. I found Sgt Domingo Deleon and told him that we had "found" some rations. He though it was great and everyone got something to eat.

Just before dusk, Co I linked up with Co G, 2/7, but not before losing two more men to booby traps. Resupply choppers brought in food and supplies as everyone dug in for the night. Incoming mortar rounds struck later in the evening, but fortunately no one was injured.

**DAVID "DUKE" MINTON - Co G, 2/7:** We were

only too happy to see India Company when they joined up with us. We had lost over half of our platoon on Allen Brook. One of our Marines later had a son and named him Allen Brook!

**CPL JACK PARSONS - Co G, 2/7:** Operation Allen Brook was very hard on many of us. I lost so many men, both wounded and dead, that it was hard to get past it. I have seven boys ranging in age from 28 down to 21 months, and my 12 year old son I named Allen Brook in honor of all those that fought in that battle. In 1998 we of 'Golf' company 2/7 held our very first reunion in Washington, D.C. and had 21 Marines attend. When they met Allen Brook they cried. We had 148 at our last reunion and we are still growing. During Operation Allen Brook I put Duke up for the Silver Star three separate times, but all they ever gave him was a Bronze Star. He, like so many of those brave, young Marines and Navy Corpsmen were all true American heros.

<u>15 MAY</u>

On 15 May, the control of Allen Brook was transferred to the 3rd Battalion, 7th Marines (3/7), under the command of Lt Colonel Roger Barnard. What was a little unusual was that there was not a single rifle company from 3/7 on Go Noi Island at the time. On 15 May, Co G 2/7, Co A 1/7, Co I 3/27, one platoon from Co L 3/7, and the Command Group from 3/7 were the operational units on the Island.

**CPL ROBERT SIMONSEN - Co I:** We swept towards Liberty Bridge all day and arrived at around 1700. We had found several booby trapped grenades along the way, but still no physical trace of the elusive enemy. Several more men came down with heat stroke just before we reached the bridge. A truck from a nearby base met us and brought sandwiches and soft drinks for everyone. It tasted great! We dug in and swiftly fell asleep as rain started pouring down. We woke up at midnight and left again for the Island interior.

**L/CPL DALE CAMP - Co I:** We made our way to Liberty Bridge with Golf Company. The Sea Bee's had baloney and bread for us. Golf Company broke ranks and acted like it was a food riot. We stood in ranks until dismissed and found very little left. That night we slept in a downpour and got up about midnight.

Pulling off of Go Noi was a well calculated move. Col Hall's plan was to fool the enemy into believing that all of the Marines were permanently leaving the Island. It was decided that everyone would sneak back at midnight to hopefully surprise the NVA.

**LT COL ROGER H. BARNARD - 3/7 BATTALION CO:** Colonel Reverdy Hall, CO of the 7th Marines, was convinced that after a week of 2/7 stirring up the OA (Operational Area,) we could fool the enemy into believing the Marines had had enough, make a show of pulling 2/7 out, then surreptitiously slip 3/7 back in under cover of darkness. On 15 May, Col Hall ordered 2/7 to vacate the OA with drums rolling, bands playing and flags flaring, and ordered 3/7 to prepare to be inserted into the OA that night.

As luck would have it, 3/7 was not to have any of its own rifle companies for the operation (which was to be considered a continuation of Allen Brook.) I crossed the river near Liberty Bridge at midnight, 15 May, with A/1/7, G/2/7, and I/3/27. With a Battalion Command Group of twelve Marines (CO, S-3, FSC, ALO, Sgt Maj, 4 radiomen, and 3 shotguns,) the force totaled about five-hundred Marines.

We crossed the river in a column of companies: Co A (Capt Bill Roll) led the way followed by the 3/7 Command Group. I don't recall whether Co G (Capt Bob O'Neill) or Co I (Capt Ralph) were next. The battalion moved in a single file, relying on the cover of darkness for security.

## 16 MAY

The Marines entered the Island again in the early morning hours and moved off in a column of companies. They headed off in a northeasterly direction, somewhat parallel to the Song Thu Bon River. As soon as all of the companies had crossed over, the Marines rested quietly until daylight.

**LT COL ROGER H. BARNARD 3/7 BATTALION CO:** We reached the line of departure for the dawn attack somewhere around 0300 without incident. At about 0500, a grenade exploded near Co A, an incident that made me fear our presence had been detected. There was no follow-on activity. We stood fast and proceeded with the original plan.

We crossed the line of departure at dawn on 16 May with two companies abreast; Co I on the left (east,) Co G on the right (west.) Co A was in the reserve. Our objective was a suspected NVA installation, perhaps of some strength. We had reason to believe they did not know we were there. We were hoping to execute a major surprise.

Company I's zone was mostly wooded. Company G's zone included a tree line and 100 yards into a cleared area paralleling the tree line. At about 0900 we hit a hornets nest. Company G was stopped cold and taking heavy casualties. Company I was drawing heavy fire and unable to maneuver around or through it. We received no indirect fire; only small arms and automatic weapons. Several machine guns in particular were deadly. It was like being in the butts at the rifle range; one of those times you were thankful for the craters created by air strikes and artillery.

Because of the relative shelter of the berm at the tree line, enveloping the position through Co G's zone seemed most logical. I had Co I hold fast, reinforced Co G with a platoon from Co A, and ordered an assault in the enemy position from our right (west) flank.

At around 0900 Co I came into an open field near Phu Dong. The field was surrounded by many tree lines. As a surprised enemy reacted, shooting broke out everywhere. It was difficult at first to know where to shoot. The column was so spread out that locations of enemy and friendly forces were nearly impossible to distinguish.

**SGT JON PAHL - H & S Co:** I was in the rear area with the CP group as we started to take heavy incoming fire. I told Capt Ralph that I was moving up to the firing line to work up a fire mission. My RTO (radio operator) did not like the idea of moving up across an open area under fire, but he prepared himself to go.

I hollered up and requested a heavy return fire to cover us. As an M-60 and several M-16's opened up, I leapt forward with enemy green tracers at knee-high trajectory coming in on both sides of me. I didn't stop until I hit the deck between a couple of riflemen behind a small rice paddy dike.

As I worked on getting our position and line of direction by orienting my compass on Hill 148, a burst of fire knocked the compass from my hands. Someone gave me another compass (I still have it today) and I shot a quick azimuth. I located my position and turned to Bruce Curtis (RTO) to give him the info to relay to the 155 Battery at Liberty Bridge, but Bruce wasn't there. He was back several meters, where he had sought cover during the run up to the front lines. We gave him some more cover fire and he managed to get close when a huge volume of fire came down on him. He hit the ground again and at first I thought he was shot. Then, he started to wriggle out of his radio harness and I screamed for him to get the radio to me. He rolled over and grabbed the radio by the straps and hurled it towards me. He said, "Fuck you, you want it, you get it yourself." Curtis was with me on my first tour and I new he was a good field Marine. If he moved any further, I'm sure he would have ended up in a body bag.

I requested a spotter WP round. My mix was right on, and a small adjustment would bring a 'fire for effect' right on target. It was at this time that the NVA must have figured that I was the FO and they began to pour in fire on my position. I couldn't raise up high enough to control the fire mission. I hollered over to the other FO team (CPL Hoffman and his RTO, L/CPL Riddle) to control the fire. Adjustments were made and eventually things quieted down and everyone was able to regroup.

**HM MIKE LUTZ - Co I:** One of our guys took a round through the neck. He couldn't feel his hands or feet, so we feared a spinal injury. Two Marines and myself placed him on a board to keep his neck stabilized and moved him to the rear to try to get a medivac.

We found a Major working two phones at the same time. We were all shocked when he told us, "Sorry Doc, we don't' have enough casualties to warrant a medivac yet."

Every Marine-157

After trying to link back up with India Company, we decided to return to the 2/7's rear area to help with their wounded. Actually, there were very few WIAs. Most of the injuries had been fatal with quite a few head shots.

CPL ROBERT SIMONSEN - Co I: A radioman in the third squad was hit almost immediately. First and second squads set up in a tree line to the left. S/Sgt Shelby E. Monk spotted an NVA right in front of us in a bomb crater and shot him. We finished him off by tossing in grenades.

L/CPL DALE CAMP - Co I: We marched onto the Island under cover of darkness. Later in the morning the column began taking fire. Our columns were spread out and we couldn't tell if the bullets flying by were from Marines or the enemy. First platoon with Lt Thompson, his radioman Cpl Jan Mitscher, and S/Sgt Shelby Monk, moved forward with 1st squad in the lead. We moved into a tree line and found several new fighting holes. One still had a small e-tool in it. These holes had square corners and sides that were straight up and down with perfectly smooth sides. Very different than ours. Because of the e-tool and a camo hat lying there, we got the impression that the NVA had just gotten up and ran. We all got into a trench line facing an open area with a small house in the middle. An NVA in full uniform with a rifle walked out of the house and was going to our left across the field. We all jumped up to shoot, but S/Sgt Monk said "I'll do it." He shot and critically wounded the NVA. Two grunts disarmed and retrieved the wounded NVA and brought him back to the trench. At this time Cpl Mitsher pulled out his .45 caliber pistol, and said, "This is for Neilson," and shot him in the face. We stood there in shock, but we all remembered Neilson, our friend, who had lost a leg to a booby trap a few days before. We also knew that Mitch had only done what we all felt like doing. Immediately after this we were ordered to assault the opposite tree line.

First Platoon, Co I, under 1st Lt Stephen B. Thompson, then probably made the smartest move of the day. Although no enemy could be seen, they began sweeping on line and firing into the approaching tree lines. The hidden NVA, not knowing that they hadn't been observed, started returning fire.

**CPL ROBERT SIMONSEN - Co I:** All hell broke out. We were receiving fire from all directions except from the rear. We threw grenades at them and they threw chi coms right back. We were so close that we could hear them talking to each other. Cpl Jan Mitscher, 1st Platoon radioman, traded his radio for an M-79 and quickly knocked out an enemy machine gun team. Pvt Carleton Hinden and L/Cpl Dale Camp both got confirmed kills.

**SGT JON PAHL - H & S Co:** I worked my way back to the CP group where I was briefed by Capt Ralph. It appeared the NVA had fallen back to regroup. We continued to assault and heavy contact was again made. A radio comm from the first platoon actual (Platoon commander) requested a "corpsman up." Capt Ralph calmly turned to E-3 Corpsman Glick and told him to move up to the front. Now Glick wasn't a boony rat. This was his first time in the field under fire and he knew his corpsman buddies were probably down. Glick just coolly gathered up his unit one, strapped on his helmet, checked out his .45 and started to move out. I told the skipper that I knew the way to the front lines and that I would escort Glick up. As we moved out, I remembered hearing something, somewhere, at some time, about never volunteering!

**PFC JUAN 'SPEEDY' GONZALEZ - Co I:** I was shot in the leg almost immediately. I managed to crawl over to one side of a bunker where I thought it would be safe. I then heard gooks talking on the other side of the bunker so I decided to toss a grenade over. My big mistake was not letting any time fuse go down because two NVA jumped on top of the bunker and shot me two more times before running off. They must have thought that they had killed me.

**CPL ROBERT SIMONSEN - Co I:** I was shooting like mad into a tree line to my immediate front where I had seen movement. Coles and Henderson (Pfc Vincent S. Coles and Pfc Jack Henderson, Jr.) were both shot and killed, one on each side of me. Suddenly, everything went blank.

**CPL JAN 'MITCH' MITSCHER - Co I:** I was standing to the rear of Simonsen and saw three automatic rounds hit the dirt in front of him and a fourth round strike his head. He fell to the ground and didn't move so I was sure he was killed.

**CPL ROBERT SIMONSEN - Co I:** An AK-47 round had gone right through my helmet sending fragments into my head. When I regained consciousness, three of the guys were by my side. Doc Glick patched me up and I was moved back twenty yards to relative safety. My nose was bleeding a lot and my head hurt like hell but no one could see any head damage through my thick head of hair. Speedy and I were lying together. He had been hit three times. Choppers couldn't evacuate us because the shooting was still too intense. To make matters worse, air strikes dropped bombs extremely close to our positions, and Speedy was hit again by flying bomb shrapnel. It was late afternoon before we were medivaced to the 1st Medical Battalion in Da Nang. There were ten killed and ten wounded on the helicopter. The load was so heavy that we had to throw out all extra gear before we could take off. Since it was determined at the hospital that I was the least seriously wounded, I had to wait, laying stark naked on a hard table, while the others were treated. X-rays were finally taken late in the evening. A doctor took out several pieces of metal from my head. I was given a bed (my first in three months) and quickly fell asleep.

L/CPL DALE CAMP - Co I: We were all firing as we crossed the open area. As we moved into the tree line we were firing forward of us but couldn't tell if we were taking incoming. At one point Pfc Vincent S. Coles and I were taking cover next to the remnant of a brick wall. We were being hit in the face with little sand grains or something. I remember looking at Coles and asking what was happening. He didn't know either. All at once we noticed that bullets were hitting the bricks, inches from me and we were being splattered with pieces of brick. This was when we first knew we were taking incoming. We got the hell out of there and moved forward to an NVA bunker. We took cover behind the bunker, a mound of earth 3 feet tall and 6 feet wide, and began firing. The NVA were only 50 feet or so in front of us, in bunkers, trenches and bomb craters. As Coles raised up to fire over the top of the bunker, he was shot once in the center of his chest and died immediately. He was a good friend who kept me laughing and tormented me with his descriptions of food dishes he learned to prepare in school.

As I resumed firing I noticed dirt popping up from an NVA muzzle blast. I could not see the soldier firing but there was what looked like a small sign, shaped like a 'T'

"Cpl Robert Simonsen, WIA"

in front of his position. I just kept firing at that area until I hit him. I hit him in the neck and his head just fell forward. Until then I had not seen him. I remember thinking when I saw him fall that it looked just like the movies. My next thought was that I was getting very weird. Very soon after this I heard shouting to my left. Guys were yelling for a new Private to get down. He was standing up behind a banana tree, firing away. They didn't tell him at ITR (Infantry Training Regiment) that a banana tree wouldn't stop a bullet. We finally got his attention and he hit the deck. We were actually laughing at him. What a strange place to find yourself laughing. I think right after that was when Cpl Bob Simonsen was shot. I looked to my left just as the bullet hit his head. It threw him backwards through the air and he landed in a heap. This was my second good friend to die in the last few minutes and I just couldn't believe they were gone.

We kept on fighting. Lt Thompson urged us forward. Marines were running from bunker to bunker, throwing grenades along the way. An enemy grenade went off within 10 feet of me but I wasn't hit.

I was behind a bunker reloading the magazines for my M-14. I had fired more than 100 rounds on single fire and only had one full magazine left. The FO with me was on his third M-16 because of malfunctions. Lt Thompson was yelling for us to move up, but the only place to move up to was the NVA bunkers. We weren't going anywhere, but Pfc Juan Speedy Gonzalez jumped up and ran forward to a bunker. The FO started firing, but his M-16 had a malfunction. He grabbed my M-14 and continued firing. He said that an NVA on top of the bunker had shot Speedy. I wrestled my weapon away from him just in time to draw a bead on an NVA as he ran from behind the bunker. Just as I was about to fire, the FO yelled. "Don't fire, that's Speedy." I hesitated because he did kind of look like Speedy. He had black hair, a green uniform, cartridge belt, and rifle. When he came out of his Ho Chi Minh sandals, I started firing. I don't know if I hit him or not. While others covered us, Mitch, another guy and I ran up to get Speedy. He was shot up pretty bad. Mitch and the other grunt dropped their gear and picked up Speedy. They ran back with him to one of our bunkers. I grabbed all the gear and ran back to the same bunker. We were getting shot at the whole time.

    We had killed or run off all the NVA in the bunker complex and had advanced 100 yards or so. While searching a bamboo grove on our right flank, I discovered a pack with uniforms, sandals, medicine, etc. One of the guys gave me the AK-47 of the man I had killed. It was covered with his blood. I think it was Pvt Hinden who passed out NVA cigarette lighters he had taken off their dead. During this time some of us were holed up in a pagoda that was to the front of the bunker complex. When we moved back, I found Sgt Deleon and showed him the pack and rifle. He thought we had done great. He was just going on and on about how well we fought. I reminded him of our dead and he told me that Simonsen was alive. You could have knocked me over with a feather. I found Bob laying down with bandages on his head. As soon as I got over to him he told me to go get his helmet. I found it and was amazed to see an entry hole, dead center in front, and a big exit hole in the rear. When Bob and I were looking at it we saw that for some reason, the bullet went around the inside, between the liner and the steel pot. Bob was the luckiest guy I ever knew.

    **SGT JON PAHL - H & S Co:** As Glick moved from casualty to casualty, I started to concentrate on the fire fight. I saw an NVA move his RPD (machine gun) over a bunker and as he shot at Speedy, I got off a burst

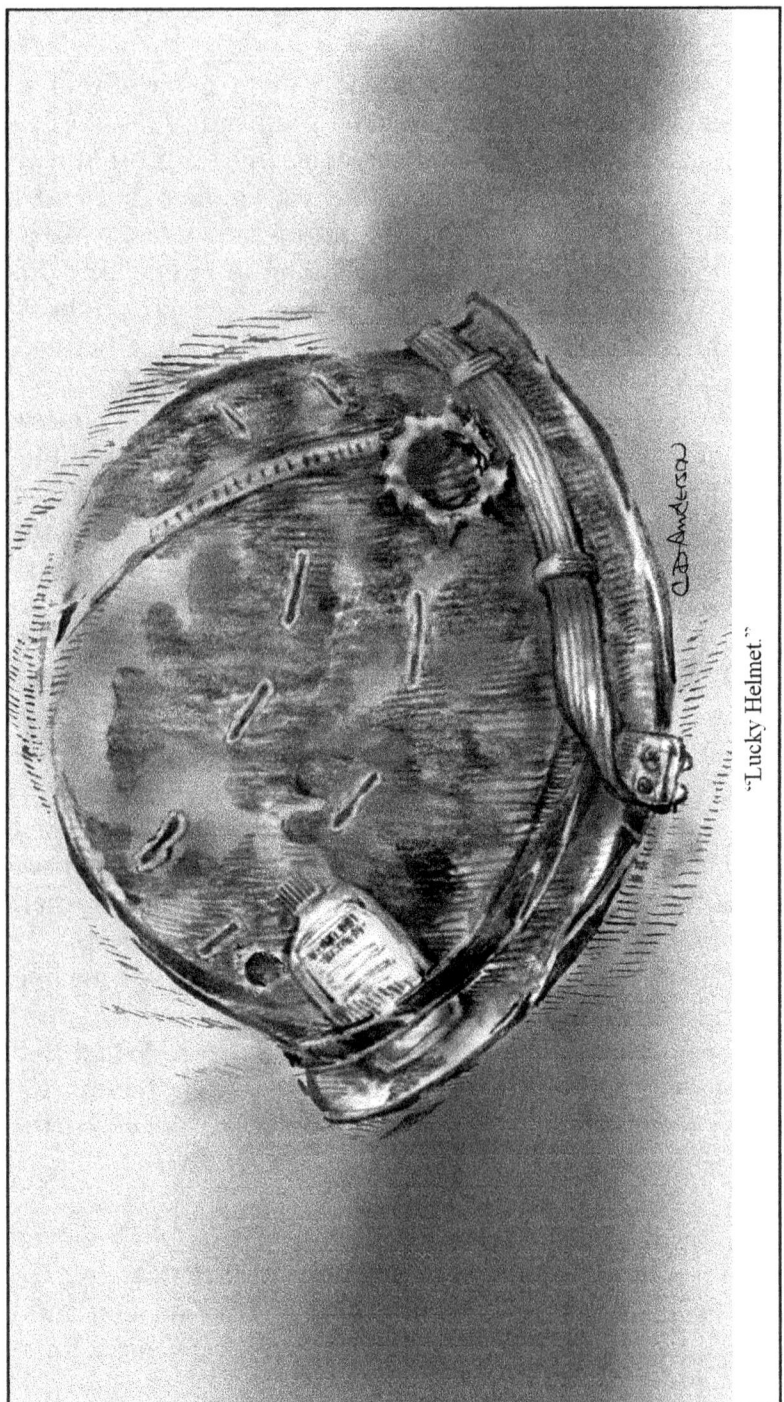

"Lucky Helmet."

in his direction. I snapped in a new mag and came around a hootch foundation in a crouch where I got into a Mexican standoff with this NVA. Banana leaves were falling all around me from his fire and we both took cover. We both came out again and my M-16 jammed! I quickly grabbed a KIA's rifle and once again, the buffer springs were broken. I then ran over to where Glick was working on a wounded Marine and grabbed his M-16. This time, he was slow in anticipating my move and I was able to hit him in the shoulder. He screamed and dropped his RPD. As he took off I aimed in on his back, but fuck, I was out of ammo! An M-60 gunner, cradling his machine gun in his wounded arm in a sling, moved up to my right along a row of bamboo. Suddenly, a burst of M-60 fire rolls the RPD guy into my front and I put a mag into him just to make sure. The gunner said he found him trying to jack a mag into an AK-47 with one arm, as my previous shot had all but blown his other arm off.

L/CPL ALLAN CIEZKI - Co I: We were in squad files and I was carrying the radio for third squad. Henderson was in front of me and Sgt Whyte was just behind me. Rounds started flying in every direction but mainly from the right flank. I saw Henderson go off to the right into some banana-like trees for cover.

I was near a corner off of a small tree line where I spotted a spider hole. I tried to jump into it, but with the radio on my back my feet never hit the bottom of the hole. I was taking fire from both the left and right front. I couldn't believe they didn't hit me! I managed to get out of the hole and took off in the direction where Henderson went.

As I crawled another 10 meters or so, I saw Henderson get hit in the stomach. I then took aim at an

NVA in a bomb crater but another Marine just opened up and really put a lot of holes into him. I next spotted some movement near a half-standing brick building about 50 meters in front of my position.

    PFC Burke and Doc Finch joined me from the rear and as Doc crawled over to Henderson, Burke stood up and started spraying his M-60 machine gun all over the brick building area. The NVA fire started to die out and Burke took off to the left flank while I went over to help Doc.
    Henderson was in shock. There was no blood around the two holes in his stomach. He tried to get up and kept saying, "I don't want to die." We put him on a poncho and carried him to a rear area where Simonsen and Speedy were sitting wounded side by side. As we put him down, we realized he had died.

    **L/CPL STEVE EASTON - Co I:** During the fire fight, Pfc Leonard L. Yazzie took an incredible hit. A bullet went through the front of his helmet and out the back. It then turned downwards and went through his pack. He wasn't injured at all. It was unbelievable!

    Adjacent to Co I, Marines from other units fought bravely against the estimated 200 NVA located in fortified positions. Two men stood out amongst their peers during the fighting. Petty officer Robert M. Casey (Co G, 2/7 Navy Corpsman) and 2nd Lt Paul F. Cobb (Co A, 1/7) sacrificed their lives in heroic efforts. Continuing to fight aggressively and aid their comrades, both men would be given posthumous Navy Cross medals (the nation's second highest award for valor.)

**LT COL ROGER H. BARNARD - 3/7 BATTALION CO:** We needed more resources than we had for the situation. We had used artillery prep and supporting fires, but now close air support carried the day. Without them, we might all still be there. I was told later that the fifty-two (or maybe it was fifty-four) sorties we requested and received were the greatest number of sorties ever delivered on a single target in RVN, at least up to that date. The air support was mostly USMC, some USN and a few USAF.

The enemy was identified as elements of the 308th Division which had been newly infiltrated into the area. The 308th Division was a crack outfit that took part in the final assault on Dien Bien Phu in the closing stages of the French war in Indochina.

**LT COL ROGER H BARNARD - 3/7 BATTALION CO:** I don't recall the hour when all enemy resistance ceased, but once the dust settled it was clear we had been in a major fight and had achieved a significant victory. The suspected NVA installation was indeed an NVA regimental headquarters with attendant security and a major staging area for supplies for the forthcoming 2nd Tet Offensive. We uncovered so much material we weren't able to evacuate it all to the rear. We were able to get all our casualties out by helicopter and we received water and ammo resupply.

I don't remember our exact casualty numbers for 16 May. I do remember that for both 16 and 17 May we lost forty-eight Marines KIA and our total enemy killed was one hundred sixty-two.

I remember thinking at the end of 16 May that we had done our job and that we would surely be withdrawn that night. Col Hall had been at the division CP at the height of the action and had been listening to the radio traffic. He was beside himself with the success of his plan to move the battalion in under the cover of darkness and surprise the enemy at dawn. I have always wondered if the surprise would not have been more complete if that grenade had not gone off at 0500 that morning. Understandably, Col Hall wanted to continue destroying the NVA. He issued orders to move south the next morning.

HM MIKE LUTZ - Co I: When I learned of our own KIAs and WIAs, I felt as low as a piece of shit for not being there with them. I vowed to myself that I would never get separated from my platoon again.

PFC TOM HANSON - Co I: We moved up into the area that Golf had been in and I remember the members of Golf hurling the cast-off gear of their casualties into a pile. Their rage was evident on their faces and in their actions.

We walked out to the area that was being used as the LZ and medivac zone and I remember the sad sight of eleven ponchos laid out in a row covering the bodies of the dead.

We were ordered to cross the LZ and dig in because this was going to be our stop for the night. We began digging in as dusk fell and Chinooks came in bringing food, ammo, water, and some mail. The water was most appreciated, of course, and we all filled our canteens from big plastic jugs. We had just settled in when the word was passed to saddle up again. We were going to make a night march. I remember being depressed because we had to slash those big plastic jugs to deprive the enemy of them.

We set out on the night march. I don't remember how long we marched, but I do remember that I was dog-tired. We were told that there would be 100% sack-out when we reached our destination. Whenever we stopped for a break most of us fell instantly asleep. You had to make sure you woke up the man behind you when starting out again or the rest of the column would be left behind. We finally reached our destination, laid out in rows, and got some well needed sleep.

LT COL ROGER H. BARNARD - 3/7 BATTALION CO: At dusk we moved SSW about 400-500 meters in a column of companies, leaving two Marines behind to detonate the supplies and equipment that had to be abandoned once we cleared the area. The detonation was successful, as near as we could tell, and the two Marines safely rejoined the column. The order of movement was Co I, 3/7 Command Group, Co A and Co G. After making a show of going into a perimeter defense inside a tree line, we moved out after dark into a erimeter in the clearing.

CPL FRED STUEBE - H&S Co: After the contact was over, we were told to dig in for the night and we dug deep. I remember seeing five bodies that afternoon. Capt Ralph had seen my 'Hot Springs, AK' on my helmet and came over to talk to me that night. After it got dark we were told to move out. Carrying all of the heavy 81 gear, we made a lot of noise. The grunts hated us for being so loud. One of our guys had an asthma attack and we had to carry his gear, too. Capt Ralph chewed us out for delaying the march. We finally stopped and set up near a ville.

CPL RAUL FONSECA - Co I: I can only remember bits and pieces of what happened on the 16th. I saw Sgt Monk shoot an NVA in a spider hole. I also saw Coles get hit in the chest. I can still hear the AK shooting all around us that day and the phantoms dropping their bombs close by. Shrapnel was flying all over and Speedy was hit by one of the stray pieces. That night I remember wondering why they (NVA) zeroed in on my ass but failed to hit me. My poncho liner was blown to hell. We were then ordered to move out at night. The weapons platoon made way too much noise. They were carrying a lot of heavy gear. I ended up helping to carry some of their stuff. I prayed that nothing would happen. We stopped for about an hour and then moved on again.

**SGT JON PAHL - H & S Co:** Sometime later in the evening, I learned that my earlier fire mission had been adjusted onto some Marines on our left flank. This info hit me like a kick in the groin. I had always taken pride in doing everything possible to help the grunts. All I could do now, and still be combat effective, was to block it out of my mind. I expected to be treated like a pariah, but the grunts seemed to take it in stride as 'shit that happens.' God, how I wanted someone to scream and cuss at me. I was reckless but not foolhardy. A foolish person has no idea of the consequences of his actions while a reckless person knows well what's going on but still pushes it to the edge of his limitations.

I still live with a deep sadness and pain that I was responsible for friendly casualties.

\* \* \*

On 16 May, the rest of 3/27 was alerted, except for Co M, to be prepared to move by truck convoy to Liberty Bridge, and to then move on foot to the area of operation.

**1ST LT BILLY C. STEED - H & S Co:** I'd been an instructor at the aerial observer school, so I had a number of friends who had taken the class or who had been instructors with me, who were now flying as aerial observers for the 1st Marine Division. As they flew across our position, they used to check in to ensure they had clearance to proceed across our TAOR. I was talking to one of them and he had just come from Go Noi Island where we had attached India Company 3/27 to 3/7 to do a search and clear operation. He had indicated that he had been running numerous flights of air and controlling artillery and there was a big firefight going on down in that area.

I had numerous friends in India Company. We didn't know the fate of India at that particular time. We knew that something big was going on because the aerial observers were directed where we had Marine units in contact. I think it took a couple of days before we found out what was really going on. It came down in a sitrep from the regiment and then I think Lt Col Woodham went to the regimental headquarters and got briefings. Then it was decided to insert the rest of the 3rd Battalion, 27th Marines into Go Noi Island to help clear out, what the intelligence report said was believed to be, at least a regiment of NVA down there.

CPL BILL JUNG - Co K: We spent all day getting ready. After making sure our weapons were again spotless, more grenades and ammunition were passed out, along with C-Rations. Last minute letters were written and sea bags were put back in storage. Lt Belser (1st Lt Joseph H. Belser - 3rd Platoon Commander) briefed the platoon honchos on what to expect.

I was far from religious, but on that night I looked at the sky and prayed for my men, my family, and for strength. I felt as if God was listening. I could feel his presence.

* * *

On the eastern part of Go Noi Island, ARVN units had also begun their operation called Hung Quang 1-38. Two battalions of the 51 Regiment under Colonel Truong Tan Thuc, plus the 21st and 37th Ranger Battalions, were the operational units. They would stay on the Island until 25 May.

* * *

It was late afternoon before hostilities finally ended on the Island. Jets had provided assistance and eventually helped to force the enemy to withdraw. Co I had been engaged in the first major battle against the NVA by 3/27 troops since arriving in Vietnam.

**LT COL TULLIS WOODHAM, JR. - 3/27 BATTALION CO: Since Co I was under control of 3/7, and because of the loss of virtually all of their key personnel, I learned very few details about the battle on the 16th until years later.**

## 17 MAY

The morning began early for Marines both on Go Noi Island and at the 3/27 Cau Ha Base. At the Battalion CP, Co K, Co L, and H&S Co prepared to be taken by trucks to Liberty Bridge. Once there, the plan was to cross over to the Island and move inland by foot along the main road running west to east until contacting 3/7 and, of course, Co I.

**CPL BILL JUNG - Co K: In the morning we had our last hot chow. After saddling up with all of our gear, we waited in the sand and heat for the trucks. The trucks finally arrived and we climbed aboard. We swore at the**

Marine Corps' usual tactic of fitting us in only half of the number of trucks we needed. At 0830, the trucks departed and swung left down the Tu Cau Road, crossed the bridge, and then turned onto Highway 1.

\* \* \*

Back on Go Noi Island, Co I, Co G, and Co A arose at dawn and headed out, still in a southerly direction. They moved towards a series of village hamlets, north of route 537.

**LT COL ROGER H. BARNARD - 3/7 BATTALION CO: We resumed movement at dawn on 17 May, again in a column of companies. The order of march was the same as the previous night with Co I leading. We were in open country, without a defined objective. That is the reason for my decision to move in a column of companies. Upon making contact, my intent was to use Co A as a maneuver element with Co G in reserve. This made sense to me then, and it makes sense to me today; using a column in moving to contact, deploying on making contact.**

L/Cpl Lewis Carpenter (Co I,) the point fire team leader, noticed a woman gesturing and shouting vigorously to some unseen persons in a hamlet. Yelling for the squad to follow, Carpenter's fire team raced to the hamlet, surprising a platoon of NVA at their meal. As the Marines opened fire, the enemy soldiers fled while the women screamed and vainly attempted to retrieve the NVA rifles from their hiding places in the village and throw them to the fleeing soldiers. In a few moments the one sided fight was over. More than a dozen NVA bodies lay scattered through the hamlet and the women, later identified as members of a medical unit, had been taken prisoner.

Apparently the NVA were totally surprised. They left

packs and weapons behind as they quickly headed to safety. Some enemy elements did manage to send off a few mortar rounds to protect their withdrawal, which found their marks among Co I Marines. Several men were wounded and evacuated to the 1st Medical Battalion.

**CPL RAUL FONSECA - Co I:** I was one of the few E-4s left and Sgt Monk made me Platoon Sergeant and Guide. We woke up early on the 17th. My squad was on point when we came to the ville. We saw three NVA eating and we stopped the rest of the Company to get orders on what to do. While we were talking over the radio, they spotted us and started running away. We killed one but the others escaped. We were then given the order to move out, but another group took point.

**L/CPL DALE CAMP - Co I:** We moved out early with India on point. Just before dawn we were moving down a trail with trees and jungle on each side. Up ahead we began to hear and smell the sounds of morning. Pots and pans were rattling, people were talking, cooking fires were smoking and I smelled Vietnamese tobacco. A young woman laughed. All hell broke loose as fire erupted ahead of us. We hit the deck and looked for targets, but saw nothing. Up ahead there was a pretty good fire fight going on. Bullets zipping by kept us down. To our left we heard the mortars fire. We waited and listened. Soon they whistled down on top of us. We were somewhat protected by the depression of the trail, but their mortars walked down the trail and I heard the Marines ahead of me cry out as they were hit. For one of the few times in Nam, I prayed for God to protect me.

**L/CPL ALLEN CIEZKI - Co I:** We came to a ville just as daylight broke. I wasn't up front but I could hear gooks talking and then M-16's and AK's talking. Suddenly I saw movement and we all opened up. It was a sight to see all of those muzzle flashes at dawn. I hit one as he grabbed a heavy pack and tried to run. My magazine was empty and I think it was Maxwell who finished him off.

There were NVA laying everywhere in the ville, most were dead. I saw one young NVA, shot through the legs and stomach, rolling in a camp fire. There was enemy equipment and weapons everywhere you looked. Then, all of a sudden, mortars started coming in all around us. Maxwell and Bryant were both hit.

Sgt Whyte told me to stay with the wounded while just about everyone else took off into some elephant grass.

**HM MIKE LUTZ - Co I:** As we entered a wooded area, several mortars came in and slightly wounded two Marines. Their wounds weren't serious but they were both peppered with small pieces of shrapnel. After applying a couple of battle dressings, they were sent back to the rear area.

Next, we had to cross through a large field of elephant grass. We waited for an air strike to get down and then moved out.

**CPL FRED STUEBE - H&S Co:** Early in the morning, India headed out towards the ville. Capt Ralph told us to stay in the rear to establish an LZ in case it was needed. India went through the ville and headed out towards another. We spotted and captured three civilians in the village after India had passed through it. We couldn't tell if they were VC or not. Members of Golf, 2/7, approached us and took charge and left with the prisoners. We then heard shooting and mortars in the second ville. We caught up to the tail end of India and received word over the radio to go back to the first ville to set up an LZ.

Upon heading back we saw gooks in the open area and knew that 'Charlie' now owned the ville.

\* \* \*

**CPL ROBERT SIMONSEN - Co I:** I was laying in bed at the hospital when three or four guys from India Company came walking through with bandages covering their various wounds. They spoke of surprising the gooks that morning and then how they were hit by mortar shrapnel. None of them seemed wounded very seriously.

\* \* \*

**L/CPL DALE CAMP - Co I:** The mortar attack ended abruptly. First squad had 2 or 3 walking wounded and so did other squads. First squad was assigned to take them back to an LZ for evacuation. My squad was down to 4 with Cpl Massey (Tex) as squad leader. The rest of the company moved on. We delivered the wounded and turned back to catch up. By now in the operation I think I was starting to loose my nerve a little. I ask Cpl Massey how we could get back to the company because we had to go back through the scene of the fire fight. He yelled at me to shut up and get going.

**SGT JON PAHL - H & S Co:** We moved into open ground that divided a tree line and Le Nam. It was covered with stick-like stems from some previous farming endeavor. It was still cool and quiet when Capt Ralph brought the company to a halt about 200 meters from the ville and requested an air sortie to prep our entrance point. He had wisely figured that the enemy encountered earlier was an outpost for a possible large force in Le Nam and was sure they would be expecting us. Air came on station (two A-4's) and dropped their ordnance. I informed Capt Ralph that our FO team had arty registered on grids inside Le Nam.

We moved out with first and second platoon on line as the assault force. Next came the CP group, divided into two sections, followed by the third platoon in column as reserves.

The sun was just hitting the grunts as I watched them come to a dry river bed at the edge of Le Nam and dropped over its edge. It promised to be a hot day as one could already feel the heat building. Next, I saw the command group move out of sight except for their radio tape antennas, when all hell broke loose. As I hit the ground, I saw machine gun bullets kicking in the sand just inches away. No one behind me was hit but I could tell by the volume and type of fire that our forward platoons and Capt Ralph were in deep shit. The fire was almost all from the NVA.

L/CPL DALE CAMP - Co I: Just as we caught up with tail-end charlie, the point was ambushed. There was a tremendous amount of shooting and explosions up there. It was terrifying. Massey said we must catch up with our platoon and we ran all the way across the huge open field that sloped down to the ambush site at the river. We passed Golf 2/7, and some of India and made it to the river bank. The incoming was tearing the place up. Bullets were hitting all around us and cutting down the tall grass. We were laying in some shallow tank tracks. There was no cover at all. The bodies of dead and wounded were laying all over.

L/CPL ALLAN CIEZKI - Co I: I left the wounded with some corpsmen and headed into the elephant grass. About half way through, I heard a great battle taking place to my front. 50 meters later, I came into the open next to a large dry river bed. I quickly saw bullets flying everywhere and Marines were either running or were down, wounded. Marines were dying trying to save the wounded. I hope someone remembers them in their prayers. I know I still do!

In a tree line to Co I's front, nearly a battalion of NVA lay hidden in fortified positions. Deadly accurate snipers waited in trees ready to pick out selected targets. One Marine after another went down. Some were killed instantly while others lay wounded in the open under the hot sun. The snipers used the wounded as bait. They left them alive, knowing that the Marines would try to rescue them. Men screamed for help, for their mothers, and even offered money for someone to come get them. Many went out to help and they too were hit.

**LT COL ROGER H. BARNARD 3/7 BATTALION CO:** I don't remember exactly when Co I made contact. They ran into an extensive, well fortified position of significant width. At the time of the contact, my command group was moving with Co A. After reports from Co I indicated the position was as formidable as the one of the day before, I ordered Co A to deploy to the right (west) flank. The terrain was flat and covered with tall grass. There was no vantage point for observation. Company G was ordered forward to a position directly behind Co I.

As on the previous day, artillery and close air support were requested to the maximum. For a reason I don't recall, on this day we had to rely mostly on artillery. We received very little air support. I had the FSC and ALO calling mission after mission while we were moving west through the tall grass to the tree line with Co A.

One really has to analyze the earlier action of surprising

the NVA quietly eating their breakfast. Several Marines who were there swear that it was a total surprise and that overtaking the village was, although small, quite a victory. Traditionally, the NVA set traps for the Americans. They were willing to sacrifice several lives in order to achieve a resounding victory. It can be argued that the fleeing NVA did lead Co I right into a fortified ambush with disastrous results for the Marines.

It is also hard to believe that the NVA Commanders would not have scouts and observation posts out in front of their lines. There had been a major battle the day before and over one-hundred NVA had been killed. There were numerous jet sorties attacking the Island just a short distance to their north. The NVA knew the Marines were out in force and ready to fight. The Marines even admitted that they had made quite a bit of noise traveling that night, especially since they were carrying the heavy 81 mortars.

Surprise or not, this day's overall battle belonged to the NVA. It wouldn't be until later that night that the Marines would be able to force the enemy to withdraw.

\* \* \*

**LT COL TULLIS WOODHAM, JR - 3/27 BATTALION CO: While 3/27 proceeded to Go Noi Island by trucks, the NVA had set up to ambush any likely units using the route from Liberty Bridge. Utilizing its monitoring capabilities, Division and the 7th Marines were aware of the intentions of the NVA along the 'red line' (road) but did not inform me or, to the best of my knowledge, Colonel Schwenk, of this deployment. I have been told that this information was classified 'close hold' so as not to compromise the fact that our intelligence gathering agencies had locked on to their tactical net. At the time I was informed of this series of events my perspective regarding the 'intelligence big picture' was considerably in conflict with the non-**

committed monitors. As fate would have it, 3/27 would never get down that road as planned and into the probable ambush.

\* \* \*

**CPL RAUL FONSECA - Co I:** We started moving through a large field of elephant grass. We were about three quarters of the way through when the shit happened. Marines were shot and killed all over. I saw one dead sergeant who was killed trying to dig a hole with his hands. That really pissed me off.

**PFC TOM HANSON - Co I:** When we moved out in the morning there was some fire up in front of the column. The lead had made some contact. Some men were detached to deal with the contact and the rest of the column moved on.

We moved through a tree line and crossed a sandy plain, the only vegetation on which were some scraggly little bushes. We came to a dry river bed, beyond which was another tree line. Captain Ralph put the whole company on line in two ranks and we started across. I was in the rear rank and though the river bed was for the most part dry, there was water in front of me and off to my right. I remember thinking about how I could avoid getting my feet wet, but then started sloshing through the water. At that moment the whole opposite bank erupted in gun fire. Geysers of water were going up all around me and several men ahead of me went down. I was closer to the bank we had left and since there was water in front of us, I whirled around and headed back. A small group of men off to the left (as we were going across) did make it to the bank with the tree line. The safety of the bank we'd left now seemed about four miles away. There was a set of track impressions in the sand left by an amtrac or tank, and though they were only inches deep, I threw myself into one of them and turned to face the enemy. Doc Price threw himself next to me on my left. He had been hit in the hand and had a few of his fingers dangling. Steve Easton dove in on Doc's left and Sgt Phillips landed on my right. I guess we were all a little stunned because Sgt Phillips had to yell, "Return fire," at which point we all opened up.

Because we'd been in virtually constant movement for several days, my M-16 was now dirty. After each shot, I had to smack the forward assist to get the bolt to seat. I had to do this on the first three or four rounds in the magazine. After that there was less pressure on the magazine spring and the bolt could strip off rounds and fire on automatic. We had to be careful not to traverse too far to the left because, as I said, some men were on the opposite bank.

L/CPL STEVE EASTON - Co I: I ran down the slope and out into the dry river bed. Bullets were flying everywhere. I dove into some deep tracks in the sand for protection. A bullet went through my helmet. Later, I was able to run back and dove into the tall grass.

SGT JON PAHL - H & S Co: I turned to Curtis, whose face was tight with fear, and told him to get fire on our preplotted targets. The 155 battery at Liberty Bridge quickly responded. I adjusted fire to cover the area to our front as I tried to move up to the firing line of the first and second platoon. Every time I moved, very accurate enemy automatic fire came down on me. Some fool even sniped at me with RPG's. I had to drop back to where Curtis and Cpl Hoffman were. Hoffman was tracking every adjustment as we didn't want any short rounds this time.

**L/CPL DALE CAMP - Co I:** Hospital Corpsman, Mike Lutz, was with us. He saw a wounded Marine down in the dry river bed and told Massey that we had to get him out of there. Massey said "Come on Camp" and Lutz, Massey, Ciezki and I ran down the tank tracks to the river. Dead Marines were laying along the tracks as we ran and they reminded me of photos of Marine dead laying on the beaches of WWII. How could my mind think of that with so much going on around me? Lutz was yelling for us to get the guy up and make him run. We didn't stop running ourselves as we swooped him up and ran for the safety of the opposite river bank. With only 20 feet or so to go we all fell. That was it for me. I only had one thought and that was to get out of that river. I will always live with the guilt of leaving my squad and crawling for my life. Bullets hit all around me as I crawled like a madman. When I reached the shelter of the bank I heard Lutz yelling for me. He was still a little ways out in the river and was wounded. I ran to him and grabbed his arm, where blood was shooting 6 feet in the air. I wanted to put pressure on this arterial bleeder as we had been taught. Lutz was so cool. He told me to get his unit one and apply pressure bandages to the wounds. The bullet hit him behind the left thumb, on his wrist and traveled through his forearm and blew out his elbow. He was bleeding from 3 arteries. I used one bandage after another and they all became soaked with blood. I asked Lutz if we should use a tourniquet because I was afraid he would bleed to death. He told me no because he knew if we did, he would lose his arm. I questioned his reasoning but he told me he knew what he was doing.

**HM MIKE LUTZ - Co I:** I had been hit through the left arm. While laying there, I pulled my burning arm and saw that with every heart beat, a spout of blood came out of each hole. I knew it was an artery. I stuck my fingers into the holes and managed to stumble to the far bank.

Dale Camp now became 'Doc' Camp. Starting with me and using my Unit-1 kit, he tended to the wounded the rest of the day.

**LT COL ROGER H. BARNARD - 3/7 BATTALION CO:** The reports from Co I were not good. I ordered Co G to press forward vigorously to relieve the pressure on Co I, but they were to make very little impact. In the meantime, we (Co A and the 3/7 Command Group) spent far more time in the tall grass than I had anticipated. The tree line was farther away than first estimated. It was during this movement that the CO, Co I, went off the air; KIA.

**CPL JACK PARSONS - Co G, 2/7:** On the morning of the 17th, my platoon was ordered to crawl out over the burning hot sand across an open area over a quarter of a mile wide to help out a company of Marines (Co I) that were pinned down by murderous fire. The temperature that day was around 115 or so they tell me. I lost most of my platoon to heat stroke attempting to low crawl to the trapped Marines. What we saw when we got there was a scene out of hell. I had never before had so many dead and wounded Marines. As we moved forward, the tree line opened up with the same fire that had cut all those Marines down. The worst part was that this unit was there to save us. They were a reactionary force that landed to pull us out of the fire and they landed in a death trap. Between setting up the LZ for the helos's to come in, calling and adjusting air cover and working on the wounded, I was very busy. I lost most of my men to heat as I said so we only had six Marines to help drag the wounded into fighting holes so our Corpsman could work on them. Every time we called in the medivac choppers they would be shot out of the LZ. It took us all day to get the few wounded we could save to safety. As it grew dark we were able to clear out the tree line and begin the horrible task of moving the dead to the LZ. It took my men until 2200 that evening just to move the bodies and we were spent. When 1st Platoon of Golf company reached us that evening we were told to just sit down and rest. It was the very first time my platoon did not have to stand post in my year in country. We slept four to a hole with our feet in the hole and our helmets resting on each other. One of my men, Duke Minton, never got over that day, and he lost it trying desperately to rescue as many as he could.

      PFC TOM HANSON - Co I: After a short while it was decided we should try to get back up on the bank, and one by one, Doc, myself, Easton and Phillips withdrew. When we got up on the bank Phillips said, "I think I'm hit." He pulled up his trouser leg and he had a flesh wound on his calf. "Yup," I said, "you've got a Purple Heart." I took his battle dressing and bandaged it for him.
      The little bushes around us were really not protective cover and barely qualified as concealment. It seemed that anyone who moved got hit. People lying wounded in the river bed had to be told not to move or they would get hit again.
      The fire fight had been going on for a short while and I just happened to be by Capt Ralph. He said, "The only way out of this is an assault. Pass the word." Now at this time communications and unit integrity had been shot to hell. We were scattered all around.
      We waited a sufficient amount of time for word to be passed and then Capt Ralph said, "Let's go!" and I stood up. I looked to my right and no one else was up. I

looked to my left and only Capt Ralph and his radioman were up. The three of us immediately got back down (thus ended the only charge of India company that I saw that day.)

I was swearing because my rifle was still not working right and the platoon commander asked me what was wrong. I told him and he exchanged rifles with me but his was doing the same thing.

A man to my front had been hit badly and was doing a great deal of screaming. Capt Ralph told him to, "Be quiet, Marine," and like a good Marine he died quietly.

We were taking automatic fire from a small building in front of us on the opposite bank. Capt Ralph had called for air support and some Phantoms appeared. They started bombing and I watched the building get taken out by rockets. They were so close that we had our backs turned to the bomb runs and I remember the 'z-z-z-z-z-k!' sound of the shrapnel as it flew past us and hit the sand.

The day began to get hotter and water was beginning to be a problem, especially for the wounded. I shared some of my water with a wounded man and was down to one canteen.

A strange thing was happening. Despite the fact that anything that moved got hit, L/Cpl Gibson was up on his feet and running around. God knows what he was doing but everyone was telling him to "Get the fuck down!" Gibson had recently lost his job as radioman for being foul-mouthed and insubordinate over the air.

Apparently our platoon commander had been hit and some of the men had improvised a bit of shelter for him with a poncho liner. I was looking at the group of men gathered around him when an explosion erupted immediately to their rear and all went down, killed or wounded by a mortar round.

By this time I was feeling pretty light-headed because of the heat. I was up on my knees and I remember faintly hearing an explosion to my right but it didn't seem to register in my brain. After what seemed like a long time after the explosion it felt like someone hit me in the side of my head with a piece of angle iron, knocking me over. I yelled, "I'm hit!" and put my hand to the side of my head. It came away covered in blood and I imagined that half my head was blown away. I knew that all the corpsmen were either busy or down and I tore out my battle dressing and slapped it to the side of my head. My eyeglasses had been blown away and my whole world was now just a blur (my eyesight is 20/200, probably bad enough to keep me out of the service in times of lesser emergency.)

L/Cpl Gibson was by me, having apparently been hit by shrapnel from the same mortar round (there may have been more rounds dropped on us but the above two are the only ones I remember.) He had been hit in the face and was blinded and in considerable pain. He couldn't see and didn't want to be left alone, so for the rest of the day when I felt like moving, he would hold on to me and we would crawl around together. Don't ask me why we moved. There sure as hell wasn't any place to go.

By this time Capt Ralph was dead and I knew our lieutenant was wounded. I can't see more than eight inches in front of me, I'm wounded, as it seems is everyone else, and the point of the exercise is beginning to be lost on me. The amount of fire had diminished to virtually nothing. I yelled, "Will somebody get us out of here?" No response.

I shared my water with Gibson. Because of the heat and our wounds we were ravenously thirsty. A bit of time passed and I again yelled, "Will somebody get us out of here?" No response. A bit more time passed and I heard somebody yell, "Will somebody get us out of here?" This time Sgt Phillips yelled. "Shut up, Hanson," and I replied, "That wasn't *me!*" I was perfectly willing to take responsibility for my own bitching, but not somebody else's.

The heat was really taking its toll on me and I was now lying motionless on my back. I had to urinate but standing up was somewhat impractical, so I just let go in my trousers. That turned out to be a good thing because the evaporating urine cooled me and gave me some relief from the heat.

I kept fading in and out, for how long I don't know. A slight breeze would come along every so often and I kept concentrating on waiting for that breeze.

Eventually, I looked over at Gibson, lying to my left beside me, and saw that he was dead. The other wounded man to whom I had given my water was lying on my right, boots by my head and his head by my feet. He was dead, too. I remember being angry because I'd given them my water and it had been wasted. Selfish, no?

S/SGT SHELBY MONK - Co I: We received word over the radio that Capt Ralph wanted "all platoon commanders up." Lt Thompson and I slowly worked our way through the grasses to link up with the CO. It was just before we got there that Ralph's position took heavy automatic fire and just about everyone was hit and killed.

SGT LUPE MONTALVO - Co I: When the corpsman went to give aid to Capt Ralph, machine gun fire ripped both of them to pieces. Ralph was a special friend and we had previously both served together in the 28th Marines.

CPL FRED STUEBE - Co I: We asked where the

CO was and we were told that he had been killed. I crawled up the river bank and saw dead Marines all over. I asked who was in charge and Sgt John Pahl (Forward Observer) replied that he had no idea. Guys from 81's started bringing up water to the front. Everyone was hurting from thirst. The heat was very intense. One of the water holes was booby trapped by the NVA. That afternoon we didn't see any other units. We set up a perimeter with the remains of India while gun ships and Phantoms struck the nearby tree line. The bombs were so close you could read the wording on the sides of the canisters.

**SGT JON PAHL - H & S Co:** When word came down that Capt Ralph was hit, Lt Cummins started to move up front to take over the company. I thought "shit, he's moving into hell with it's mouth wide open." I saw grim determination on his face as I told him I would also move up to give him covering fire. I just started to move when a single bullet struck the Lieutenant in the heart. Some fucker in that tree line sure could shoot!

I dropped back to my team and found that the FAC team had air on station so we checked fire on our arty. Two Phantoms dove in and dropped their bombs first and then followed up with rockets and 20mm cannon fire.

The sun got higher and hotter and, despite the supporting arms we were bringing in, the gooks maintained a murderous fire.

When Cpl Mark Smith's (Co I) platoon came under fire, the primary radio operator was wounded and subsequently evacuated. Although Cpl Smith was not a trained radio operator, he unhesitatingly assumed the operator's duties and, despite intense enemy fire, maintained reliable communications with the command post throughout the day. When his platoon commander was mortally wounded, Cpl Smith, displaying exceptional composure under fire, calmly relayed all vital communications. He was awarded the Bronze Star for this action.

Captain Ralph, the Commanding Officer, had been killed along with two other officers (1st Lt Lanny Dee Cummins and 2nd Lt Marc Guy Fiebelkorn.) The Company's men were spread out and separated. For several hours, men fought alone or in small groups and just tried their best to stay alive. Snipers were waiting for heads to stick up to check out the surrounding area. The temperatures rose to ungodly heights and there was very little water left. It was difficult to keep the seriously wounded alive and medivacs were out of the question.

**SGT JON PAUL - H & S Co - FORWARD OBSERVER: Capt Ralph was the best Marine officer I ever served under and I still grieve today for his loss.**

**Just minutes before he was killed, he stopped me from making a fuck up that would have haunted me to my grave. I had pulled up my M-16 to fire at three individuals in black pajamas fleeing down a path at the edge of the tree line we had just come through. I fired twice and was going to full auto when Capt Ralph said, "Sgt Paul, those are women!"**

**SGT RAY ALLISON - Co I: I helped to evacuate one of my men who was wounded by shrapnel. By the time I returned, I lost contact with my platoon and it seemed as if much of Co I had been decimated at a dry river bed area. I managed to cross over the river bed with several other Marines. Myself and another guy went back out and pulled in a wounded man. Marines on the other side were trying to suppress some of the fire that was coming in on us.**

Sgt Nate Lee was in a depression on the other side. I thought he was dead. Late in the afternoon, the heat started getting real intense and we were hurting for water. Then across the way, I saw Nate starting to move. We yelled at him to lay still because the snipers were still shooting and picking us off. As he was moving, he was shot again and he died right there. Nobody knew that he was even alive until he started moving. He had probably laid there for two or three hours in the sun. I though that he had probably been shot and lost consciousness before trying to move.

\* \* \*

**SGT GARY HARLAN - Co I:** I had been ordered back to the states on May 5th, two weeks prior to Allen Brook. I was in California when I received a letter from Haugen telling about the NVA ambush and that Sgt Lee and Lt Fiebelkorn had both been killed. Later I would learn from Nate's brother, Tony, that on the same day that he had been killed, the entire Lee family had gathered to celebrate Mrs. Lee's birthday. It wasn't until three days later that the family learned that Nate had bled to death on the battlefield on the day of their celebration.

\* \* \*

Meanwhile, the truck convoy was diverted to the 27th Marines Command Post by Colonel Adolph G. Schwenk, the Regimental Commander. Information had been received indicating heavy casualties with a tremendous loss of Co I Officers and Staff NCO's. After a map reconnaissance, Colonel Schwenk and Lt Col Woodham made a decision to leave the trucks and heli-lift 3/27 to an area south of Go Noi. The convoy arrived at the CP at 1045 but there was some delay with the arrival of the helicopters.

**LT COL TULLIS WOODHAM, JR. - 3/27 BATTALION CO:** Sometime into the motorcade, I received word from the Regimental Commander to report to the command post. When we got to the CP, Col Schwenk informed me that Capt Ralph had been killed, along with several other officers and men. It was decided that we would now helicopter in to relieve Co I. We sat down and picked out coordinates that we thought would be appropriate to the situation. It was an area just southeast of where Co I was fighting.

Finally, at about 1300, the first elements of Co K were airborne. There was then another delay when a coordination problem arose for the air preparation of the landing zone.

Co K, Co L, the 81mm Mortar Platoon (-), and elements of H & S Company that provided security to the command group were heli-lifted into the vicinity of An Tam (1). Battery D, 2nd Battalion, 13th Marines, was located at Liberty Bridge and provided fire support from that location. An Engineer Team remained attached to the Command Group and would be utilized on an as needed basis by the rifle companies. Each company had an Artillery Forward Observation Team assigned to them.

**SGT WES LOVE - Co K:** I was a 3.5 Rocket Launcher squad leader. I was on the first chopper in the first wave headed for Go Noi Island (to us Happy Valley.) When the pilot asked for the senior man, I stepped forward. He handed me a map and asked where we were going? I had seen the location of Go Noi on the map in the 1st Sergeant's office, so I pointed to it.

**CPL BILL JUNG - Co K:** We boarded the Sea Knight choppers and headed off southwest. I put a magazine in my rifle and my men did likewise.

* * *

On the Island, the Co I Marines were still fighting for their lives. Once realizing that several officers had been killed, 1st Lt Stephen Thompson took over as the Company CO. The Lieutenant would later be awarded a Bronze Star for his courageous action that day.

**SGT JON PAHL - H & S Co:** We started getting heat casualties at our position as the heat of the day increased. First Cpl Curtis, then the FAC and his RTO fell to day's sun. We moved Curtis back to where Sgt Black had his 60 mortars and he took over his care. Gunny Dyrdahl (Gunnery Sgt Vernon Dyrdahl,) who had calmly moved from position to position to make sure everybody was doing their job, had now moved into a low shade covered area where he could watch our left flank and keep an eye on the company. Gunny told me to move the FAC and RTO (Cpl Harley) over to him.

Upon returning to my former position, I heard 'cowpoke one' trying to raise us on the FAC net. I told him what was going on and he responded by saying "It was my show now." I told him that air was dropping ordnance too deep into the tree line and that the gooks were right at the banked edge of the dry wash. I requested napalm as close to friendly troops as possible. Two F-4's came screaming in at tree top level and dropped their canisters of napalm. Hell, I could even read the lettering on those babies. "Take that, you slopehead bastards."

Now, Cpl Hoffman was overcome by heat exhaustion. As Riddle passed him back to me, a gook put a bullet through his shoulder and I got sprayed by a bunch of blood. Hoffman came to and was okay. After a battle dressing was applied, he was able to continue controlling the arty. Eventually, I was able to contact the Company RTO (Tony Roberts) and Lt Thompson, who had taken over the company.

Doc Glick managed to make it back to the Gunny's position. The cheeks of his ass were badly laid open by small arms fire. I couldn't believe that anyone else could possibly survive on that exposed slope.

In one sector of the action, Pfc Robert C. Burke began a one man assault against the enemy. He climbed to the edge of the riverbank and singlehandedly started assaulting various bunkers and delivering such a high volume of suppressive fire that he temporarily relieved the pressure on the forward elements of the company enabling some of the casualties to be pulled to safety. Observing an NVA bunker that was pinning down one of the friendly elements, Burke, oblivious to the rounds hitting around him, aggressively assaulted this fortification with such deadly accurate fire that three NVA were seen fleeing from the position. These soldiers were quickly killed by Burke with a burst of machine gun fire.

At this time, a group of hidden snipers began directing all of their fire on this Marine. Although suffering from the 110 degree plus heat, he began covering the area with fire by walking laterally up and down the line of fire. He suppressed much of the enemy fire until his M-60 machine gun malfunctioned. Moving back to a covered position, he handed his weapon to a wounded comrade and took a casualty's M-16 rifle and magazines and grabbed as many grenades as he could carry. He proceeded back up the bank and into the midst of the enemy fire. Disregarding his own safety, he repeatedly exposed himself to the enemy fire as he lobbed grenades at the enemy bunkers and positions with little effect because of the heavily fortified complex.

Seeing yet another pocket of resistance, Burke aggressively assaulted it, firing his M-16 rifle from the hip until he had knocked out the position.

Observing that his M-60 machine gun was now functioning, he threw two belts of ammunition over his shoulder, grabbed his repaired machine gun, and once again returned to his precarious position at the top of the riverbank. He again made a valiant stand as he saturated the area with well placed bursts of machine gun fire. It was there that an NVA sniper found his mark and mortally wounded Pfc Burke.

Throughout the battle, his presence of mind and heroic efforts were an inspiration to all who served with him. Burke repeatedly exposed himself to the enemy fire that day, knowing full well that the NVA were very accurate, and of the danger to his own life. At a time when others were hesitant to move, he set an example by calmly moving from position to position. He would be awarded a Medal of Honor (the nation's highest award for valor) posthumously. He was the youngest (18 years old) recipient to receive this medal in Vietnam.

**SGT RAY ALLISON - Co I: Burke was on the far left hand edge of the river bank. I told him not to leave the river bank. He had an M-60 and somebody came and told me that Burke was going out to get one of the sniper positions. I said, "No! Stay here at the bank and provide us with security." The next thing I knew they said Burke had left. I don't know when his body was retrieved, but it was later that day.**

**L/CPL DALE CAMP - Co I: About this time grunts down to our left started yelling for a Corpsman. Since I had the Unit One I ran down to see if I could help. It was my friend Robert Burke. He had 4 or 5 bullet holes**

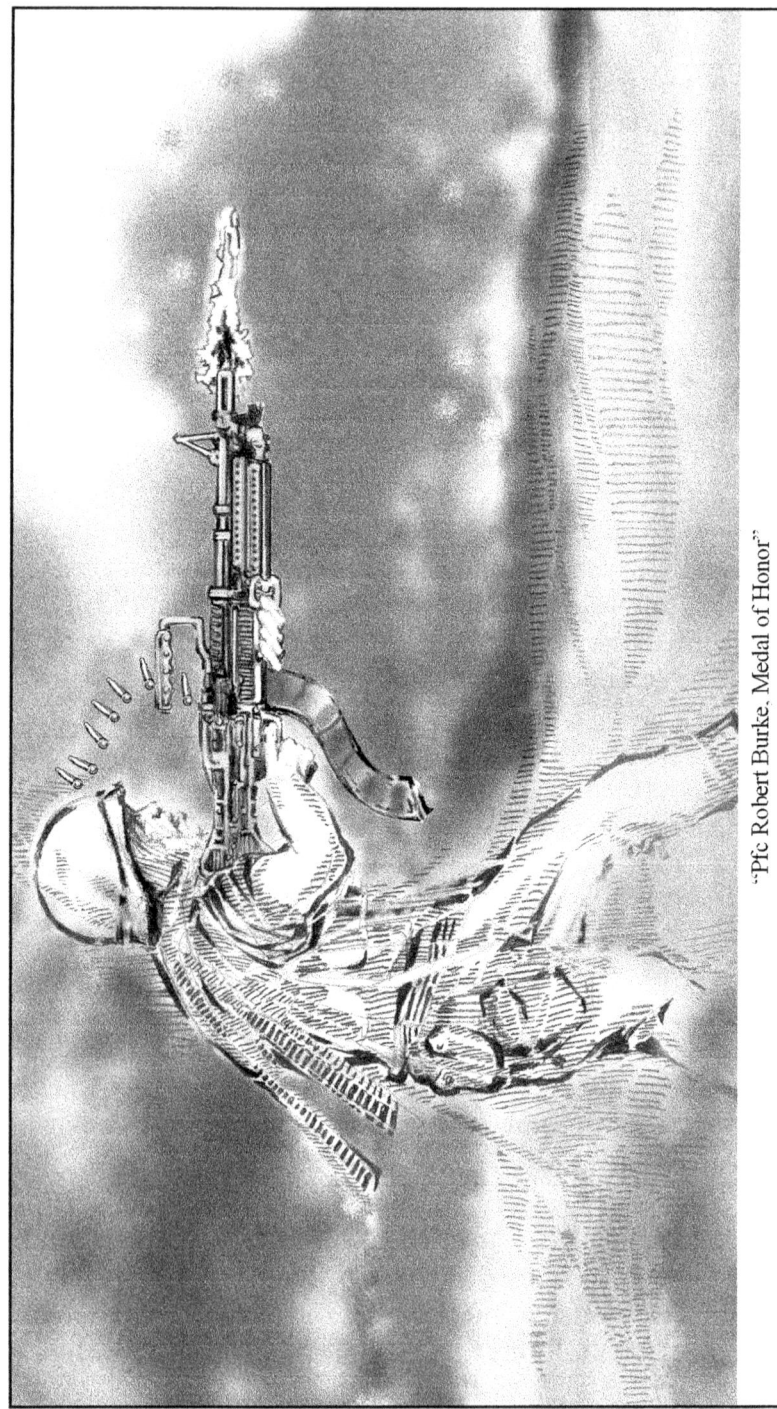

"Pfc Robert Burke, Medal of Honor"

in his chest and was already dead. We all know the story of his bravery. I believe that many of us would not have made it across the river without his help. He died so we could live. When I got back to Lutz, he was really hurting. He told me to reach in his pocket and get the morphine he kept there. I gave it to him in his left shoulder, and in a while he felt a little better. Of the 4 of us who ran into the river after the wounded guy two were hit, Lutz and Massey. The wounded guy was hit again but survived. Ironically, Massey was also hit in the wrist but not as bad as Lutz. When I gave him morphine for his pain he laid a guilt trip on me that has lasted all these years. I guess he was mad about me not helping him out of the river, cause he told me to quit looking out for myself and to start looking out for others. I still feel like I let him down even though he and I didn't like each other. He was making the hard decisions that I was afraid to.

   The battle raged on around us. The NVA behind us were pouring fire across the river into India and Golf. The sniper on our right flank was hitting one grunt after another. Men were screaming, crying, begging for help, asking for their mothers. And we who were safe behind the riverbank felt helpless. Our leadership gone, we just didn't know what to do. We talked about what to do but no one seemed to know the answer. All I really knew was, I wanted to survive this. Artillery screamed into the NVA bunkers behind us but didn't seem to slow them down. Marine jets showed up and we laid out colored panels on the bank above us. We lay against the bank as they started their dives. They looked like they were coming down at us. The NVA fired up at them as they came down and quit just before the jets dropped their loads. When those bombs went off 100 feet behind us the earth rolled under us like waves on the ocean. They made run after run to no avail. The snipers continued to kill Marines.

All our water was given to the wounded and now the incredible heat was trying to kill us. A Marine across the river just stood up and started walking away. We all yelled at him to get down but he was crazed by dehydration and heat and just walked away. Our friend 'Senator Mudflap' from Joplin, Missouri had been laying in the river bed all day and everyone thought he was dead. He started yelling at us, telling us that he was going to run to us and to cover him. We were very afraid that he would be killed and we told him to stay put. He moved a little and the sniper shot him in the ass. 'Senator Mudflap' quit moving.

L/CPL ALLEN CIEZKI - Co I: Late in the afternoon, NVA nurses and doctors in white uniforms ran out into the river bed. Their bunkers must have been smashed by air strikes or they were moved out by Co K making their advancement. Marines at the far bank shot at them and they eventually ran back into the tree line.

Pfc Melvin Cox (we called him 'Senator Mudflap') ran out and was shot crossing the river. He laid still and we thought he was dead. Two hours later, he moved and was hit again. At about 1500, we heard him say "It's me, I'm coming over." He got up and was shot a third time. He laid hidden in a tank track until it got dark and he finally made it over. He was very thirsty and we gave him a whole helmet of water.

L/CPL DALE CAMP - Co I: I had sat next to Lutz all day, talking to him and checking his bandages. I had 13 pressure bandages on his arm and the bleeding had stopped. My clothes and his were soaked in blood and the smell of blood that day stays in my memory. We had all run out of water and I started to get delirious. I realized that I was crying. I remember thinking that I shouldn't be crying cause I was a Marine, but I couldn't stop. Some one threw water in my face and I snapped out of it. They gave me a drink and I came back to my senses. Some of the guys were getting water from a dirty little pond on our right flank. Grunts would fire into the trees and where we thought the sniper was and others would run out and get water in their helmets. It saved our lives. Many trips were made to the pond as we fired cover fire. Phillip Miller our 1st squad radioman tried to get water without cover fire and was shot by a sniper. We got him back to the bank but he was shot through the right lung and died a short while later. Many of the men on my side of the river were wounded but one stands out because of his special wound. He had been shot in the balls and the bag looked like it had been opened by a surgeon. The testicles were untouched. We rigged a shade over him and every time someone went by he asked them to look and see if his balls were going to be all right. In typical grunt black humor we thought this was somewhat funny. Only one person came across the river to us during the day. He was a young officer who was the FO. He ran across and asked for water. He never said another thing all day and we all knew that he had gone over the edge from the horror of that side of the river. The hot, tragic day drug on. The other companies from 3/27 were dropped behind the NVA bunker complex and started moving toward us. We could hear the battle raging. This action flushed out some NVA doctors and nurses who tried to escape by crossing up river from us. They ran into the dry river bed still wearing their white gowns and we all jumped up and tried to kill them. They ran back the way they came. Firing in our area had slowed down and the sniper had been killed by fire from the grassy field. Darkness was coming.

L/CPL ALLEN CIEZKI - Co I: We tried

everything to get to the water, which was in an exposed area. We tied boot laces together and threw canteens over into the water but it didn't work very well. Our best method was to run out under cover fire and fill up our helmets with water.

Later, an FO officer ran across the river bed, but he was so spaced out he wasn't of any help. He brains were fried from the heat.

**CPL RAUL FONSECA - Co I:** We came to the dry river bed and I waited for the right time to move my squad across to the dike area. I had located possible enemy positions and I covered my fire teams as they crossed over, with my M-16. I was the last to get across. I got on the radio to the Company CO to let him know the enemy positions in front of us. The radioman told me that both the CO and XO had been killed.

I decided to take charge of everyone at the bank. I told the radioman to call for backup to sweep in from the opposite direction while I was going to direct support from wherever I could find it. We had to get out of this mess. I switched radio channels to 105's. I gave them my location and that of the enemy. I asked for a spotter round first and then corrected them after that. When I finished with the 105's, I also got some Huey gun ships to come and help. We spotted with red smoke and the Hueys opened up with rockets. It was a good feeling after the shit had stopped.

We still had to stay where we were until nighttime when Kilo linked up with us. I told every man at the dike to remember the location of the fallen men in the river bed and on the other side so that we could pick them up later on. The heat was also a big factor in loss of life that day.

I remember one Marine getting up from the elephant grass and running to the right yelling his head off.

He ran fifty yards and then collapsed. He wasn't shot. It was the heat that got him. I returned later that night with the help of others to pick that man up. He was dead. I can still picture all of the body bags in line on the ground.

After that night, there is little that I can remember about Allen Brook. I can't explain why my memory is gone.

      L/CPL JOHN GEORGE - Co I: 17 May 1968 was probably the scariest and bloodiest day of my experience in Vietnam. As I remember it we started a sweep toward a tree line with a dried up creek bed in front of it. L/Cpl West was to my left. We crossed the creek bed and were almost to the other side when the NVA opened with automatic weapons directly in front of us. West fell immediately. I fired into the tree line and turned to go back. I felt my leg jerk to the side and I almost fell but managed to get back to the other side of the creek bed.

We laid down in the weeds and started firing back across the creek bed. About that time a bullet hit my helmet, it must have been at an angle because my helmet flew off my head and I never found it in the grass. For a few seconds I thought I was badly hurt but it just stunned me for a minute. My left leg finally started to hurt enough for me to look at it and I saw a bullet hole through the top of my boot. A Corpsman came over and took my boot off. He started to tie a bandage around my leg when a sniper shot came very close to him. He threw the bandage to me and said, "Here, put it on yourself." He crawled away and I didn't blame him at all. There were Marines hurt a lot worse than myself anyway.

Someone told me to try to crawl back to the bomb crater we had passed on the way, because the wounded were being taken there for a medivac. I had only crawled a short distance when a bullet hit the ground in front of my face so I decided to stay where I was. It got extremely hot as the day wore on, and at times the gun fire was so heavy, it was a steady roar. I thought if I didn't die that day from a bullet, I would surely die from thirst. Sometime in the afternoon Sgt Ray Allison came by with canteens of water he managed to get somewhere. He gave me two of them and I drank them both. It was the best drink I ever had. I have always felt that Ray should have gotten a medal for risking his life to get the water because I think he saved some lives that day. Sometime after dark, the wounded were medivaced to Da Nang.

**L/CPL ALLAN CIEZKI - Co I:** There was one guy back on the other side to our right who should have received some kind of medal. He was in a good fighting hole and had an M-60 machine gun. He kept shooting all day and probably prevented the gooks from overrunning us on our side. At times, I could see guys throwing him belt ammo throughout the day. I never did find out who he was.

* * *

**LT COL ROGER H. BARNARD - 3/7 BATTALION CO:** I was advised mid-to-late afternoon that 3/27 would be landing by helicopter to the south of the point of resistance that afternoon/evening. This was most welcome news because it seemed as though the enemy position, plus the size of the maneuver area (i.e., the distance to the point at which an envelopment could begin) presented a challenge of exceptional proportions. I don't recall the time Co A reached its enveloping position, or the time that 3/27 arrived in the landing zone. I only remember that Co A was too late to begin its envelopment (it never took place.) The arrival of 3/27 precluded the commencement of the envelopment.

That evening, I was in direct radio contact with the CO, 3/27. Later that night, I was ordered to proceed to Liberty Bridge at dawn, 18 May.

\* \* \*

**LT COL TULLIS WOODHAM, JR. - 3/27 BATTALION CO:** Although we had no helicopter team loading plans, I thought we did a good job. We circled over our LZ for quite a while before landing. I saw my first Go Noi casualty shortly after we had landed. This Marine was about fifteen yards away and was hit in the neck by shrapnel. A corpsman performed a tracheotomy right there while we were moving along.

The inbound helicopters finally landed at 1500 and the Battalion immediately launched its attack to the north to link up with Co I. Co K was on the left, Co L on the right and the Command Group with H&S elements following. The attack did take pressure off of Co I as enemy units had to divert much of their attention to the newly arrived Marines. Automatic fire and mortar rounds were brought to bear on the Marines as they began their attack.

**CAPT JOEL D. PARKS - Co K CO:** My company was the initial company inserted. We landed on a slight hill south of Go Noi Island. My XO went in on the first wave and started to establish an LZ for the Battalion.

India Company was in a pretty dire situation and the Colonel pushed hard in getting me there. I initially had some problems in having my people released from landing zone security duty and then getting everyone on line for our attack.

**LT COL TULLIS WOODHAM, JR. - 3/27**

**BATTALION CO:** We caught the enemy by surprise in the area where we landed because we were to the rear of them and our direction of advancement was over their backs. They were caught between us and Co I and 3/7. We attacked with Kilo on the left, Lima on the right and the Command Group following in trace of Kilo. It did not take the enemy long to realize that we were there. We came under mortar attack and long range machine gun fire. The Division placed us under operational control of the 7th Marines (Colonel Reverdy Hall.)

The landing zone became so hot that the last helicopter, containing elements of the command group, had to be diverted to Liberty Bridge where the 27th Marines were establishing a forward command post.

**SGT GARLAND SISCO - Co K:** We came in on the first wave of helicopters and set up security. It seemed like a couple of waves came in before we started taking mortars in our LZ.

**SGT WES LOVE - Co K:** After a ten minute flight, we landed 75 to 100 yards away from a tree line. I was the first off the chopper. At the time, I had Roach, my M-79 man; Don Hill, 3.5 man; Lewis, M-60 man; Parker, ammo humper and rifleman; and lastly Edney, a Navy Corpsman. These people were with me all through the rescue of India. After several hours of rocket, mortar and small arms fire, we entered the tree line at about 2000.

**L/CPL LEROY R. DRIFFILL - Co K:** As the choppers landed and the rear ramp let down, we unloaded as fast as we could as bullets whistled over us. We spread out and awaited orders. We were told to dig in at first, so we grabbed our entrenching tools and started to dig a foxhole. I remember the ground being as hard as concrete, and after twenty minutes myself and Cpl Twilling had

"Hot LZ"

maybe dug in four inches. Mortar round began to fly in, but the enemy fired only four rounds at us. We were then told to move out. We moved to a large dry rice paddy and all companies were lined and facing a tree line about three hundred meters to our front. The command sent four point men walking toward the tree line. As they neared it, all four Marines went down by enemy fire. It almost looked like a firing squad had cut them down. The Companies then began an assault on the tree line. The intense firing from both sides was so tremendous that it seemed the ground rumbled and vibrated. The enemy positions and snipers pinned us down for hours but towards nightfall the Marines broke through to the tree line. Around ten to fifteen of us, including myself, were separated from the main body. We continued to have small contacts with the enemy forces, and began helping our wounded to the best of our abilities. Medivac choppers were called and flight after flight began removing the wounded. We worked well into the night retrieving our fallen brothers. We would load the wounded first and then the heart wrenching task of loading the dead. I will never forget the sadness felt by us as we had to throw, as if they were garbage bags, our dead brothers over the back of the choppers rear gate, piling them up as high as we could stack them. On completion of the medivacs, we set up a small platoon base and rested the best we could.

**L/CPL DAVID STEFFENSON - Co K:** We were taking mortar fire when we landed. We scattered and went for some existing trenches. We were told not to get into the trenches but to dig in sideways because the trenches were zeroed in on. After the mortaring stopped, we moved forward. Then one of the officers said that we had to get a radio into the tree line, but he didn't give a reason.

We were going through a graveyard and I noticed that there were tunnels. The engineers started blowing a few of them up. We kept going forward and right in front of the tree line I felt like I was stung by a bee. I fell down and was bleeding. I felt the pain in my side and then I was shot again in the side. Two guys came over to help me. One was shot in the groin and then, I guess, shot in the head. He didn't make a sound except when he was shot in the groin. He was screaming, then nothing after that. Then Steve Young, the guy who really helped me, was bandaging me up when he was shot in the forearm. Then he just keeled over. He too was shot in the head and died instantly.

It seemed that both sides were just shooting. I didn't know if I was more afraid of our guys or them. I used Steve as a shield. I just got behind him and laid there. Then two guys came up. I don't know their names. One was a squad leader and a grenadier, and they started firing. All I remember was the squad leader saying "We gotta get out of here. We'll just have to run and crawl, run and crawl." When he said go we ran, then dove down, crawling through this heavy, deep, thick mud. We had to do this for maybe two hundred yards.

When we made it back, we waited till evening before being medivaced out. There was just me, the squad leader and the grenadier. I thought everyone else was dead. Christ! The choppers were so filled with casualties from the first day that they were just throwing the dead in the back of the helicopters that were there. I remember looking at them. I can still see them. They looked like mannequins, upside down. We got out that night and I was just praying to God they wouldn't shoot down the helicopters. There was one medivac after another.

**SGT GARLAND SISCO - Co K: After L/Cpl**

Michael Kuhse and Pvt Young were killed trying to help Steffensen, Johnson and myself went out to try to help. I lobbed M-79 grenades over him to try to keep the enemy heads down. Years later I would talk to Steffensen and as soon as he heard my voice, he remembered it was me who helped get him back to safety that afternoon. He remembered the M-79 rounds being very close and said I hoped you were good and knew what you were doing. I preferred to think that I was very good.

       L/CPL ART RIORDAN - Co L: The first and last time I flew on a CH-53 was into Go Noi Island. I can't remember landing in a chopper where we weren't getting mortared or fired at. We were supposed to link up at the 3 o'clock position with the team that landed ahead of us. We came into a Hot LZ and linked up with anyone that was there already. The CH-53 barely hovered two feet off the ground and he was taking off again. We were taking mortars and small arms. As the chopper was lifting and about 20 feet in the air, I saw a body coming out and I rolled to avoid him landing on me. He was an FNG. I was amazed when he told me he was afraid he would get separated from his platoon so he jumped. He could have been a casualty without a shot fired. This is just another fine example of Esprit de Corps on Go Noi Island.

       CPL BILL JUNG - Co K: As more choppers came in, NVA snipers opened up to our front. Our platoon poured bullets at them and the enemy fire stopped. We received word to move out. Two of our platoons were up front in the assault and on line with Lima. Our 'third herd' brought up the reserve. Mortars began falling to my right as more choppers came in. We started to descend from the high ground with the company spread out in combat formation. Below us was a wide stream. On the other side were paddies and a thick tree line. Somewhere over there were the remnants of India.

Several hours into the battle, 3/27 encountered an unmapped stream across its avenue of attack. It was too deep to allow a quick negotiation. A decision was made to send Co L to the east to search for an easier crossing and then go northwest to link up with Co I.

**LT COL TULLIS WOODHAM, JR. - 3/27 BATTALION CO:** It was about 1500 when our lead elements were stalled at a dam area. Col Hall (7th Marines CO) got on the net and started haranguing me to get help to 3/7. He just couldn't comprehend what we were up against.

**CAPT JOHN ERNEST - Co L CO:** We were ordered east after we hit the stream. We spent the rest of the afternoon and evening with very little contact. Kilo did a great job in linking up with India.

Co K located a small dam which allowed the men to cross over the stream but it had to be done single file and in a very precarious manner. While Co L met little resistance, Co K was still seriously engaged with the NVA. Air and artillery missions continued to be called in for support.

**CAPT JOEL PARKS - Co K CO:** We came to a river and had to shift to the right before coming to a passable ford. We crossed, shifted back left, and then tried to establish where India was. By pyrotechnics, they appeared to be on our left flank but actually were much further away. We pushed off on our attack and started receiving mortar rounds resulting in our first casualties. We couldn't utilize supporting arms except for machine guns because we didn't know the exact position of India and the enemy was between us and them.

At first I thought we were going up against a squad but soon realized that it was at least a platoon because as soon as we knocked out a position, reinforcements moved in. They were fighting from trench lines and houses.

First platoon took pretty heavy casualties and the platoon commander requested to be replaced so he could regroup and take care of his wounded. I then moved up the third platoon from reserves. Second platoon, by this time, had taken 2 KIAs and 3 WIAs but were still moving quite well despite being under heavy automatic fire. Sgt Kalka initiated the use of gas by throwing in four gas grenades and this broke up the attack and the NVA fled the area.

**CPL BILL JUNG - Co K:** The company began crossing the stream over a stick dam. As we waited, a mortar round landed to my left and three men went down. Pvt Franklin H. Metzger was struck in the head by a piece of shrapnel and died instantly. Tracer rounds were flying everywhere and we could see many friends falling, either dead or wounded. We used everything on the tree line. Jets, mortars, artillery and even gun ship helicopters strafed the area with rockets and machine guns. We continued moving as dusk started to fall around us.

As Co K continued its attack, and came under intense NVA fire, Pfc Vincent Chiofolo commenced delivering a heavy volume of rifle fire into the fortified positions. This action enabled a machine gun team to move forward and engage the enemy. In the ensuing fire fight, the team became pinned down, and when the M-60 machine gun malfunctioned, Pfc Chiofolo fearlessly maneuvered across the fire-swept terrain in an attempt to draw the fire and attention of the enemy away from his comrades. Delivering accurate fire into the hostile emplacements, he succeeded in diverting the enemy fire, enabling the Marines to maneuver to positions of relative safety. Alertly observing three NVA soldiers launching a determined assault upon his comrades, he boldly exposed himself to the intense hostile fire and aggressively engaged the enemy soldiers, killing two of them. Although seriously wounded by a hostile sniper, he ignored his painful injury and steadfastly remained in his hazardous position, until forcibly restrained and moved to a covered position by fellow Marines. For this bravery under fire, Pfc Chiofolo was awarded the Silver Star.

**SGT GARLAND SISCO - Co K: We moved across a small stream and began crossing a large open rice paddy where we started taking hostile fire from the tree line. My squad took one WIA and two KIAs at this time. We finally secured the tree line and then moved on through the area. I remember seeing huge bomb craters from an earlier air strike. We then dug in for the night with our backs to the river. At about 2400 or after, we took eight to ten mortar rounds into our company area.**

**SGT WES LOVE - Co K: By the time the third or fourth chopper dropped it's human cargo we were in deep shit. Mortar, rocket, machine gun, light arms (AK's) in heavy volume were incoming. Moving forward was extremely difficult. It didn't take us very long to learn their snipers were very accurate. We had covered maybe half the distance to the tree line when I noticed I didn't hear the M-60 to my right talking anymore. I glanced just to see S/Sgt Dan O'Conner take a hit and drop. I thought he went to grab the M-60 and fire back, but later I found out he was grabbing for the bag with the glove wrench and spare barrel to replace it. The 60 barrel was already red.**

Two gunners had been hit in less than a minute and I was getting concerned cause his was the closest 60 that was covering my field of fire. That really changed plans for advancement. Lewis took his M-14 off his back and started firing his chlorine and CS gas grenades into the tree line. Only after a long and hostile afternoon did we finally enter the tree line. Just as we entered I picked up an AK-47, looked at it (then looked at mine) shook my head and slung it over my back. While they were busy checking bunkers and fighting holes, I calmly sat down to un-jam my Mattel toy. As we made our way into the trees the devastation was everywhere. We found dead bodies of the NVAs, gear, packs that they had left behind, and torn up ground everywhere as we headed for India Company.

\* \* \*

**HM3 PAUL BENECH - Co I:** I remember carrying our Executive Officer to safety and tending to his wounds. Then I dragged two Marines suffering from heat exhaustion to a small pond. After that, I didn't know who I was patching up. I was just running everywhere I heard Marines yelling for a corpsman. Halfway across an open field, the enemy opened up on me. One round hit my pistol. Other bullets ripped through my pack and parts of my flak jacket. One round tore a huge hole in my helmet and creased my head, knocking me unconscious. When I woke up on the helicopter, I thought I was in heaven. I'm thankful to be alive.

**L/CPL DALE CAMP - Co I:** With darkness we prepared to cross back over the river. Although we were in the safest place on the battlefield, we felt cut off from our company, and felt a strong need to get back to them. We picked up our wounded and started to the other side.

Lutz, who was pretty high on morphine, wanted to walk by himself. He passed out when he stood up and another grunt and I carried him across.

Bodies lay everywhere. Some were already lined up under ponchos. I found Lt Stephen Thompson who was the only India Company officer left alive. He grabbed me and told me that he had been told early in the day that I was dead. It was great to see him. We added our dead to the line. The wounded were medivaced. I looked for the only other member of my squad and found out that he had broken his leg carrying wounded back from across the river. I was the only one left from 1st squad. I dug a shallow hole, crawled in and went to sleep. The worst day of my life had ended.

HM MIKE LUTZ - Co I: 'Doc' Camp had hit me with some morphine and the rest of the day is somewhat hazy due to the blood loss and effects of the morphine. As the day wore on, I must have passed out. When I awoke it was after dark and medivacs had started. At the LZ, Jan Mitchner told me that hardly anyone was left. The chinooks came in and took us to the hospital in Da Nang.

PFC TOM HANSON - Co I: I heard someone crawling around me, and not knowing if we'd been overrun, I played dead. Then I heard English being spoken. I yelled out, "Hey! Is somebody there?"

A man replied, "Yeah, I'm here, buddy."

"Listen," I said, "I don't know how much strength I've got, but if you help me I think I can move." While I'd been out, the line had moved back, so with the help from a man from Golf 2/7 (I believe,) I crawled back to a small gathering of men in the rear.

Some brave souls had gone off and returned with water-filled canteens. God, did that water taste great! We were going to move back further and proceeded to do so when one of the Marines said, "Hey, will somebody help me with this guy?" I thought the man he was talking about was dead and told him so.

"Naw," said the Marine, "he's not even wounded. He's just passed out from the heat." I rolled the man over and checked his wrist for a pulse. None. I pulled his shirt open and listened for a heartbeat. No sound. Then I looked at his mouth. There was a ring of sand around his mouth and nose. How tragic. His buddy had dragged him back but had lain him face first in the sand. Unconscious, he'd suffocated. I'll never forget the look on that Marine's face when he realized what he'd done.

A medivac zone was established and I remember one incongruity as night fell. So many of our buddies were lying dead a short way away, yet someone had a transistor radio out and we sat listening to country-western music on AFVN.

When night came the medivac choppers landed. In my recollection they took some small-arms fire and at first would not land. When they (CH-46's) did set down we began to load the stretcher cases, which filled two or three loads. When they were all loaded and off, a gunnery sergeant told me he wanted me to be the first one on the next chopper out. When I finally got on and lifted off, words cannot express the relief I felt getting the hell out of there. I was also feeling sad because I had learned what had happened to my friend Bob Bauer. At the medivac zone someone asked if anyone knew Bob. I had said I did and the Marine told me, "He died in my arms."

We made a short hop and came down at an aid station, similar to a MASH unit. A corpsman took me off and put me on a stretcher. As the Chinook took off the corpsman took off his shirt and used it to protect me from the rotor wash. I'll never forget that bit of kindness after the ordeal we'd been through.

I was carried in and had my wound examined. A small bit of shrapnel had gone through my ear and lodged in my skull. They dug that out, cleaned me up and sent me to x-ray. Aside from a slight concussion, I was in fairly good shape.

I got on another chopper and was flown to NSA (Naval Support Activity) in Da Nang. After a few days they sutured my ear and head wounds. They gave me new glasses and after a few weeks of healing I returned to India company.

L/CPL ALLAN CIEZKI - Co I: When it started to get dark I could see Marines on the other side. We yelled at them to get down, but the NVA had already moved out. I was exhausted but I managed to help some wounded move across the river bed. I must have fainted because the next thing I knew, it was morning and two guys were trying to pick me up, thinking I was dead.

I looked back across the river bed and saw Marines picking up KIA's. They were stiff like boards and hard to put into ponchos because of the positions they were in. Equipment was piled all around the LZ, but somehow I was able to find my rifle and radio.

\* \* \*

CPL RICHARD SNELTZER - Engineer attached to 3/27: I remember that our choppers landed late in the day and we were immediately hit with NVA spotter rounds. That night 175mm artillery was fired over our heads and into the tree line. When the sky would light up from the explosions, we could see bodies flying above the trees.

\* \* \*

**CAPT JOEL PARKS - Co K CO:** We moved into the tree line with about one and a half platoons and then waited for darkness before trying to link up with India. We moved in a platoon vee with half of a platoon to the rear in a column. We went about 300 meters and then took about 500 rounds of automatic fire. We didn't receive any casualties and after the fire stopped we continued on our movement. We went another 400 meters due west and then crossed a stream bed and moved into India Company.

India had about 23 dead and many wounded. They were completely disorganized and had no holes dug. I told them to take care of their wounded while I set up security around them. India hadn't eaten for two days and they were pretty tight on water. We got resupplied with water that night and I let India have it all.

**CPL BILL JUNG - Co K:** Darkness was now upon us, and the jungle to our front was quiet. We peered at the blackness and waited for the enemy's next move. One wounded man somewhere to our rear began screaming for God, mercy, mother and just out of pain. We felt sorry for him but his wailing started to get on our nerves.

Our left flank was trying to link up with S/Sgt William O'Hara. As men called out his name, hidden NVA joined in on the chorus. Christ! It was scary. Our company was finally linked up and we began sweeping in the dark looking for India. Slowly, we stumbled through the darkness, bamboo thorns and ditches. We halted, linked up again, and then turned left and moved out in a single file. It was around 2200 when we finally joined up with India and Golf, 2/7.

**SGT WES LOVE - Co K:** By my calculations we should have been at the India base camp at 2200. I popped a green flare so we could locate each other and I scared a perimeter guard only 10 yards away. Somebody has to remember that I was the first to reach them that night. Oh, how I remember it well.

PFC Johnny G. Johnson (Co K) was born a Marine. His father fought on Guadacanal and was wounded on Pelilu during World War II. Johnson idolized and imitated his father. At seven, he was digging foxholes in the front yard and he grew up knowing that he was going to be a Marine. He learned to drink his whiskey straight, just like his 'old man.' Johnson had joined 3/27 (his father had also served in the First Marine Division) in late February. Initially he was assigned as a clerk, but after several weeks of bitching, he managed to get out in the field as a grunt with Kilo Company, 2nd Platoon.

**PFC JOHNNY G. JOHNSON - Co K:** I moved into a tree line on point. A mortar landed a few yards away and I was knocked down, but luckily no shrapnel hit me. My adrenaline was running on high. In the moonlight, I saw rows of dead Marines. It was a very eerie sight. We moved into a long trench line for the night. I was scared to death that the gooks would launch a counter attack through the open trench. I was the first one they would hit.

**SGT WES LOVE - Co K:** Inside India Company's perimeter, for the few of us that had reached them first, we started relieving them from the perimeter and the gruesome task of retrieving the dead Marines. We spent most of the rest of the night lining them in two rows for a medivac the next day. A very bad feeling I had earlier had returned; though we had kicked ass to get here, I still felt they had opened up to let us in and without our knowledge had just shut the door. I quickly checked my people and all were OK. Just the usual 1000 mile stare. You never get used to it but a certain numbness that makes you oblivious or feel like you are not a part of the carnage you're in the middle of. You see a commercial jet leave the Da Nang air field headed for the real world and pray you'll last long enough to be on one, and you think of a person or yourself back home on a bar stool wondering is he happy or is he bitchin' about the war. Shots break the silence, it's a VC storming the perimeter. A S/Sgt took a hit in the side. Two or three rounds hit him and he still kept coming. Then I heard a .45 go off and he ran no more. The rest of the night was quiet and dark, real dark. You couldn't even see a hand in front of your face.

SGT JON PAHL - H & S Co: During the medivacs that night, the Gunny knelt down by Cpl Cox (Mud Flap) and said, "Cox, you tough bastard, how's it going!" Cox yelled back, "Gunny, get this green Marine Corps shit off of me."

As I remembered, about 35 flights of fixed winged air craft dropped ordnance and I can only estimate that 300 to 400 rounds of arty were fired in direct support that day.

HM3 RAUL KELLEY - CORPSMAN - Co K: When it got dark I heard a Marine yelling for help so I moved out to get him. Once I patched him up, we realized we didn't know where the CP and medical evacuation area were. We hid behind a dike and soon five or six other wounded joined up with us. Eventually we were able to call in and get help from other Marines from the CP. Back at the CP, we started separating casualties into priorities, ranking everyone from serious to routine.

Control of Operation Allen Brook had passed from 3/7 to 3/27 at around 1900. As the companies settled in for the

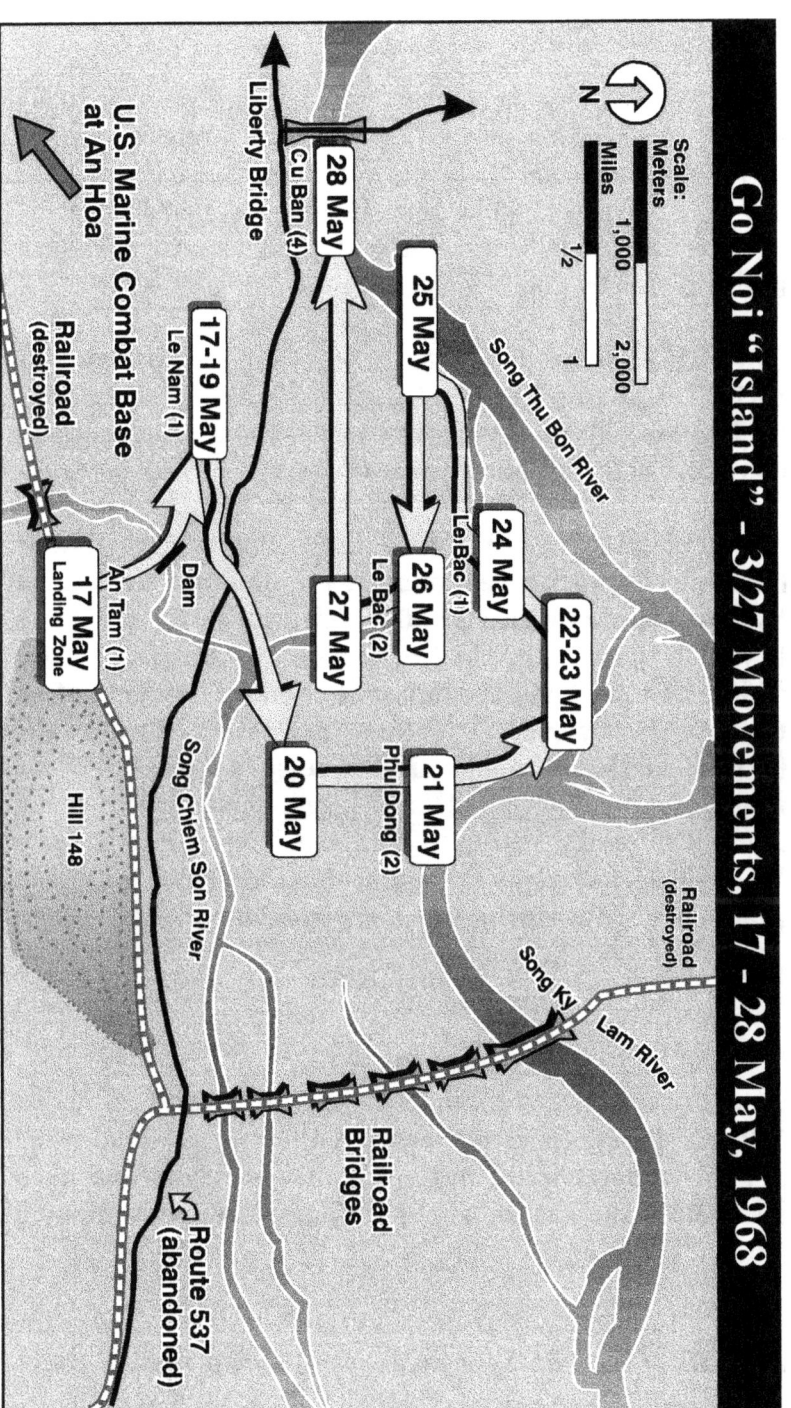

evening, the Command Group was situated in a rice paddy south of the no name stream; Co K and Co I remained in the Le Nam (1) area; and Co L was to the east. Casualties for the day were twenty-one killed and sixty-eight wounded. Enemy casualties could not be accurately assessed due to darkness but fifteen bodies had been found.

**CPL BILL JUNG - Co K:** As I moved through our perimeter looking for the Lieutenant, I came across nearly twenty dead Marines lying in two rows. In the moonlight, it was a grisly and ghostly sight!

**SGT DANA HARPER - Co K:** Quite a few times I have questioned my reasoning for signing a waiver to go back to Vietnam with 3/27 after three purple hearts on my first tour with 3/1. Go Noi Island was the same place where 3/1 took a large number of casualties on Operation Union I, exactly one year before Allen Brook. I was in the hospital at the time and my entire squad was killed or wounded. I know I had guilty feelings about not being there. I think that's why I justified my decision to go back again. God has plans for me in this life. I was wounded again on 17 May during the initial action on Allen Brook.

\* \* \*

**CAPT BLAKE K. THOMAS - Co M CO:** My company was TAD (Temporary Assigned Duty) to the 1st MPs for Danang airfield security when we received word at approximately 2200 on 17 May that we would be moved out at 0630 the next morning to reinforce the Battalion on Go Noi Island.

**SGT EDWARD BENAVIDEZ - Co M:** On the morning of the 17$^{th}$, I got up about 0700 and went to chow.

**Right after morning formation, I went after some ice for the club. I got back by 1000 and I was reassigned as a squad leader. We had some replacements come in and we are almost at 100% strength. Lt Tilghman was the platoon leader. I stayed around my tent all day. At 1800 we had a briefing. I was the 1$^{st}$ squad leader but the squads were switched around so I actually had the 3$^{rd}$ squad with Nowlin as 1$^{st}$ team leader. At 1930, I took my squad out to the point on outpost duty. I sent one team out on an ambush at 2100. About 2300 we got word to get ready for an operation. I Company has been hit hard and we are going in to help. I left one team at the outpost and the rest of us went in to pack.**

## 18 MAY

3/7 marched off the Island in the early morning hours of 18 May. They had relinquished control of the operation the night before. The next night, 3/7's combat base was mortared and both Lt Col Barnard and his XO were wounded.

At 0615, the 3rd Battalion, 5th Marines, commanded by Lt Col Rexroad, was placed OP CON to the 27th Marines and arrived on Go Noi Island. They would operate mainly to the east of 3/27 throughout the month of May.

**CAPT JOEL PARKS - Co K CO: I called in air and artillery in the early morning to prep the areas prior to the command group joining up with U.S. NVA were still shooting at the jets as they came in for their bombing runs.**

At 0830, Co L moved from its night position to link up with Co I and Co K. At the same time, the Command Group with one Co K platoon, also began moving to the rendezvous point near Le Nam (1) and Cu Ban (3). At 0940 the

Command Group joined the other companies. The 81mm Mortar Platoon, under 1st Lieutenant Roy Casteel, was given the task of a reconnaissance patrol to establish positions for the Command Group.

**LT COL TULLIS WOODHAM, JR. - 3/27 BATTALION CO:** In the morning, the rest of the Battalion Command Group joined Kilo, India and 3/7. We crossed over the area where the enemy had been when they were set in position for the ambush of India and 3/7. It was a most unusual morning in that it was quiet, sunny, and as clear as it could be. There was no activity and it was extremely hot. We began to police up the battlefield and evacuate casualties.

While organizing and consolidating our positions, it became apparent that Co I had been rendered combat ineffective. They had heavy casualties in the ranks and almost total annihilation of their officers and staff NCO's. Co I was for all realistic purposes combat ineffective. Co M had been alerted the previous day that they would, in all likelihood, be joining the Battalion on Go Noi Island. The plan was to evacuate Co I with the helicopters bringing in Mike Company.

**CPL RICHARD SNELTZER - Engineer attached to 3/27:** As we were waking up, everyone looked to the south at what looked like dozens and dozens of people standing there waiting to attack us. It turned out that they were just shadows from erosion ruts in a mud bank.

\* \* \*

Co M was acting as security for a POW compound on the outskirts of the Da Nang airfield. The Marines began their battle preparations and moved out to an LZ. They would wait several hours in the hot sun before the choppers arrived.

**CPL MARLIN 'JACK' JACKSON - Co M:** Everyone was laying against their packs as we waited for the helicopters. We had learned that we were headed into a very tight battle. This was my second tour and I had been into the Arizona Valley before. It was considered 'injun country,' and it wasn't a very nice place to be.

I was part of a three man Forward Observer (FO) Scout Team. Cpl Orville Brettman and I shared radio duties under the leadership of 1st Lt John Williamson. We were told we were going against just one NVA battalion. I thought to myself, where have I heard that before! As we waited, we cleaned and checked our weapons. I couldn't help but wonder how many men wouldn't return alive.

\* \* \*

**L/CPL DALE CAMP - Co I:** I awoke early on the morning of the 18th. The realization of what happened on the 17th hit me hard. Guys were up and moving around in confusion. The row of bodies was sitting right in the middle of our area, and everyone was quiet, tired, and sad. I was assigned to a detail to search for our dead and we fanned out along the riverbank. Bodies were scattered through the grass. We knew all these guys and it was tough to see their bodies twisted in rigor mortis. We remembered some of them had pleaded for help and we took note of their wounds. We gathered up their weapons, and carried the bodies back to our row of dead. We found men who had died of minor wounds and men with no wounds at all, who had died of heat and dehydration. Survivors told tales of Marines so desperate that they drank their piss mixed with Kool-Aid. We worked quite a while until we were satisfied we had found everyone.

India Company was told that we would be extracted because of the loss of our officers and so many men. We really weren't capable of doing much right then. We staged near the LZ, and started putting the dead on choppers. I don't know how many of us were left but it looked like less than a platoon. Each of us had about 6-10 weapons that we were responsible for taking on the choppers with us, and it was a real impressive pile of rifles.

**LT COL TULLIS WOODHAM, JR. - 3/27 BATTALION CO:** I sent Roy Casteel and some elements of the 81 mortar platoon over to scout out a location for a command post as we tried to consolidate the battlefield area. Lima Company was still coming in from the east and was in sort of a turning movement. We started hearing sporadic rifle fire from our right front, where the 81 platoon had gone. It soon turned into intense fire and before we knew it, we were engaged in a full scale conflict with an unknown size enemy force. Lima had them pinned on the right and Kilo took position on the left.

**CAPT JOEL PARKS - Co K CO:** My company took one half of the perimeter and Lima took the western half and started moving into the tree line. They started taking heavy machine gun and sniper fire within a few minutes. I didn't realize how serious it was until the Colonel told me to move up on Lima's left flank to help bail them out.

**CPL FRED STUEBE - H&S Co:** Our Lieutenant, Lt Roy Casteel, joined us on the 18th. That morning I found an NVA canteen and picked it up as a souvenir. It had words and pictures etched on it and I still have it today. Eighty-one's were sent off to look for a CP and we ran into deep shit. The fire was intense and we had many casualties. We were able to pull back while we were being relieved by Kilo or Lima.

    Co K now moved out to the north and Co L, moving from the east, soon began taking small arms fire. Initially, it was thought to be one or two snipers, but it soon became clear that a major enemy force was involved. The volume of fire became increasingly heavy. Lead elements of both companies were pinned down and could not be extracted. The NVA bunker positions had been established with the intention of fighting it out until absolute necessity dictated otherwise. They showed no desire to abandon the battlefield despite the intensity of the mortar, automatic weapons fire, artillery and air strikes thrown at them.
    The area where the NVA were dug in was the same place that Co I had surprised the enemy on the morning of the 17th. They had swept through this area and it's amazing that they had not seen any of the fortified positions. It was never determined if these NVA were remnants from the battle of the 17th who had escaped and repositioned themselves or if it was an entirely new unit.

    **CAPT JOEL PARKS - Co K CO: I kicked off with two platoons up, each moving in a wedge. The platoon on the left started taking numerous heat casualties. It was around noon and 112 degrees. They had no water and started to wilt like flowers. Third platoon had more water and made it to the tree line but took 14 wounded. The Lieutenant left his platoon sergeant to handle the wounded and entered the tree line with just 9 men.**

    **HM3 RAUL KELLEY - CORPSMAN - Co K: There were more heat casualties than we had anticipated. Almost all of the Kilo company corpsmen were evacuated due to heat because they were all working so hard to help**

with the wounded. Men were placed in a river to cool off and the more serious ones were evacuated to the rear. Usually, they would return in two days.

\* \* \*

L/CPL DALE CAMP - Co I: Before all of India Company could get off Go Noi, the battle started up again. Down to our left flank, one of the other companies of 3/27 started into it with the NVA and it just grew and grew. Bullets were zipping through the LZ and we spread out and lay down. Gunny Dyrdahl was sitting on a stack of C-Rations while the bullets flew by us and we yelled at him to get down. He looked at us with weary eyes and said "I'm too old to get down, get up, get down." He just didn't give a shit anymore. We were in awe of the man.

As the battle heated up, more and more casualties were brought to the LZ and less and less India Company grunts were extracted. There were a great many heat casualties due to the extreme weather and when they made it to the LZ, we took them into the nearby pond to cool them off. Some of them were out of their heads.

By now only casualties were being evacuated and India Company was moved into defensive positions. We were very anxious to get out and this was a crushing development. Members of India Company still on Go Noi, spent the rest of the day manning the LZ perimeter and helping with casualties.

\* \* \*

S/SGT WILLIAM OHARA - PLATOON SGT Co K: As we started out after another tree line, one platoon ran into a mine field and another came under heavy fire and took several casualties. We pulled back and then called in artillery and air support.

      **SGT WES LOVE - Co K:** We started to patrol away from India's position and walked into a mine field. What they had were chi coms, which were low grade Chinese dynamite grenades, tied up in the tall elephant grass and then one attached to another. Set one off and you set them all off. I was the chief instructor of the Viet Cong orientation and booby trap trail on Camp Pendleton, so I knew what to do. Three factors governed the mine field with the Marines. 1. If you can back out of the field, do so! 2. If you are to scared to move, then don't! 3. If moving would set it off, don't move! Three backed out. That left about six or eight. I repeatedly entered the field and brought them out one by one until all were retrieved.

      The choppers started coming in to medivac the wounded and dead from India, Kilo and Lima. All hell broke loose, RPG's (rocket propelled grenades,) mortars, machine guns, light arms, everything you could think of was going off all at the same time. I figured now was the best time as any and hollered "Fire in the hole" twice as loud as I could and tossed a grenade into the mine field and off it went. I turned toward the incoming choppers and the sight was something to see. Puffs of gun powder smoke, streaks of tracer smoke, were leaving vapor trails. I then noticed Marines getting off the choppers from Mike Company. Without thinking I replied, "Where the fuck have you guys been?" Someone just glared at me and kept going. Arty out of Da Nang was pounding very close and the air strikes were too close. Napalm drops were making us very hot now, a couple even got burned. As we finished up I heard, "Sgt Love! You still alive?" I turned around to see the big smile and friendly face of Lt Belser. He asked what I had left in manpower and I said I lost my corpsman hitting the tree line. I had Hill, Roach, Lewis,

Parker and myself. I then asked him a dumb question, "How many Kilo are left?" He said he was taking a head count and numbers didn't look good. With a smile and a "Hang tough," he was on his way.

Sporadic fighting continued. Lt Sutherland came up to me and told me to get on the chopper, since by this time I couldn't breathe. I told him I wasn't leaving my men. He assured me in no uncertain terms that I was leaving. Then I too was headed for NSA leaving behind my men and my newly acquired AK-47. The heat and my asthma had finally gotten to me.

**CPL CHARLES HUKABY - Co K:** People were dying and we couldn't get to them. At one point the platoon commander could see people only 25 meters in front of him, but we couldn't help them out.

As the battle continued, heat began to take its toll. Heat casualties soon exceeded the number of battle casualties. Temperatures rose near the 120 degree mark. Flak jackets were discarded and water became an increasingly critical item. Rumors circulated that the temperature was 130 degrees.

**L/CPL ART RIORDAN - Co L:** Every tree line held a well hidden enemy. We had just finished eating our C-rats when we got the word that the 1st squad, 1st platoon was to take point. That was my squad. We saddled up and started weaving through the 81 mortars who were getting their gear together. I remember wondering why they were so far up front. We were headed to a tree line directly in front of us. To our right and parallel to our march was another smaller tree line. Pfc George Botes, who I shared many fighting holes, was walking point that morning. I was either 4th or 5th in line. We didn't get 200 feet when all hell broke loose. Botes got hit instantly. A corpsman, right next to me, took a round in the helmet and two rounds to his body. We were getting tagged by snipers. I buried my nose in the dirt and started rolling towards the smaller tree 25 feet to my right. Rounds kept hitting to my left and I kept rolling right. Someone had me in his sights. As I neared some brush, I dumped a magazine into the tree line, aiming at nothing. The platoon behind us was firing into the tree line. We had rounds coming in both directions, sticking your head up was deadly. Bullets were flying everywhere and M-79s were hitting close. Pfc Botes was out in the open and getting hit repeatedly. As I reached down to change magazines, my helmet slid down over my eyes. At that same instant a round or shrapnel blew up my front hand grip, cutting my hand, arm, lip and splattering the front of my helmet. Thank God my helmet slid down. I moved a little deeper in the tree line and came across a Marine leaning against a tree, in the sitting position. He was talking on a radio and didn't appear to be from a line company. I tried to tell him about the snipers when he took a round and his head blew up. I did a rapid low crawl deeper into the tree line and came across a wounded Marine. He was shot in the pelvic area, I put him over my shoulder and carried him back to where they were setting up a triage. As I was going back up front I came across the 81 mortars who were going out in the open. I told them the dinks had snipers in the tree line. They had their orders and as they were setting up their tubes they were getting hit. One Marine got hit in the shoulder. A young private and myself put him in a poncho liner and took him back to the triage. As I was going back up the tree line I remember seeing the Sgt Major with black grease under his eyes and in the standing position, firing into the tree line. I think he was the only Marine I saw in the standing position, everyone else was hunched down or in the prone position. Air strikes were called and I believe napalm. It was so hot that day the napalm sucked the little remaining oxygen in the air, out of our lungs.

\* \* \*

PFC MARVIN W. LIPPS - Co L: The first five men into the tree line were killed or wounded including my squad leader. The rest of us were pinned down by snipers.
At first we thought it was just a small fire fight but later learned we had hit three or four companies.

PFC STEVEN BROOKS - MACHINE GUNNER - Co L: We operated in three or four man teams. We carried about 1,500 rounds for each machine gun and a spare barrel. Our main job was to cover our company so that they could advance on the enemy.

CPL RICHARD COUSINS - Co L: I was shot in the leg around noon. My squad was in a bomb crater. I believe it was at this time that Mike Company landed and the air strikes started.
I had 42 days left in the corp for my four year enlistment. I decided to drag myself back to the LZ and go 'home.' I crawled into one of the fields of fire and a burst of gun fire came from my right rear. The rounds hit ten feet away from me. I rolled left and headed back into the tall grass.
I will never stop believing that the NVA soldier had let me go. He was only 50 yards away and the way the NVA where shooting Marines, they rarely missed.

\* \* \*

SGT GARLAND R. SISCO - Co K: The NVA had

quite a few snipers in trees. When one was killed, another replaced him. One NVA actually had a mortar tube up in a tree. They were quite well equipped.

**CPL BILL JUNG - Co K:** The heat began to become unbearable. The sand and tall grass we were in turned into a frying pan. The heat was so thick it was hard to even breathe. The weaker men started to fall from it. Pfc William 'Little' Lestage was one of the first to go. His body grew hotter and hotter and then snapped. Going crazy with the heat, he kicked and thrashed all over the sand. It took five of us to hold him down. We gave him water and salt and carried him to an LZ for evacuation.

**LT COL TULLIS WOODHAM, JR. - 3/27 BATTALION CO:** I had to make a calculated decision on whether to get rid of our flak jackets and gas masks due to the extreme heat. I called the Regimental CO to see if it was feasible to do this. He left it up to me. The decision was to drop the flak jackets and gasmasks.

**PFC JOHNNY G. JOHNSON - Co K:** It was very hot and we started filling our canteens in a dirty creek. I would get dysentery the next day from the tainted water. We started assaulting a tree line. I lost my hearing after the shooting started so I didn't realize that our platoon had stopped. I charged ahead, not knowing that I was all by myself. I went through tall elephant grass and made it into the enemy tree line. After I realized that I was alone, I was afraid to move back because I thought I might be shot by my fellow Marines. Napalm drops came in so close that my eyebrows were singed. It was so hot that fluid started running out of my ears. I finally made it back to our lines after constantly yelling "Don't shoot! Don't shoot!" An officer told me to get on the next chopper to be evacuated as a heat casualty. I refused the offer. I couldn't leave my platoon.

**SGT GARLAND SISCO - Co K:** We moved to an area across another stream (kind of a sandy area in the open) and we began to take heavy gun fire. An air strike was called in. Later on, some of us suffered heat exhaustion, including myself. We were medivaced to the 5th Medical Battalion at Da Nang. I spent 24 hours there having fluids pumped into me.

**L/CPL ART RIORDAN - Co L:** Go Noi Island had to be the hottest place on earth during May of 1968. I heard a rumor of the temperature teaching 128 degrees fahrenheit. If it wasn't, it was damn close. I became a 'heat casualty.' My skin stopped perspiring and I was getting dizzy. I remember laying down in a puddle of water to cool off. I must have rolled face first because someone pulled me up and I was on a helicopter. As soon as we got in the air the cooler temperatures revived me and by the time we reached Da Nang Aid Station I was feeling fine. I have never liked hospitals. When we landed two, very large corpsmen met the chopper. They asked me where I was hit and I told them I wasn't and I was going to go back to Go Noi. They grabbed me by my elbows and raced me into a room, my feet never touched the ground. I was placed on a table and all my 'good luck' clothes, including my 'good luck' boots were cut off me with scissors within seconds. I was getting pissed. A doctor asked me where I was 'hit.' I said, "I wasn't fucking hit! The blood stains on my clothing were not mine. It was other Marines." They shoved needles in both arms which were attached to bottles and wheeled me into a hall. I pulled one needle out and another very large corpsman was going to introduce my wrists to velcro. I needed one arm free and he reluctantly agreed to one bottle at a time. I had a fear of hospitals which I have to this day. The next morning I found some clothes and made my way back to Ca Hau. I put on another pair of semi 'good luck' clothes and went to the Armory to have my M-16 repaired. They told me the barrel was to badly dinged and they would have to give me a new M-16. I just wanted a new front grip. I remember him telling me that if I fired it, the barrel could blow up in my face. I told him I must have fired a 100 rounds since. He replaced my 'good luck,' de-blued, three-pronged flash suppressor M-16 with a newer one. In combat, if you survive, luck plays a major roll. I felt totally luckless and I was on my way back to Go Noi.

* * *

**MAJ ERNEST T. FITZGERALD, S-3 OFFICER - H&S Co:** The heat was a major problem. We did probably lose more men to it than we did to the enemy fire, even though small arms and machine gun fire continued throughout the day. We called in air, snake eye bombs and napalm and they did a terrific job. It was close. I remember one run that the heat from the napalm burned our faces. The enemy was no more than seventy-five yards away. In the two tours that I had, including Operation Starlight in '65, that was as hairy a fight as I had been in and the companies did a magnificent job.

1st Marine Division assets were promptly given in support of the battle. This included the combination of every available artillery piece which could be brought to bear by the Division Fire Support Coordination Center. It was also augmented by Marine aircraft striking enemy lines with rocket fire, 500 and 1,000 pound bombs and napalm drops. The

Command Group's advanced location aided command and control of the engaged companies, but it put them in a precarious position of being dangerously exposed. They were subject to many hazards, especially from friendly air and artillery strikes.

With NVA forces located between 3/27 and supporting Division artillery fire, it was necessary to direct artillery from northern batteries as well as support from the Liberty Bridge site. Firing from north to south toward 3/27, shells had to land just short of them and into the enemy forces. This called for extremely precise coordination among forward observers and supporting batteries. Since several friendly units were in close proximity to the entrenched enemy, it was not possible to bring in supporting arms on all NVA locations. The battle and heat continued as many Marines still could not withdraw to safety.

**LT COL TULLIS WOODHAM, JR. - 3/27 BATTALION CO: We were getting quite a bit of support. Artillery from the 11th Marines was coming from our left at Liberty Bridge, and Division artillery was coming from the north, along with air support. On one napalm run I lost most of my eyebrows and the front of my hair from the intense heat.**

**CPL BILL JUNG - Co K: I crawled to a fox hole near the rows of dead that I had seen the night before. The death smell was sickening by now. A pair of skinny ankles stuck out from under a poncho. I was sure they were the ankles of my lanky friend Slim (Cpl Robert Simonsen - Co I,) but I didn't want to pull back the poncho and see the truth. Later I would learn that Slim wasn't dead but had been wounded in the head on 16 May.**

The fighting was getting heavier. The NVA were not only in bunkers and spider holes, but also in trees. From equipment later found, it was determined that the NVA forces were from the 16th and 38th Regiments of the 308th NVA Division. One Marine platoon captured so much enemy gear it needed two transport helicopters to remove the weapons and ammunition.

**CPL JOHN HAZELWOOD - Co I:** We found six .50 caliber machine guns, three AK-47 rifles, one M-16, three carbines, a .30 caliber machine gun, two 7.62 light machine guns, a 60mm mortar and 25 mortar rounds, 4,000 rounds of small arms ammunition and five gas masks. We also found 12 packs that had been thrown aside by the enemy. Guess they must have been in a hurry to leave.

**CAPT JOEL PARKS - Co K CO:** Our mission was changed and we were ordered back to protect the Battalion's rear. Both my men and myself were now suffering from the heat. We set up a reaction force of a provisional platoon but it was never committed to action.

**L/CPL LEROY R. DRIFFILL - Co K:** The next morning we prepared to move through the tree line, but were told to hold tight and take cover as a bombing run was coming to hit the tree line. We were maybe 100 meters from this tree line and the jets came in and dropped 500 lb bombs. Luckily none of us were hit by it. We proceeded through the tree line and in reaching the other side found two rows of bodies awaiting medivacs. These were Marines of I Co, 3/27. When we got to them, there were 17 Marines left out of a full company. I sort of felt like we should have been there sooner, or been there with them. Things might have been different. I believe Kilo Co was in reserve the next day, as heavy fighting was occurring in the next set of tree lines. We awaited orders and cleaned weapons, and wondered what lay in store.

* * *

The helicopters finally reached the LZ to pick up Co M. The flight lasted just a few minutes and the Marines exited into a hell storm at 1500. They were sent off to support Co K, which had suffered a considerable number of battle and heat casualties. Most of Co I was evacuated in the choppers delivering Co M and were returned to the 3/27 Cau Ha Base.

**CAPT BLAKE THOMAS - Co M CO:** We sent the third platoon in first in a CH-53. The landing zone was very hot so the rest of the company had to come in on smaller CH-46s.

Once we were in, my mission appeared to take what men I could muster and get my third platoon, which had been committed, back out again. They had become pinned down along with the parts of both Lima and Kilo Company. We basically were a relief force.

My command group came in on the second wave and as we waited for more Marines to arrive, it became evident that the third platoon had been chopped up pretty bad. They were separated into two groups and the platoon commander (2nd Lt Joseph Weiss) had been killed almost instantly.

**SGT EDWARD BENAVIDEZ - Co M:** In the morning after chow, we packed everything up. D Company 1/27 relieved us. We went to regiment HQ to wait for choppers. At 1300, 3$^{rd}$ platoon took off on the first wave. My squad was on the second wave with the company CP. The rest of my platoon was on the third wave. It was a hot LZ. 3$^{rd}$ platoon was already pinned down and my squad was the only one there from 1$^{st}$

platoon. The rest of the company was directed to another LZ. The CO directed me to take my squad to the left of 3rd platoon and assist.

L/CPL EDWIN VELEZ - Co M: As we got on the SeaKnight Helicopters, we were scared. I looked at the door gunner and he just shook his head in a negative movement. He had been into the LZ and knew the situation. As we got closer to the battle zone we could see craters, smoke and even some bodies. We jumped out of the helicopters and some men were hit immediately. It seemed that there were only a few Marines left alive.

There was a Staff Sergeant (I can't remember his name) who was hit by shrapnel in both his back and chin. I heard him calling for help so I went to him but he was to heavy for me to carry alone. A corpsman came to help out. The Marine could hardly speak but kept asking for water. We told him no, because of his severe chin wounds, but he insisted. The water came pouring out through his chin. We finally removed him to safety and Sgt Campora took over.

CAPT BLAKE THOMAS - Co M CO: As we got more reinforcements, I sent in Lieutenant Richard Tilghman and 8 men across an open area to link up with one of my trapped squads. Under the cover of artillery and hueys, they were able to gradually withdraw this unit.

It had become evident that the snipers must be shooting from above the ground so I ordered the men to turn their fire up into the trees. My radioman, Cpl Eddy R. Cramm, was the first to kill a sniper and we eventually shot 5 or 6 NVA up in the trees in our immediate area.

CPL MARLIN JACKSON - Co M: We landed in CH-46 helicopters. There were dead and wounded spread all over the LZ. A Gunnery Sergeant from another company walked by me, all bandaged up and kept repeating "What happened to my company?" I knew right away that this operation was going to be bad.

We set up in a dried out creek which was being used as an aid station for the wounded. It was 115-120 degrees. If you were in the elephant grass you could probably add another 10 degrees. The humidity was 100%

I looked over the creek bank and saw a Marine helping a wounded comrade. I jumped up and helped them get into safety. It turned out to be an FO from India. He said things were pretty bad up front so I asked the Lieutenant if I could go up to help out. He said OK. I grabbed two ammo cans and took off following two others. The heat was extreme. There were blood trails all over. I quickly passed out the ammo. You couldn't see where you were shooting at through the tall grasses. I saw two wounded Marines and helped them back. We stayed off all trails which were all in areas of enemy kill zones. Back at the creek, the Lieutenant told me to stay put after I told him what I had observed.

As I waited, I spotted the Battalion Sgt Major. He was sitting on a rise, like he was at the rifle range, and calmly picking off NVA snipers. I gained more respect for him that day due to his courage.

**L/CPL MIKE SWAGERTY - Co M:** I remember like yesterday coming off the chopper on that 'island.' The first thing I saw was a Sgt Major, black under his eyes, like I had worn as a receiver for my high school football team just the year before in Azie, Texas. He was yelling, "Drop your gear and get up front." It wasn't hard to determine where the 'front' was; the firing was incessant, hot and heavy. We dropped our gear, ran to the elephant grass and hit on our bellies, crawling through the thick growth until we were close to the edge, where the grass ended and a clearing began. We were a hastily formed line facing across the clearing to a tree line about 30 meters away. I fired a few rounds into the tree line, then stopped firing, trying to see where the enemy was. On my left, Sgt Benavidez was yelling, "Fire, fire." I asked him at what? He said, "Just shoot in the tree line." So I did.

**HM3 RICHARD J. SCHMIDT - Co M CORPSMAN:** I was in the 3rd platoon and we were sent up to help with the wounded. We became pinned down and as I was helping a man, wounded by a mortar round, I became a heat casualty. I got back and cooled off in the river and then went out for more.

**CPL RICHARD BUCHANAN - Co M:** When we landed on May 18th we were under fire. I was told to "get those snipers" by Col Woodham. He was standing tall and steadfast, in the dry river, like no one would dare shoot at him. He helped me put a bandage on a young Marine who I think was his radio man. We worked over the tree line with thousands of rounds concentrating on anything in the trees big enough to be a gook. Now and then someone would yell, "I got one!" The tree line was about 90 yards away. I was with Hayes, Noble, and Joe Shaw. As we were told to fall back, we could see the jets coming in and we felt the heat from the blast. What a show! We didn't recover some of the bodies until the next day and a lot of them were badly burned. Among them was Noble. I helped bag him, his arm was up in the air as if to fend off something, but what, I'll never know. Later on the 18th, a large piece of a 105 shell hit my M-16 where the metal meets the stock and just broke it all to hell. I picked up another M-16, from the stack of hundreds, next to the bodies which were all lined up like on review. I looked at

Noble's bag, but don't remember feeling anything.

* * *

**1ST LT BILLY C. STEED - H & S Co:** We inserted the command element and the other rifle companies first and I was to bring in the rest of H & S Company. I think it was on 18 May when I got down there. We were flying in a 46 and I could see close air support being run and a lot of smoke. You could see artillery fire and mortars going off. I was on the intercom with the pilot. They didn't really know where the safe zones were, so they had to go ahead and drop us in, but unfortunately they dropped us right on top of the enemy.

As we were coming off the helicopter, the first guy I saw was Lt Roy Casteel. He was a mortar platoon commander and he had fired up all of his mortar rounds and his mortar men were now in hand-to-hand combat and of course using their weapons as best they could. It was really what we call a sandwich. We now had people being dropped in by helicopter and it took awhile to get them organized. We were trying to put medivacs back on those helicopters, so it was the normal chaotic thing that you get in a situation like that when you're amongst the enemy.

I tried to find out where the front line was and to get people to direct fire towards the enemy. I got a team together of stretcher bearers to help load the dead and the wounded; mainly the wounded because we had so many wounded you couldn't worry about the dead at that particular time. We finally got those helicopters out as they were receiving fire and taking hits.

I finally linked up with Lt Col Woodham and the rest of the command by going from position to position to find out where the CP was located. It was then getting along toward dark and we finally got people consolidated again and into a defensive perimeter. Most of the people had all arrived and had now joined their parent units.

L/CPL TOM FULEKY - H & S Co: We were getting organized for Allen Brook and I was told that I wasn't needed on the operation as a sniper, so I volunteered to be a grenadier. I didn't want to be left behind and wanted to go on my first operation. Little did I know what I was getting into. I was driven back to Regiment HQ waiting to get choppered out when they finally landed and lowered the ramp. First we had to unload all the bloody helmets, flak jackets, and firearms. Then we took off with a television crew and reporters and flew into the operation. I had heard that India Company had taken heavy casualties and to be careful not to drink water out of the wells because they were contaminated.

MAJ ERNEST T. FITZGERALD, S-3 OFFICER - H&S Co: The command group was not in a very advantageous position (right out in the open) and we took small arms fire and some mortar fire as well. We were trying to evacuate India's casualties during this time. At one point in the afternoon the small arms got to be such a nuisance that the Sgt/Maj grabbed an M-16 and tossed it to me and then took one for himself. He indicated we should shoot into the trees off to our right front. We both fired several rounds and sure enough, a body came out of one of the trees head first. The small arms into the CP ceased pretty much after that.

LT COL TULLIS WOODHAM, JR. - 3/27 BATTALION CO: Sgt Major Snyder was a Marine's Marine. He had come from force recon and was a real hard charger. The troops may not have known it, but he greatly cared for all of them.

Sgt George Hight (H & S Co) was a radio operator with the tactical air control party. He volunteered by leaving his relatively safe position with the command group to aid the growing number of casualties. Disregarding his own safety, he ran across the fire swept area with a medical kit and moved from one casualty to another using his own body to shield his fellow Marines, as he administered first aid treatment. After two hours, he expended an entire medical kit and twice rendered mouth-to-mouth resuscitation. He finally collapsed from heat exhaustion, but he eventually returned to the hazardous area and continued to give aid. Sgt Hight would later be awarded the Navy Commendation Medal for his actions.

\* \* \*

**CAPT BLAKE THOMAS - Co M CO: As we moved up we came across about 25 men from other companies. Most were heat casualties, a couple were wounded and some were just lying there confused. I found a senior man and told him to get his people moving. As he stood up to get everyone organized, he was shot in the stomach. Accurate sniper fire was coming in from a tree line about 150 meters away.**

**I moved my people up and set up a base of fire with two M-60s and M-16s. We then started evacuating the wounded people. We had to slap and yell at them to get them moving. The healthy ones were given a rifle and moved up on the lines. HM3 Walters distinguished himself by moving back and forth under fire and evacuating the wounded. I put him in for a silver star.**

As L/CPL Thomas Thuesen's Co M platoon was moving to reinforce other units, they came under intense fire from a well camouflaged enemy force, wounding several

Marines. L/CPL Thuesen rapidly began delivering a heavy volume of machine gun fire, enabling several of the casualties to be treated and evacuated.

When his ammunition was expended, he ignored the hostile fire and moved to another position where ammunition was located and then resumed firing until his resupply of ammunition was expended. Realizing the serious condition of the wounded and their urgent need for medical care, he crawled across the fire-swept area, obtained a medical kit and additional personnel and ammunition and guided a small relief force back to his position. Repeatedly exposing himself to the North Vietnamese fire, he completely disregarded his own safety as he moved to positions to deliver more effective fire. When his weapon malfunctioned, he remained exposed to hostile fire as he dismantled the machine gun, cleared the malfunction, reassembled the weapon and resumed firing. After a second malfunction, he ran across the fire-swept area where he obtained another weapon and continued to bring accurate fire to bear against the enemy. Although he had been moving constantly in the intense heat throughout the five hour battle, he refused to withdraw until all the casualties had been evacuated. When his platoon was ordered to break contact, he provided covering fire until the withdrawal was completed. L/Cpl Thuesen was awarded the silver star for his actions.

1st Lt John Zalipski, a mustanger with Co M, was informed that a squad from another unit was pinned down and had taken many casualties. He unhesitatingly led six other Marines across a fire-swept terrain to the besieged squad's position. Moving about and shouting encouragements, Lt. Zalipski directed their withdrawal to relative safety. He personally rescued one casualty under intense fire and would later be awarded a bronze star for valor.

**CAPT JOHN F. ERNEST - Co L: I first met John Zalipski on the drill field in officer's training. He was an**

enlisted instructor. Ski was one outstanding Marine and I was glad to see him show up in 3/27 as an officer.

      **L/CPL CHARLES SWAGERTY - Co M:** I'm not sure how much time passed, but in what seemed like less than an hour, I heard someone crawling through the grass to my right, coming in my direction. I turned my weapon towards the noise prepared to blow away a gook.

      Then came the yelling, "Don't shoot, don't shoot, I'm a Marine." A man crawled through to me. He was small in stature, but soon would become one of the largest men I've ever seen in my life. He told me he was from India company, and he and a few others had just about made it across the clearing when the gooks opened up on them. They were all hit, and holed up in a bomb crater on the other side of the clearing. I turned to my left and told Lt Zalipski what had happened. He immediately made the decision that we would get the wounded. He asked for volunteers, looking me straight in the eye, an obvious order or challenge. I said I'd go, as did a corporal and two others. The Lt told me to crawl out leading the way. The Marine laying beside me, already badly wounded, now said "No, I know where they are, I'll lead the way." And that brave hero did. We crawled across that clearing, him at point. I never knew who that incredibly courageous man was, but he should have gotten the Navy Cross or Medal of Honor. He led us to that bomb crater, and we all crawled inside. I believe one of our hastily formed rescue squad got hit crawling across the clearing, and that in itself was remarkable. We were totally exposed and rounds were kicking up all around us. Halfway across, crawling as low as I could, my canteens turned under me. In the middle of the clearing, I had to stop and take that belt off before continuing. Once inside the crater a quick survey showed that all three or four men there were indeed, hit.

Now we had real problems. We were in this crater, the NVA were in bunkers about 10 meters in front of us, and our friendlies were about 20 meters behind us. So, besides the enemy knowing where we were and trying their best to get to us, both the enemy and our friendlies were shooting over our heads at each other. Raising up over the edge of the crater, with the intense fire from both sides only inches above you, meant risking losing your head.

We were too busy to consider our predicament, but it was clear our future did not appear promising in that crater. I would peer over the edge and fire at enemy trying to make it to our bunker. The corporal spotted snipers in the trees and was having a field day picking them off. He actually had the advantage there, our position at the lowest level allowing him a clear view up into the trees. I manned the front of the crater towards the bunkers. Others were treating the wounded and manning the sides. I gathered all the frags and began throwing them at the bunkers, getting the fastest peak I could at the holes before letting fly with the grenades. Time passed slowly, but wore on into late evening. The NVA were throwing frags at us but they were falling just short of our position. The heat was unbelievable, exaggerated by our plight. I recall watching a horse fly land on my forearm. For some reason I just watched the fly as it bit me, never moving or shooing it away. A small amount of blood, mixed with the sweat of my arm, slowly flowed towards my elbow. It's weird the things you remember, isn't it? The Lt was towards the back of the bunker on the horn, desperately trying to get us air support. I recall a helicopter flying overhead and firing into our hole, rounds kicking up dirt between my legs. Either he mistook us for the enemy because we were in their lines, or his support fire was a tad close. Everyone else was busy making stretchers to carry the wounded back. More time passed and it was getting very late into the day. The Lt called back to get help to get us out. He was told that we would have to hang on until morning.

I guarantee you, when I heard that news, this young Texas boy knew that dog wouldn't hunt. Although only a L/Cpl at that time, I told the Lt in no uncertain terms that we wouldn't make it until morning. My opinion was quickly reinforced by all. We knew that, even with the daylight we still had, it wouldn't be long before they got to us. And when dark came, we knew we were all dead men. The Lt was up on the horn, yelling that we had to get out of there.

He was finally told that an air strike was coming. We were to have the wounded ready to move and immediately after the jets dropped their load, we were to pick up and make a run for our lines. It sounded like a plan to me. Not a good plan, as I didn't relish the idea of running upright back across that clearing, laden by the wounded we would be carrying. But it was definitely a better plan than staying in that hole.

Within minutes we heard the roar of the jets. I looked up to the right and saw a plane dive down towards us. I kept my eye on him, and watched those silver canisters roll down towards the ground. This was the only time on Allen Brook that I was absolutely sure I was about to die. The napalm was being dropped just too close for us to survive. I lay my head down on my left forearm and called on my faith (something I thought I had given up on) and said the world's shortest prayer, "Jesus!"

When they exploded it was, for a brief moment, like someone had sucked all the air out of me. But then it passed just as quickly, and we were somehow alive. We immediately grabbed up the wounded and took off across the clearing, running as hard as we could with our load. Not a soul was hit, and we were met at the edge of the elephant grass by men who took the wounded off our hands. Drained, both mentally and physically, I dropped to my knees. The word came that we were pulling back to set up a perimeter. We started gathering the wounded and dead to take them to the 'rear.' The first person I got to was a Lieutenant. He was dead, shot in the forehead, straight between the eyes. I think he was my Lt but I don't recall his name. We carried the wounded and dead to the rear as it began to get dark. We then pulled back and set up the lines. I think it was Sgt Benavidez who passed the word to fix bayonets. I recall that order as being both absolutely frightening and then exhilarating, having never engaged the enemy close enough to put my hands on him. We were 100% on the lines, and the night passed uneventful.

**HM3 RICHARD SCHMIDT - Co M CORPSMAN:** One poor man had been injured by a grenade and while one corpsman was working on him, he was hit again, along with the corpsman. Then another corpsman went out there to help and they both were hit again. Then I went out to help and he was hit a fourth time. All you had to do is move the grass and the NVA would shoot at the bottom of the grass.

As we were carrying him out, he was shot in the neck and died. The other two Marines helping me carry the guy were also shot.

**SGT RICHARD PELKEY - Co M:** When we got off the choppers one of the squads had gotten pinned down at the tree line. We were trying to get them out. All I could see was the elephant grass because it was so tall. We were lying down in the elephant grass and sniper and weapons fire were real heavy. You could hear it coming all around us. A couple of choppers came in and shot some rockets off. Napalm was also dropped. The machine gunner that was attached to my squad got hit. He was just up to the left front of me. When he got hit, a couple of corpsmen that were with him put him on a poncho and were carrying him back to the rear. We were dragging him at that point because he was heavy and there was but two of them and myself. One other person grabbed a corner of the poncho and we began carrying him back. The Skipper called out to me so we stopped. I squatted down and he asked me if I knew where I was going. I told him that I did and he said "OK, Go."

Just as I was standing up again, a round hit me in the tail (hit me in the right buttocks) and I just gave way. My legs just went out from underneath me. The corpsman was right there. That was no problem. He came over and I said "I'm hit." He came over to me, took some scissors and cut off my pistol belt and trousers. About that same time someone said that the machine gunner got hit two more times. I said "Doc, I'm bleeding." He said "Don't worry about it I've got my finger in it." Ri--ight, I needed that! He turned to the machine gunner and then said to me "Don't worry about him, he's dead, I can't help him." So he came back to me and put a bandage on me and gave me a shot of morphine. He found out later how I got hurt and said he shouldn't have given me the shot because the bullet went through the intestines. Apparently they're not supposed to give you morphine if you have an intestinal wound. He didn't realize it at the time and thought I only got hit in the buttocks.

They rolled the machine gunner off the poncho, rolled me on and carried me back to where the corpsmen were in a little gully or swell. It was lower than the surrounding terrain. They had everybody lined up that had been wounded waiting on the choppers. We waited what seemed like a long time, but probably wasn't. There was so much small arms fire that the choppers couldn't get in. Every time they started to come in they couldn't take it. They'd have to go back up because of the intense ground fire.

It seemed like quite a while later, but finally one of the choppers came in. They picked us up like cord-wood, throwing us into the choppers trying to get us out of there. They flew us from there to Da Nang, hauled us out, took me inside, put an IV into me and took me straight to OR. I don't remember anything until the next morning when I woke up. I thought "Christ, I went into the OR and with one little old bullet hole and came back out with a big one inch wide hole," which they'd cleaned out with soap. My stomach was cut wide open because they had gone into my intestines. I had colostomy, which I didn't even know what it was, and a drainage tube hanging out of me. I said "Jesus Christ, what happened?" I went in with just one little hole and came out looking like a zipper.

Sgt Pelkey would later receive the Navy Commendation Medal for his continuous excellent service while serving with Co M, 3/27. His flight home would take him to Japan and finally to the Naval Hospital in Jacksonville, Florida, where his parents were waiting for him. Quoting Pelkey, "You can trust me on this one, I was one happy S.O.B."

\* \* \*

**LT COL TULLIS WOODHAM, JR. - 3/27 BATTALION CO:** I received a call from Col Schwenk saying the Division wanted to know "What in the hell was going on down there." They had five specific questions that they wanted answered. I started writing down the questions while we were under heavy incoming fire. After copying the third question down, I asked Schwenk to

"LT COL Tullis Woodham, Jr., Silver Star."

handle it. I told him "I'm fighting a God Damn war down here and I'm up to my ass in Indians!" He said fine, he would take care of Division.

\* \* \*

**CPL MARLIN JACKSON - Co M:** An officer came up and asked if anyone had been to the front. I said yes and he told me to lead four Marines up to the fighting. I got more water and ammo and headed off. 30 feet into the grass, we took automatic fire and one Marine was hit. Shooting was going on all over. I bandaged up the wounded guy, and then we continued, leaving him behind. I shot at least two magazines before seeing one of the others get hit in the stomach. I grabbed him and we went back and picked up the man we had left behind. We eventually made it back to the creek.

I found more water and ammo and took off again. The NVA were shooting at anything that moved in the grass. When I reached the front I passed everything out, grabbed another wounded Marine, and headed back. I almost got lost. They kept shooting at me and we would hit the ground. We came across another very badly wounded Marine. I bandaged him up but I couldn't stop his bleeding. I knew he would die if I couldn't get him back. I was able to get him on my shoulders and grabbing the other guy around the waist, we took off under fire. I just hoped we were going in the right direction. It had taken nearly an hour to get from the front lines to the creek.

\* \* \*

**LT COL TULLIS WOODHAM, JR. - 3/27**

**BATTALION CO:** Capt Robert R. Anderson was the H&S Co Commandant and, as such, was in charge of the command post security. In the afternoon he made several trips to the front lines to help evacuate wounded and heat casualties. Eventually, he succumbed to the heat, too. He passed out and we evacuated him to the Regimental CP where they had set up trailers with ice and water. The heat victims were dumped in so their body temperatures would go down. Andy recovered and was on the first chopper back in the next morning.

\* \* \*

**SGT RAY WATKINS - Co M:** Operation Allen Brook was about the worst of the twelve combat operations I was involved in. I was a squad leader for the 3rd Platoon when our company landed in a field of elephant grass. We immediately realized that we were taking incoming fire from the NVA in the tree line. My Platoon Sergeant told me that our Platoon Commander (2nd Lt Thomas J. Weiss, Co M) was dead. He also said that we had about twenty WIA's near the tree line. My squad dropped our packs and low-crawled to the wounded. Each man pulled a wounded Marine back to safety. The battle continued until dusk when we were able to recover our dead.

I killed my first NVA during the operation. I carried an M-79 grenade launcher. The NVA soldier was in a trench line about 50 yards in front of my platoon position. As he raised his head to look our way I fired. The round landed next to him and he died instantly. We lost a lot of good men so maybe this was payback for our guys.

Sgt Ray Watkins, Co M, was a squad leader when he moved his squad forward to relieve the lead elements of

"Capt. Anderson. Heat Casualty."

his platoon which had sustained several casualties. He unhesitatingly maneuvered his squad to provide covering fire so the wounded could be treated and evacuated. For his initiative and bravery, he was awarded the Navy Commendation.

    **PFC LARRY FRYE - Co M:** I had just joined 3/27 in April fresh out of ITR at Camp Pendleton. I was 18 years old and really green in country. I had made only two friends since I had been with Mike Company: Blanchard and Jones (Pfc David M. Blanchard and L/Cpl Donald B. Jones.) We were on the 3rd chopper to leave that day for Allen Brook. I had five canteens of water on my cartridge belt. We landed in a hot LZ and the temperature was 130 degrees to boot. We landed in elephant grass with incoming all over the place. It was like landing in Hell. I jumped off the chopper and the first thing I saw was dead and wounded Marines laying all over the place. I can still hear them saying "Water, water." Their mangled bodies had guts laying out. In ten minutes I had used all five canteens of my water helping these guys by pouring water on the gut shots and drinks to the others.

    Both Blanchard and Jones were killed. I helped put Jones on the chopper. We were carrying a body in a poncho and when I looked down to see who it was I couldn't believe it. We were sniped at while we were loading him. Blanchard was killed going after a bunker with his M-60. He was listed as an 0311 (rifleman) but he carried an M-60 in Nam. He was my best friend and the first one I made over there.

    I remember Phantom F-4's dropping napalm on the NVA positions and the beauty of watching their awesome power and thinking that no one could live through it. Then the NVA would get right up again in the elephant grass and start shooting. How could they possibly live through those napalm drops? I remember seeing dead NVA for the first time, some fried by napalm, and not feeling pity for them. I wished they were all dead.

**PFC RICH LEWERENZ - Co M:** I was a pointman on Allen Brook with 1st Platoon. I don't know how I survived. The napalm strikes were so fuckin' close that I knew I was going to burn up. I remember the smells and the five foot high pile of discarded helmets and flak jackets.

\* \* \*

**CPL BILL JUNG - Co K:** Doc Rahn (HM3 Donald 'Doc' Rahn) was killed. Our company went out on 17 May with eight corpsmen and by the end of the operation, only one was left.

We finally formed a skirmish line to assault the tree line on Lima's left flank. We moved through the sand and high grass with bullets and mortars crashing around us. There was screaming as Cpl Kenneth Benoit fell wounded. One of my fire team leaders fell to my right. He dropped his gear and hobbled back toward the evacuation point. Benoit lay on his back bleeding severely from multiple shrapnel wounds. He turned pale and started going into shock as the pain and heat got to him at the same time. God! It was hot. I put Benoit over my shoulder and started carrying him back. I had to keep stopping and soon all of my strength gave way. Finally, some other men came by and took over carrying Benoit to the choppers.

I walked over to where Captain Joel Parks and the Samoan Gunny were sitting and I asked for orders. They said little, so I went on my way. I then saw my machine

"Mute Testimony"

gunner buddy, Cpl Richard Bennett, and went over to talk for a while. All of a sudden he went blank and passed out from the heat. He was evacuated and they say it took him a week to get his memory back.

**SGT GARLAND SISCO - Co K:** First Lt James M. Kent was a mustanger in his second tour. He was an excellent field leader. If anyone helped to organize Kilo on the 18th, it was Kent.

* * *

**CAPT JOHN F. ERNEST - Co L:** We were sweeping the tree line and didn't meet any resistance until our point squad was practically on top of the NVA positions. We got some of the bunkers with rockets, but it became apparent we needed air support. We had to relay information between the men who were pinned down and the aerial observer overhead.

**L/CPL BRUCE DILLINGHAM-FAO - Co L:** We lost communications with the lead squad and because of the heavy fire we were unable to get up to their positions.

**L/CPL ROBERT BARCROFT-FAO - Co L:** We had to shout up to the point squad to toss a smoke grenade to mark their position so the aerial observer would know how close to direct the air strikes.

Marine F-4 Phantom jets dropped 250 and 500 pound bombs within fifty meters of the trapped Marines, allowing them to pull back.

To help Co M pull back so that artillery and air strikes could obliterate the entire tree line, Sgt Richard A. Aghamalian (Co L) directed rocket and machine gun fire into the NVA bunkers to the left of Co L.

**SGT RICHARD A. AGHAMALIAN - Co L:** Those bunkers were so low to the ground that the only way we could get rounds in on them was to fire right over the heads of Co M. Most of the rounds were fired only about eight inches above their heads.

**CAPT BLAKE THOMAS - Co M CO:** Lima Company had extricated their people and had moved up to our right rear to provide suppressive fire. They fired LAWS and M-60s about 8-16 inches over our heads as we moved back. We were able to get back just as it started to get dark. We had taken about 5 KIAs and 20 WIAs.

Realizing the seriousness of the situation, L/Cpl Gary Much quickly moved to the point of heaviest contact and, standing in the open exposed to hostile fire, began delivering 3.5 inch rockets into the enemy position. Ignoring the enemy fire all around him, he steadfastly maintained his position in the hazardous area until he had expended all of his ammunition. Obtaining a resupply, he then continued to deliver a heavy volume of accurate fire on the enemy fortifications, sufficiently suppressing hostile fire to enable the beleaguered Marines to move to positions of safety. For his courage, bold initiative and selfless devotion to duty, L/Cpl Much was awarded the Silver Star.

**L/CPL GARY W. MUCH - 3.5 ROCKET MAN - Co L:** I fired about 35 rounds of Willey Peter to provide a smoke screen for the pinned down Marines. This allowed them to move back so we could call in air strikes.

**L/CPL ART RIORDAN - Co L:** On Go Noi Island we were pinned down by a machine gun that was in a heavily fortified cement bunker. There was a call for "Rockets" and a Marine fired two LAW's rockets which had little to no effect. Cpl Gary Much, an old school rocket man, put his 3.5 tube together. Cpl Much sported a rather large, non-regulation moustache like the kind a Walrus grows. I was standing right next to him and we were about 200 yards from the bunker. He took aim, yelled "clear" and fired. If I hadn't witnessed this first hand I wouldn't have believed it. That rocket found a small firing slit in the bunker and blew it all to hell. There was a loud cheer and Cpl Much just shirked his shoulders and modestly said it was a luck shot. He made a believer out of me and was always a welcome sight in the bush.

Pfc Burton Bower picked up twelve Light Antitank Assault Weapons and his rifle and unhesitatingly moved to the point of heaviest contact. Completely disregarding his own safety, he stood in the open exposed to hostile fire and began delivering accurate rocket fire into the enemy positions. Although the North Vietnamese concentrated their fire against him, he steadfastly maintained his position in the hazardous area and was painfully wounded in his shoulder. Undaunted, he continued to deliver rocket fire into the hostile emplacements until he had expended his ordnance.

He then began delivering a heavy volume of accurate rifle fire and received a second wound and was medically evacuated. Pfc Burton Bowers was also awarded a Silver Star for his actions.

\* \* \*

**CPL MARLIN JACKSON - Co M:** Lt Williamson told us we were going to advance and aide the front lines. After a short distance, we had to hit the deck. Too many

"L/Cpl Gary Much, Silver Star"

were being wounded as we advanced.

The Mike Company CO, Capt Blake Thomas, asked for a radio and as the operator reached over to give him the handset, he was shot in the chest and died almost immediately.

Division was running low on HE (High Explosive.) We called for everything they would give us and then used smoke to cover our withdrawal. In the meantime, the FAC (Forward Air Controller) called in napalm. The first strike was too close and we could hear the FAC trying to cancel the second strike, but it was too late. We knew we were going to fry! My hair curled and my exposed skin was burnt, but fortunately no one was seriously injured.

The smoke mission allowed us to retreat to the riverbed. Another company to our rear was firing over our heads to provide additional coverage. It's a wonder that no one was hit. The gunners were very good. The enemy bugged out too.

That night I took stock of myself and reflected how lucky I was not to have been hit that day. I had nicks and holes all over my clothes and equipment.

* * *

**L/CPL DALE CAMP - Co I:** Darkness was coming on, and it hung over our heads like the 'sword of Damocles.' Unless we got off soon we felt like we were doomed. All at once a chopper landed. For the first time in hours there were no casualties to put on it. Gunny Dyrdahl ran up the ramp and told the crew chief that they could take us out. The crew chief objected because his mission was to pick up casualties, but the Gunny insisted. We ran on board with our arms full of rifles and the chopper lifted off. There were 6 of us, including the Gunny and the S/Sgt from Weapons Platoon. As we gained altitude, I had a tremendous feeling of relief. I was going to survive.

We landed at 3/7 battalion rear on Hill 55, because it was close, and the chopper went back after wounded. The Gunny led us to the Battalion office and made arrangements for food and transport. While he was inside some Marines from 3/7 saw our appearance and wanted to know what in the hell we had gotten into. When we told them about the battle on the 17th they freaked out. Misunderstanding what we said, they thought the CO of India 3/7 had been killed. The CO of India 3/7 at the time was Capt Charles Robb, the son in law of President Johnson. No wonder they freaked out.

When the chopper arrived at 3/27, I don't remember anyone meeting us. Back at the company area it was quiet. Only a few of us had made it back off Allen Brook. In my squad tent I could feel the ghosts of Coles and Miller. Their seabags were sitting at the end of the hooch. I felt very lucky and very guilty to be the only one there. For years I had survivors syndrome and felt guilty for not getting hurt or killed. I felt that I must not have done my job right since I wasn't hurt doing it.

\* \* \*

As darkness fell, the fighting stopped almost as suddenly as it began. The NVA forces withdrew from their reinforced bunkers and escaped into the night. Air and artillery rained down on the enemy positions to finish off anyone left behind. All 3/27 units pulled back to defensive positions established by Co K. Ironically, the positions were basically those occupied by the NVA forces when Co I and 3/7 fell into their ambush of the 17th. Friendly casualties for the day were placed at 15 KIA, 78 WIA, and 6 MIA (Missing in Action.) 94 were evacuated as heat casualties. Accurate enemy losses could not be determined, but at least 20 were killed. A farmer who was found the next day said he had seen NVA dragging back many dead and wounded during the night.

**CPL FRED STUEBE - H&S Co:** The Colonel pulled India off the Island but not the 81's. That evening we found a gook bunker and decided to spend the night in it, that is, until some officers decided to claim it for themselves. A few minutes later, they came running out of the bunker yelling "Snake!" Everyone started shooting at the snake but I think it got away.

**CPL BILL JUNG - Co K:** The 18th ended and I fell asleep exhausted. I wondered what tomorrow would bring. Today had been pure hell. Only three of my squad answered to muster that night.

**LT COL TULLIS WOODHAM, JR. - 3/27 BATTALION CO:** The battle went on most of the day and into the evening. We fired everything that we could get hold of. We fired up almost all of the artillery ammo that the Division had for its allocation. It was incredibly hot and we lost many Marines to the heat.

It was later determined that we had hit one or more NVA battalions. They had buried themselves into concrete bunkers and allowed our forward elements to move in close, and then pinned down the rear follow up troops. This left the forward element to be caught between friendly and enemy fire.

Contact was broken at 2000 and we fell back to the original enemy (Co I) ambush area. Kilo was already there along with portions of the 3rd Battalion, 5th Marines (3/5.) To my chagrin, 3/5 was in the process of policing up the remnants of the enemy weapons and equipment that had been abandoned as a result of the engagements between

3/27 and the NVA forces. In as much as they had no part in the various actions, they had no proprietary rights to any of the enemy equipment and I directed their removal from the consolidation area. An uneasy calm settled over our defensive perimeter that evening.

**RON McCARVILLE - Co K, 3/5:** On the 18$^{th}$ we left Liberty Bridge and humped about 1500 meters where we encountered the remnants of a large battle field. The site was one of utter destruction. Enemy and Marine dead were piled up everywhere. 3/27 Marines had that 1000 yard stare. I can't describe my feelings but I know I will never forget the Marines of 3/27.

<u>19 MAY</u>

On 19 May at 0630, patrols were sent out to the battle area to finish picking up equipment which had not been retrieved the previous night. At the same time, units within the Battalion Command Post (CP) began a detailed search of the area.

**LT COL TULLIS WOODHAM, JR. - 3/27 BATTALION CO:** That morning, we checked out the battle field area. A number of NVA bodies were recovered and it was obvious the enemy had sustained heavy casualties. We were informed by local Vietnamese villagers that the NVA had left the area the night before, carrying wounded and dead with them. The rest of the 19th was devoted to consolidating our forces, evaluating losses and being resupplied. I then started planning our next movement.

Large quantities of captured and abandoned enemy equipment and armaments were evacuated by helicopters, destined for Regiment Headquarters, but I understand little actually reached its intended destination.

**CPL BILL JUNG - Co K:** Soon after daylight, parties went out to collect the rest of our dead. There were many over by the northeast tree line. Our Skipper, Capt Parks, said that what he saw over there brought tears to his eyes. A lot of Marines died heroically.

**L/CPL CHARLES SWAGERTY - Co M:** When morning came, we got on line to assault the tree line, fully expecting to meet the resistance we had left only hours earlier. But there was nothing. The NVA were gone (only temporarily, we would soon discover.) We began policing the battle field, gathering gear, weapons, and dead. As Sgt Benavidez and I neared one dead Marine, we found something that would haunt me the rest of my life. A dead Marine, laying prone in the tree line, propped up on his right elbow, frozen in death. In his right hand, covered in plastic, was a picture of a woman and child. That Marine's final act in life, obviously knowing he was dying or about to, was to pull out a picture of his family. He died that way, looking at what must have been the people he loved most in life. He was fried by the napalm that had passed over us in that crater. Being in that hole had apparently been our saving grace, the depth allowing the fire to pass over us. Whether or not he was already dead when the napalm got him we'll never know. I can't speak for Benavidez, but I can tell you that sight has stayed with me forever, indelibly etched in my troubled mind. How I wish we would have taken the time to gather that picture, identify the man, and notify that Marine's family, letting them know that their husband and father's last act in life was to gaze on a picture of them! What comfort that could have been to them. But we didn't have the luxury of the time to even consider such an action. After speaking to Benavidez at the Hot Springs reunion in 1998, it was apparent that neither of us knew who this man was, and no family member ever found out about his dying act of love and devotion.

In the tree line we found the bunkers, incredibly reinforced by ingenious methods in the use of bamboo. There was a mass grave, the dead stacked on top of each other, feet sticking out of the top. I joined others in using our hands to uncover and take souvenirs; something in later, more mature years I would regret.

L/CPL ART RIORDAN - Co L: We were on a sweep through an area that had previously been involved in some serious fighting. The wounded had been evacuated and we were just picking up the dead. A Marine with a look of anguish on his face was gingerly trying to retrieve the Dog Tags from a fallen Marine. He had taken a serious hit in the chest and the Tags were imbedded deep in his chest cavity. I looked down and said "Hey Man, he don't feel a thing, he's dead." The Marine looked up at me and without saying a word, just the look in his face told me, "I know he's dead, asshole, it hurts me." We all hurt that day.

CPL FRED STUEBE - H&S Co: I remember Lt Casteel chewing his little cigar. He asked the radioman to bring him the radio. The radio operator said "Sir, I've been bitten by a snake." Casteel didn't believe him, but when he stood up to walk, he collapsed and went into a coma. Then the Lieutenant saw the Bamboo Viper near the radio. He shot at it with his .45 and the snake took off into the bushes.

CPL BILL JUNG - Co K: Our hillbilly from Arkansas, Cpl Donald Hill, had caught a bullet in his rump the day before, but continued to stay with the company. It got so that he could not even sit down, so he finally was flown out. Hill was a fine Marine.

**LT COL TULLIS WOODHAM, JR. - 3/27 BATTALION CO:** On the 19th, the men were more afraid of the Bamboo Vipers than the enemy.

**PFC JOHNNY G. JOHNSON - Co K:** On 19 May, we cleaned up all of the gear in the combat area. Snipers hit two or three men and we were able to kill one of them.

**HM3 RICHARD SCHMIDT - Co M CORPSMAN:** We were sitting in a trench line waiting for the platoon and company to form up when the CO came over and told us to help look for bodies.

We started across to the next tree line and one of my friends spotted a sniper popping up and down out of a hole. We started shooting at him with 16s, M-79s and LAWs.

I took it upon myself, along with two others, (PFC Edwin) Velez and a machine gunner named (Cpl Duane) Pounder, to check out the position and retrieve the body. On our way across, two more snipers opened up on us about twenty feet away. I fired about 5 rounds on automatic before my 16 jammed up. I think I hit one man before I made my 'didi' back to a trench line. We later checked out the area and found bloody field dressings and enemy equipment.

When asked later about lessons learned from his experiences on operation Allen Brook, HM3 Schmidt replied, "I learned not to play Marine!"

**CPL FRED STUEBE - H&S Co:** On the 19th,

Weapons Platoon borrowed a captured NVA flag from the Colonel and we took a group picture with Lt Casteel.

Air and artillery missions were called in onto the tree line of the previous day's action. At 1100, Co L left the CP and headed off to search this tree line area. They found a number of dead NVA, a few weapons and five friendly KIAs (previously listed as MIA.) By the end of the day, 3/27 had now suffered a total of 40 KIA and 139 wounded. Known enemy losses were 66 killed NVA and one VC captured. The Battalion spent the night in the same location.

**CPL BILL JUNG - Co K:** As I sat that evening in a clump of bamboo, I looked around and stared at an area blown to hell. It was complete blackened destruction. I marked the fight's location on my map: Le Nam (2), a village on Route 537. The whole area belonged to the devil.

**CPL MARLIN JACKSON - Co M:** I traded off radio watches with Cpl Brettman and helped to retrieve dead around the battlefield. I came across a very good friend who had been shot above the eye and was badly burned by the napalm drops.

That evening I heard another Marine digging his foxhole. He hit something hard and began cussing under his breath. The next morning we found a 250 pound bomb in his hole. It was amazing that it hadn't gone off.

## 20 MAY

3/27 moved eastward with Co L and Co K leading, and the Command Group and Co M in trace. While en route, there was sporadic sniper fire.

**CPL BILL JUNG - Co K:** We were in elephant grass overlooking a river. The heat was ungodly. A lot of men were hurting from it. In the distance, we could see some Marines in a tree line. We hoped they didn't find any NVA. It was too damn hot to fight.

In the early afternoon, Co M found 15 to 20 civilians suffering from wounds and ruptured ear drums. They were treated by a corpsman.

Upon reaching a night defensive position, the Battalion formed a perimeter with the three companies. There had been no significant contacts and casualties of both enemy and friendly remained unchanged.

**L/CPL LEROY R. DRIFFILL - Co K:** The next several days we encountered our second enemy, heat. We had many casualties due to the tremendous temperature we were faced with on an everyday basis. I can remember my head pounding from the heat and I reached and pulled out my canteen, unscrewed the cap and went to take a drink but the canteen was so hot I could not put it to my lips without burning them. The water was too hot to drink. I even tried to pour a little inside the canteen cover to help cool the water but with no success. To add to the heat, no wind was blowing and if it had, it would have felt like a hair dryer blowing on you while sitting in an oven.

**LT COL TULLIS WOODHAM, JR. 3/27 BATTALION CO:** We had only traveled a few miles east from our 18-19 May positions but it was obvious to me that the intense heat was seriously affecting the readiness of the Battalion. I called a halt to our movement about mid-day and set into defensive positions for the night.

During the evening I received reports from our outposts that 3/5 was proceeding in the same general direction as 3/27 and was in close proximity to our left flanks. I notified the 3/5 CO of this and expressed my concern over mistaking each other for the enemy. His response was that no 3/5 Marines were in the vicinity of 3/27. I told him "then they must be NVA and if they don't disappear shortly, 3/27 is going to take them under fire." Strangely enough, shortly thereafter, those 'enemy' forces were removed. The Regimental Commander, having monitored this exchange, and being aware of my anger over the 3/5 policing of the battlefield incident of the 18th, directed us to hence forth conduct operations in widely separated areas. 3/5 moved east towards the railroad tracks and 3/27 turned to the north and west of the tracks.

Each evening thereafter, along with the S-3, Major Fitzgerald, I would plan our course of action and direction of attack for the next day and call it into Colonel Schwenk for his concurrence and approval. His support and confidence in his Battalion Commanders allowed us a great amount of freedom in movement in accomplishing the mission and task assigned. You could not have asked for a more responsive Commander.

CPL CHARLES HUCKABY - INTERPRETER - Co K: That night we had an outpost out that let a squad of NVA walk right through them. When they realized that they had walked into our lines, they made an abrupt left turn and ran into the tree line. The last man didn't turn and he ran right across our perimeter. I think he was a track star because no one could catch him. L/Cpl Brady chased him and fired five rounds before his rifle misfired. The NVA turned around and sprayed several AK-47 rounds but didn't hit anyone. I think Lima Company shot him when he made it to their area.

CAPT JOHN F. ERNEST - Co L CO: Cpl (David

C) Jenkins put his rifle down and picked up a .45 and shot the NVA in the arm. He held him down until help came. We learned a great deal of valuable information from the NVA.

**MAJ ERNEST T. FITZGERALD, S-3 OFFICER - H&S Co:** I was sitting on the ground untying my bootlace when I heard bare feet running. I looked up and saw this silhouette of a man carrying an AK-47 and running like mad. He ran right past me and I gave an alarm. Someone shot him. A good shot, too, in both arms. When he was treated and questioned it turned out he was deserting or trying to. He got lost and ended up inside our lines. What he was trying to do was get the hell out of South Vietnam. I remember talking to him through an interpreter. He said he was a farmer from outside Hanoi. He was in his thirties, with a wife and two children. I saw the picture of his family. He had been drafted into the army and was not that happy with his lot, especially after our pursuit of his regiment. He was carrying some documents as I remember, but I don't recall if they were of any importance.

During the interrogation, the detainee stated that his unit, 2nd Battalion, 38th Regiment, had been in Vietnam only three or four days. The prisoner was probably in the 36th Regiment but had recently been transferred from the 38th. The unit had infiltrated from the North through Laos taking nearly a month. The prisoner said that he had been in the service for only one year prior to coming to South Vietnam and that the only training he had received were instructions on how to fire and maintain his weapon (AK-47.) He was told that the operational area was to be used as a training base for his battalion until they made contact with U.S. forces. His unit had received no warning that U.S. forces would be operating on Go Noi Island. The size of his battalion on arrival in South Vietnam was estimated at four hundred men. He further stated that many men in his unit had died as a result of a recent engagement with Marines (probably the encounter of 17-18 May.) Morale in the battalion was reported as being low due to a shortage of food and medical supplies. The enemy battalion did possess three heavy machine guns but to his knowledge they did not have mortars.

**CPL BILL JUNG - Co K: During the night the NVA tried to infiltrate our lines. One broke through and ran across the perimeter, firing as he went. A bullet in both arms brought him down. He was big, and an insolent bastard too. The rest of the night passed with the usual flares and distant artillery.**

**L/CPL TOM FULEKY - H & S Co: One night an NVA ran through our perimeter and Marines opened up from all directions hitting him three times. I got the job of guarding him for the night and I could speak a little Vietnamese. He seemed to trust me and I shared my c-rats with him and carried him out to the LZ in the morning. The helicopters brought in much needed supplies and one of the things I remember was a garbage can filled with soft drinks floating in ice. One of the Marines reached into the garbage can with his empty cup made from a c-rations can to scoop out some ice water. A Staff Sergeant knocked it out of his hand as he was taking a drink cutting his face. That's one E-6 I wish we had smoked.**

<u>21 MAY</u>

The Battalion moved out the next morning heading north to the village complex of Phu Dong (2). The heat was still unbearable. Most of the men had given up their flak jackets, but heat casualties still hampered the march. Several men had to be evacuated. As enemy bunkers were found along the route, combat engineers were dispatched to destroy them along with a recently discovered 250 pound bomb. At approximately 1355, the lead elements began receiving small arms and sniper fire. Artillery and air strikes were called in on the enemy positions. The Battalion set up and prepared night defensive positions.

Resupply helicopters flew in water, food and replacements. Most of the replacements were new men just arriving from the states. Everyone was glad to get new people but inexperienced Marines were also another problem.

For the second night in a row, an NVA found himself running within the Battalion perimeter as the Marines were settling in for the evening. He ran right past the command post and the Sgt Major yelled a warning. The enemy soldier was quickly subdued and he was evacuated to the rear.

At 2235, Co L received five or six rounds of 60mm mortar fire. At the same time, Co M took small arms fire and six incoming 81mm mortar rounds. The Marines responded with small arms fire and artillery missions were also called in on the suspected enemy mortar positions. 5 Marines were wounded in the action.

**L/CPL ART RIORDAN - Co L: We were setting up a defensive perimeter across from a tree line. There were bomb craters everywhere but we were not allowed to use them unless we probed for booby traps. I was digging in on a slight knoll next to the 60 gun team. It was late in the afternoon and the hottest part of the day. I took off my gear and started digging. The gun team was laying down and playing cards in some grass when all hell broke loose. Small arms fire was coming at the gun team and me on the knoll. The dirt kicked up all around me, a round went between my legs and one came so close to my right ear it**

sounded like an explosion. I spun around and dove into a bomb crater head first and tore the skin off my nose. Myself and another Marine were in the crater. Neither one of us could believe we weren't hit and after checking each other out for holes or leaks, I reached out and grabbed an M-16 and cartridge belt. He said it was his weapon and I said, "It's mine now." I started firing in the direction of the tree line. I saw some movement and started firing at the NVA who had gotten off a few mortar rounds. Their firing stopped long enough for the gun team to set up. Once the gun went off the NVA beat feet.

**CPL BILL JUNG - Co K:** During the night, the NVA sniped at us. I hugged the earth while tracer rounds were going over my head. Then the rain started, so I slept under a torn piece of tin.

**L/CPL TOM FULEKY - H & S Co:** Capt Thomas had my sniper team go on to an LP about 150 meters from our CP. We hid in a clump of bushes looking into a tree line about 200 meters to our front. It was about my 5$^{th}$ day on Allen Brook and I had not slept very well. We switched guard about every 1-2 hours and it was the most difficult night of my life. It took every ounce of strength to stay awake knowing that if one of us fell asleep we would both be dead.

**PFC JOHNNY G. JOHNSON - Co K:** At dusk, we started receiving incoming small arms fire and I took a round in my right thigh. We couldn't get a medivac that night so I had to wait until the next morning. When I was put on the chopper, I was told I would get a Bronze Star when I got back. I never returned and never got the medal. According to news reports, I was the only survivor of my platoon. I do not believe this. I was medivaced to

Da Nang, then Cam Rahn Bay, and finally to Yokuska, Japan. I was discharged shortly after getting out of the hospital.

**CPL MARLIN JACKSON - Co M: That night I found some tin sheeting and I made a small shelter. There was a small hole near by which I thought to be adequate. Later, we started taking incoming and I dove for my hole. It was way too small! In the light of exploding flares, everyone around me could see my head in this hole and my ass sticking out. Laughter broke out all over.**

## 22 MAY

At 0835, on 22 May, the Battalion moved out to sweep from its night positions north to An Quyen (2). Preparatory fires were called in to clear tree lines in advance of the approaching Marines. Sniper fire slightly wounded two men as the Battalion continued its advancement. The Battalion reached its night defensive position at 1452 after stopping occasionally to prep potential danger areas with air and artillery and to suppress sporadic sniper fire.

Co K had been left behind approximately 800 meters with several heat and battle casualties. They were also protecting some supplies and equipment that had not been picked up previously. As soon as the men and equipment had been loaded onto helicopters, Co K rejoined the Battalion.

**CPL BILL JUNG - Co K: We had been eating only at night for the past three days. During the day, we would get water from shell holes, craters, streams and wells.**

At about 1630, a six-man scout team from the S-2 section departed the perimeter on a reconnaissance patrol to the village of An Quyen (1). The team observed two young

Vietnamese males who, when they saw the Marines, ran away into the tall elephant grass adjacent to the village. They also observed pools of blood and fresh drag marks. The patrol pursued the individuals physically and by fire and, in the process of searching in the grass for them, discovered seven fresh camp fires and signs of recent occupancy of about thirty-five people. The patrol returned to the CP position while artillery was ordered upon the area around An Quyen (1).

**LT COL TULLIS WOODHAM, JR. - 3/27 BATTALION CO: Whenever we came to open areas in front of tree lines, I always brought it under prep fire. Also, I put myself in the position as the enemy commander and tried to figure out where he would place his CP. I then would direct that this area be brought under 81mm fire or request artillery support from our supporting batteries.**

**It should be emphasized that the intense heat, often 110 - 120, was probably the single most important factor governing our rate of advance and distances traveled each day. Each Marine had a green towel, basically hung around his neck, that was soaked in streams or wells when we were fortunate enough to come upon them. This aided immeasurably in overcoming the heat problem and cut down significantly on heat evacuations.**

<u>23 MAY</u>

The Battalion remained in position the entire day. At 0800, Co K and Co M commenced an offensive sweep north toward the Song Thu Bon River. It should be noted that this river had many different names. An aerial observer reported sighting 27 fresh graves in an area that had received air strikes and artillery missions on 22 May.

**CPL BILL JUNG - Co K:** We found an NVA horribly burned by napalm. The man smelled terrible. Our platoon started sweeping along the southern bank of the Ky Lam River. We would fire into any suspicious hedge or tree line. Further upstream, Lt Belser decided it was time to clean up. With one squad as security, we stripped and washed off in the river. It felt great. As we started back to the CP, it started raining again and it would not stop until the next morning. I was soaked and cold, but you get to a point where it doesn't bother you anymore.

**CAPT BLAKE THOMAS - Co M CO:** We found several areas where the enemy had built small campfires in overgrown fields. We also found and destroyed a fiberglass boat like the Marine Corps used that was probably utilized by the NVA to ferry across the river.

Neither of the two companies made enemy contact and both returned to the Battalion's position by late afternoon.

**SGT GARLAND SISCO - Co K:** I remember telling Pfc Edward J. Gaffney that he could change holes that night because he got flooded with big red ants all over his body. He was cussing up a storm.

## 24 MAY

The 24th of May would be a day of heroes for 3/27. No less than four Bronze Stars, six Silver Stars, and two Navy Crosses would be earned during the day's ferocious fighting.

At 0700, the Battalion moved southwest from its night position towards Le Bac (1). Co K and Co L led the way with Co M and the Command Group following at a distance. The

Marines pushed through mostly deserted and overgrown rice paddies, farms, and villages. Some villagers were located and upon questioning, it was revealed that an undetermined number of NVA had passed through their hamlet several days earlier carrying about twenty dead. This group was also reported to have several women with them who were thought to be nurses.

The companies continued their march passing about a dozen fresh graves. At 1130, after crossing a dry riverbed, the lead units began to receive sporadic small arms fire from a tree line to their front. The tree line and beyond were brought under fire by artillery and mortars.

**CAPT JOEL PARKS - Co K CO: I received reports of a sighting of 5 NVA. I called in artillery and the battery made a 200 mil error and I lost seven men to a short round. I called the Colonel to get air support and he replied there was none and that artillery was still trying to get unwired. I then started to prep two positions with my 60's and 81's.**

**First platoon started moving out on the left flank and was told to set up a base in a pagoda to their front. We ran across the open field to the tree line shooting from our hips. We only took one casualty in the crossing. First platoon then came under heavy sniper fire from hidden spider holes with AK-47s and machine gun fire.**

**L/CPL TOM FULEKY - H & S Co: We had just crossed this dry riverbed when short rounds dropped in on men from K Company. We went over the bank and started bringing back some of the wounded. I was sort of joking with one, saying he was going home early.**

**The first four men in my squad of scouts were told to go up further to bring more wounded back. We were all busy retrieving the wounded and KIA's and carrying**

them back across the riverbed to a staging area. The Navy doctor was working like crazy to keep as many men alive as he could. It was getting worse by the minute. The heat, sweat, blood and the exhaustion was taking its toll on everyone. There were four of us carrying a badly wounded Marine in a poncho liner. Two Marines were in front and Major Fitzgerald and I were on rear. Our hands were starting to slip when Major Fitzgerald pulled out his .45 and threatened to shoot anyone who dropped his corner! All we needed were more casualties.

As soon as the front of my squad went ahead of us, they ran into real trouble crossing spider traps. Three out of four had head shots. My squad leader Limey Kincad got shot in the neck and looked real critical. Our corpsman David Klasen had his mustache shot off and my best friend, Guy Gibson, was shot in the back of the head, splattering Bill Boyd with bone fragments and brain matter. Gibson was put in line with the KIA's and I went through the rest of Allen Brook thinking he was dead. When I got off the Island, I heard he was still alive and at the hospital in Da Nang. I dropped everything and hitched a ride to see him. He was a tough kid from Winsville, Missouri and I try to keep in contact with him often.

**CPL BILL JUNG - Co K:** Sawyer's squad was sent ahead to scout while we followed at a slower pace. We swept across the sandy riverbed and continued up the next rise through dirt and grass to a hedge line. We climbed through the hedges and came to the edge of a plowed field where we stopped. Fifty meters in front of us was a recently battered tree line. Then a terrible mistake happened. Three short 105 mm rounds of our own came crashing down on us. The explosions shook the ground, sent shrapnel flying everywhere and showered us with dirt. When we got up, seven of the men were wounded. As the

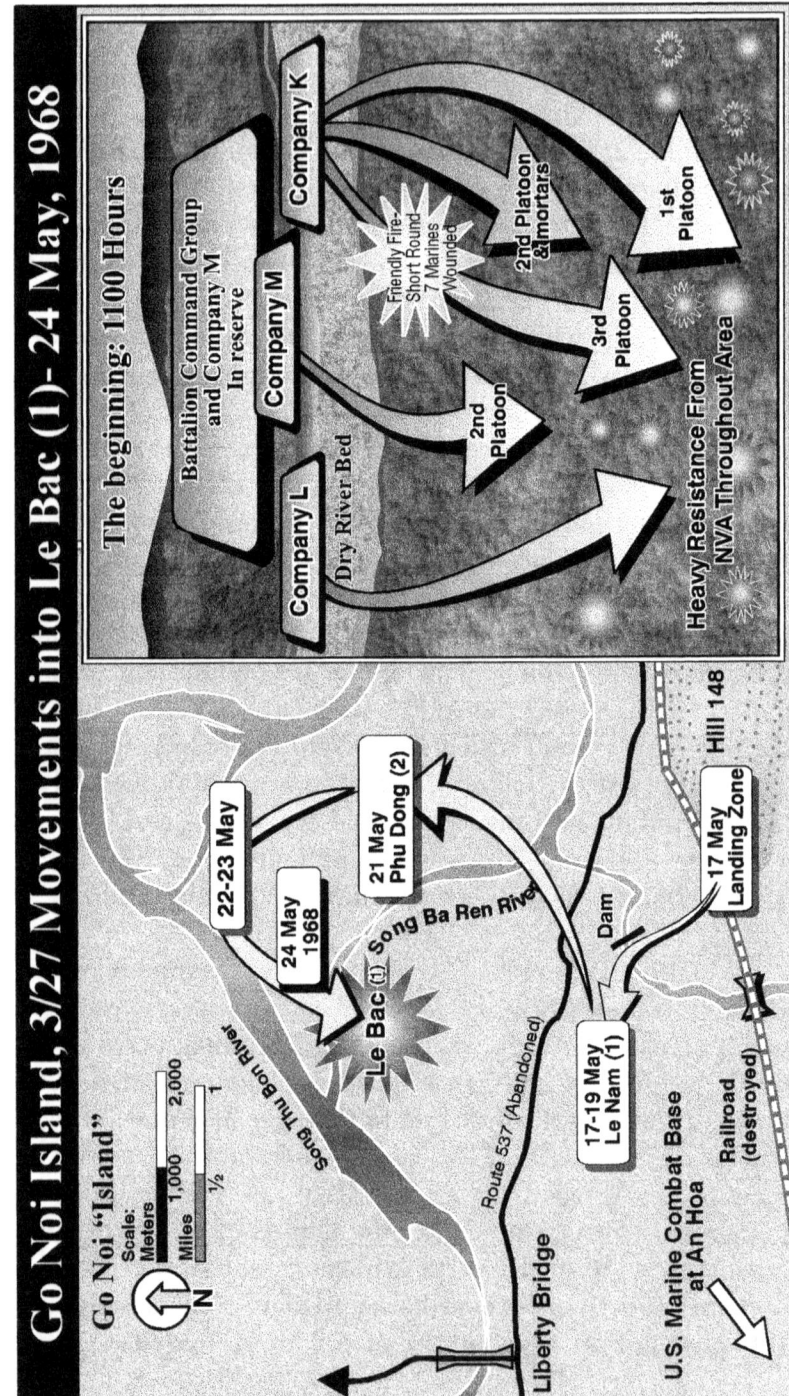

wounded were taken to the LZ being set up back in the riverbed, we regrouped and prepared for an assault.

Co K and Co L continued to move forward until 1230, when they encountered heavy resistance from fortified positions in Le Bac (1).

\* \* \*

**CAPT JOHN ERNEST - Co L CO:** Our mission was to protect the Battalion's right flank in case the NVA tried to envelop us. Kilo Company got into a good fight on our left. We ran into a bunker complex and came across one with two NVA inside. We were ordered to get them out alive. We did everything in our power to do so even throwing in tear gas, but they had gas masks. Every time we approached them, rifle fire and grenades came pouring out. We dug holes in the side of the bunker but again received rifle fire through the holes. Finally, after several hours we plugged the holes with grass and lit it on fire. One man was killed and the other one crawled out. He told us that they were pretty fed up with American fire power.

\* \* \*

**CPL BILL JUNG - Co K:** The 1st Platoon was on our left, Co L was on our right and 2nd Platoon was in reserves with our 60 mm mortars. We rushed across the field firing our weapons from our hips. Bullets were flying everywhere. I could see several men from 1st Platoon falling. Then, as luck would have it, I fell into an unseen trench and sprained my ankle. I spread my men out as we took cover behind rubble and trees.

**L/CPL LEROY R. DRIFFILL - Co K:** We moved up to a dry riverbed and spread out in line facing a tree line. We noticed movement within the tree line and tried to request the commanders to pound the area with artillery. The mortar section of the weapons platoon fired a few rounds of 60mm at the tree line, but that was it. The order came down the line to advance by fire. We began to cross the riverbed with us all shooting into the tree line, when heavy weapons fire from an enemy machine gun position opened fire on us. Glancing to my left I saw maybe six Marines going down from left to right. Looking back at the tree line, I could see where the fire was coming from as the smoke gave their position away. Without hesitation I dropped to the prone position and opened fire with my M60 and eliminated the enemy position by firing the entire ammunition belt I had loaded in my gun. I remember looking up and seeing that everyone had made it into the tree line with exception of the wounded or killed and myself. I found myself in the middle of the riverbed with no cover and about 50 yards of riverbed to cross. I jumped up and ran with all I had, zig-zagging back and forth and praying I wouldn't get my ass shot up in the meantime. We found enemy positions within fifteen to twenty yards from us. They were in foxholes, pagodas, and even trees. Cpl Twilling tried to move up on the foxhole positions and was shot through the leg. I laid down cover fire and he was pulled to safety. We tried to pitch grenades into the foxholes until we ran out of grenades. As the enemy would stick their heads out to see what we were doing, I would open fire on their positions, but we received word that our fellow Marines were on the other side of the enemy's positions and were in our line of fire. It became quite confusing as to where we could shoot at the enemy because we didn't know exactly where our people were!

**SGT GARLAND SISKO - Co K:** We started walking in the direction of LeBac. Strange as it may seem we were traveling in a column instead of in line like we did in search and destroy ops. Before we ever got there it seemed deathly quiet. Someone asked, "Why is it so quiet?" The response to it came from someone, "It's the quiet before the storm." If I remember correctly, it seemed like we walked across an open flat area and when we got to that point it seemed like the whole world opened fire on us. There were some explosions, either B40 rockets or 82 chicom mortars. As I began to get my men in the second squad spread out and undercover from the intense gunfire, there was an explosion about ten meters in front of me. I was knocked down by the blast and wounded. The next thing I knew the corpsman was working on me. I was ambulatory so they told me to walk to the LZ where the medivac was, which was back the way we came in. I remember I just picked up my rifle and helmet, got up and walked through that hail of bullets to where the medivac was coming in. I was not hit once in spite of the intense gunfire. I was medivaced and never was returned to the bush. I was sent out of Nam because of the Marine Corps order of twice-thrice wounds.

\* \* \*

**CAPT JOEL PARKS - Co K CO:** I decided to try to out flank the spider hole positions with two squads from the third platoon. They were about two hundred meters away from the pinned down first platoon.

**CPL CHARLES HUCKABY - INTERPRETER Co K:** Each NVA machine gun bunker was covered by at least 4 spider holes. To get to the bunker you had to eliminate the spider traps or you would get pinned down by one or more of them. The NVA planned their defense very well and I respected them a lot. We took quite a few casualties that day.

1st Lt Belser, Co K, 3rd Platoon Leader, received word by radio that the 1st Platoon was pinned down by snipers. He took his radio man and one squad and attempted to outflank the enemy. Belser went right into an enemy ambush. Two Marines were killed and several were wounded, including Belser who was shot three times in the arm. Heavy automatic fire continued as Belser called for the rest of his platoon to move up.

**CPL BILL JUNG - Co K:** Belser called by radio for us to come help. He was obviously in pain. Enemy rounds surrounded us as we went forward through the tree line. We didn't know exactly where our unit was. We probed forward and then fell back, a little confused. We started to inch forward again with Pfc Jerry Lee Hilbert on point. We lost contact with Hilbert and would find out the next day that he had been killed. Then Belser's people fired up a green flare, so we knew where to head for. I shook my head and said "Fuck it!" I stood in a crouch and yelled for my squad to move out. I ran across some rubble and a four round burst was fired at me. One bullet passed through the flesh of my upper left arm and knocked me off of my feet. Bullets kept snapping around me as I continued to crawl toward the ambushed squad. They were in bad shape, Pfc Gary Purcell was dying. Lt Belser had three bullet holes in his arm and the 3rd squad radioman was shot in the back. The platoon radioman, L/Cpl Joseph Schaler, was shooting away. Sgt Terry Sawyer, our machine gunner, Pfc Michael Cunningham, and a few others were also there.

Lt Belser moved from position to position informing his men of the situation and directing their fire. At one point in the battle, he called in artillery within 30 feet of his own position. Belser kept the artillery coming in as he withdrew, taking the dead and wounded with him.

**CPL BILL JUNG - Co K:** We kept firing and throwing grenades. We saw the gooks trying to surround us some more, so Sgt Kalka had me fire two phosphorus grenades into the nearby brush. The brush caught on fire and prevented the NVA from sneaking up. Mike Co was trying to get us out but they ran into some NVA machine guns. We decided to get out on our own. We threw smoke grenades for cover and took Purcell and the other wounded out as fast as we could. We finally linked up with the company. I had used up nearly all 300 rounds of ammunition that I carried and all of my grenades. My arm had stopped bleeding. Little Lestage had bandaged it up during the fight. Kilo Company continued fighting, shooting at the dug-in NVA from a trench. Officers were even manning one of the machine guns. To our right, Lima Company was also engaged in a fight. Sgt Kalka told me to leave on the next medivac. My ankle and arm were painful, but I hated to leave the company. I boarded a CH-46 and we were soon taking off. Several dead men and wounded were on the floor. My old friend Chief was among them, both of his legs shot up. I could see the Island as we left. The tree line where the fight was going on was a cloud of dust and smoke. The devastation and rubble of the Island passed beneath us as we headed north to a hospital.

Cpl Bill Jung would receive a Bronze Star for his actions on 24 May.

\*   \*   \*

**CAPT BLAKE THOMAS - Co M CO:** We were in reserve as Kilo and Lima moved towards Le Bac (1). Kilo became pinned down and was taking heavy casualties. I moved my first platoon, under Mr. Tilghman, to the left flank to relieve Kilo one.

**CPL MARLIN JACKSON - Co M:** We were told to stay put as Kilo and Lima advanced across a large dry river bed. We soon heard tremendous fire and knew they had 'hit the shit.' We were told to drop our packs and to advance to the battle area. As we crossed an open area, we started taking fire and two men went down. When we reached the bank, I looked down at the tree line where the main shooting was going on. Marines were pinned down everywhere. Since Brettman had the radio, I went out and grabbed a wounded man and a heat casualty and brought them behind the bank and to relative safety of the dry river bed, which was about 3/4 of a mile from the front lines.

I took some water and ammo and headed back to the dike. There were three boot black Marines who looked scared to death. I told them to hang tough as I moved out towards the tree line. After I gave out the ammo, a Marine in front of me took a hit and fell backwards into my arms. A corpsman bandaged him up and I carried him back to the bank where we fell right on top of the black Marines. I asked one to help me carry the wounded guy back. We moved just a few feet when I heard a burst of fire and a scream. One of the blacks had peeked over the bank and was shot in the chest. I told his buddy to grab him and we took off to the rear. We had to stop 5 or 6 times. The Marine with the chest wound stopped breathing and we had to yell at him to get going again. It worked every time and we finally made it back.

**PFC LARRY FRYE - Co M:** We were on a hill and Kilo was pinned down. They were in deep shit. We were sent to help them out but I had passed out from the heat. They were going to medivac me but I said no. I remember humping the 3.5 rocket rounds. It was a bitch. I was glad when we changed to LAW rockets.

\* \* \*

**L/CPL LEROY DRIFFILL - Co K:** After a few hours M Co personnel were sent forward to assist us. One group arrived at our position and was, it seemed to me, anxious to attack the NVA positions. There was a 3.5 rocket launcher team with them and I asked them to take out the pagoda to our front, but the only rounds he had were WP. I told him and others that the enemy was well concealed and to keep down. Out of nowhere these Marines charged the enemy positions and were quickly cut down by small arms fire. These men were not only wounded or dead, but were near enemy positions, making it nearly impossible to retrieve them safely. Four of us, including myself, volunteered to crawl in front of the enemy positions. We were given grenades and told to get as close to the enemy as possible. We pulled the pins and on "three," we threw the grenades toward the enemy positions. One of the grenades thrown hit a tree and bounced back to our position. The explosion went off very near to me the best I can remember. I received no shrapnel, but the corpsman felt I had a concussion as my head hurt extremely bad and I was disoriented. I was pulled back off the line and medivaced to Da Nang, where I spent three days in recovery.

As L/Cpl Charles Swagerty's Co M squad moved into assist a Co K unit, they came under intense fire from snipers. Several wounded Marines were dangerously exposed to the hostile fire. Swagerty boldly advanced across the fire-swept terrain and located the enemy positions. Despite the fact that his rifle was struck by enemy fire and damaged, he fearlessly exposed himself to the sniper fire and skillfully hurled numerous hand grenades at the enemy emplacement. He silenced the NVA fire and allowed his comrades to evacuate the wounded Marines. He was awarded a Bronze Star for his actions.

**L/CPL CHARLES SWAGERTY - Co M: On 24 May, we moved to assist another unit that was pinned down. There were several Marines that had been hit and lay exposed in a clearing. We moved to a ditch immediately adjacent to the clearing. The enemy was in 'spider traps,' dropping everyone that moved into their fields of fire. Anyone who raised up out of the ditch was getting hit. Several of us tried to move out to get the wounded. My weapon was struck by enemy fire and exploded in my hands. The impact was bone breaking hard. We returned to the ditch. The corpsman worked feverishly on the wounded in the relative safety of the depression of the ditch. Our rifle fire wasn't getting the job done. I grabbed as many frags as I could and moved to a position where I could chunk them at the spider holes. Others were firing their weapons and throwing frags, trying to suppress the fire enough to get our wounded out. Our aggressiveness seemed to slow down their fire for a moment, and we charged across the clearing to the wounded, two or three men stopping at each downed Marine. There was no time to make even a cursory inspection of their wounds. We picked them up and hauled ass back to the ditch. I remember dropping down**

beside the first Marine I brought to the ditch. A corpsman immediately began working on him. He'd been shot in the head. I recall him moaning almost unintelligibly saying, "Momma, Momma."

   L/CPL THOMAS THUESEN - Co M:  We were reinforcing another unit on our right flank which was engaged in heavy contact. We took four casualties crossing an open area, but we managed to get into the tree line where the point element was. There were NVA soldiers all over the place, but they didn't open up on us until we were ten feet in front of them. They pinned us down with machine gun and sniper fire. I worked over the reinforced concrete bunkers as best I could with my machine gun, but it didn't have much effect. I started concentrating my fire on the snipers in the trees.

   Marine helicopter gun ships and jets were called in to pound the NVA positions. Some of the bombs and rockets hit within 30 meters of the Marines.

   L/CPL THOMAS THUESEN - Co M:  I knew we had to get help. So I ran, crawled, and slid back to the rear. I got a corpsman to treat the wounded and picked up another squad. We managed to get back to the trapped men. I directed fire of three machine guns at the bunkers while the casualties were pulled back.

   As the Marines continued sweeping forward, under heavy machine gun and sniper fire, Pfc Bruce Richardson (Co M) positioned his gun team to provide covering fire.

   PFC BRUCE RICHARDSON - Co M:  The NVA were real close. They were throwing hand grenades from trench lines concealed by thick grass. Then my Gunner was killed.

The Assistant Gunner, Pfc Larry G. Fones, took over the gun despite a shrapnel wound in his right wrist.

**PFC LARRY FONES - Co M: Bullets were coming from all directions and one even creased my nose but I kept firing.**

Fones began to run low on ammunition so Richardson raced back to get more ammo. On the way, he was shot in the hand.

**PFC BRUCE RICHARDSON - Co M: When I reached the supply point, a corpsman put a battle dressing on my wound and told me I was going to be evacuated. I just grabbed some belts of ammo and started back. Just before I reached the gun, I caught a glimpse of something that reminded me of an old submarine movie I once saw. There were periscopes extending 20 feet above the enemy bunkers. It enabled the NVA to see us over the thick tall grass so they could adjust their fire when we moved. I gave Fones the ammo and then moved to tell our squad leader about the periscopes and bunkers. He had been wounded too, but still managed to call in artillery and air strikes on the bunkers.**

**CPL MARLIN JACKSON - Co M: On the way back from another trip to the front, a mortar round hit right behind me and threw me in the air and into the dry creek. I was pretty dazed and the next thing I knew I was on a chopper with a tag on me. Although I had blood all over my back, I didn't think I was wounded that bad so I jumped off before it took off.**
Grabbing water and ammo again, I headed back

towards the tree line. I took incoming fire the entire way. My rifle stock was hit and I was blown to the ground. As I stood up another round hit my pistol grip. I came across another wounded Marine who had been shot in both legs. I reached for my canteen but found it too, had taken a hit. I grabbed the Marine and threw him over my shoulder in a fireman's carry. As we were moving out, fire came pouring against us. The wounded man was hit on the butt. We hit the ground and I fired at an NVA with one hand, hitting him in the head. We continued back to the LZ. The wounded Marine kept saying, "Shot in the ass, my wife will never believe it." We both started laughing so hard I almost couldn't walk.

* * *

Pfc Herbert Jester (Co K), although fully realizing the danger involved, made three trips into an enemy infested area to help move his injured comrades to safety. On one trip he noticed an NVA machine gun position. Crawling to within ten feet of the bunker, he killed two soldiers with hand grenades. Next he observed an NVA firing from a spider hole. He aggressively attacked and killed the enemy with rifle fire. He continued throughout the day delivering water and ammunition and he remained with the last group to leave in order to provide covering fire. He was awarded a Silver Star for his bravery.

When Lt Belser's platoon rejoined Co K, he was ordered to move to the rear and be evacuated. He refused, volunteering to lead the reinforcements back to the Marines pinned down. He led a group of Marines from both Co K and Co M back into the action.

**1ST LT JOSEPH BELSER - Co K: We ran into some bad trouble and I soon found myself with about eight**

**men who could still function as a unit. It was during this rescue that I was shot in the right leg by a .50 caliber shell. At the time it happened, I really didn't think about it. I just put an e-tool on it and kept going. My only thought was to save those men.**

Pvt Charles R. Yordy's (Co K) was part of Lt Belser's platoon. As the Marines moved up on the flank of the enemy, the unit came under intense automatic weapons fire from several North Vietnamese bunkers and spider holes, pinning down the platoon and inflicting numerous casualties, including the platoon commander who fell directly in front of an enemy machine gun emplacement.

Without hesitation and with complete disregard for his personal safety, Pvt Yordy rushed across the hazardous area firing his M-16 rifle from the hip and succeeded in reaching the side of the injured officer. Picking up a wounded man's M-79 grenade launcher and ignoring the enemy rounds striking around him, he fired directly into the aperture of the bunker silencing the hostile fire. Observing another enemy bunker nearby which had pinned down his company, he crawled to the emplacement and destroyed it with several hand grenades.

As the platoon began to withdraw, Pvt Yordy selflessly remained behind and covered the withdrawal of his unit by throwing hand grenades and firing his grenade launcher at the hostile position, abandoning his precarious position only when he was assured that his fellow Marines had reached relative safety. For his heroic actions, Pvt Yordy would be awarded the Navy Cross.

Lt Belser, after seeing to the safety of the other casualties, agreed to be evacuated, with the assistance of Pvt Yordy. He would later lose his leg at the NSA hospital in Da Nang. He was awarded a Silver Star for heroic actions that day.

\* \* \*

**2ⁿᵈ LT BILL PRISH - Co I:** While recovering at Philadelphia Naval Hospital, I met Joe Belser. He sure downplayed his role on Allen Brook, only saying that the guy he rescued wasn't wounded nearly as bad as he was. He even joked about it.

I also met Al Guhl, a 2ⁿᵈ Lt with Mike Company as well as Chesty and Mrs. Puller who were visiting their son Lewis. What an honor, but what crappy conditions!

**CAPT BLAKE THOMAS - Co M CO:** Kilo's right flank was a much different story. Kilo three was in a lot of trouble and had taken many casualties. I sent my second platoon, with the third platoon in reserve, into this area to help them out.

Second platoon jumped out and went right into a box-shaped ambush. The platoon commander, platoon sergeant and most of the squad leaders were killed or wounded.

**CPL RICHARD BUCHANAN - Co M:** It was a box-shaped ambush. We unknowingly entered from the south end. Washington was point man. As he entered the hedgerow-lined compound about 60 feet from where Mike Company entered, he was gut shot from a spider hole no more than four feet in front of him. I opened fire on a spider hole adjacent to me in the middle of the compound at the same instant. The ambush was coordinated. The NVA were well-equipped and hidden. I was the seventh or eighth in line of 17 Marines. The spider hole had three NVA in it, armed with clean AK-47 assault rifles. It was covered by a woven mat of bamboo, dirt and a small bush. I saw the weapon sticking out of a slit in the mat just as it fired. L/Cpl Clark, the radioman was killed in front of me with a single gun shot to the head. I fired through the mat. The two NVA I could see were dead before the sound of the shot that had killed Clark stopped echoing. I turned my back on the hole, took the radio off Clark's body as John Hayes reached down and pulled the mat off, exposing a third NVA posed to shoot me in the back. Cpl John Hayes, with one clean shot, dispatched the NVA soldier and then moved to a pagoda to the right of our direction of march. Having no more than two round in my magazine, I moved to the left as everyone else moved to the right. I approached an L-shaped trench in the far left corner of the compound. I fired my last two rounds killing two NVA, one holding the other one who was wounded in front of him. As I lay next to the hole, a third NVA started to move and I killed him using the butt of the M-16. The L trench was 22 feet wide, 5 feet deep with the sides dug out two feet from the bottom for storage and additional security. It was manned by four NVA soldiers. A .30 cal machine gun had been mounted on a ground mount over the center of the L trench. The main body of the L-shaped trench was 7-8 feet long and parallel to our direction of our march. The short end of the trench went left, out away from the center of the compound about four feet ending in the hedgerow. I tried to use the .30 cal machine gun, but a fourth body lay at the bottom of the hole tangled in the ammunition belt which was over 15 feet long. After a dozen rounds it stopped. I could not move the dead body with the other two piled on top. The 115 degree heat had taken most of my strength. At this very moment a loud blast erupted behind and to my right.

    Cpl Michael Stoppa was located towards the rear of the column. As the ambush erupted, he observed a hostile automatic weapons emplacement. Cpl Stoppa seized a satchel charge and with complete disregard for his own safety, began maneuvering towards the enemy position. Ignoring the intense fire impacting around him, he crawled next to the fortified emplacement and hurled the explosive charge inside, killing several NVA soldiers and silencing their weapons. He then moved back to this unit's position and administered first-aid to his wounded comrades until he too was seriously wounded. He was awarded the Silver Star for his actions.

**CPL RICHARD BUCHANAN - Co M: I rolled out of the trench as a sniper placed three rounds next to me. I was able to see all three rounds strike the ground within inches of my face in a neat pattern.** I did not move for several minutes, then slowly lowered my hand to my belt, removing a fresh magazine and a grenade. I knew that the sniper was directly in front of me in the left corner of the compound behind the hedgerow in the trees. I was determined to eliminate him. I got to my feet and slammed a magazine into my M-16. I pointed in the direction of the sniper and pulled the trigger on full automatic, but it jammed, leaving me with just the grenade. I lobbed the grenade over the hedgerow at the spot where I knew the sniper to be. The sniper fire stopped. Two days later when we worked our way back to the ambush site I learned that the sniper had a spider hole in the corner, one of four spider holes across the back of the compound. The sniper got out of the hole and into the trees to shoot. When I threw the grenade it landed in his hole, which he had just retreated to. I then turned my attention to a Marine holding a body 20 feet behind me and to the left of the hedgerow. I yelled for him to "get out before you get killed," but he wouldn't leave. I yelled again and he yelled back, "I'm not going without the lieutenant." I yelled louder at him to leave. He yelled back, "I'm not going to leave him." I told him, "If you don't leave, I'll kill him myself." But he stood fast, ready to defend the man he was protecting against anyone or anything. I now know that the Marine I was yelling at was Charles Yordy K Company. I did not understand what took place between that other Marine and myself during those few minutes in the field, surrounded by a well-armed and entrenched force desperately trying to kill us. Now after talking to Yordy 31 years later, I believe it was like two football players passing the ball, two men on the same team, both of the same strength, character and stature. One exhausted, passing his determination on to the other. Had Yordy not cleared the way for me, the outcome of the battle on May 24, 1968 would have been much different. At that moment another Marine came from behind Yordy in what appeared to be a John Wayne approach, rifle held high, moving to the left then the right. He got about ten feet before an NVA dropped him with a single burst of automatic weapons fire which hit him in the legs, dropping him. He lay still as I turned to find the source of the automatic weapon fire. I determined it had to be from the same hole that the shot that Washington took came from. I keyed the radio and a helicopter gunship answered. I told them what I was going to do next and asked if someone would say something to my parents if I didn't make it into the pagoda. Leaving all my gear, with the exception of my last grenade and the radio, I crawled to just in front of Washington and threw the grenade up and over the hedgerow. It landed on the edge of the second spider hole across the back of the compound. I picked Washington up under the arms and continued across the compound past the third hole and into the pagoda. Washington's screams still haunt me after all these years. "Lord, please take me, Lord, Lord, please Lord." This went on for over an hour non-stop until he passed out and remained that way for the next 3 hours. I believe Washington died of his wounds several days later.

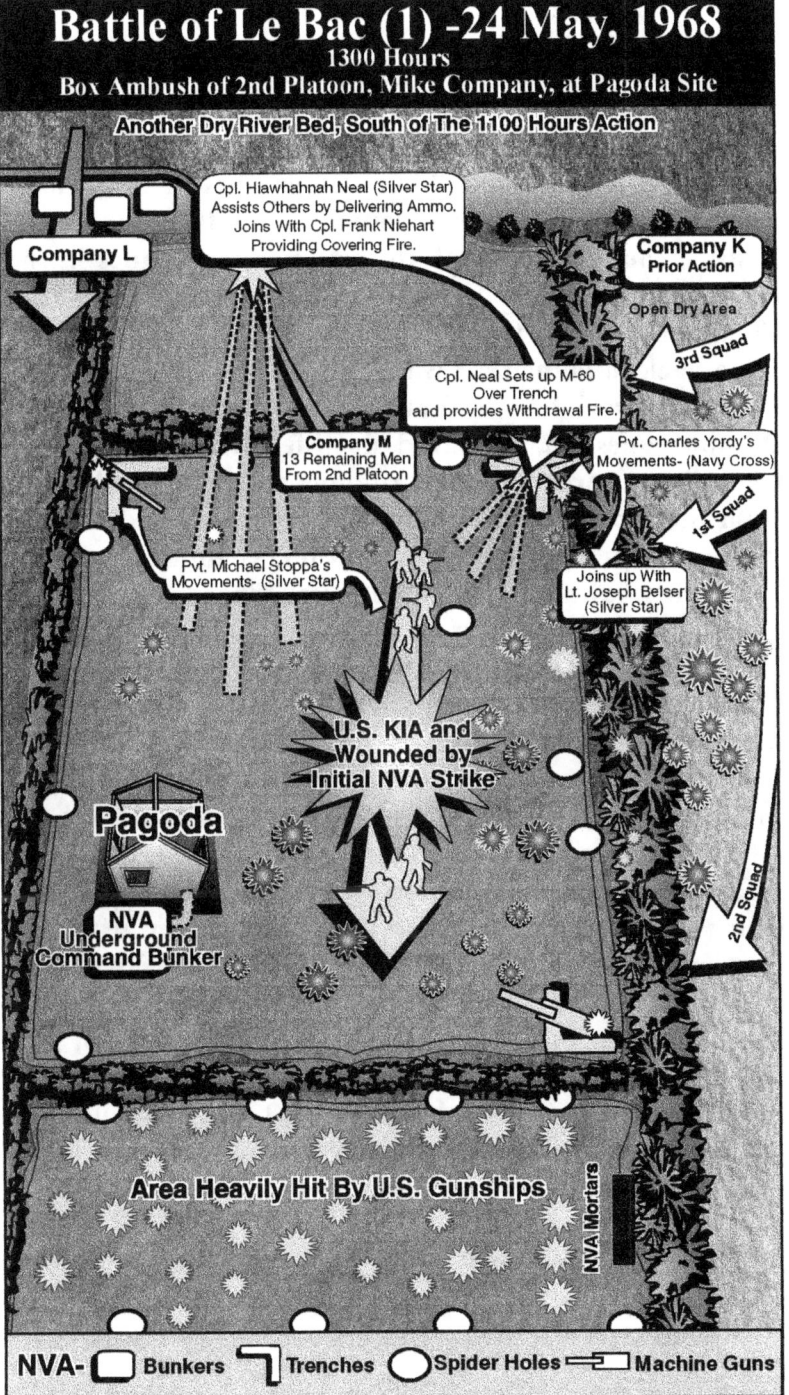

Once I got in the pagoda, I found what weapons I could, gathered every Marine that could move and set up a defense, covering the windows and open areas so we would not be overrun. We numbered about ten Marines. The majority of us were wounded and there were five dead. I found another M-16 and several grenades in the open, near Clark's body and went for them as Cpl Clinton Chapman stood to throw a grenade as cover. As his arm came back to launch, he was shot. He did manage to throw the grenade even though he was mortally wounded. Without question, he saved my life. As I helped Cpl Chapman, a corpsman came running across the field of fire from the same direction that Mike Company had entered the compound and started to treat the wounded. I've seen brave men but none that could match what this corpsman did. Crawling back into the pagoda, I discovered that the M-16 I had retrieved was also jammed. I must have said something, because the corpsman who had just arrived and was treating Cpl John Hayes for some serious chest and face wounds, handed me his .45 cal pistol. This corpsman continued to expose himself to hostile fire throughout the afternoon, going from Marine to Marine as needed. Cpl Chapman's grenade landed close enough to stun an NVA which allowed me to get a round into him with the corpsman's .45 cal pistol. My first round hit the wall just under the window, about an inch below the sill. It made a hell of a hole in the wall. The second shot I got off, traveled the twenty feet over the NVA command bunker that was attached to the backside of the pagoda and into the hole in the hedgerow, hitting the NVA in the head, which knocked him down into his spider hole.

L/Cpl Robert Dyer was a radio operator for Co K. The Kilo command post was situated about 75 meters away from the pagoda.

"Cpl Richard Buchanan, Navy Cross."

**L/CPL ROBERT DYER - Co K:** At that point, myself, Corpsman Walters and one other Marine who I did not know volunteered to go up to the pagoda. I left my PRC-25 radio in the woods next to our CP and the three of us moved left along the hedgerow/tree line forty or fifty yards under fire and then we dashed up into the pagoda with bullets flying everywhere. I have to say I was dumbfounded when we go to the pagoda. To the best of my memory, when we got inside we found Richard Buchanan and several other Marines, some wounded and several dead or dying. I remember trying to keep my head down below the window ledge or sill and the bullets zinging into the stucco from what seemed to be all directions. There was no sense of any command structure at the pagoda, only a sense in all of us that we had to get out of there.

**CAPT BLAKE THOMAS - Co M CO:** We couldn't communicate with the men in the hooch because their radio handset had keyed out when a dead Marine had fallen onto it.

I switched my radio to button vermillion, the medivac common frequency, in an attempt to contact the gunships in the area to help us out. By some quirk of fate, Cpl Buchanan also switched his radio over to the medivac station and the two of us were finally able to communicate and coordinate close in gunship support, often within just a few feet of their position.

**L/CPL ROBERT DYER - Co K:** After a while I noticed a PRC-25 radio on the floor and mentioned to the other Marines that I was a FAC radio operator and would seek air support from the UH-1E's that were flying around. Richard Buchanan told me where the enemy fire was coming from and I attempted to call the helicopters on

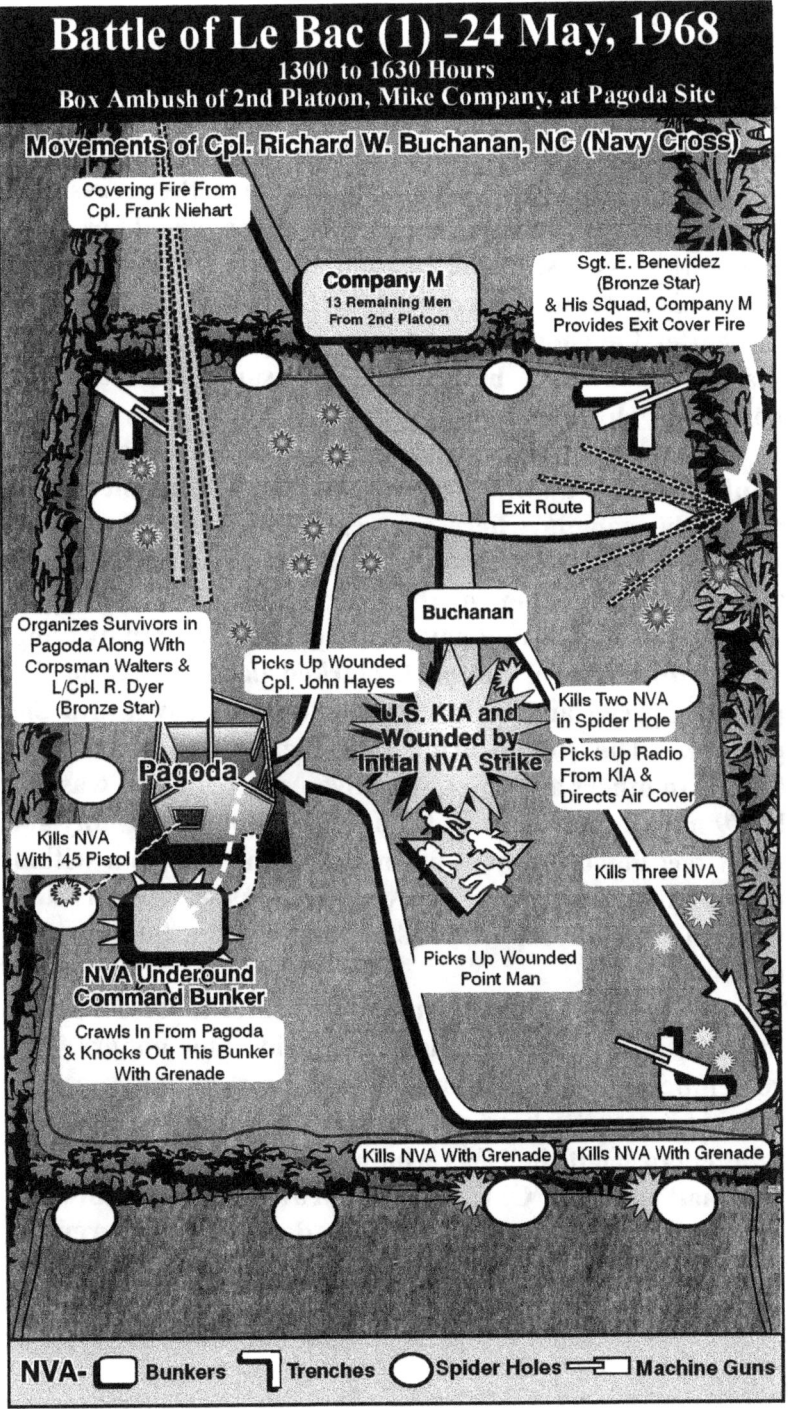

the radio which had been on the floor of the pagoda. After failing to get in contact with the choppers, I heard the CO of M Company, Capt Blake Thomas, acknowledge me on the radio. I asked Capt Thomas to have the hueys fire rockets and machine guns alongside of the pagoda as close as possible because of the location of automatic and sniper fire which we were receiving. He agreed and shortly thereafter the choppers made a couple of runs and we felt that perhaps they had eliminated some of the NVA positions. However, we continued to receive fire.

At that point someone suggested that we enter the bunker which ran alongside of and had an entrance from inside the pagoda where we were pinned down. At the time we were probably thinking that we should call in the hueys right on top of the pagoda and if we were underground we would have more protection than by lying on the dirt floor of the pock marked pagoda. All in the pagoda agreed and we proceeded to move down into the pagoda. The first Marine into the bunker was a Pfc known to others as 'Chief,' a native American who was the M-79 man in one of the K Company platoons. He only got a few feet down the steps when shots rang out from within the bunker. There were NVA in the bunker. He was shot in both legs. We pulled 'Chief' out of the bunker and regrouped.

The decision was made to someone to frag the bunker and Richard Buchanan did the honors. I remember one of the longest moments in my life was waiting (after Richard threw the grenade down into the bunker) to see if the NVA who were inside the bunker and who had shot the 'Chief' would throw it back up into the area where we were hunkered down. The grenade detonated with a thump and we proceeded to develop a plan to get out.

CPL RICHARD BUCHANAN - Co M: The helicopters strafed with rockets and M-60 fire very close to us. I had forgotten just how close and many until just recently. Lots of dirt, smoke, and loud, very loud. We laid flat on the pagoda floor. Lots of big hunks of rockets, bullets and dirt/rocks went through the roof of the pagoda and hit the walls. What leaves were left on the trees were cleared. It went on for a long time, the better part of 40 minutes, but none of us were hurt from our own fire.

L/CPL ROBERT DYER - Co K: We again had Capt Thomas have the hueys make a strafing run close alongside the pagoda. After the strafing and as part of our strategy to get out of the pagoda, Doc Walters and I took the 'Chief,' who by now was in terrible pain, shot in the legs by the NVA in the bunkers and attempted to exit the pagoda towards the tree line. We only got a few feet outside and we took intense small arms/sniper fire from just outside the bunker area alongside the pagoda. One thing you never forget is the pop of a weapon when it is fired in your direction at close range. We did an about face and crawled back into the pagoda.

I recall getting on the radio and asking either Lt Kent, the K Company XO or Capt Thomas to get us two M-60's down alongside of the hedgerow and that they had to lay down an intense base of fire alongside of the pagoda (both sides) for us to get out. Whoever was on the radio (Kent or Thomas) agreed. I indicated that when they were in place that they should commence firing and at that point we would come out with everyone alive or wounded. At this point, half were wounded including the 'Chief.' After a couple of minutes we were notified on the radio to get ready. Every Marine in the pagoda grabbed someone wounded, dead, or otherwise and when the firing from the M-60's started we ran like hell to get to the hedgerow. Doc

Walters and I had the 'Chief' and I remember thinking how painful it must have been for the 'Chief' to endure the bouncing as we tugged him towards the hedgerow. We made it to the hedgerow and the first person to meet me was Lt Kent. He was right in the thick of it, directing fire by the other Marines and with his M-16 smoking. I'll never forget Lt Kent for that day.

At least two gun teams moved up to help, one from Company M and another from Company L.

**CPL DAVID HEIN - Co M:** The 2nd Platoon of Company M was pinned down while trying to take the village of Le Bac (1). We took many wounded and dead. Corporal Neal, with complete disregard for his personal safety, climbed on top of an enemy bunker and gained fire superiority with his machine gun. He was constantly exposed to enemy automatic fire and grenades. In the process of keeping several enemy positions silenced, his machine gun malfunctioned.

**CPL ROBERT DICKEY - Co M:** Corporal Neal then ran across an open field of enemy fire and retrieved a machine gun and ammo from a fallen gun team. Returning to the top of the bunker he again gained fire superiority until he ran out of ammo. Once more he braved the heavy automatic fire of the enemy to secure ammo from a wounded ammo man. He returned to the bunker and kept the enemy's heads down until he again ran out of ammo. He then helped with the evacuation of the dead and wounded. He stopped only when we medivaced him due to heat exhaustion.

Corporal Neal would later be promoted to Sergeant and would receive a Silver Star for his efforts on 24 May.

**CPL RICHARD NEAL - Co M:** I was carrying 700 rounds of M-60 ammo and wished I had a lot more. My gun took a direct hit that bent the site all to hell. I finally grabbed a wounded lieutenant and got out of there. I remember that Frank Neihart (Co L) was the other gunner. I ended up at the Marble Mountain Medivac Station. After a few days, my First Sergeant came by and saw me. He was thoroughly surprised because I was reported as missing!

**PFC FRANK NEIHART - Co L:** Neal kept telling me not to spray, but to shoot straight ahead. He knew the NVA were in the hedgerow to our front. We took our helmets off and put them under our M-60 gun mount to get it high enough to shoot over the bank. Neal was moving everywhere. He was one tough Marine.

**SGT EDWARD BENAVIDEZ - Co M:** We were in a trench line when two Marines jumped in and told us they saw some wounded men in a large crater up ahead near a pagoda. Lt Tilghman had me take my squad up to assist the wounded. We took all the smoke grenades from the platoon and plenty of frags. We moved in under fire and got them out.

**L/CPL ROBERT DYER - Co K:** After getting out, I assisted in the evacuation of the 'Chief' and others to the area where the helicopters were medivacing dead and wounded and returned to the hedgerow to provide fire towards the pagoda and surrounding area.

One unmentioned hero in this entire episode and a person I want to acknowledge is the efforts of Corpsman Walters to provide aid to dead and wounded Marines before the pagoda incident, during the pagoda incident and afterwards. He was fearless and a man among men. The best corpsman I ever had the experience of serving with and I felt like he was a true brother to those of us in M and K companies who were in the area of LeBac (1) and (2) on May 24.

After some time it seemed all the dead and wounded were removed and I remember Lt Kent telling me that we should pull back across the rice paddy/field to the area where the Company (and the battalion) was regrouping. It was late in the day, near dusk.

On a lighter note, at the time I remember being incredibly thirsty, not having had any water or food for some time that evening. Some of the pallets of supplies which had been dropped by the helicopters had laid out in the sun for hours. That night I had drawn the 0300-0600 AM radio watch assignment. When I was awakened that early morning for my radio watch, I was reliving the episode in the pagoda during my sleep and I was startled by Cpl Potkalypski when he woke me. I locked and loaded and I almost killed him with my M-16 in my confusion in being awaked. In any event, once awakened, Cpl Potkalypski (Capt Park's radio operator) and I broke into the provisions on the aforementioned pallets and I drank an entire tin (approximately 2 gallons of grape juice) during my radio watch. Later in the morning on the following day, I had what I thought was indigestion and leaned over to discharge what I thought would be some intestinal gas. I proceeded to shit the entire 2 gallon of hot grape juice all over my utilities.

Both Robert Dyer and Edward Benavidez earned Bronze Stars, while Richard Buchanan became the second Navy Cross winner for actions on 24 May, 1968.

Co M had finally linked up with Co K at 1400. The two companies started to withdraw north to allow supporting arms to neutralize the enemy positions. By 1630, all friendly units were clear of the area and air and artillery fire were called in on Le Bac (1). Once disengaged, Co M, Co K, and Co L pulled back north toward the Battalion CP. Reconnaissance elements were dispatched to the vicinity of Phu Tay (2) to locate a suitable CP site.

**CAPT BLAKE THOMAS - Co M CO:** In general, it was hard not to write everyone up for a decoration in my company. They did an outstanding job on the 18th and 24th. No matter how hairbrained a scheme it was, someone was willing to try it if there was a chance.

* * *

**CPL RANDY RICHARDSON - Co K:** After the fight, I reached for my cigarettes attached to my helmet and found a bullet had ripped through them. Later in the evening, I unrolled my poncho liner that had been strapped to the top of my pack and found five more bullet holes. Like they say, close only counts in horseshoes.

**SGT GARLAND SISCO - Co K:** Doc G.L. Graymire did a super job. Between 18 and 24 May he was constantly risking his life, helping to aide one wounded man after another.

**L/CPL LEROY R. DRIFFILL - K Co:** One of the most important people to any grunt is their corpsman and we lost one of the finest during Operation Allen Brook. Richard Carl Fina was my friend. He was killed on 24 May 1968 and was one of the corpsman attached to the 1st Platoon. He died trying to do his job by going out into an open riverbed during heavy enemy fire because there were wounded Marines dying out there. He is only one of many heroes of Vietnam. To a Marine grunt every corpsman is, and will always be, a hero to all of us who fought in that conflict. These brave men with total disregard for their own safety, and due to their undying courage, saved many Marine's lives. I know that God will have a special place for them in his kingdom.

At about 1700, all units commenced moving to the new nighttime position in the vicinity of Phu Tay (1). Perimeter defenses were established and resupply missions were undertaken. During the night, about 100-150 rounds of small arms fire and 4-6 rounds of 60 mm mortar fire were received in the Battalion's position, inflicting minor wounds on two Marines.

A few hours later, twenty rounds of mortar fire fell outside the Battalion's perimeter. It appeared as though the enemy was attempting to locate the CP position. They were confused since the Battalion had not returned fire in response to their earlier harassing fire.

**LT COL TULLIS WOODHAM, JR. - 3/27 BATTALION CO:** That night we set up our CP on a high bluff overlooking a dry riverbed. Up to this time, every evening when we set in the defensive night position the enemy would harass us with small arms fire or sporadic mortar rounds. We would respond to them and we would have this intermittent activity throughout the night. That night, I directed our units not to return any probing fire. When we did receive machine gun and small arms fire, everyone held back as ordered. Since there had been no response, the NVA Commander started to shift his fire down into the dry riverbed and elephant grass area assuming, as I had hoped he would, that we had moved our forces there.

**CPL MARLIN JACKSON - Co M:** Later that

evening I had a corpsman look at my back. He found and removed a couple pieces of shrapnel. My priority that day had been to help the wounded. I was tired and pretty fed up. Later in the evening I moved over to our 'head' area, pulled down my pants, and started my business. All of a sudden we started to take incoming mortar rounds. I just stayed where I was and finished up. I just didn't give a damn!

The day ended with 9 Marines KIA, 35 WIA, and 38 evacuated as heat casualties. 45 NVA were killed and one was captured.

\* \* \*

Back at the Cau Ha Base, Co I prepared to return to Go Noi Island after reorganizing and receiving fresh troops from the States.

**CAPT JOHN ERNEST - Co L CO:** I couldn't believe that they were sending India back into combat after just one week of reforming. If it were World War II, they would have been given several months to form up and retrain.

**2ND LT BILL PRISH - Co I:** On my first full day in-country I was driven from Da Nang to the regimental HQ. While waiting to meet the Colonel, I sat outside his tent and faced directly towards a large casualty board. I couldn't help but read the numbers of KIA and WIA and the companies that had apparently took a beating. It was May 24, and I now know that the casualties were from Allen Brook. The colonel came out and caught me looking at the board. The only words that I can remember him saying were, "Lieutenant, is there any question where you're going?" My response was, "No, sir" as I stared at 'I' company on the board.

It was late afternoon when I got to 3/27 at Cau Ha. 1Lt Steve Thompson was the acting company commander. He was also the only officer left in the company. Steve told me that there was no hurry to meet my platoon (2nd,) as there would be time for that in the morning. At about 3:00 a.m. I was awakened by a lot of activity around the area. I quickly learned that I Co was going back to Go Noi, and there was a real seriousness and even a type of fear permeating the area. I hadn't even heard of Go Noi. I quickly went to the 2nd platoon area, assembled the men and introduced myself. A hell of a way to begin. My words were basically, "I'm your platoon leader and won't be wearing any bars, so just do as I say." Within the hour we were trucked to Liberty Bridge. There were 26 of us when we rejoined the operation on May 25.

## 25 MAY

Beginning at 0712 on 25 May, preparatory artillery fires were called on Le Bac (1). These were followed by air missions at 0845. Again at 1000, more arty prep fires were called in on the target area and shortly, Co L was ordered to move out towards Le Bac (1). As Co L moved out toward the objective, another air strike was made. At 1045, Co M, Co K, and the command group again reached the dry streambed just north of the village. Co L moved through the objective approximately 150 meters to the front.

At 1205, Co L took one casualty due to small arms fire but avoided heavy contact by withdrawing and calling in another air strike. Co L was not about to be sucked into another NVA trap. At 1220, the Battalion CP group received mortar and small arms fire from its rear.

\* \* \*

**CPL MARLIN JACKSON - Co M:** As we moved thru a dry riverbed, several of us stopped and started talking and smoking. A mortar round came in right into the middle of our small group. Unbelievably no one was hurt badly.

\* \* \*

**LT COL TULLIS WOODHAM, JR - 3/27 BATTALION CO:** It became apparent to me after our stand off with the NVA on the 24th that we were again, on the 25th, butting our heads up against a dug in enemy in entrenched defensive positions and facing a situation that could easily result in a scenario similar to the one we found ourself in on the 17th and 18th of May. There was no doubt in my mind that we could, and would, win with our superior forces (professionally speaking) and fire power but I was not convinced the price we might have to pay, justified immediately assaulting those dug in forces.

I decided to disengage from the Le Bac (1) entanglement and moved the Battalion westward towards the Song Thu Bung River where we could regroup, allow our supporting arms to further soften up the target area, and then launch subsequent attacks against the enemy under more favorable conditions. I considered that the most practical, tactical, move at the time and still hold fast to that view and decision now.

The command group and all companies moved west towards the river. Once there, everyone started digging in for the night.

At 1330, Co I together with 2nd platoon Co C, 1st Tank Battalion and some leading elements of 1/27, joined the

Battalion and were integrated into the defensive positions. Co I was now led by 1st Lt Julian W. Parrish, who had been the Battalion Adjutant.

**LT COL TULLIS WOODHAM, JR. - 3/27 BATTALION CO:** That afternoon and evening we held beach call at the river. Everyone got a chance to bathe in the water. It greatly helped our spirits. Regiment had decided to send India back, along with a tank platoon. Later that evening, we started getting mortar fire from the northern river bank between Hill 55 and us. I brought the tanks around and directed their fire across the river. The enemy's harassing fires stopped.

**SGT ED BENAVIDEZ - Co M:** We all then moved down the river about 1500 meters where we met India company, which had received reinforcements, and five tanks. We set in around the river and got resupplied. Tomorrow we'd go back to the tree line with the tanks and would try again. We have to recover our KIA's which were left behind. I was sent to the $2^{nd}$ platoon to give Sgt Hein a hand. $2^{nd}$ Platoon got ten new men. I was no longer in the $1^{st}$ platoon. We had a chance to clean up in a pond by the river. The river is too dangerous because the gooks fired on us from the other side. During the night we sent out one squad from our platoon on an ambush and they killed a couple of gooks.

**CPL ROBERT SIMONSEN - Co I:** In the hospital, I swore that I would never go back to Go Noi Island again, but guess what? We went by trucks this time! Rain, rain and more rain. The nights were very cold and miserably wet.

**CPL CHARLES SWAGERTY - Co M:** That evening

as we were setting up for the night, word was passed for me to report to the CP. I was told that I was to report to the rear to join a CAP unit that I had applied for earlier. I wish I could express to you the feeling of elation I had upon learning that I was taking the next chopper out to the rear. I wish, also, that I could say that I was saddened to leave everyone else on that island. But that would be a lie; my only feeling at the time was the sheer joy of getting the hell off that island. I choppered to the rear, but failed to get there before the next CAP school started. You talk about 'skating' duty! I was transferred to Headquarters Company, where I became a gate guard for about a month. Then when the 27th was about to go back to the world, I was transferred up north to B 1/3, 3rd Mar. Div., and back into the real war. I was promoted to E-5 and was a squad leader with them until I got shot December 26, 1968.

    I recall an awful lot more that happened on Go Noi, but mostly those are other people's stories. Once, though, while linking up with India company for an assault, I was the end element of Mike company that was to link up with the end of India. Their end Marine was Paul Michael Brannon, a boy I had grown up and gone to high school with, with whom I had joined the Corps on the 'buddy' plan. We'd gone through all of our training together, but had been separated when we went to the 27th Marines. Our joyous reunion was short-lived. We fought a lot of war together in the next two days, two high school buddies far from home, in a world alien to the sticks we were raised in. But Paul left early when, after being allowed to go a squad at a time into the river to bathe, snipers opened up on them and Paul was hit.

    **CPL CHARLES HUCKABY - INTERPRETER Co K:** Since we were very short handed I was sent out on an LP. There were three of us and later that night we saw several NVA to our front. I called in and the CO told us to return to the lines. I said I thought it would be safer for us to lie low and for our lines to fire machine gun fire right over our heads. The CO didn't like this idea so we pulled back out.

Resupply was completed by 1516 and further air and artillery prep fires were zeroed in on Le Bac (1). At 2124, a Co M squad ambush observed 3 NVA in front of their position and heard movement in a tree line. They opened fire and killed 2 NVA.

## 26 MAY

At 0720 on 26 May, Co L and Co M, along with tanks, started moving back toward Le Bac (1) from west to east. Air and artillery continued to fire on the objective. At 0940 Co L found seven dead NVA and twenty-two freshly dug graves which were opened up and found to contain NVA dead. Co L then started receiving mortar fire, which wounded six men. The Battalion's mortars returned fire on the suspected enemy positions and an artillery mission was also called in.

**PFC WILLIAM K. HOPKINS - Co L:** I was a rifleman in the first platoon. We came across several dead NVA and three Kilo Company Marines. They were shot in the head and their bodies had been mutilated. It was horrible to see our fellow Marines like that.

**CPL MARLIN JACKSON - Co M:** We swept back towards Le Bac (1). The area was totally destroyed with craters and blown up trees everywhere. We came across an area where the fight on the 24th had taken place and we found a live Marine sitting. He had been missing for two days. There were 3 to 5 dead Marines around him.

**SGT EDWARD BENAVIDEZ - Co M:** In the morning we got lined up. Lima company on the left and Mike company on the right with India and Kilo companies bringing up the rear. The tanks were in front. We moved all the way up to where we got hit Friday. We found our KIA's and we were getting ready to move again when we got mortared. Seven men from the 1st platoon got hit. Later after the medivac, the gooks opened up on us again with machine guns, rockets and mortars. One machine gun nest was knocked out and some spider holes were crushed by the tanks.

* * *

**L/CPL ART RIORDAN - Co L:** We were set up in a tree line across from a ville. There was a field/rice paddy separating us. We had a Tank with us and it was raining and cold. The Tankers were not happy because they had recently lost a Tank to RPG's. I knew the Tank Commander and I told him I was going to get some shut-eye under his Tank and out of the rain. It was night and I wasn't under there long before we started getting small arms fire from the ville across the field. The tank started reving up and the turret started moving in the direction of the ville. I got out from under it in a hurry and just as I did they fired two rounds. I remember it being louder than hell. I did not like losing my hearing out in the bush The next morning we swept through the ville to take a body count. We found dead animals and holes in everything including leaves on trees, but no bodies. I heard the tanks had fired 'bee hive' rounds. There wasn't much in that ville that didn't have a hole in it.

At 1325, Co M made contact with an unknown size enemy force. They received small arms and automatic weapons fire from the enemy as well as RPG rounds directed at the supporting tanks. Co M returned fire, called in air strikes on the enemy positions and directed close-in tank fire, all of which resulted in suppressing the enemy. 28 NVA were killed and one was captured.

**CAPT BLAKE THOMAS - Co M CO:** We started off in the morning heading back to Le Nam (1) from the northwest to the southeast. Lima was on the left and Mike was on the right. We retrieved the dead that we had left on the 24th. When we ran into the NVA again, it was a different story because we now had tanks.

I had three tanks attached to my company. I had them loaded with 90mm rounds, two with canister and one with delay. I fired the canister rounds first and then the delay into the ground. The first volley scared them, the second volley caused them to get up and run and the third volley wiped them out.

**LT COL TULLIS WOODHAM, JR. - 3/27 BATTALION CO:** We jumped off and went east towards the railroad tracks. We had not gone far when we again hit the NVA. It was close combat and the tanks were heavily engaged. I remember Lt Williams, the tank platoon commander, was killed standing up in his turret during the fight. He was due to rotate home in just a few days.

**CAPT BLAKE THOMAS - Co M CO:** During the battle, the tank commander stood up and pointed to an NVA in a spider hole and was shot in the chest and killed. One of his people went into shock due to the heat. They were not used to it like we were. This left no one in the tank who could operate it. Fortunately we had two former 1811s (tank MOS) with fourteen months experience in tanks. These two were able to take over and operate the tank.

**L/CPL TOM FULEKY - H & S:** One of the tank commanders got killed, and Capt Anderson took over the tank. I offered him my assistance to be the machine gunner, but he turned me down. During the operation, Capt Anderson used me as a runner to make physical contact with the company to our right. That made me nervous because everyone was getting a little testy by then.

**1ST LT BILLY C. STEED - H & S Co:** I remember one specific incident. We had a large bunker we were going against and we were receiving heavy automatic weapons fire. We brought up a tank and as we were directing it, the tank commander was shot with a machine gun right across his chest. I can still remember it to this day. Most times when you see a guy wounded he's down on the ground, but the Lieutenant was laying across the turret of the tank with about half his body out and a lot of blood running down the tank. We were trying to get him and the rest of his people out of the tank. They had hit the tank with an RPG and we lost some other people attempting to get him out. We finally got somebody in to drive the tank backwards and get it in a relatively secure area.

**CPL MARLIN JACKSON - Forward Observer, Co M:** I left for the front to help retrieve wounded and dead. As I advanced towards some tanks I received heavy fire from my right. I dove for cover and then crawled around thru some brush. I saw an NVA in a bunker. I ran up to it and shot off 15-20 rounds into the bunker. As I pulled the pin on a grenade, I saw two bloody hands coming out of the bunker. I captured and tied him up and took him back to the rear.

He was a drafted college student and had only been on Go Noi Island for 4 or 5 days. I would like to go back to Vietnam some day and look him up if he is still alive.

The captured enemy soldier indicated that he was a member of the 2nd Bn, 68th Regiment. He claimed his unit was armed with four 82mm mortars, nineteen 60mm mortars, nine heavy machine guns, 15-20 light machine guns, RPGs, 20-30 BARs, and numerous AK-47s, over half of which were new. Morale in his unit was low due mainly to air strikes. He added that many men wanted to 'Chieu Hoi' (give up and change allegiance) but didn't know what procedures to follow. His pack was fairly new and was well stocked with supplies.

**CAPT BLAKE THOMAS - Co M CO: We started taking RPG and heavy fire on our right flank later in the day. A platoon from India was assigned to me to help strengthen this side. One tank was hit, but it remained operational. The tank commander, although wounded from shrapnel, turned his turret around and shot delay rounds into the trench line where the NVA were firing from. We saw legs, packs and other equipment flying in the air but we were never able to check this area out.**

\* \* \*

**CPL CHARLES HUCKABY - INTERPRETER Co K: As we moved back in following the tanks, I realized that I had never seen an area more devastated in my life. This was my second tour, including operation Hastings and Harvest Moon, and I couldn't believe what I saw.**

**The bunkers were built with iron railroad rails and wooden ties, bricks, heavy lumber, sandbags and earth. Direct hits from jets were about the only thing to knock**

them out. There was NVA equipment laying all over the place. I picked up an NVA pack for myself.

**SGT CHARLES C. KALKA - PLATOON SGT - Co K:** I don't believe we could have taken the ville without the tanks. The infantry would throw out enough small arms fire at a bunker to keep the NVA from setting up their RPGs and then the tanks would knock out the bunkers.

\* \* \*

**1ST LT BILLY C. STEED - H & S Co:** The radio operator and myself were in a bunker complex and we received fire from a bunker so we threw a CS grenade in there. We were still receiving fire, so we knew that they all had gas masks. We then threw a frag grenade in and finally got one guy out. We wanted to capture some of them so we could get intelligence from them. I was standing on the side of the bunker and when one ran out, I jumped on him and he unfortunately had a grenade but he hadn't pulled the pin. It was quite a show for a while. I was wrestling with the guy, who was attempting to pull the grenade, and the other troops couldn't shoot him because we were in such a close situation. We finally did capture him and got numerous amounts of intelligence from him. I wrestled the grenade out of his hand and they just subdued him.

\* \* \*

**CAPT BLAKE THOMAS - Co M CO:** While we were medivacing our casualties, we took about 12 rounds of incoming 60 mortars. 7 more of my men were wounded during this attack. I called in an arty mission and a low charge round hit a tree, wounding 4 more of my Marines.

**CPL RICHARD BUCHANAN - Co M:** I was sent out of the field by Col Woodham on the last chopper with the dead on May 26$^{th}$ when he found out I had less than two weeks before discharge. I was home in the bay area with my family on June 4$^{th}$ with my discharge papers. Thirty years later, I had a heartbreaking phone call from Cpl Chapman's daughter. His wife was pregnant when he left for Vietnam and he believed she was having a son. She had twin girls instead! The first thing she asked was, "Is he really dead?" I told her how he died in my arms after he had thrown a grenade at an enemy soldier who was trying to kill me.

At 1520, a torrential downpour halted further advancement. The enemy also broke contact under cover of the rain. They withdrew toward Le Bac (2), which was located southeast of Le Bac (1). An air mission was requested and artillery was fired into this area. Defensive positions were established south of Le Bac (1) and the Battalion prepared to spend the night.

\* \* \*

**CPL ROBERT SIMONSEN - Co I:** I took out a three man Listening Post (LP) that night about 200 meters in front of our lines. We were to warn the others in case of a night attack. Everything was quiet until around 0200 when our LP was hit by grenades. Luckily, we had located our LP in a thick clump of bamboo and all of the shrapnel was stopped. I radioed in and asked for permission to return to our lines since our position was known to the enemy. Permission was granted and, after tossing grenades behind us, we ran all the way back to the CP.

"Grenade!"

* * *

**LT COL TULLIS WOODHAM, JR. - 3/27 BATTALION CO:** Every evening we looked for a CP area where we could spread out our maps and have all the radios set up. We found a large bunker that looked perfect. The Sgt Major and a radio operator went in first to check it out, but they came out a lot faster than they went in. They had seen a cobra which had curled up and was ready to strike. We did not use that bunker that night!

* * *

**L/CPL DALE CAMP - Co I:** We went out on a night patrol and we could hear the NVA countering our every move. We found NVA comm wire all over the place. We also found a bunch of SKS rifles when an underground bunker collapsed.

* * *

**L/CPL HAROLD O'NEAL JR. - Co L:** At 10 that night, I went out on an LP about 300 meters in front of the lines. We set up in a tree line and then heard movement fairly close to us. Our radio didn't work very well so it was hard to call back to the CP. Seven rounds of automatic fire came fairly close to our position but we didn't return any fire since there was only three of us.

Around 0200 artillery started landing very close to our position. I was able to call in and stop this firing. Next we heard a lot of movement all around us. I think they were moving bodies out of the tree line. I told everyone to stay low and keep quiet. Later, I received permission to leave the LP. We moved out fairly fast, but had to keep stopping and hitting the ground every time a pop flare went off. We finally made it back and set in with our company's line.

*   *   *

During the night, three grenades were thrown into Co K positions, slightly wounding one man. The Command Post received approximately twenty rounds of 82mm mortar shells. Artillery was again called in on suspected enemy mortar positions. Two Marines were wounded in this action.

**CPL CHARLES HUCKABY - INTERPRETER Co K:** I was loaned out to one of the platoons that night and stood line duty. I was with L/Cpl (Dale R) Byrd and L/Cpl (Jerry K) Ray. I taught them some Vietnamese while standing our watches. Later, the NVA hit us with about 10 grenades and several mortars and both Bryd and Ray were wounded. Ray, whom we called 'Pony,' had to be evacuated.

*   *   *

**CAPT JOHN ERNEST - Co L CO:** We received one of the fastest and most furious mortar attacks I have ever experienced that night. We took nearly 25 incoming rounds but we were well dug in and only had one casualty.

**CPL MARLIN JACKSON - Co M:** Later that night, Cpl Brettman woke me out of a deep sleep as we were being mortared. Just as I got into a hole, a round landed exactly where I had been sleeping.

**L/CPL TOM FULEKY - H & S:** We were settled in trying to get a little sleep when the red tracers came flying over my face and mortars were being lobbed in at the same time. I remember yelling out "Oh my God! and another scout, L/Cpl Anderson, a Mormon from Salt Lake City, thought I was hit and threw me into a foxhole covering me with his body. I saw a lot of these types of actions in my six months in Vietnam; many unselfish Marines willing to give up their lives to save yours.

<u>27 MAY</u>

It was another hot day in hell. Orders from the 27th Marine Regiment were received indicating that one company from the 1st Battalion would be helilifted into the area and two companies from 3/27 would be taken out. The exchange began at 0938 and was essentially completed at 1435. Co C of 1/27 was brought in while both Co K and Co M were retracted.

**CAPT BLAKE THOMAS - Co M CO:  We were evacuated after having been well shot up. There were only three officers and two staff NCOs left. Mike Company Marines did a fantastic job.**

**CPL MARLIN JACKSON - Co M:  As we were flying back to our base, the helicopter started dropping. I looked at the door gunner and his eyes were as big as saucers. The pilots were moving their hands all over the controls. I got pissed knowing I was going to die now, after having survived hell the last two weeks. The pilots, somehow got the chopper going again and we made it back to Cau Ha.**

Cpl Jackson would be awarded a Silver Star for his actions on Go Noi Island.

**SGT EDWARD BENAVIDEZ - Co M:** In the morning Lima and India companies started sweeping and we brought up the rear. The gooks had fled during the night. We found all kinds of NVA bodies, equipment, weapons, etc. Kilo company was relieved by a company from 1st Battalion, 27th Marines. About 1000 we were relieved by another company from 1st Battalion, 27th Marines. We flew back to our Bn area in choppers. The operation was over for us, for a while anyway. We now had to regroup because we lost a lot of men out there. The rest of the day was spent getting cleaned up. We then got word that we had to send out a squad size patrol tonight. What a blow! We sent out one squad from 2nd platoon. I got drunk with Lozano, Bilberry, Hein, and Bean. Seventy percent of the men who came over in February had been wounded or killed.

\* \* \*

In the meantime, Co I and Co L continued to search Le Bac (1) and at about 1005, elements of Co L captured another NVA. The NVA, however, was severely wounded and died prior to evacuation. A number of weapons, ammunition, documents, rockets and rocket launchers were discovered and evacuated to 27th Regimental Headquarters.

At 1130, the 27th Marines assumed OP CON of the 1st Battalion, 26th Marine Regiment (1/26.) 1/26 was given the mission of operating in the area south of Route 537 to prevent infiltration and escape of enemy forces to and from Go Noi Island. They would remain in the area until 6 June and would have only sporadic enemy contact.

At 1220, Co L discovered five dead NVA, together with large quantities of rice and peanuts. At 1400, Co I found 22 fresh graves. They were uncovered and the remains of recently killed NVA were found wrapped in plastic.

At 1505, a CH-34 helicopter made a forced landing near the Marine's location. A platoon from Co C was dispatched to provide security for the downed chopper and crew. At 1600, the Command Group and two rifle companies commenced moving to a new location and arrived approximately a half an hour later. Preparations for night defensive positions began immediately. Helicopters completed resupply missions and the Co C platoon returned after the downed helicopter was retrieved.

CPL Matthew Raible (Co L) had fought to get out of the company office and into the field. From 18 to 27 May, he performed his tasks admirably as a radio operator. Time and time again, he provided communications under heavy fire and also assisted in the evacuation of casualties. As a result of the oppressive heat and weight of his radio, he became a heat victim on 18 May. Realizing that his unit was short of radio operators, he refused medical evacuation and remained in the field, despite sickness and recurring dizzy spells. For his Allen Brook service, Cpl Raible would be awarded the Navy Commendation Medal.

**CPL MATTHEW RAIBLE - Co L: We were sweeping toward the end of the day before setting into positions for the evening. Captain John Ernest (CO - Co L) wanted to go into the tree line because he thought it would be cooler there. We started digging foxholes in a graveyard. I hit a grave and said there was no way I was going into that hole. We also spotted bamboo viper snakes in the area. Earlier in the day, we were given orders that we didn't have to wear our flak jackets if we didn't want to. It was so hot carrying that radio and everything else that I shit-canned mine right away.**

**We had set in for the evening. We took shifts of four hours on and four hours of sleep. I was on my off time and I just crapped out when a mortar round hit a**

tree and that was it. It was one round and it hit dead square. They must have zeroed in on my radio antenna which I had running up a tree. I thought I had that bloody son-of-a-gun camouflaged enough but they hit it right on the button. The CO's radio reported four serious and two critical. I imagine I was one of the critical and I sort of remember being put in a poncho. The shrapnel hit me in the lower abdomen, left foot, left lung, and two vertebrae of the neck. My injuries left me a quadriplegic. They medivaced me to the nearest base camp and then to the NSA Hospital in Da Nang. At the time they were rushing me down the gangway, my arm fell off of the litter. That's when the Doc said "Can you feel that?" I said "yeah" and then he just gave me a shot. I woke up the next morning or maybe it was the next day.

* * *

**1ST LT BILLY C. STEED - H & S Co:** We continued day in and day out like that. You always got fire and mortar rounds at nighttime and you had to send out combat patrols and OPs. You normally got harassing fire at night. If you did have time to get some rest, it was interrupted. The troops were so tired it took all the supervisory people (platoon commanders, XOs, company commanders and squad leaders) checking the lines every 30 minutes just to ensure that people were awake because they'd been fighting continuously for four or five days. Some of them would actually fall asleep standing up. You just had to continue to go around, but your leaders got less and less sleep, so you took little catnaps during the day. At nighttime you'd sleep a little sitting in a foxhole.

It's a question of knowing what you've got to do, so you've got to reach down and get self discipline, and it's hard to do that. You've got to stay focused because you know people are depending on you; your troops are depending on you to do the right things and your seniors are depending on you to accomplish the mission. It's one of those things that you're trained to do, but nothing like that is easy and it's hard to explain how chaotic it is to people who have never witnessed it. You don't have time to think about yourself, home or your family. When you're in the midst of combat, the only thing you're thinking about is how to accomplish the mission, save your people, getting supporting arms, and suppressing enemy fire. That's all that goes through your mind (which is what should be happening.)

    L/CPL RAY FISHER - Co I: We had walked quite a ways with no enemy contact. It was afternoon when we finally stopped. By this time it was very hot outside. Shortly after we stopped, a rainstorm went through the area and cooled things off. It was only a short-lived relief because the steam and heat returned immediately when the sun came back out. We set up a perimeter around H & S Company with a few tanks inside the perimeter. My fire team was made up of Leonard Yazzie, Philip Wyatt, and Steve Sullivan. While setting up we found some fresh pineapple and enjoyed eating it. Next, Sullivan and I also discovered a spider hole camouflaged inside the perimeter and requested permission to blow it in place. Permission was soon granted, so we both flipped grenades in the hole blowing up a well-concealed NVA hiding inside. I remember getting a grappling hook from either the H & S or from one of the tanks and pulling the blown up body out of the hole.

    Later that evening, while it was still daylight, we saw three NVA coming toward our position. They would disappear in and out of the elephant grass and reappear where the cover was not as dense. They did not see us. At last, we opened fire on them a few hundred yards out. The CO and the FO came up to our position to see what was going on and fired a mission into the area where we saw the NVA. They also walked rounds into the tree line behind the elephant grass. That night I remember a few rounds being fired, but no one suffered any casualties.

## 28 MAY

Orders were received indicating that 1/27 would relieve 3/27 on 28 May and that the two forces were to effect a link-up in the vicinity of Liberty Bridge. As a result, the Battalion moved from its night position at 0805 on the morning of the 28th with Co I and Co C forward with tanks and the Command Group and Co L following in trace.

At 0915, in the vicinity of the small village of Cu Ban (4), Co I made contact with an enemy force entrenched in a tree line. Second Platoon was in a fight for their lives. Tanks were sent in to help bail them out. One tank was quickly knocked out with an RPG round, which also wounded three men, while another tank was blinded.

**LT COL TULLIS WOODHAM, JR. - 3/27 BATTALION CO:** A number of our Marines were from tanks. They were able to move them when the tank crews were injured. Gunnery Sgt Frank Smith, our acting S-2, was a former tank crew chief and he manned one of the disabled tanks during the encounter.

**2ND LT BILL PRISH - Co I:** On the morning of May 28 we were on the move, and 1Lt Parrish who had taken over as I Co CO called me up to 'speak' to three Vietnamese who had appeared in our path. I had gone to High Intensity Language School in Quantico for ten weeks. But, that was two months ago and I had forgotten most of the little I had learned.  After some painful dialogue, I reported to Lt Parrish that they were saying that there were some North Vietnamese in that tree line, which I pointed to.  He said, "Good, that's who we're looking for.  Your platoon has point, get them on line."

There was about 300 yards of open field, flat as a pancake leading to the tree line.  We got on line with Hazelwood's squad spread out on the right with Platoon Guide Sgt Whyte and Givens' squad on the left with Platoon Sgt Allison.  I was in the middle with my radioman, Jim Howard. I remember our machine gun squad, led by Corporal Wilkie, was to the rear.  It was a very hot day.  When we got within about 70 yards a number of shots rang out and we all hit the deck.  The CO radioed and wanted to know what was going on.  Before I could answer, someone radioed back that there were a couple of snipers ahead.  I knew better because over a half dozen shots passed near me and they were close enough that I could tell from the sound and angle that there were more than a couple of snipers.  I radioed back that there were at least four or five snipers ahead.  The order came back, "We're sending up some tanks, get into that tree line!"  We were still hugging the ground.

The sniper rounds were less frequent now, but I couldn't reach my squads on the radio.  Just then Sgt Whyte came running over and slid down by me, "What are we going to do Lieutenant?"  I gave him our orders, told him to give the order to Hazelwood and get back to me.

Three tanks came up, we stood up to get on line, and all hell broke loose!  There was literally a wall of fire.  We hit the deck again, and fired back.  I started firing into the trees because a lot of the incoming rounds came at an angle.  The noise and confusion was enormous, and Howard still couldn't reach anyone on the radio.  Then a tank got hit with a RPG.  Before I knew it the tanks were pulling back, leaving us there on the deck in a real mess. I think they thought we were all dead. Every time Howard or I moved, rounds went over our heads or peppered the ground around us. I thought he was hit several times, but he kept raising his head trying to establish radio contact with our squads. Finally, we crawled back at least 100 yards until we fell into a bomb crater. God, it was hot!

The CO radioed and wanted to know about casualties. I told him there were some, but I didn't know how many. He said, "I'm sending back the tanks, go find out." I picked Wilkie, Leffew and Martinez and made them volunteers to go forward with me. They weren't happy. I just knew we were going to die so I told them to forget their rifles (no sense arming the NVA,) and to just bring water for the wounded. Well, we went forward next to, but mostly behind the tanks. I was on the TI (tank intercom) phone, but couldn't get a word in. Those tankers were talking to one another and were excited/scared as hell. They put out such a volume of fire, machine gun and cannon, that I don't recall taking even one incoming round. My group of 'volunteers' didn't find one man even though we got within 40 yards of the tree line. I later learned that Sgt Allison had gotten behind the other tank and retrieved some of our KIAs. The rest were retrieved by another Company after they enveloped and drove the NVA from the tree line.

With the loss of those killed and heatstroke victims, the platoon was down to 14 members again.

2nd Lt Bill Prish was awarded the bronze star for his actions during this engagement.

**L/CPL RAY FISHER - Co I:** We saddled up and began to move out in the direction of where we saw the NVA the night before. My fire team was on point and we crossed a dry riverbed. On the other side, we found bunkers that had not been vacated very long. There was food, some packs, and other equipment left behind. Yazzie picked up a NVA K-Bar that was in one of the bunkers and gave it to me. He told me he already had one. After going through the bunkers, word came down to get on line. We were going to sweep into the tree line in front of us. Our platoon moved out on line. As we walked through the elephant grass my fire team located a communications wire running from the bunkers we had just come from. The wire was running in the direction of the tree line that we were heading for. We were told to pull it up and follow it. Yazzie and Wyatt were on my left with Wyatt in the middle. Sullivan was also close by on the right of me. We had about ten yards or so between us. I had the comm wire in my hand pulling it up as we walked. It was barely covered by the dirt and grass. I could get about thirty yards of it pulled up in front of me at a time. We were then told to advance by fire team rushes. Givens, my squad leader, was far to my left with only three other Marines in that fire team. Hazelwood's squad was to my right but behind a ways. Somewhere behind us was Sgt Whyte, a gun team, and the platoon commander, Lt Prish. Sgt Allison was behind me to my left somewhere behind Givens. As we came out of the elephant grass there was approximately 70 to 100 yards of open clearing to cross to get to the tree line. It was my fire team's turn to advance at that point. When we got about halfway across the open area, the NVA started firing. My helmet was shot off and Yazzie was hit in the chest but was not killed instantly. He kept yelling for Sully to help him but the fire was too intense for anyone to get to him. We were so exposed that none of us could even move. We were stuck out in the field and had no cover at all. Wyatt, Sully, and I opened up and we could see the NVA moving back and forth in

# India Company Pulling Off Go Noi "Island" - 28 May, 1968
## South West of Liberty Bridge - Cu Ban (4) RVN

Bombing Runs

Bunkers

Machine guns

NVA Positions

Machine guns

Machine guns

Machine guns

Open Grassy Field

Tanks Fired Upon by RPG's

India Company Attack

3/27 Battalion Reserves

Locations of Dead Marines
Locations of Live Marines

the tree line. During the next twenty minutes the volume of fire started to increase and during that time, Yazzie went silent. Wyatt was lying directly in front of a machine gun emplacement and the NVA were pouring rounds at him and me. Sully moved forward a little to throw a grenade but after throwing it and hitting the ground I saw an NVA fire an RPG and it exploded on the ground close to Sully's midsection. He looked to me to be killed instantly. Wyatt and myself were still returning fire and I saw at least two NVA fall that Wyatt had shot. I yelled to Wyatt that I was going to try to get the gun emplacement with grenades and told him to cover me, which he did. On my last grenade, Wyatt was up on one knee giving me cover fire but he was hit and killed instantly. We did knock out that gun but I was the lone survivor in my fire team. I could hear fire from behind me but at this point, I could not see anyone alive around me. Things seemed to quiet down for a second and luckily I was able to dig with my bare hands a hole big enough to get my head and shoulders below ground level. I knew that any minute I was going to be hit because they were really zeroed in on me. At different times the NVA tried to come out of the tree line to get equipment off the dead, but fire from the rear of me would turn them back, thank God! I never saw anyone move up on my left where the volume of fire was not so heavy. I never did understand that. Then all hell broke loose on my right, when Hazelwood's first fire team charged the tree line. They were going right for a fortified automatic weapons position. They were on a dead run. It looked like two were hit and two made it into the tree line. Not far behind them, and to the first team's right, the second fire team sprinted into the tree line. They had some casualties, but it was hard for me to see. When Hazelwood's squad hit the tree line, it forced some NVA out of their positions. I still never saw anyone moving up to my left but I knew that the NVA were going to come out and sweep into our unguarded left flank. If they did, I was a goner. After Hazelwood's squad moved up, the fire died down for a while. I could hear guys shooting at random.

Corporal John E. Hazelwood dashed forty yards under enemy fire to the back of the second tank and directed its fire until several NVA gun emplacements were knocked out. Still under fire, Hazelwood ran back to his men and organized a counterattack on the tree line held by the enemy. Through the ensuing battle, he moved from one man to another offering words of encouragement and directed accurate fire at enemy positions until he was mortally wounded. Hazelwood would be awarded a posthumous Silver Star for his courageous actions.

**L/CPL PAUL A. WOODS JR. - Co I:** We knew they were in the tree line and we were ordered to attack in fire team rushes. We ran in there and just got wiped out. They (NVA) were really good with machine guns and RPGs. I wish we had dropped napalm on them first.

**SGT RAY ALLISON - Co I:** Cpl Thomas Mills was killed the same time as Hazelwood. They put us on the line assaulting a tree line. Tom was killed in the initial fire, but I don't know exactly when. When we recovered his body it was swollen because he laid out there pretty much the whole day. Both Hazelwood and Mills had made it fairly close to the tree line before being killed.

L/Cpl Stephen 'Sully' Sullivan was also killed during the tree line assault. We were on line and moving out when they opened up with a barrage of fire. Sully was hit in the abdomen. He was a close friend. He was dead when I got to him. I helped to carry him out right away.

As we started the assault, the infantry was in front of two tanks. As the return fire started, we dropped to the ground and the tanks moved up. I got behind one tank and it took a rocket hit and caught on fire. Another tank came back and one of the tankers jumped from it and onto the burning tank. He managed to back it out of danger. I went back to where there was a big depression in the vegetation and where the tanks and Company Commander were at. The CO told us to go out and retrieve anyone that was injured or dead. I took out a group of people along with a tank. We threw men onto the tank and got most of them out. They then called in the air strikes.

L/CPL RAY FISHER - Co I: At that point I heard tanks coming up from the back of me. They were firing as they advanced toward the tree line. I could count three tanks on line. There were Marines behind the center tank. I could not tell who was behind the tank on the far left. The tank on the right only had Sgt Whyte behind it. Sgt Whyte saw me, and I was then able to relay enemy positions to him. He directed some deadly fire over the phone from the rear of the tank into the tree line. I was still lying in front of the tanks. When they fired, I was lifted off the ground and the blast deafened me. The burnt powder covered me and I could feel the heat from it. The fire at this time was the heaviest. With me in the middle, shots were coming from both the front and the rear. However, the tanks were putting a deadly barrage on the enemy now. From behind one of the bunkers directly in front of me, an NVA stepped out with an RPG, fired it, and hit the tank to my left. The tank caught fire and stopped in its tracks. It knocked the commander out of the top of the gun turret. One or two Marines jumped out of their tanks. They ran across a deadly field of fire to get to the tank that was just hit and started it back up. Sgt

Whyte asked me where Hazelwood's squad was. I told him they were to his right and in the tree line. I pointed right where I had last seen them. The other tanks started to back up. I watched as Sgt Whyte ran in the direction of Hazelwood. I never saw him again. He was killed in front of the tree line. With the tanks breaking contact and the guys backing up with them, I thought for sure they were just regrouping. But they backed out of sight and things got quiet. I could hear some firing from Hazelwood's squad and by this time I was almost out of ammunition myself. At this point, I started to move to my left toward the direction that I had seen someone shooting up the green pencil flares. I was hoping to hook up with them. I moved to that area and I could not find a soul.

It was not too long after the two tanks came up the second time. They appeared to be in the same area where I had been earlier. There was no fire from the tree line and I could see Marines handing bodies upon the tanks. However, I was concerned about the NVA that I had seen earlier still between the tanks and myself so I stayed where I was. I was reluctant to move also because I was running out of ammo. I thought that our guys would make another push and I would be able to hook up with the left-hand unit as they moved up into the tree line. But the tanks backed away toward the dry riverbed and everything became extremely quiet. I knew no one had gotten up to Hazelwood's squad position. I just knew some would be back, but those tanks faded out of earshot. While everything was quiet, I started to move back toward where I had last seen Hazelwood's guys.

Sgt Charles J. Whyte was the platoon guide for the pinned down Marines. He braved the incoming rounds to move from one position to another, also encouraging the Marines and directing their fire. Joining a group in an assault against a tree line, he maintained its momentum by remaining in the forefront of the squad, firing his rifle until he fell mortally wounded. He was awarded the Silver Star for his bravery and selfless devotion to duty.

**CPL RAUL FONSECA - Co I:** Prior to Allen Brook, I had been under Sgt Whyte. His death bothered me for a long time.

**CPL STEVE EASTON - Co I:** We moved into an open field and could see the NVA running around in a tree line. They didn't surprise or ambush us. We knew exactly where they were. I saw their RPG man maneuver and fire off his rockets towards the tanks. Yazzie was killed close to the tanks. We were then told to make a frontal attack, which seemed crazy, but we didn't question the orders. We assaulted by fire teams, leap-frogging, firing and maneuvering. Marines were hit all over but my team didn't stop until we were fairly close to the tree line. Pvt Eli C. Villegas and Pfc William Oster were with me along with another man I can't remember. We were pinned down for three hours. I told everyone to keep their head up and stay alert for the NVA. I knew we were going to die. We were in grass with no other protection. Bullets kept going over our heads. I could see the NVA making probes to try to find us. We stopped shooting so they couldn't pinpoint our location. I kept wondering why the NVA didn't throw grenades into the grass. They would have gotten us for sure.

Bombs and napalm were being dropped in the tree line. They were working the drops closer and closer to our position. I told the others we would wait until they bombed directly in front of us and then we would get up and run. I started seeing several NVA sneaking up closer to our position. I rolled over on my back and tossed several grenades over my head towards the enemy. Finally, a bomb went off next to us and debris flew right over our heads. We got up and started running for our lives. When I stopped, I looked around and I couldn't see anyone. I called out for the others but no one responded. I was out of water and was very thirsty. I planned to find a river and float down it until finding American troops.

Suddenly, I heard gook voices and I thought the NVA were sweeping the grass to finish everyone off. Then I realized the voices were coming from an airplane flying overhead delivering propaganda to the enemy. I waved an air panel at the plane hoping they would see me. It started raining and I was able to collect enough for a drink. At about this time, I made contact again with Oster.

We observed a high spot with green uniformed men walking around. We gambled that they were friendly forces and headed off in their direction. They were Marines, but not from 3/27 (probably 1/27.) They asked if I would lead them back to where we were pinned down and I agreed.

The NVA had stacked our bodies and had set up a cross fire ambush around it. These Marines were good fighters and quickly eliminated the enemy. We found one Marine who had been purposefully shot in the muscles of both arms and then shot in the heart. I finally got out of there. I had been missing in action for over eight hours. I think Villegas also got out, too. It was a hell of a day and I will never forget it.

**L/CPL RAY FISHER - Co I:** I saw a huey gunship fire a Willie Pete rocket into the tree line toward the area of Hazelwood's squad. It was not long after that, that two phantoms showed up. They dropped napalm and it hit toward my right almost directly on Hazelwood's position. I remember the wind it created, pulling everything loose into the blazing fire and feeling the intense heat of the blast. The powerful wind was so strong it felt as though it was dragging me in the direction of the fire. After that, I saw two more Phantoms starting to make a bomb run. I knew at that moment I had to get up and run to my left to get out of the marked area. As I did, a couple of NVA must have been thinking the same thing. We did not have much time to worry about each other because we were running for our lives away from the air strike. With no more than a few seconds the first Phantom shot down the tree line and dropped two 500 pounders. When they hit and went off I swear it blew me six feet into the air. The concussion disoriented me and I thought both eardrums were busted. I remember the huge chunks of the bomb falling and there were pieces of dirt as big as a half of a 55-gallon drum. The dust was so bad that it blanked out the sun. The second strike did about the same thing but it was further away. I remembered being very disoriented. I do not know how long I sat there before I checked myself out and discovered I had only sixteen rounds left in my rifle and that was it. Since no action happened for some time, I figured that no one was coming back for the rest of us left up in or near the tree line. I decided to make a break in the direction that I had last seen and heard the tanks heading. I had to run like hell for a long while. Spotting the tanks again, I finally caught up to the last tank. My memory faded in and out during this time. I also do not know why I did not get shot when I came busting out of the brush alongside the tank. I do remember a couple of Marines pulling me up from the rear of the tank.

**CPL ROBERT SIMONSEN - Co I:** We could hear heavy fighting going on to our front on the other side of a tree line. We were in a column and all of a sudden, a chorus started from the front and continued past us and into the rear. The words "Chaplain up, Chaplain up" were repeated over and over. I never did know if the Battalion Chaplain (Lt M. P. O'Neill) ever got the word and responded. All I knew was that someone was dying in the fight up front.

Second Platoon, Co I, was ordered to withdraw from the battle site at 1140 so that air and artillery could be fired at the enemy positions. However, contact with eleven Marines was somehow lost. Only three of these men were later found alive. The 8 Marines killed from Co I would be the last 3/27 men to die on Phase I Allen Brook. In addition, 2 Marines were wounded and 12 NVA were killed.

**BRUCE BLEY - Co C 1/27:** I remember all to well May 28, 1968 when we were told that there were some MIA's from India, 3/27 at a village called Cu Ban (4). Charlie Co, 1/27 was assigned to locate them.

When we got there, I think we found eight KIA's from India and I know three guys were alive because I helped them on to a tank.

I often think about those three guys and wonder how they are doing today. One of them said that they had to play dead, because Charlie was all around taking gear off the dead.

On June 5th we went back to that same ville for the third time and lost eight KIA's and 17 WIA's from Co C 1/27.

After reorganizing Co I, the Battalion moved along a dry stream bed towards the Song Thu Bong River and then southwest to Liberty Bridge. A link-up with lead elements of the 1st Battalion was made at 1335. Just prior to the link-up, the Command Group received two 60mm mortar rounds resulting in 3 more wounded Marines. The wounded were placed on tanks and evacuated. The column reached Liberty Bridge at about 1400.

**LT COL TULLIS WOODHAM, JR. - 3/27 BATTALION CO:** The battle on the 28th bothered me more than the enemy Commander could have known. At the time, I was only interested in getting everyone off the Island and not to take any more casualties.

One thing that bothered me for a long time was that some of our guys turned up missing. I was ordered to withdraw but I told Col Schwenk I wouldn't leave without getting all of our men out first. I was assured that 1/27 would take care of our men. It would be their number one priority. I was told that we had to leave ASAP so the timing of our withdrawal could be met.

We finally worked our way through and broke contact with the enemy. I believe the NVA Commander knew that other forces (1/27) were approaching towards his rear and that they were in a perilous position. We reached Liberty Bridge and were ferried across the river.

**L/CPL TOM FULEKY - H & S:** Finally we started marching off Go Noi Island and I was totally wiped out. We were struggling along in single file and I remember my poncho liner was dragging on the ground behind me and this tank came along with Capt Anderson's head sticking up through the driver's hatch with a big smile on his face. "Come on Fuleky, get your ass up here." For some reason the guy liked me. The feeling was mutual.

**CAPT JOHN ERNEST - Co L CO:** I had lost nearly 20 pounds on Allen Brook due to the heat and a bad case of dysentery. My company lost 8 KIAs and 24 WIAs in the operation, but I feel that we hurt the enemy far worse than he hurt us.

**CPL ROBERT SIMONSEN - Co I:** As we approached the bridge, Co I was given unbelievable orders. We were to stay on the Island and help 1/27 with security. We were totally pissed off as we saw our 3/27 brothers leave Go Noi without us. We turned around and started moving back inland with 1/27. A downpour of rain began and continued off and on throughout the afternoon.

**SGT ANDREW BOYKO - 81 MORTARS - 1/27:** We left the 3/27 CP by truck and drove to the river. The bridge to Go Noi Island had been destroyed earlier and was still smoking, so we had to be ferried across on barges, ever watchful for the enemy.

I was attached to 81mm Mortars as a demolitions man during this time. The mortarmen had their rounds unpacked from the fiber containers and strapped to their backpacks due to the imminent contact we anticipated. When we hit the Island, a sudden cloudburst of rain that lasted for about 15 minutes drenched us and also soaked the exposed mortar rounds. We continued marching and when the rain stopped I saw several men approaching us from the interior. They were trudging toward us and looked as if they were in shock. The tanks accompanying them were covered with the bodies of dead Marines. I spotted Cpl Eggers, one of my former fire team members, and asked him what had happened. He said "The elephant grass is so thick, the gooks can be three feet away from you and you'd never know they were there." This was all he said as we passed one another.

I suddenly felt chilled and didn't know if it was from the rain or from fear. I fell in behind a tank going toward the interior of the Island, trying to stay warm from the exhaust. The area we were in had been heavily bombed and the terrain was pock-marked with craters so big, you could drive a tank into them, put a man on top of the tank and still not see him.

The column was halted and I was informed there was captured enemy ordnance that needed to be destroyed, along with our own 81mm mortar rounds that had their increments soaked from the rain. I placed all the ordnance in the middle of the road and blew it with the C-4 that I carried.

We continued on till we found what was left of the rest of India Company. Many bodies were wrapped in ponchos. When the chopper came in, I ran to the nearest body, and another short, skinny Marine (Cpl Herrera, Co A, 1/27) ran up with me and we opened the poncho to find a bloated blackened body that appeared to have been lying in the sun for several days. The body was large and too heavy and neither of us felt we could carry him, so we opened the next poncho. The Marine looked like he was asleep. His face was clean, his fists were clenched to his chest and he still had color in his face. We picked up the poncho and ran to the chopper. As we were running across the field, I was kicking the man's head, so on the run I opened the poncho and said "Sorry 'bout that," and continued running and kicking until we threw him on the bird with the rest of the bodies. I never found out who he was.

After the chopper took off, I started to walk away feeling helpless and angry that our guys were getting killed. I remember seeing a dead gook lying on the ground who had caught a round in his face. The back of his head was blown off and I was so mad I wanted to kick him in the head to see how far the rest of his brains would splatter. For a long time I didn't understand why I didn't do it.

\* \* \*

**1ST LT BILLY C. STEED - H & S Co:** I was really impressed with Lt Col Woodham and how he handled the situation on Allen Brook. He made sound tactical decisions, utilized his supporting arms, and he probably saved many, many lives and of course killed and routed the NVA. We were finally relieved of duty there on Go Noi Island and Operation Allen Brook. As we rotated back to our former CP, knowing that the 27th Marines were soon going to deploy back to the states, I requested to go up and fly with the AO section. Lt Col Woodham was gracious enough to let me go a little ahead of time, before the Battalion and the Regiment went home. Some of us who had been back in the States more than a year had to spend the rest of our 13 months in Nam and that was one of the places I wanted to go. It was an area I was trained in and wherever the fighting was going on, that was where you were. You were directly involved in action at all times and you could provide the infantry guys with close-air support, artillery, medivacs and intelligence.

**RICHARD SNELTZER - Engineers attached to 3/27:** I thank the Lord for watching over me while I was on Allen Brook. I still have vivid memories of walking through an area that was completely void of any vegetation or buildings, due to the bombing and artillery fire. I remember seeing an old woman rocking back and forth on a rocking chair where her house used to be. The devastation was horrendous.

**L/CPL RAY FISHER - Co I:** On the morning of May 29$^{th}$ I was told that no one else survived and if they did they were missing in action. I did not know until later how many men we lost or what kind of shape our platoon was in. It was shock to my system because I arrived in Da Nang on May 24$^{th}$. I had been in the country for only five

**days and had been baptized under fire.**

## 29-31 MAY

The three days Co I spent assigned to 1/27 went by swiftly. The rains continued as the Marines, constantly on the move, went out on a never-ending series of sweeps, patrols and ambushes. Finally, on 31 May, Co I was helilifted back to join their 3/27 compatriots. They were met by plenty of cold beer and soft drinks. The Co I totals stood at 36 dead. They were the first company on the Island and the last to leave. They suffered as many losses as the other companies combined.

## PHASE I REMARKS

3rd Battalion, 27th Marine's May battle against the NVA had been a very bloody and costly one. 67 enlisted men and 4 officers had been killed. Another 247 were wounded in action. There were hundreds of heat casualties, but most were returned to the field in just a few days. Known enemy losses were put at two hundred and twenty-five and six were captured. Accurate enemy totals will never be known. Supporting arms probably thoroughly wiped out several enemy concentrations. Whenever possible, the NVA removed and buried their dead. Although Operation Allen Brook would continue for several months, it can be said that the back of the enemy on Go Noi Island had been broken by 3/27 Marines. The Battalion had met a large NVA force for the first time. They had fought very hard and with much courage. They attacked time and time again against superior numbers and fortified positions. They always did their best to rescue trapped Marines and to recover all casualties.

The North Vietnamese Army had proven to be a formidable foe. Time and again they withstood an onslaught of everything the Marines could bring down upon them. They, too, died bravely. Although there was hatred between them, both sides respected each other.

At no time during the operation did the enemy launch any significant ground assault. At night he limited his operations to attacks by fire with mortars, grenades, and harassing fire by automatic weapons. Many of these attacks were utilized to cover his movement. Most of the night probes were probably conducted by local guerrillas rather than NVA personnel.

During the 27th Marine's Regimental control of Allen Brook (17 May-06 June, 1968,) close air support was used extensively. A total of 586 fixed wing sorties were flown which expended 2,628 rockets and 1,584,800 pounds of bombs.

**LT COL TULLIS WOODHAM, JR. - 3/27 BATTALION CO: Capt James Foster was our air officer. I called him 'Birdman.' He was a F-4 Phantom pilot who served with our Battalion. He was the link to all our air support, the various air force missions and controlled the Tactical Air Control Party (TACP.) He was so good, I assigned him as a Company Commander shortly after the first phase of Allen Brook. I changed that assignment before it was effected because I decided it would be misusing my assets.**

In addition to the air power, 660 artillery missions were fired. These missions involved 105mm, 155mm and 8" Howitzers. A total of nearly 17,000 rounds of various artillery ordnance was expended, most of which was high explosive.

3/27 returned to their Cau Ha Base in the sand and started to refill their ranks with new men. They would continue to patrol the rocket belt around Da Nang until receiving the call again. 3/27 would return to Go Noi Island.

## 3. OPERATION ALLEN BROOK
## (PHASE II)

During July, 1968, land clearing operations were underway in the Go Noi area east of the railway line. The on going mission was to provide security for an extensive land clearing operation designed to deny the enemy harbor sites and to disrupt and interdict the enemy lines of communication. Aerial herbicide drop (Trail Dust) missions, demolitions, and extensive use of bulldozers operated by the 1st Engineering Battalion were utilized for the land clearing.

The basic technique to furnish infantry security for the engineers was to first provide long range protection by having a screen of company and platoon sized units positioned 1,500 to 3,000 meters surrounding the engineering unit. Next, a platoon of infantry was placed in a defensive perimeter at a distance of 150 to 200 meters around the clearing operation to discourage snipers. Finally, a third inner screen was established in the immediate vicinity of the bulldozers to provide close in security. The officer in charge of the land clearing security would position himself with the Engineer Officer in charge of the operating equipment to ensure that positive close liaison was established at all times.

The area east of the railway consisted of thickly wooded areas and wide open grassland. The terrain was flat with mostly grass and dried up paddy beds. The land had been used for farming rice and other vegetables.

On 8 July, 3/27 was alerted to make preparations for a deployment back to Go Noi Island to support the land clearing operations.

On 12 and 14 July, visual reconnaissance flights were conducted over the objective area to familiarize key Battalion personnel with the terrain. During both flights, brief stops were made at the 2/27 Field Command Post who had operational control. Lt Col Woodham, the Sergeant Major, S-3, Headquarters Commandant, Company Commanders and selected company officers participated in these over flights.

Prior operation intelligence was gathered from enemy defensive position overlays supplied by III MAF and 1st Marine Division G-2 and from information received from 2/27 during their occupation of the assigned area prior to 3/27's arrival.

No overall estimate on enemy strength was known. Sightings of groups of four to fifteen VC were often observed, but it could not be determined if an organized NVA unit was operating in the area. One captured document revealed that the AK 25 (unknown unit) had occupied the area prior to 3/27's arrival. Most enemy sightings were movements in a north to south direction. There were more booby traps located on the Island than during the May phase of the Allen Brook Operation. This was probably due to the fact that the main enemy was now VC and not NVA. Most enemy contacts were quick probes with the enemy breaking contact almost immediately.

## 16 JULY

**CPL BILL JUNG - Co K: We returned to Cau Ha from a patrol in the early morning hours of 16 July. We received official word that we would be returning to Go Noi Island where Operation Allen Brook was now in its second month. We spent the morning getting our gear ready. We were given the option of leaving our flak jackets behind and most of us did so. We Go Noi veterans remembered well the heat in May and the benefits outweighed any wounds the jackets might prevent.**

At 0730, 3/27 commenced a helilift from their Cau Ha base to the 2/27 field command post. The order of movement was Co I, Co K, Command Group B, Co L, Command Group A, and Co M. As the helicopters took off, sporadic small arms enemy fire was received. Suppressive

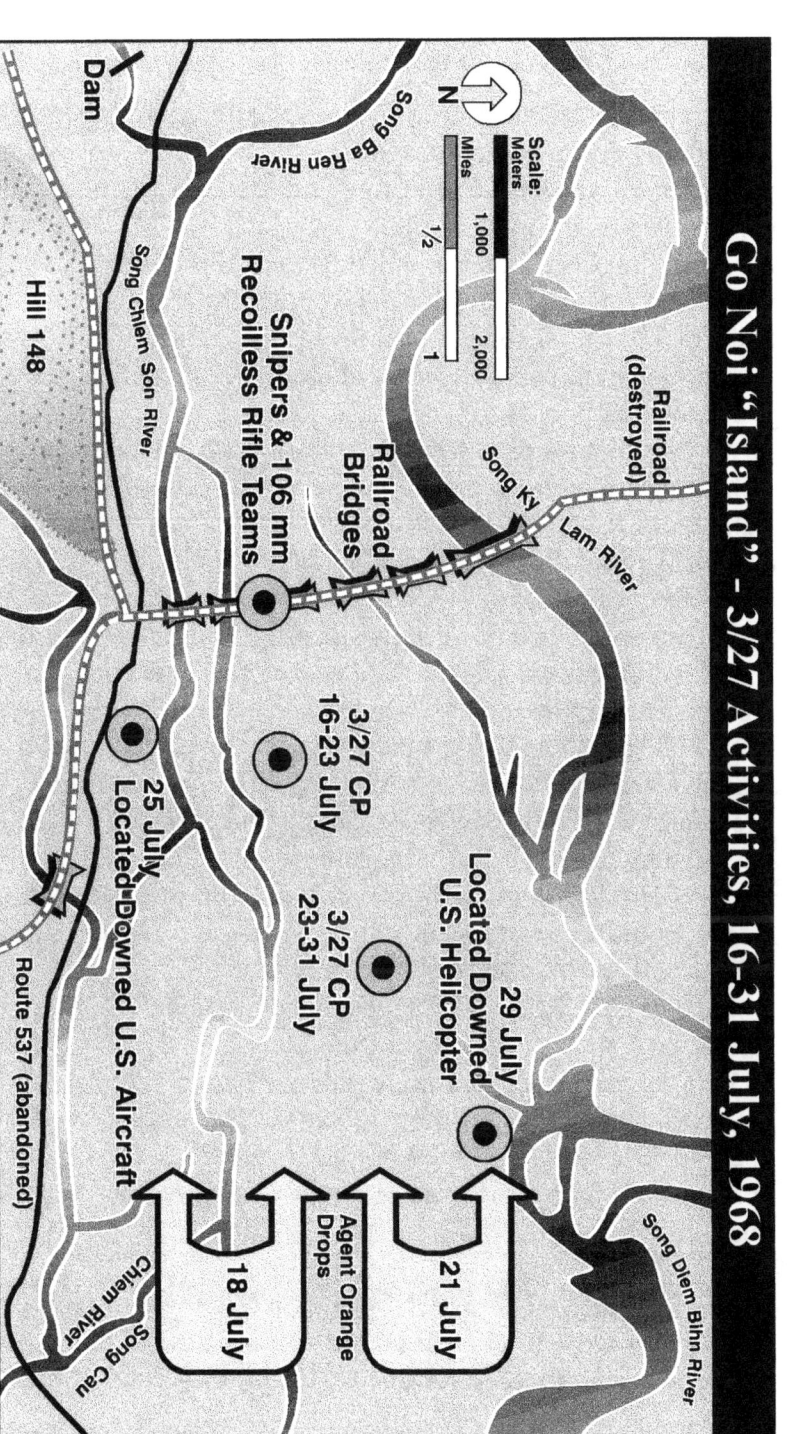

fires were directed at suspected sniper positions by both escort aircraft and personnel in bunkers around the base's sand berm perimeter. By 1145, the majority of the Battalion's forces had completed their movement. At 1200, 3/27 assumed responsibility once more for Allen Brook. 680 Marines, along with 16,000 pounds of equipment, were transported during the helilift. The initial combat load for the Battalion's troops was a light marching pack with a basic load of ammunition. Flak jackets were optional.

    Simultaneous with the Battalion's helilift, a detachment from H&S Co, under the control of Major E. T. Fitzgerald, the Battalion Executive Officer, arrived at Liberty Bridge to establish a rear Fire Support Control Center (FSCC.) The detachment consisted of FSCC personnel, a section of the H&S Security Platoon and two sections of 81mm Mortars. Liberty Bridge was located approximately 11,000 meters to the west of the operational area.

    Throughout 3/27's operational involvement, artillery support would be utilized to a high degree. Prep fires, contact fire missions, night defensive fires and harassment and interdiction ( H & I) fires were utilized on a daily basis.

    From 16 to 22 July, the majority of the Battalion's forces would be positioned within range of F Battery, 2nd Battalion, 13th Marines' 105mm Howitzers.

    On 23 July, most of the Battalion would be displaced further east and out of range of the 105s. At this point two 155mm towed howitzers were attached to F Battery and provided long range artillery support. During 3/27's July operational control, a total of 3,907 rounds of combined 105mm, 155mm, 8-inch and 175mm were fired in support missions.

**CPL MARLIN JACKSON - Co M: I was not happy to be going back to Go Noi Island. In my gut, I had a bad feeling. I remembered all of the dead and wounded faces**

that I had seen. As we landed there was a lot of dust from the land clearing operation. It looked like a big housing project was going on.

From an artillery standpoint, with the land clearing going on, we could see the enemy and where our rounds were landing. We could now get a physical body count of our work.

**HM3 DAVID 'DOC' WATSON - Co M:** In mid-July, I was told to go to the BAS (Battalion Aid Station) and draw extra battle dressings, morphine and plasma. We were going on Allen Brook II!

As we approached Go Noi Island, all of the stories of hot LZs that I had heard from the old salts came back to me. Strangely enough, I don't remember if the LZ was hot or not. I just got the heck away from the chopper and waited for the rest of the guys.

\* \* \*

**CPL BILL JUNG - Co K:** Soon we were circling over the Island and below I could see the ravaged land pocketed with craters of all sizes. The choppers landed in a sea of dust. As soon as we ran off, the men from 2/27 who we were relieving, scrambled aboard and were quickly airborne. There was no doubt that they were happy to leave. We spent the rest of the day and that night on Battalion lines around the engineer's base camp.

Upon arrival in the objective area, Co L assumed security of the land clearing operation. Co L, Co K, and the H&S Security Platoon formed a Battalion perimeter while Co I and Co M established patrol bases.

\* \* \*

**L/CPL LARRY FRYE - Co M:** The first things that struck me were no elephant grass, bulldozers, mud, and very little vegetation.

\* \* \*

**CPL ROBERT SIMONSEN - Co I:** We returned to Go Noi Island in the morning by helicopters. This was my third trip to the Island and this time I was a squad leader. I was now responsible for the lives of eight others, none of whom had been to Go Noi before. I saw Marty Nowak (2/27,) an old friend from Camp Pendleton. We talked for a while before his unit departed. My squad was sent out on an afternoon patrol to scout out the area and to look at a potential site for a future Battalion CP. We headed east and along the way we passed a dead NVA who had been rotting for several days. The smell was awful. The dead had a unique smell and we could always tell when we were close to one. My point man was Pfc Dewayne Williams. He had a great sense of direction, even at night. He would later receive a Medal of Honor after 3/27 rotated back to the States. He jumped on a grenade and was killed, saving three others from injury. We came to a small hooch with an old Mama San by herself. We checked out the hooch and continued on our patrol, now heading south towards a river. The patrol was uneventful except we did find some Vietnamese documents which, upon returning to our base, I handed over to the Company CO. He asked several questions about the terrain we had traveled and then dismissed me.

\* \* \*

**HM3 DAVID 'DOC' WATSON - Co M:** While patrolling, I stubbed my foot on something and bent over to see what it was. It was a Foo Dog from some shrine. I picked it up, cleaned it and put it in my pack. Even though it was only 2 or 3 pounds, by the end of the operation it seemed to weigh 30 pounds. I still have it.

## 17 JULY

**HM3 DAVID 'DOC' WATSON - Co M:** While on a patrol, movement was observed in the tree line to our front, too far away for small arms fire. The Lieutenant called in artillery, but the rounds were short. This was the first really intensive incoming I had experienced. I hit the deck and shut my eyes. I then heard someone scream and I crawled over to him. He had a penetrating shrapnel wound above his right leg. As I was bandaging him, we heard another salvo coming and we hit the deck again. The same Marine received a similar wound on his other hip. I received two small pieces of shrapnel in my left upper arm. He was medivaced and I never heard what happened to him.

\* \* \*

**CPL BILL JUNG - Co K:** After an early morning sweep and patrol, we returned to our lines and rested in our foxholes. The engineers were blasting nearby, destroying a tree line to our front. Sometimes they blew a few hundred pounds of explosives all at once. The earth shook and debris and dust flew everywhere. No one could rest in that mess, but at least with the tree line gone, the NVA would have a harder time sneaking up on us.

\* \* \*

**PFC DAVID BURNS - Co L:** We moved north

from the OP site at the railway trestle. It was my first time on point and kind of scary. Artillery shells landed to the west of us as we walked and pieces of shrapnel whizzed by our heads.

* * *

**LT COL TULLIS WOODHAM, JR. - 3/27 BATTALION CO:** Lt Billy C. Steed was an excellent officer. At one time or another, he was XO in three different Companies. He was someone I could count on. During this phase of Allen Brook he was flying as an aerial observer. His call sign was Cowpoke One Zero. It was great to hear his southern drawl on the radio flying over us on Go Noi.

**1ST LT BILLY C. STEED - Aerial Observer:** Every time I flew I always checked in with 3/27 to make sure they didn't need anything or, if they did, to help them out. It was always rewarding to me to be able to help the old infantry guys out and especially the ones that I had fond memories of in the 3rd Battalion, 27th Marines.

## 18 JULY

At 0515 on 18 July, the Battalion Command Group, Co K and Co L headed off in a northerly direction. At about 0700, when all units except 1st Platoon, Co L were north of the 540 grid, Air Force elements made an herbicide run (Agent Orange) between the 52 and 54 grid lines.

**CPL MARLIN JACKSON - Co M:** We thought the Agent Orange drops were great. Anything to take away the enemies cover was a plus. Little did we know the long term effects of this herbicide.

**CPL BILL JUNG - Co K:** We headed off in a northerly direction at 0500. We were moving off at a rapid pace and didn't know why. The Battalion's Sergeant Major (Sgt Major R. F. Snyder) was yelling at us to get our asses in gear. All of a sudden we looked back and saw Air Force C-123s flying at treetop level over our vacated area, spraying defoliant.

After the herbicide run, the Battalion's units returned to its established positions and conducted normal daylight activities.

\* \* \*

**CPL BILL JUNG - Co K:** Later in the afternoon I took a patrol out. We had a sniper team along with us, and dropped them off at 1,000 meters out. We continued northeast, constantly looking for the hidden gooks we knew were holed up close by. We reached Ky-Lam Nam on the south bank of the Song Ky Lam. As we followed the river, Indian (Pvt Danny Welch) suddenly swung to his right and began firing, hollering that he had seen three or four gooks and downed two. We turned to the east and began quickly sweeping ahead. We wanted those gooks that went down. Indian saw one crawl into a bunker. Suddenly there was an explosion and screaming to my right. Virgil, a new man, had tripped a booby trapped 60mm mortar round. Pfc James Blondi, my friend and radio operator, had gone down with the blast, too. Both were seriously wounded and an emergency medivac was immediately called in. I located an LZ and was soon talking to the chopper pilot. It was getting late after the medivac, so we headed back towards the bridge. We finally rejoined our friends at the bridge minus two men, a lot of ammo, and sweat.

Evening positions were secured with Co L, Co K and the Command Group forming a perimeter.

The Battalion perimeter received 10 rounds of 82mm mortar fire at 2130, with no resulting casualties. At 2100, just prior to this incident, a Co I squad patrol received numerous incoming grenades. Artillery and flare ships were called and a relief platoon was dispatched.

<u>19 JULY</u>

During the morning of 19 July, Co I, Co K, and Co M conducted offensive operations in their assigned zones of responsibilities.

**CPL MARLIN JACKSON - Co M: I was carrying the radio as we came up over a rise and saw Mike Company sweeping thru a paddy in front of us. I carried my handset attached to my helmet so I could monitor all radio traffic. I heard a mortar mission for a tree line to our front but the coordinates just didn't seem right to me. I told Lt Williamson and he confirmed that the mission was being called in right on top of our forward elements. We started yelling incoming but it was too late. WP and HE rounds landed, wounding several Marines.**

\* \* \*

**CPL ROBERT SIMONSEN - Co I: We went out on a company size sweep and about midday, my squad was dropped off in a clump of trees to make sure no one was trailing us. We stayed put for about three or four hours when we were told to rejoin the company.**

**Along the way we saw a spotter plane flying over head and we waved to the pilot. He must have thought we were NVA because he shot off a WP round about 25 yards**

from our position. My squad all panicked because they knew artillery rounds or bombs would soon be following. I yelled for a radioman and called in right away. I'm sure they could hear the tension in my voice as I tried to abort any firing mission that had been called in. Everything worked out OK and we were able to join our unit just before dusk.

## 20 JULY

On 20 July, the rifle companies conducted sweeps and patrols in assigned areas of responsibility. Co K took over the security of the land clearing operations and provided one platoon to permanently out post the railroad trestle. This platoon provided protection for both the sniper team and the 106 Recoilless Rifle Team.

**CPL BILL JUNG - Co K:** We were acting as security for the bulldozers. I felt my squad by now was a well disciplined and good team. At one point, the CO of Headquarters Company came over and praised us as being one of the best rifle squads that he had seen. The heat bore down unmercifully. As we guarded the perimeter, dust from the dozers settled on sweaty skin and added to our general filth. All of us had a smell comparable to our dirty appearance. When fresh water ran out, we went to the bomb craters or old wells for more.

*  *  *

**CPL ROBERT SIMONSEN - Co I:** We came into a deserted village with my squad leading the way. We found several bags of rice in a bunker. What was unbelievable was that stamped on the bags were the words 'Donated by the United States of America.' We also found a new Mickey Mouse T-shirt in the bunker. We torched the village and continued on our way.

## 21 JULY

A second Trail Dust mission was scheduled on 21 July at 0715. In preparation for the herbicide run, the Battalion consolidated its perimeter and cleared the area between 53 and 55 grid lines. Co I returned to the Battalion CP at 0645 to clear the Trail Dust operational area. At 0730, a squad observation post from 2nd Platoon, Co K spotted twenty to thirty VC moving south. An artillery mission was called in, but clearance was denied due to the Trail Dust mission. At 0730 an unknown type of explosion occurred within the Battalion perimeter causing five wounded Marines.

**L/CPL MICHAEL J. LITTLE - Co L:** I was hit by shrapnel in both of my legs and my collar bone was broken. This was my second Purple Heart and I would be evacuated to Yokosuka, Japan.

Investigation revealed that a CBU device from the Trail Dust had apparently been accidently dropped into the perimeter.

\* \* \*

**HM3 DAVID 'DOC' WATSON - Co M:** While on a patrol, one of the Marines found some buried urns containing rice, uniforms, documents and a bunch of piasters (Vietnamese money.) As we were trying to figure out what to do with the money (I was making about $135 a month) we realized that it was old and out of circulation. It was worthless. We sent the documents to the rear and destroyed the rest.

* * *

Evening activities were established with Co K and Co L in the CP. The other companies set in for the night in their own patrol bases. During twilight hours, observation posts (OPs) along the southern boundary of 3/27's area of responsibility observed fifteen to eighteen VC in three separate sightings. Artillery and small arms were fired but the river barrier precluded a physical search of the area.

* * *

**CPL MARLIN JACKSON - Co M:** That afternoon, Brettman volunteered me for a night ambush. This was a running joke we had with each other. We patrolled to our designated coordinates and set up in high grass. There was a tree line off to one side. Later in the evening we saw lights and heard voices and clanging metal over the tree line. We called in a fire mission but canceled it because the lights started moving thru the tree line and headed right for us. We knew we were vastly outnumbered so we just sat tight and hoped no one would see us. It was very eerie having gooks all around us as we sat there in the grass.

* * *

**HM3 DAVID 'DOC' WATSON - Co M:** That night it started raining. The only thing dry I had was the top inside of my helmet and the inside of my medical kit. I tried to take a rain shower to get my filthy clothes and body clean. I was then clean, wet and cold. By the next afternoon, I was wet, muddy, wet, miserable, wet, hungry, and wet. Everyone started getting immersion foot and jungle rot. The only decent memory I have of that rain was sitting under a poncho shelter drinking C-Ration coffee, hot chocolate mix, sugar and creamer mixed together and heated by an acrid fumed heat tablet. Some of the Marines started getting coughs and sniffles and I had nothing to give them.

## 22 JULY

The daylight activities for 22 July consisted of sweeps, patrols, and OPs. Co M's CP received twenty rounds of harassing fire at 0820 from approximately 400 meters. Three separate booby traps killed one and wounded two during the morning hours.
Corporal Frederick Dale Stephenson, Co M, would be the last 3/27 Marine to perish on Go Noi Island.

**CPL MARLIN JACKSON - Co M:** A Marine stepped on a booby trapped artillery round right in front of me. I can still remember the blinding flash.
Later, we were on a patrol and the lead elements had passed thru a tree line, when we heard an explosion. The point man had found an unexploded fire cracker round and had thrown it over his shoulder, not knowing its potential danger. The man behind him picked it up and threw it off into the brush where it exploded. No one was hurt! These fire cracker rounds were relatively new. When dropped from an aircraft, they broke apart and actually bounced on the ground, exploding in the air. They were very effective when catching the enemy in the open. They had us arty guys give a class on the danger of these rounds if they were found unexploded.

\* \* \*

**HM3 DAVID 'DOC' WATSON - Co M:** On all of

our movements with acting platoon sergeant, Sgt Campora, he insisted that we wear flak jackets, zippered up and buttoned. He rode us hard to think, move, think, beware, and think! I asked him why he was such a hard ass 25 hours a day. His reply was, "I hate to lose Marines."

While on patrol, two Marines tripped a white phosphorous booby trap and things got interesting. Quickly I mixed some Copper sulfate solution to neutralize the large pieces and on some of the Marines we put mud packs on the small pieces of phosphorous to cut the air off. As I was getting ready to give the wounded Marines some morphine, a sniper opened up. Fortunately, Pvt Hamilton got him with his M-14 before any damage was done.

\* \* \*

**LT COL TULLIS WOODHAM, JR. - 3/27 BATTALION CO:** One day we started getting artillery fired from north to south over the Island. It was obviously coming from the batteries belonging to the Korean Marines located to the north of Go Noi. I asked that they check their fires because we had ongoing helicopter operations in the area. The Koreans insisted they were not firing missions over us. With that information, I told the Division Fire Support Coordination Center that in as much as the Korean Marines denied responsibility, it must be enemy fire and 3/27 was going to execute counter battery fire. Division must have transmitted our intentions to the Koreans because the shelling mysteriously ceased.

During the afternoon and evening, the sniper team and the 106 Recoilless Rifle (RR) Team engaged fourteen VC on the trestle with small arms fire and 106 RR Beehive and HEAT (High Explosive Anti Tank) resulting in five VC and one NVA killed.

**CPL BILL JUNG - Co K:** It rained most of the day, a welcome break from the heat. Soon we found ourselves not only wet, but very cold. We did take advantage of the rain by stripping down and taking a shower, courtesy of Mother Nature. One would try anything to rid oneself of his own stinky presence.

### 23 JULY

The movement of equipment and supplies to a new CP began at 0645 utilizing engineer otters and organic mules. This new location was further east and out of the range of the 105's. The move continued until 1100 when the Command Group arrived at the new CP. Co I assumed security for the land clearing operation and the OP on railroad trestle. Co M moved to the new CP while Co K and Co L moved east and north to initiate daylight activities.

**CPL BILL JUNG - Co K:** Kilo left the Battalion area in the morning and stuck out on our own. Captain Joel Parks picked my squad to take the point. We entered an area that the dozers hadn't reached yet, but one that still bore the ugly face of desolation. The company perimeter for the evening was set up in an over grown grove of destroyed bamboo. We dug fox holes and watched an air show as jets dropped bombs and napalm on suspected enemy areas. During darkness, heavy torrential rains came which would last for two days.

At 1430, a Marine tripped a large surprise firing device within the Co I area, injuring four men. Between 1715 and 2000, the sniper and 106 RR teams on the trestle made four separate sightings totaling 13 VC/NVA. On each occasion both small arms and 106 RR beehive, as well as HEAT rounds, were fired at ranges between 800 and 1,200 meters. The results were eight VC and three NVA killed.

*  *  *

**L/CPL LARRY FRYE - Co M:** I remember once getting juice and ice cream choppered to us by mistake. We loved it. It was like a piece of heaven out there in the boonies.

*  *  *

**CPL ROBERT SIMONSEN - Co I:** We brought our resupplies from the chopper over to the platoon area for distribution. We opened a box and found four or five steaks that were probably destined for some supply sergeant with good connections. Being good Marines we told no one and divided the steaks up. I think everyone in the platoon got one bite, but it sure tasted great!

## 24 JULY

Land clearing operations continued on 24 July during heavy and cold rains.

**CPL BILL JUNG - Co K:** Morning found us soaked. Getting dry was impossible. Then there was the cold. We couldn't believe how cold it was during those rainy days in July. With the rain came mud, which only added to our filth and discomfort. I was so wet that my skin began to ripple and even peel off, sticking to my rifle. I just don't know what was worse. The heat or the rain!

*  *  *

**CPL ROBERT SIMONSEN - Co I:** We were patrolling in squads about 150 meters out from the bulldozers when we spotted a cardboard box in the middle of an open field. We approached cautiously and probed all around the box, finding no apparent traps. Someone finally got the nerve to pick it up and we all opened it. It was a case of new socks, probably dropped by mistake from a resupply helicopter. We couldn't believe it. We were soaking wet from the rain and we hadn't changed socks in one or two weeks. You can't imagine the feeling of dry clean socks on our wet cold feet. We divided the socks up with the platoon. Everyone got one or more pairs.

**CPL MARLIN JACKSON - Co M:** It was raining and cold all day. My skin started sloughing off and my feet were in tremendous pain.

\* \* \*

In the afternoon the sniper and 106RR teams again observed 18 VC in three separate sightings. Eight of the enemy were killed. Units established night positions with Co I and Co M in the Battalion CP. At 1830, the tank and mortar pit positions received ten incoming 82mm mortar rounds. Eleven Marines were wounded and evacuated. The suspected mortar site was taken under fire by 81mm and Marine artillery with unknown results.

**2ND LT BILL PRISH - Co I:** We had battalion perimeter duty and all dug in, pretty deeply. I noticed Sgt Allison had a textbook foxhole, narrow and real deep; mine wasn't textbook. We were milling around just before dusk when all of a sudden we took incoming from mortars. Two or three had already hit before we realized what was happening. I ran for my foxhole and found Sgt Allison in it. I said, "Get out of there!" and he naturally said, "Go find another one lieutenant, someone's in mine!" Well, I never even got down on the ground because it was over almost as soon as it began. Fortunately, at least for me, all the rounds hit the middle or back side of our position.

\* \* \*

**CPL BILL JUNG - Co K:** We went on patrol and the night was black, with the clouds and rain making matters worse. We were to go out 1,200 meters to set up an ambush. Friendly artillery was supposed to have shelled the site a few hours earlier in an attempt to dislodge any enemy troops. We moved through a huge overgrown cemetery and then crept into a jungle of brush and bamboo. It quickly became apparent that we were being surrounded by unseen enemy forces. We could hear them everywhere. We threw a couple of grenades in a suspected area and heard several people running off at a fast pace.

By the time we had traveled 800 meters, I received permission to set up the ambush where we were. Suddenly, the entire world around us began to disintegrate. Explosions filled the night and shrapnel started falling around us. It seemed that the prep fire that was supposed to come in way before our patrol was now coming due to an error. It's a good thing we hadn't traveled all the way to the proposed ambush site or we would have all been killed. As it was, we hugged the ground for dear life. Then it stopped, almost as quickly as it started. Miraculously, no one was wounded. We returned to our lines, still hearing the enemy following us along the way.

<u>25 JULY</u>

Contacts remained light and scattered on 25 July. Squad patrols made sightings of small groups of VC moving on a north/south axis at ranges of 2,000 to 3,000 meters. Co I provided security for the land clearing operation. At 1145, an element from 2nd Platoon, Co L, observed five to ten VC on the northern bank of Song Ky Lam River which was out of the Battalion's area of responsibility. Scout/snipers fired with unknown results. At 1345, a Co I security post on the railroad trestle observed an OV-10A aircraft in flames, shot down south of the Battalion's area.

**CPL RAUL FONSECA - Co I: Our squad was acting as security for the snipers and the 106 team. Earlier in the day, a corpsman was wounded by a booby trapped grenade. He lost his right eye and we medivaced him out. We found several other booby traps and we took care of them. Later on, several NVA were spotted in the hills coming out of a cave. The 106 team loaded up a beehive round and zeroed in on those suckers. You should have seen them go down. Right after that, we saw a spotter plane shot down.**

**LT COL TULLIS WOODHAM, JR. - 3/27 BATTALION CO: I recall when the first OV-10 was shot down in Vietnam. It occurred in our area of Go Noi. The spotter aircraft was probably lower in altitude than he safely should have been because he received a number of rounds through the bottom of the plane, causing it to go down. It landed south of us across the river in 'indian territory.' Division directed relief forces to retrieve the occupants of the OV-10 and to salvage the plane's sophisticated and classified equipment and manuals. I set up 106's at the river bank as a base of fire to suppress enemy fire when our air support made striking runs over the crash site. There was virtually continuous close air**

support for Mike Company as they attempted to carry out the rescue mission. The NVA would shoot at our planes as they pulled out of their runs and we would throw 106 beehive rounds at the NVA to frustrate their efforts. That was about as close to an 'air show' as I'd seen in Vietnam.

After extensive prepping of tree lines leading to the objective area by Marine air and artillery, Co M with a heavy section of tanks crossed the river at 1530. They reached the aircraft at 1645 and found the bodies of the two crew members and recovered small miscellaneous aircraft parts. By 1935, Co M had returned to the operational area and set up for the night. Co I and Co K provided Battalion perimeter security.

**CPL MARLIN JACKSON - Co M:** The cowpoke tipped its wings at us as it passed overhead and crossed over a river. It then swung around and made a low pass over a tree line where it took tracer fire. The plane tried to gain altitude but more rounds poured out of the tree line and soon we saw smoke. The plane crashed right into the trees and we knew the pilots were killed.

Mike Company was told to retrieve the bodies and we first prepped the area with artillery. We forded the river and soon found the plane debris and the two pilots scattered in an area of fifty feet in diameter.

**HM3 DAVID 'DOC' WATSON - Co M:** We left to find a downed observation plane, along with some tanks and amtracks. That was the first time I had seen air support and napalm up close. We found the crew dead and returned them and some personal effects. I kept waiting for a sniper or a NVA unit to open fire, but nothing happened.

<u>26 JULY</u>

The rifle companies conducted daylight activities with little contact.

**CPL BILL JUNG - Co K:** They let us sleep late that morning. When we did crawl out of our trenches, a clear sky met us instead of rain. There was extra water around so we turned our helmets into sinks and shaved a few days whiskers off, after being told to, of course! Shaving was never popular in the field. We then started cleaning our weapons.

\* \* \*

**L/CPL LARRY FRYE - Co M:** I remember sitting down eating C-Rations when an old Mama San came out of the bush in a daze. The whole side of her head was an open wound with maggots crawling all over. I puked right there. It was the most revolting sight I had ever seen. She had been injured by our artillery. I also remember being in a small deserted village and all of a sudden getting hit with heavy machine gun fire and a bunch of AK-47s for about ten minutes. Then there was a Co M Marine who was shot in the ass sitting in the window of a hooch. He was pissed and we all laughed at his wound.

\* \* \*

**CPL BILL JUNG - Co K:** As our platoon walked along the east bank of a stagnant pond, gooks on the opposite bank opened up on our column with small arms fire. We quickly returned the fire and soon a sharp fight was in progress. I observed one of my new men sitting upright in the open grass, just looking at the gooks without firing. I yelled at him and he soon snapped out of it and joined in on the fight. Soon, mortars came crashing down on the commie positions and the fighting ceased.

* * *

**HM3 DAVID 'DOC' WATSON - Co M:** The other corpsman, Smitty and myself were holding sick call; treating jungle sores, cuts and severe cases of athletes foot. I hated the leeches the most. To this day I don't like to fish with black plastic worms.

After we finished, we went on a sweep thru a deserted village and some Marines wanted to eat some of the wild bananas that they had found. Most of them ended up with diarrhea.

We took some heavy machine gun fire for a few minutes and I kept waiting to hear my name called. Corporal Dupard got the machine gun with his M-79.

Later, we were on Battalion security perimeter duty. Patrols were constantly going out. Some of the Marines were so exhausted from the heat and continuous patrolling that I didn't see how they could function. They seemed to draw on deep down reserves to go out one more time. Fortunately, very few were hurt, so Smitty and I had very little to do most of the time.

* * *

Night defensive positions were established with Co I and Co M at the Battalion CP. Co K and Co L set up patrol bases in the outlying areas.

## 27 JULY

On 27 July, the companies conducted normal daylight operations with very little contact. Co K's night defensive position received twenty rounds of automatic weapons fire from a range of 600 meters. An artillery mission was called and assigned to a Naval gunfire support ship.

**CPL BILL JUNG - Co K:** As the sun began to set on another day of war, heavy enemy fire suddenly began zipping in on us. Soon the company was firing back with rifles and machine guns. Contact was broken quickly and all was soon quiet. Then all of a sudden cannon shells began raining on us. They screamed and screeched, coming in fast and low. We dove for cover as the shells exploded around us. It was over in a matter of seconds and the familiar cry of "corpsman up" was heard. Three men were wounded from the 2nd Platoon. It had been an accidental shelling from a U.S. Navy ship off the coast. I was madder than hell.

**HM DICK SCHMIDT - Co M Corpsman:** During operation Allen Brook we were 'relaxing' in a creekbed or wide ditch. Some were wearing flak jackets and some weren't. We were cleaning our weapons, eating some c-rats, and just catching our collective breath. Someone called in some arty on our own position. A S/Sgt named Feliciano from 3rd plt, M Co dove across two Marines that weren't in their flak jackets and stayed there until the 'friendly fire' stopped. I would like to locate that S/Sgt and thank him and get his heroism recognized. I can't name any witnesses to verify my statement but I would swear to that fact on a stack of Bibles.

<u>28 JULY</u>

The rifle companies completed night time activities at dawn on 28 July with only Co K receiving one light probe during the evening. Daylight activities again consisted of platoon patrols, squad ambushes and OPs. Night defensive positions were established with Co I and Co M providing Battalion perimeter security. Co K and Co L established patrol bases.

\* \* \*

**L/CPL STEVE EASTON - Co I:** I sent out an LP about two hundred meters in front of the CP. During the evening, the LP called back that they had movement to their front and asked permission to open fire. The OK to shoot was given and we heard all kinds of firing for the next few minutes. The LP then called back and asked for more ammo, so myself and another guy volunteered to take it to them. We went out, dropped off the ammo and returned.

The next day, everyone wanted to know, what the results were. We searched the area and found no bodies, blood trails, or anything. Then someone found pig tracks. The entire fire fight had been against a couple of pigs!

\* \* \*

**S/SGT SHELBY MONK - Co I:** The lead squad heard something at the edge of a village and the platoon commander told them to check it out. They moved up to and old building and saw some kind of movement. Receiving permission, the Marines opened up with rifle fire and then began a search for bodies. They felt something wet and sticky and called back to the company CO reporting that they had wounded someone. Checking it out further, they found to their great surprise that the building was a pig pen and that they had killed several 'VC' pigs.

<u>29 JULY</u>

The Battalion's scout section discovered the fuselage of a crashed CH-46A helicopter. The bodies and miscellaneous 782 equipment were found in the area. At 1600, a helicopter extracted the bodies.

**CPL BILL JUNG - Co K: The company's new position was around a deep watering hole. Not far away one could see the twisted wreckage of a CH-46 Marine Sea Knight helicopter sticking out of some tall grass. It was found by Mike Company and had been missing for nearly a half a year. We heard it had been shot down with a load of wounded aboard. Only bones were found of the missing Marines.**

**CPL MARLIN JACKSON - Co M: It felt strange as we evacuated these bodies. I was sorry for the men but at least now, their families could rest at peace better.**

Night positions were established with Co I and Co M providing Battalion perimeter security. Co K and Co L set up patrol bases for the evening hours. Co I started making preparations to leave the Island.

<u>30 JULY</u>

At 0900 on 30 July, Co I commenced a helilift from the Allen Brook area back to their Cau Ha Base. The remaining three rifle companies conducted daylight activities with Co L sweeping from its patrol base to the Battalion CP.

The advance party from 2nd Battalion, 7th Marines, arrived at 1430 and departed at 1515 after a short liaison visit. A battery of howitzers arrived and were positioned within the Battalion perimeter. The Battalion made preparations for relief on the 31st. Night positions were established with Co L and Co M at the Battalion CP and Co K at a patrol base.

## 31 JULY

At daybreak on the 31st of July, Co K began an offensive sweep from its night patrol base to the Battalion perimeter. All companies and the Command Group began preparations for their relief. The 2/7 Command Group was helilifted into the CP area at 0900. At 1000, a helilift began utilizing CH-53 and CH-46 aircraft to return the three remaining rifle companies and the Command Group back to its base headquarters. At 1200, the 3/27 FSCC at Liberty Bridge terminated its operation and returned to the CP by trucks. The Battalion Command Group departed on the last helicopter at 1315, having turned over operational control of the land-clearing operation to 2/7. It was ironic that 3/27's first contact with Go Noi Island and Operation Allen Brook was with Co G, 2/7 back on 14 May.

**CPL BILL JUNG - Co K: Soon our turn came to board. We ran through the dust kicked up by a big Sea Stallion helicopter. A few seconds later, we were flying away from and saying good-bye to Go Noi Island, its heat, its endless wreckage and all the bad memories it created. We got the night off back at our base. I had two hot showers, a hot meal and plenty of cold beer.**

**CPL MARLIN JACKSON - Co M: When we pulled off the Island, it looked like a big parking lot from the sky.**

**LT COL TULLIS WOODHAM, JR. - 3/27 BATTALION CO: When we left the Island after the land clearing operations, I don't believe a sparrow could have flown across it without packing a lunch. We cleared so much of the area there was not any place for the enemy to stage troops, supplies or equipment. I have been told, however, by those who followed on after us, that the**

problem arose again and once more it became a NVA/VC stronghold.

## PHASE II REMARKS

**LT COL TULLIS WOODHAM, JR. - 3/27 BATTALION Co:** The field deployment on the second phase of Operation Allen Brook was a most successful and effective operation in support of the land clearing program. Security provided by 3/27 prevented any engineering personnel or equipment casualties. The company and platoon-sized patrol bases, patrols and outposts effectively prevented the enemy from concentrating on an offensive effort.

Significant combat results were obtained from the employment of a 106 Recoilless Rifle along with a sniper team. Once an area was located and found to be an enemy route, the sniper team would fire and spot in conjunction with the 106RR. On several occasions, the sniper would fire first, striking one of the VC. When the enemy would group together to carry off the casualty, the 106RR would fire, inflicting multiple kills.

**CAPT E. MILES KEEFE, JR. - 3/27 S-3:** I came up with the idea of placing the 106 Recoilless Rifle with the sniper team. You should have seen how excited everyone was when we had our first success.

One Marine was killed and another 41 were wounded in action during this phase of Allen Brook. The enemy lost 35 VC and 10 NVA for a total of 45 killed.

It is significant to again mention that 3/27 Marines were exposed at least twice to Agent Orange drops. Although they moved out during the actual drops, the Marines went right back into the affected areas.

The land clearing operations would continue under 2/7 and Operation Allen Brook would officially cease on 24 August.

# 4. OVERVIEW OF OPERATION ALLEN BROOK

Throughout the two phases of Operation Allen Brook, 3/27 suffered a total of 4 officers and 68 enlisted men killed in action. A total of 282 Marines were wounded and another 123 were listed as non-battle casualties (mostly heat victims.)

The known enemy losses by 3/27 forces were put at 270 NVA/VC. This total does not reflect an additional 146 NVA killed on 16 and 17 May while Co I was assigned to the 7th Marines and was responsible for many of these KIAs.

Through their effective teamwork, aggressive fighting spirit and many acts of individual bravery, the Marines of 3/27 dealt the enemy a severe blow and in doing so, demonstrated valor and professional skill in keeping with the highest traditions of the United States Marine Corps. For this action, 3/27 was awarded the Meritorious Unit Commendation.

The Go Noi Island action was also specifically mentioned in a Presidential Unit Citation given to the First Marine Division (reinforced) for the period between 16 September 1967 to 31 October 1968.

Many acts of valor by 3/27 Allen Brook Marines were rewarded and many were not. The average Marine would simply say he was "just doing my job." There were several Bronze and Silver Stars given out, two Navy Crosses and, of course, Robert Burke's Medal of Honor. Everyone who served on Go Noi Island deserves a medal of some kind, just for existing amongst the heat, blood, sweat and fears that were encountered.

Robert Burke now rests quietly in his home town of Monticello, Illinois. His portrait and Medal of Honor adorns a wall of the county's courthouse. He is buried next to his mother and father. His mother never did recover from the loss of her son. Burke had led his family to believe that he was a mechanic in the rear and not a machine gunner. A peaceful town park is named in his honor. Two Marine Corps buildings, one at Quantico, Virginia, and another at MCRD, San Diego, California, also bear his name.

**CAPT JOHN ERNEST - Co L CO:** Burke's home town was near mine and on a trip back east, I had a friendly visit with his sister, Marilyn. Although I didn't personally know him, I think he exemplifies the best qualities of the guys I knew who actually served in the rifle companies.

**PFC JAMES COLLELA - Co I:** Pfc Robert C. Burke was my best friend. In Vietnam, he taught me how to survive in the jungle. He bandaged me when I was wounded May 17, 1968; the same day he died for you and me. My friend and I were only 18 years old. I never expected to see 19.

When I got married in 1972, for our honeymoon my wife and I traveled to Monticello. She believed it was to meet my best friend.

All the way she kept asking me if my friend would be home when we got there. After we arrived, I went to Robert Burke's grave. I stood there with my new wife, with my life ahead of me and knelt down in prayer to thank Bob for my life.

Those of you who knew Bob are lucky. I was with him over 30 years ago on May 17, 1968. I was his A-gunner/ammo humper. I was his friend. I was with him when he gave his life.

Today, I have three beautiful daughters, who have heard Bob Burke's name all their lives. I can still see Bob's face every time I close my eyes, and remember how lucky I was to know such a selfless and courageous man.

**1ST LT BILLY C. STEED - AERIAL OBSERVER:** Pfc Burke was a motor transport guy. I remember walking over the places where Burke had done his fighting and talking to the people who had observed him and had written statements for him on his Medal of Honor. I also helped Julian Parrish get input into that citation and followed that whole evolution from the time we got out to ensure that the guy got his proper rewards. Pfc Burke was one of the ones that was recognized, but there were a tremendous amount of Marines who just did their job and didn't get recognized. Not that they needed to be recognized, but 3/27 Marines just performed magnificently day in and day out. Most of them knew that they were going to get killed or wounded before they left there, and they still went out and did their job. You never had a break from the fighting. You were always on a patrol or in a defensive position with at least 50% of the people awake every night. It wasn't like Korea or World War II, where you could bring people back and they'd have a place to relax. There was no rear.

You accepted that you may get killed. Unfortunately, it came to the point where you hoped it didn't happen to you, but it was just something you dealt with. It's called mental toughness. You get that from hard training that starts off in recruit training. That's what the main purpose of recruit training is, to teach mental discipline. All your training that you do and the drills you go through are to reinforce those things.

On May 31, 1968, 3/27 held a Battalion Memorial Service in the Cau Ha messhall for their brothers who had fallen during Phase I. The names of all KIAs were read off by the Battalion Chaplain. Hearing a recognized name sent chills down the spines of the listening survivors. As the Marines walked out of the messhall and started back to their company areas, a VC sniper opened up and shot several rounds over the CP. This shocked everyone back into thinking about the present instead of dwelling on the Allen Brook experience.

Operation Allen Brook lasted from 4 May through 24 August, 1968. The operation, which mainly involved the 27th

Marines and the 7th Marines was considered a search and clear mission to neutralize enemy forces and installations which affected the defense of Da Nang. The enemy was totally crushed on Go Noi Island. They lost 1,017 known killed while total Marine casualties were 172 killed and 1,124 wounded. American Generals have argued that forays such as Allen Brook kept the enemy off balance and disrupted his supply system and bases.

The following article was written in the December, 1968 LEATHERNECK magazine by L/Cpl Art Kibat:

> *"An ancient bell that for many years tolled out for Viet Cong and North Vietnamese soldiers has found a new home with the 27th Marines.*
>
> *While on Operation Allen Brook, 1st Lt H.D. Paterson, Jr., found the ancient masterpiece in a pile of rubble.*
>
> *After conferring with his commanding officer, Lt Col A.W. Keller, it was decided the huge brass bell would be evacuated to the battalion base.*
>
> *A Mule, a light-weight hauling vehicle, was used to haul the dragon-studded bell to the landing zone, where a Marine helicopter flew it out.*
>
> *At the battalion area, the Marines decided the bell would make a dandy surprise gift for their Regimental Commander, Col A.G. Schwenk.*
>
> *After studying the battle-scarred bell, Col Schwenk said, "This bell will be hung at the 27th Marines' headquarters at the Margarita area (Camp Pendleton, California) home of the Regiment, in memory of those who gave their lives on Operation Allen Brook."*

The bell now is located in front of the 5th Marines Headquarters, at Camp Pendleton, California.

**L/CPL ROBERT DYER - Co K: While my son was in USMC Officer's Basic School at Quantico, Virginia, I sent him an earlier edition of <u>Every Marine</u>. He told me that some of the experiences involving Operation Allen Brook were utilized in their classroom discussions.**

Operation Allen Brook was followed by Operations Meade River (December, 1968) and Pipestone Canyon (May 1969) in the Go Noi Island area. The enemy seemed to love the Island as a staging and training sanctuary. Time and time again the NVA were wiped out, but always at a severe cost to the Marine lives. It seems as if it were a constant exercise in futility for both sides. For years, blood flowed along the dry river beds, tree lines and elephant grasses of Go Noi Island.

COL A.G. 'Dolph' Schwenk, the former 3/27 Regimental Commander, was the G-3 (operations officer) for the Division during Operation Meade River. He was credited with the major roll in conceiving, planning and executing the Operation. 1,589 enemy NVA were killed, 362 captured and 445 weapons were brought in during the successful encirclement of the Go Noi area during Meade River.

In the April 1991 Vietnam Magazine, former Marine and Secretary of the Navy, James Webb, remembered Go Noi Island as a 'very bad place.'

**LT JAMES WEBB: In May, 1969, my platoon took 3/5 into Go Noi on a night move and was torn up. It was during the kick off for Operation Pipestone Canyon. There was a natural movement for the NVA to come down out of the Que Son Mountains into those villages on the Island. It was covered with chest deep trenches and thick vegetation. There were some big fights on Go Noi Island**

over the years.

By the end of Pipestone Canyon, Go Noi Island's 7,144 acres were once again virtually leveled. Only scattered small shrubs remained standing. From the air it was obvious that it would be impossible for the enemy forces to return unnoticed. Of course, one year earlier after Allen Brook, the same statement was made.

**CPL MARLIN 'JACK' JACKSON - Co M:** I've talked to lots of people over the years, both former Marines and Army Vietnam veterans. Everyone had heard that Go Noi Island was a very bad place. Its reputation as a haven for NVA was well known.

**L/CPL LARRY FRYE - Co M:** I've had that Allen Brook ghost locked up in the closet for a long time. I think I have blocked out most of what really happened.

**SGT JON PAHL - H & S Co:** On the anniversary date of Allen Brook, 1991, it finally caught up with me. I simply broke down and grieved and cried like I was never going to come out of it. After four days, I finally got up and started the long march back. It wasn't just Captain Ralph, but everyone we lost. God bless them all.
A Vet Center counselor, Carl Whaley, brought me back a rubbing and photo of Captain Ralph's name on the Vietnam War Memorial wall. I'll treasure it my whole life.

# PART III
# EXODUS

## 1. LEAVING 3/27

The 27th Marines was sent to Vietnam to counter the Tet emergency situation and was initially scheduled for a three month deployment. This period was soon increased to six months but it was quickly determined that the Marine Corps could not sustain this troop level without calling up reserves or shortening time between additional tours.

The 1st Brigade, 5th Infantry Division was then scheduled to replace the 1st Marines, who in turn would replace the 27th Marines for its departure back to the United States. A delay occurred because the Army maintained it needed a full month of orientation training before it could conduct combat operations. This is especially interesting since the 27th Marines immediately began combat patrols the day after arriving in Vietnam, with over 50% non combat trained Marines by MOS specialty and no training time as a cohesive unit. It wasn't until September that the shifting of forces would finally transpire.

Senior United States officers said they did not regard the 27th Marines departure as a de-escalation of the war but its implications were obvious. Johnson's administration was, at the time, more interested in down-scaling than in winning the war.

The Regiment's strength was now at 5002 men. In its seven months of combat, the unit was credited with killing 2000 enemy soldiers while losing 245 (nearly 175 in 3/27 alone) of its own men killed. Over 2000 purple hearts were awarded (many were for second wounds.)

In late August, the word was passed among the Regiment's three battalions that members who had completed a previous tour were coming home and the Regiment would return its colors to the Fifth Marine Division. Marines on their first tour in Vietnam, who were mostly junior personnel with less than a year in the Corps, were assimilated by remaining Marine units as replacements. Other Marine units took up the combat outposts occupied by the Regiment's battalions.

August was the last full month that 3/27 spent in combat. Mines and booby traps continued to cause the majority of the Battalion's casualties. Sixty-six such devices were discovered and destroyed in place while twenty-seven were detonated by Marines and resulted in injuries. 9 Marines were killed and another 60 were wounded.

**L/CPL CHUCK SPENCER - Co L:** I felt sad, like I was deserting the men, when I received my transfer orders to H&S Co, 3rd Battalion, 1st Marines. The first night the platoon went out without me, they were ambushed. I tried to get Capt Ernest to let me go out and help but he said no. I sat down and cried like a baby, listening to the battle on the radio traffic.

**L/CPL TOM FULEKY - H & S:** Out of the original 15 scout/snipers that we started with in February 1968, I may be the only one that didn't get wounded. Nobody got killed though.

On August 14$^{th}$, I left Vietnam on emergency leave. The flight was on a C-141 just like the trip over except that there was about 80 aluminum caskets aboard. I've often wondered if some were from our great unit, the 27$^{th}$ Marines.

One final thought of my experience. I was extremely proud to be attached to 3/27 and to be a scout/sniper. Although my six months in country was not easy, I loved the people I served with and I wouldn't trade my experience for anything.

**L/CPL CHARLES SWAGERTY - Co M:** As I've grown older, I've become proud of who I was back then. Don't get me wrong. I'm not glad I was there. Like a helluva lot of other Marines, it now seems as though it was another person who did those things. I'll never forget the unbelievably heroic acts of the men I served with there. I've forgotten all the names, but I'll never forget their faces, frozen in my mind's eye at 19 or 20 years old. I learned later that after leaving Mike company, I'd been awarded a Bronze Star with combat 'V' for action on Go Noi. While proud of that, I place very little stock in it. Compared to the men I saw fight and die on that island, my acts pale in comparison. I've always felt that I was tested, however, and to some degree met the challenge. To this day, I feel humbled and proud for having served with those men.

I became a police officer for the City of Fort Worth when I came home. I'm a cop today at a smaller city south of Fort Worth. I've owned and operated a martial arts studio in Fort Worth, Texas for the last 15 years. I'm married, have four wonderful children and a very understanding wife. As is the case with many thousands of combat veterans, she's not my first wife. I hope she's the last. She is the first person I ever talked to about that place, and meeting all those brave Marines at the 30th reunion gave her a firmer understanding of who and why I am. I feel that their pain and sadness offered credibility to the stories she has had to endure.

I don't deny that I still go back to that place more than I should. I wish I didn't. Once was more than enough.

L/CPL LARRY FRYE - Co M: I was transferred to Golf, 2/1 who would take over 3/27's Battalion TAOR. In my heart I was always a member of 3/27 first. When 3/27 went home, they took a bunch of short timers from other units. I heard they had a parade in San Diego, and me and some other guys were still over there. To me, it was the first disappointment I had from stateside. I thought it was all politics and a snow job from Uncle Sam.

I heard 3/27 was the first line unit sent home. I also heard when 3/27 came home that the government said they were winding down the war. That's what we heard over there!
The guys from 2/1 thought that 3/27 had it made. Eventually, they started taking many booby trap casualties and soon gained a respect for their new TAOR. I even heard some of the 2/1 Marines say they wished they were back in their old area.

L/CPL LONNIE MILLER - Co K: When the 27th Marines went home, I was sent to Co C, 1/7. All I could think of was, "You assholes left me!" I was really scared to go to another unit.

PFC WILLIAM PRIETO - Co I: I joined 3/27 after Allen Brook. The Marines in India company took great care in teaching me the ropes. It was quite a different story when I was transferred to 2/1. They put me on point and basically left me alone. I will always fondly remember the days I spent with 3/27.

Bill Prieto would serve heroically with 2/1, earning a bronze star in the Cam Sa area. His medal and a purple heart were awarded 28 years later through the persistence of his wife.

LT COL TULLIS WOODHAM, JR. - 3/27 BATTALION CO: The 2nd Battalion, 1st Marines (2/1) came in to our area to relieve us in late August 1968. They stayed with us for a week or so to learn our roles and missions. The Battalion folded its colors and left in early September.
I was one of those who were reassigned elsewhere upon 3/27's departure for CONUS. My remaining time in Vietnam was served as Deputy G-1 and Staff Secretary III

MAF in Da Nang.

One of my fondest memories was when a group calling themselves 'Woodham's Warriors' visited with me prior to their departure for CONUS and we relived those proud and inspiring experiences shared as Marines of 3/27.

In the group were Captain Blake Thomas, Captain Robert Anderson, Captain George Eubanks (Officer in charge of the interrogation/translation team) and Lieutenant Billy C. Steed. These men were a cross section of a truly professional and dedicated band of Marines within 3/27.

I sincerely believe that 3/27 was one of the finest battalions that the Marine Corps had ever had. I feel particularly proud to have been the commander. Not only to have commanded, but to be the only commander that it had while in Vietnam.

**1ST LT BILLY C. STEED - AERIAL OBSERVER:** Julian Parrish was a Korean vet who had a lot of combat experience. He'd been in Vietnam before and when he got commissioned he was a First Sergeant and had a lot of sound experience. Jim Kent, another one of the company commanders, was just a superb combat leader and Maj Fitzgerald, who was a 3/XO, was a calm individual under fire. He was able to give proper advice to the Battalion commander. They all made a good team and that was probably why the Battalion did so well; you had seasoned combat veterans in some key positions and there was a wealth of knowledge.

I learned from Lt Col Woodham the same principles and traits of leadership I still use today, so I'm thankful that I was able to observe him and be able to do as good a job sometimes as he did.

Lt Lewis B. Puller Jr., son of the Corps legendary hero,

General Louis B. (Chesty) Puller was with Co G, 2/1 and received multiple wounds shortly after the departure of 3/27. He tripped a surprise firing device just east of the CP area on the patrol route towards the Leprosarium.

**SGT BILL JUNG - Co K:** Later in the day the main body of 2/1's troops arrived. Our company's relief was Golf Company. These men were veterans of fighting further north. Our area and it's plentiful supply of mines would be something new to them.

Naturally, we were glad to see them. But with our joy there was also a pang of sympathy for the new arrivals. Their ignorance of the terrain and it's hidden death would mean many casualties for these newcomers. We were told to help them as much as possible by telling them of the countryside and teaching them about the mines and booby traps. We decided to help 2/1 to the fullest, as much as time allowed anyway. It would be more help than we got from 2/3 in February. They made no effort to give us much advise, and all our companies suffered because of it.

Our platoon was to help their Golf Company's 3rd Platoon. In the sandy company street, our NCOs and squad leaders met their lieutenant and NCOs. They had an abundant supply of corporals and sergeants, all they rated, unusual in a Marine platoon in Vietnam. Most, like our '3rd herd,' were way under strength because of casualties.

Their lieutenant was the son of the famous Marine General Chesty Puller, the most decorated man to have ever worn a Marine uniform. Unfortunately, the young lieutenant would step on a mine later in the fall. He'd live, but as a multiple amputee.

Out there in the sandy street we told them as much as we could remember at the moment. Any bit of information was passed on. They listened and asked many questions, all of them very interested because their lives could very well depend on it. This was mostly new to them. There were far less booby traps up north. We left the meeting with the feeling that we had helped the new arrivals, but evidently not enough. From all reports that I heard, 2/1 later suffered many casualties in that hellish area. You can only tell a fellow so much about those damn mines. The rest you learn the hard way, as we did.

    That night several of us went out with this platoon into the bush. Quietly, we again taught them as much as possible. I took one of their squads on an ambush patrol, passing on countless pointers and bits of information. There's no harder or better classroom than no-man's land in the middle of the night.

    Lewis B. Puller, Jr., would later receive a Pulitzer Prize for his book <u>Fortunate Son</u> in 1992 which described his account of the Vietnam War and its aftermath in reassembling his life. In May of 1994, Puller took his life after a reoccurrence of alcoholism and the unraveling of his marriage. At his death, he was in the process of putting together a project to build schools in Vietnam as a living memorial. It was intended to be a reminder that the men who fought in the war were not just victims, but builders and shapers of the future.

*   *   *

    **L/CPL ART RIORDAN - Co L:** I was in the bush until about four days prior to my rotation date. We were under manned. Gunny Francis told me to take some 'snuffies,' fresh from the states and still in their starched utilities, to supply. I was at the point where I didn't want to get to know any more FNGs. These three were full of piss and vinegar and wanted to know when they would get a chance to 'kill some gooks.' I was getting pissed. You can hate the gooks but you had best respect them. I took them to get their jungle 'utes' which pumped them up even more. As I took them to get the rest of their gear we passed a very large pile of helmets, flack jackets and cartridge belts that had belonged to our KIAs and WIAs. Most of this gear was blown to shit; full of holes and dried blood. I stopped, turned towards them and told them, "You are issued one helmet, one flack jacket, a cartridge belt with two canteens and one first aid pack. Try to find a canteen without holes, a full canteen will save your life." Reality hit. They didn't say another word as I took them to get the rest of their gear.

\* \* \*

**CPL ROBERT SIMONSEN - Co I:** My Lieutenant came up to me and asked if I wanted to stay in the grunts or return back to my original MOS (surveying.) If he had asked me prior to Allen Brook, I would have said yes to the grunts. I now knew I had nothing else to prove to myself and that booby trap alley would eventually get me. I decided to finish my tour with an Engineering Unit.

It was strange as I boarded the truck that took me to the 7th Engineers. I couldn't help remembering all the faces that I had left behind during the last seven months. I knew for the first time in a long while that I was going to live and return back to the U.S. I was the only original member left in my platoon when I departed. I was happy to see Bill Jung (Co K) join me on the trucks as we left our Cau Ha base for the last time. I was both happy and sad. It was a very emotional trip as we drove thru our area along the MSR Road and into Da Nang.

Little did I know then, just how greatly these seven months of my life would affect me for my remaining days.

These few months still remain as the most significant experience of my life.

**SGT BILL JUNG - Co K:** On the morning of 28 August, orders came down for all of the first tour men who were to be transferred. We assembled in the sand in front of the company's huts. Besides our personal belongings, we were also taking our weapons and combat gear with us, unusual in a transfer, but fine with me. I didn't want to make my last trip out of Cau Ha without a weapon.

Saying "good-bye" to my old friends and comrades wasn't easy. A few would return with the Regiment. The rest would be sent to other outfits in Vietnam. In the following months several of them would be killed or wounded. I would later read the published casualty lists in the 'Stars and Stripes' and often see the names of old friends. Most of them, like Indian who went to bravo Company of the 7th Marines, would have a fate unknown to me. I always liked to think that they made it home.

As much as leaving pleased me, there was a certain amount of regret in my heart as I walked toward the waiting convoy. I was bidding farewell to a chapter in my life, to a company that was my home, to men who were my brothers.

I found the truck going to the 7th Engineers and I threw my seabag and pack aboard, trying not to think of Doc and all the other many faces, now long gone.

Aboard the vehicle I met up with my old friend, Bob Simonsen, from India Company. Like me, he was going to the 7th Engineers, and also like me, he had come over with the Battalion. He, too, at the end had been a lonely 'original' in his platoon.

The line of trucks started their engines with a roar and pulled out of Cau Ha. I took one last look at the sprawling compound of huts and barbed wire, surrounded by a sea of sand. I'd never see it again. My days as a rifleman were over.

SGT ANDY BOYKO: In September, we heard that the 27th Marines were going home. I had arrived in Vietnam with the 3rd Battalion, then was transferred to the 1st and now I was told that I was going home with the 2nd. After turning in my gear, I was sent to the transit area near Hill 327 to wait for the rest of the 2nd Battalion.

## 2. RETURN TO THE USA

The withdrawal plan called for the returning of the 2nd and 3rd Battalions to Camp Pendleton and again stationing the 1st Battalion on Hawaii. Of the Regiment's 4300 Marines who deployed to Vietnam in February, 740 were returned to the states, 60 returned to Hawaii, and 2000 remained in Vietnam with other units. The remaining 1500 Marines of the Regiment had either returned to the United States for discharge at the end of their enlistments, received humanitarian transfers or had been evacuated as casualties. The Regiment's ranks were also augmented by 300 Marines who had completed combat tours with other units, and were due for normal rotation. This made the withdrawal to appear to be larger than it actually was.

**CPL MARLIN JACKSON - Co M: I left with the 27th Marines on 16 September, 1968. If I ever had to do this again, I'd have to say I couldn't have done it with a better outfit. The men performed professionally, not just on Allen Brook, but for the entire seven months in Nam.**
**I did my best to forget the war. I drank heavily for nearly twenty-five years, finally stopping a few years ago. I often think about the men who died and why I wasn't killed. There probably will never be an answer.**
**When I pass by high schools today and see all of the young men, I often wonder if they, too, could serve in a war like Vietnam. At first I usually say "no way" and then I think about it and realize we were just like them in our youth.**

**SGT ANDY BOYKO: When I got to Okinawa, I was assigned to a company. Being exposed to a shower again, I couldn't get clean enough. I took three hot showers a day!**
**Our daily routine consisted of inspection and reissue of required uniforms, and drilling the rest of the day. The**

drilling was to help retrain us from field Marines to garrison troops so we would be able to march in a parade that was planned for our arrival back in the States.

Every evening, I would shower then go on liberty. A friend and I would order an entire case of beer at the NCO club. After the beer was gone we would go into town to drink more and chase the ladies! This pattern would last for four days while we were on Okinawa.

L/CPL ART RIORDAN - Co L: I was finally leaving the Nam. I had my flight date, my orders and had gone to the Medical Hooch and received my shots. The serum was chilled in a 1930s type refrigerator and was given to me by needle, many needles worth. I was good to go.

Three of my buddies accompanied me by 6x to Da Nang. It was a warm farewell and I had mixed feelings about leaving. Don't get me wrong, I wanted out of there. One guy wanted my helmet, another my flack jacket (an Army type without the plates) and the third wanted a chain that I kept around the pistol grip base of my M-16. Farewells over, I went to a staging area where they went through your sea bag and took what they wanted. Most of my souvenirs, Red Star, NVA cigarette lighter, etc. were taken by Officers under the pretense that they wanted to identify who we were fighting on Go Noi Island. Yeah right!

We stacked our sea bags in a pile on the tarmac. I found a Club and ordered a beer when rockets started hitting the Airfield. I knew where they were being fired from and wondered if our guys 'waxed' any of them.

I remember boarding a Continental Air Lines jet with about six guys from 3/27. We sat together. A 'round-eyed' flight attendant was walking down the aisle spraying a scented bug spray on both sides of the cabin. When she got to our seats she stopped and emptied both cans in our direction. What an ego deflator. I had been convinced that I wasn't getting out of the Nam. Ho Chi Minh was saving me for the grand finale. None of us said much until we were a few hours in the air and out of missile/Mig range. This was the first time that I had relaxed the slightest in months.

We landed in Okinawa and went through a week of what I now call sensitivity training. The do's and don'ts of when we return to the world. What I recall was they wanted us to know that we were returning to a hostile America and if some 'hippies' pissed us off we weren't allowed to kill them. Myself, Bill Hartmann (Cpl with Mike Co) and a few others found a 'hole' in the fence surrounding Camp Smedley Butler and received our own style of sensitivity training. I believe the ville was called Kim Village. I have a lot of fond memories of that place. How we didn't get locked-up that week is luck in itself. One hundred psychologists couldn't do the work that ville did in a few hours. For a grunt Marine all it takes is some beer, women and a few barroom brawls and they are back to normalcy. We got normal quick.

We left Okinawa and landed in Seattle for fuel and then on to L.A. where we went to El Toro for discharge. I was back to being a civilian in a very short time. I stayed on the coast for a week getting my 'shit together' before driving back to N.Y. There I made a quick transformation from a combat grunt to a partying drunk. That lasted a few months before the money ran out and I went back to work. I still lift a drink to us combat Marines. Never to be forgotten!!!

Six commercial jet liners and one Air Force jet transport were used to return the 27th Marine Regiment to San Diego, California. The leading element aboard the jet transport, landed at night on 15 September 1968, at Lindberg

Field. There were no crowds waiting to cheer or military bands to play martial music. None of the returning two tour veterans seemed to notice as they filed stolid faced off the aircraft. They were home from Vietnam, and for the moment, that was all that mattered.

On hand to greet the members of the Regiment was BGen Leo J. Dulacki, commanding general of the Fifth Marine Division, the parent organization of the 27th Marines. Col Adolph G. Schwenk, commanding officer of the returning Regiment, was the first Marine off the aircraft. He had taken the Regiment to Vietnam to begin his first tour there, and was scheduled to return to Vietnam to continue his tour after the Regiment was again installed at Camp Pendleton, the Fifth Marine Division's home base.

3/27 returned with a strength of ten officers and one hundred and fifty-eight enlisted Marines. The bulk of supplies and equipment would arrive by ship during the first week of October. Most of it was either unserviceable or in need of repair due to combat usage.

**CAPT JOHN ERNEST - Co L CO: I am probably one of the few Company Commanders who can say that he left the United States with a unit, served an entire deployment in Vietnam, and returned back to the States, all with the same unit and in the same capacity as Company Commander.**

None of the Marines filing from the aircraft commented audibly on the lack of a welcome-home audience. They knew their aircraft was four hours ahead of its scheduled arrival and that there would be time for a proper homecoming welcome later. The city of San Diego, they had heard, was planning something special for them.

"I gotta make a phone call," one corporal said, looking across the runway in search of a non-existent phone booth.

"Is the club open?" another Marine asked, running his hand across his dry lips and the stubble that had grown on his face during the 18-hour flight from Okinawa.

"Smell that good air!" a sergeant said as he inhaled deeply. "It might have a little of that L.A. (Los Angeles) smog in it, but it sure don't have any Charlies around fouling it up."

And then, the sea stories began to flow as tension eased and the Marines boarded buses for a customs inspection area. The realization of the fact that they were home again began to spread over the Marines and sporadic cheering and a loud chorus of laughter could be heard from the darkened buses.

The rest of the Regiment arrived on the following day (16 September) to be greeted by the Commandant of the Marine Corps, General Leonard F. Chapman, Jr., along with Secretary of the Navy, Paul R. Ignatius and Major General Lowell E. English, Commanding General, Marine Corps Recruit Depot, San Diego.

General Chapman also visited Marines wounded in the Vietnam conflict who were patients at the nearby U.S. Naval Hospital at Balboa, and paid two calls on dependents awaiting the return of Marines at the Reception Center. Mr. Ignatius accompanied Gen Chapman on one visit to the reception center.

The day after the 27th Marines returned, the city of San Diego staged a welcome home parade down Broadway street. It was the first time since the Korean War cease-fire that such a parade had been held in the city.

Marching units, led by the 27th Marines, came from Camp Pendleton and El Toro. Military hardware, such as the HAWK missile and towed howitzers rumbled through the streets, passing thousands of spectators who turned out to welcome the Marines. Overhead, Marine aircraft from El Toro's Third Marine Aircraft Wing flew over the crowds.

During the parade, the main body of the 27th Marines

was halted in front of the reviewing stand where ceremonies to honor the Regiment's dead were held. Col Schwenk relinquished command of the Regiment he had taken to Vietnam to Lt Col Edward L. Meyer, whose task it became to rebuild the Regiment into a unit capable of answering another call for rapid deployment.

**SGT ANDREW BOYKO:** After four days on Okinawa, we were flown to San Diego, California. We stood in some kind of ceremony and were later told there would be entertainment for us, base liberty (Marine Corps Recruiting Depot) and beer.

The next day, we dressed in our clean utilities and were trucked to a park in San Diego to stage for the parade. Before the parade started, we just sat around on the curbs or laid on the grass. The units from the States stood at parade rest while waiting.

We finally formed up and started marching down Broadway. We heard bands playing and people cheering as we continued on the route. Confetti was falling down at us from large buildings on each side of the street. At the review stand, we were halted for a speech. I don't remember what was said.

After the parade, we were trucked back to MCRD. Those of us who were being discharged were put on buses and sent to Camp Pendleton. The others were sent home on leave prior to reporting in to their new duty station.

At Pendleton, we were given a quick medical examination and told if we wanted to get out, we had to sign a release that relieved the military of future medical problems. If we didn't sign, they would keep us for a month or more for in-depth medical examinations. Most of us signed the waivers and headed for home. We were now civilians!

It is ironic that this first unit to return home received a parade given in their honor, while the thousands of Marines who followed them, received nothing. Once the war became unpopular, there were no parades or even handshakes. America wanted to forget the war. Veterans quickly learned not to even mention their Vietnam experience because they would be highly criticized. The men would simply keep their experiences to themselves, with no outlet to express their troubled feelings. Most were able to handle it, however, quite a few to this day have not yet made peace with themselves.

Troubled Marines need to seek help, preferably through veteran organizations and reunion groups.

**SGT BILL JUNG - Co K: In June of 1972, after six years of active duty, I left the Marines and returned to civilian life. During those years I had served in many units, but my favorite will always be Kilo Company, 3/27. The miserable life we led and the enemy we faced aren't fond memories, but the men I served with are. They were good men, real comrades.**

**Our souls were tired in those days. Even now on some occasions when I think back and remember, mine still is.**

In the 'letter of the month' in the April 1994 Leatherneck Magazine, former 3/27 corporal, Tim Davis, relates another important problem:

"I am a Marine corporal, retired, and Viet vet. I had a problem that I felt guilty about for years. It is a thing called 'Survivor's Syndrome.' A lot of Viet vets have it.

I lost both legs above the knee in Vietnam in 1968.

There are some vets, a lot of them my good friends, who feel they didn't do enough in Vietnam because of what happened to me. So I started feeling bad being around them because I always get most of the attention. They all have Purple Hearts, but their wounds are not visible.

I went to the dedication of the Women's Memorial in

November for two reasons. First, to say "thanks" to the people who saved my life and took care of me. Second, to see if my guilt was my fault.

I was sitting with one other wheelchair vet along with five other fellow vets who were able-bodied. Every time a vet came by, they would bend down, hug me and Mark (the other wheelchair vet) and welcome us home. They would not say a word to the other five. I came to the conclusion that the Viet vets are doing it to themselves; it is not me, it is *them*.

While at the memorial, I found my nurse, 'Miss K,' whom I've been trying to find for 25 years. We got a lot of publicity in newspapers and TV.

Watching the vets ignore each other made the experience difficult to enjoy. I am sure that most don't realize they are doing it. We decide that if a guy does not look the part of a Vietnam vet, we don't want to take a chance of welcoming him home.

Wake up, guys. We Viet vets don't have a 'look.' We all don't have that faraway stare; we don't all dress in olive drab with medals. And, we all didn't come back with obvious wounds.

It would be good to acknowledge each other's presence. "Were you in Nam, Brother? Welcome Home," or "Nice to meet you."

If you feel you don't fit in because your scars are not visible, you are wrong. 100 percent wrong. We were there; we did all we could to survive. And that is what we are doing now.

Here's some information so that we know a little more about how we are feeling, so we can take that small step to welcome home a vet who doesn't look like one of those crazy, mixed-up, terminally wounded, borderline whacko Viet vets. *Take the chance!* Extend your hand and say, "Welcome home and thanks."

**CPL DAVE STIER - Co K:** I was not a warrior type. Like many people involved, I ended up in Vietnam by default. However, I did what I had to do. When I saw a reason to do something I followed up with no excuses.

The Marine Corps taught me to accomplish a mission regardless of abilities. Just do it and do it well. Someone said that at least we were well trained. My response is that as for infantry, we were not well-trained at all. The Marine Corps trained us to do what you had to do!

Not being a military type there are a lot of things about military action that I don't comprehend. If I had a choice to do it over, I wish I would have been better informed. The worse part was not knowing. Until I became a squad leader I didn't know where we were most of the time, not even in our own area. On one occasion when everyone but me was hurt and the radio was broke I didn't even know where to go for help. I had to rely on my own sense of direction. I felt like a horse with blinders on. I followed the basic instructions and they weren't always right.

We had some very good leaders and some very bad ones. Looking back I see many occasions where people were killed and/or wounded by stupid NCOs and officers. We all made mistakes but some were blatant! The saying is, 'not everyone in the USMC is a Marine and just because you have rank doesn't make you a leader.' The flip side is that there were many Privates, PFCs, L/CPLs and CPLs who made decisions and carried out tasks that showed extraordinary abilities while considering the men and the mission. I don't know if there were too many worse places to be at where 3/27 Marines fought in Vietnam. I am proud to be with that outfit and what they accomplished. I can gladly embrace my brothers from that time.

**SGT GARY HARLAND - Co I:** For years I had recurring nightmares of either pursuing or being pursued by shadowy figures; some dressed in black, others in green; but all of them armed, dangerous and faceless.

Now that I have revisited Vietnam, I doubt I will ever have those nightmares again because I have met the enemy and having seen his face, I can see he is no longer my enemy.

**L/CPL ART RIORDAN - Co L:** In the Nam, songs conjured up memories of good times with girlfriends, dances, beaches, baseball games or just driving in your car. Generally they remind you of the better times back in the states. Conversely, back home songs can remind you of the Nam. One song in particular is the 'Ticket' by Joe Cocker. That song, in 1968, was sung by every Marine, Soldier, Flyboy and Sailor that was stationed in Southeast Asia. It was a song that depicted our flight date back to the World. We were singing that song the night we got hit by a 500 pound bomb at Anomo Bridge. Since then I cringe and change the station every time a disc jockey plays it.

**CAPT JOHN ERNEST - Co L COMMANDING OFFICER:** I pretty much kept it all to myself as there are few people around who can relate to the life of a rifle company grunt.

## 3. CONCLUDING HISTORY

Lt Colonel R.G. Hunt assumed command of 3/27 upon its return to Camp Margarita and the unit began an extensive personnel and logistics buildup. By November 1968, the Battalion strength had increased seven fold and an extensive training cycle had commenced.

During the 10-12 November, 1968, Marine Corps Birthday Celebration, 3/27 officers visited former members of the Battalion who were wounded in Vietnam and recuperating in local hospitals. Later, on 13 December, 1968, many of these wounded veterans were honored guests at a Battalion field meet.

In February 1969, one company from the Third Battalion Twenty-Seventh Marines aggressed the Twenty-Eighth Marines during its air movement/cold weather training exercise at Fallon, Nevada.

During April 1969 the Battalion conducted a demonstration of combat in built-up areas at Camp Pendleton's Combat Town for the Doctor's Symposium.

In May, Major R.D. Smith became Commanding Officer. The Battalion began 30 days of extensive field training in preparation for its aggressor role against the 13th MEB. On 4 June 1969, the 13th MEB landed over Camp Pendleton's White Beach. At this time, a demonstration was held for the Commandant of the Marine Corps as the Third Battalion, Twenty-Seventh Marines opposed the amphibious landing.

On 29 August 1969, the Third Battalion, Twenty-Seventh Marines was presented the Meritorious Unit Commendation for Operation Allen Brook by Brigadier General Ross T. Dwyer, Commanding General, 5th Marine Division, during a Division parade.

This ceremony entitled all Marines who were assigned to the Battalion from May 17 to May 28, 1968, to wear the Meritorious Unit Citation awarded by the Secretary of the Navy. (Company I Marines were also awarded a 2$^{nd}$ MUC for

May 13-17 while attached to the 7$^{th}$ Marines.)

Few of these Marines were still assigned to the Battalion. Several did make it to the ceremony and sat in the grandstands for a brief reunion.

First Lt Roy J. Casteel (H&S Co) was with the Battalion when it left the Santa Margarita area in 1968 for duty in Vietnam. He survived the bloody fighting in May where the Battalion earned its special distinction. He came back to the United States when the 27th Regimental Colors were returned to Camp Pendleton and he marched in the parade in San Diego.

**1ST LT ROY CASTEEL - H&S Co: I was in charge of a mortar platoon. There was heavy resistance as we attacked a tree line. One man was killed and seven were wounded. It was the worst fighting I've ever been in.**

Two sergeants were also in the grandstands, reminiscing old times.

**S/SGT WILLIAM W. O'HARA - Co K: It was a bad deal. We were fighting against professional troops that were dug in, determined to separate Marine infantrymen from artillery and air support.**

**SGT RICHARD MURRAY - Co M: There were 17 dead and wounded in Co M. I was a squad leader and then took over as supply sergeant when he was killed. Most of the casualties were picked off by small arms fire. This was my third tour in Nam and Allen Brook was as rough as any operation I had been on.**

**1ST LT ROY CASTEEL - H&S Co: Our team did the job. The Marines who cleared the enemy from a remote, unknown Island, will never forget it.**

With the deactivation of certain Fifth Marine Division units, the Third Battalion, Twenty-Seventh Marines began disbanding in September 1969.

The 27th Marine Regiment was deactivated on 15 October 1969, following the Presidential decision to begin withdrawing U.S. forces from Vietnam.

It is clear that the 27th Marines had been the Commandant's ace in the hole, that when there was a special need, a new contingency, or a growing crisis, this Regiment has been taken out of the mothballs and has always risen to the occasion in a spirited and highly professional manner.

And now, the Regiment along with its three battalions, rests. The surviving Vietnam veteran members of the Regiment, however, have been restless for several years. These Marines, especially from the 3rd Battalion, have been meeting in small groups, writing and calling each other and have started bi-annual reunion meetings. It is through these contacts that this book came into being. Before all is forgotten it was decided that an accurate record was needed to keep history intact and to provide an understanding of what these brave men went through.

They were called for in their youth and met the ultimate challenge of their lifetime. They will all be forever affected by the war, yet they will also be proud to claim the title of United States Marines. They had also proved, more than any others before them, that '<u>EVERY MARINE</u> is a basic rifleman.'

# APPENDIX

Every Marine-413

## HONOR ROLL

The following is a near complete list of former 3/27 Marines who perished in Vietnam. Some of these Marines were killed while with another unit or on another tour after 3/27 returned to the United States. Regardless, they will always be honored as 3/27 Veterans. These Marines will never be forgotten by those who survived. Semper Fidelis.

**H&S COMPANY**

| | RANK | BORN | KIA | HOME OF RECORD |
|---|---|---|---|---|
| CRAIG, HARRY LEE | L/CPL | 26 MAY 48 | 18 MAY 68* | ARLINGTON HTS, IL |
| JANKE, THEODORE JR. | SGT | 06 OCT 46 | 19 MAY 68* | SALINA, KS |
| KINYON, RODNEY EDWIN | HN | 09 MAY 48 | 07 JUN 68 | ROSEBURG, CA |
| LEWIS, MICHAEL LEE | CPL | 31 DEC 47 | 15 AUG 69 | FORTWORTH, TX |
| MARTIN, ARTHUR J. | HM3 | 14 OCT 43 | 11 JUNE 69 | MARRERO, LA |
| MYERS, GEORGE L. JR. | HM3 | 09 SEP 42 | 28 JUN 68 | CHICAGO, IL |
| PEREZ, RODOLFO | SGT | 17 AUG 47 | 05 AUG 68 | CORPUS CHRISTI, TX |
| PRITCHETT, GEORGORY GENE | HM3 | 06 FEB 48 | 03 MAY 68 | WALNUT, CA |
| RAHN, DONALD K. | HM3 | 01 JUL 47 | 19 MAY 68* | ERIE, PA |
| ROACH, FRED LEROY JR | L/CPL | 21 OCT 47 | 23 FEB 69 | CONCORD, NC |
| WALKER, JAMES EDWARD | CPL | 05 JAN 48 | 20 SEP 68 | NEW ORLEANS, LA |

**INDIA COMPANY**

| | RANK | BORN | KIA | HOME OF RECORD |
|---|---|---|---|---|
| CUMMINS, LANNY DEE | 1ST LT | 24 OCT 42 | 17 MAY 68* | OROVILLE, CA |
| DAVIDSON, RONALD LEE | 2ND LT | 14 FEB 43 | 5 AUG 68 | HUDSON, OH |
| FIEBELKORN, MARC GUY | 2ND LT | 25 SEP 46 | 17 MAY 68* | PAGOSA SPRINGS, CO |
| RALPH, THOMAS HENRY JR. | CAPT | 23 OCT 40 | 17 MAY 68* | CLIFTON, TX |
| ANDREWS, WILLIAM LARRY | L/CPL | 02 JAN 50 | 26 MAR 70 | MCCOMB, MS |
| BAUER, ROBERT LOUIS | PFC | 23 DEC 42 | 17 MAY 68* | PORT HURON, MI |
| BILLS, LYLE PRESTON | PFC | 20 AUG 48 | 17 MAY 68* | COUNCIL BLUFF, IA |
| BOCANEGRA, FELIX RAMON | L/CPL | 09 AUG 49 | 05 JUN 68 | VENICE, CA |
| BRIDGES, R.B. JR | L/CPL | 17 JUL 48 | 15 JUN 68 | AMERICUS, GA |
| BURKE, ROBERT CHARLES | PFC | 07 NOV 49 | 17 MAY 68* | MONTICELLO, IL |
| COLES, VINCENT SAMSON | PFC | 27 FEB 50 | 16 MAY 68* | NEWARK, NJ |
| CRAFT, EZRA DELANO | PFC | 30 AUG 46 | 28 MAY 68* | BALTIMORE, MD |
| CROOK, THOMAS HIRAM | PVT | 25 JUN 45 | 17 MAY 68* | KANSAS CITY, MO |
| DEEDS, LELAND SAMUEL | PFC | 29 JAN 47 | 13 MAY 68* | NEWTON, MO |
| EDWARDS, DANIEL LYNN | PFC | 01 APR 50 | 10 AUG 68 | CREDO, WV |
| ELDRIDGE, WETZEL LONNIE | PFC | 01 OCT 48 | 28 MAY 68* | URVANA, OH |
| GIBSON, JOHN ARTHUR IV | L/CPL | 06 JUN 47 | 17 MAY 68* | CHICAGO, IL |
| GREEN, ALLEN RUSSELL | L/CPL | 29 JUN 49 | 17 MAY 68* | HANLEY HILLS, MO |
| HAGE, MARK KELLOGG | CPL | 12 JUL 49 | 05 AUG 68 | WYOMING, MI |
| HAWKINS, ALBERT W. | PFC | 01 JAN 41 | 17 MAY 68* | COLUMBUS, OH |
| HAZELWOOD, JOHN E. | CPL | 09 FEB 44 | 28 MAY 68* | GYPSUM, KS |
| HENDERSON, JACK JR. | PFC | 30 JAN 50 | 16 MAY 68* | CHICAGO, IL |
| HIMES, BERNARD MALCOLM | L/CPL | 25 NOV 49 | 17 MAY 68* | ANITA, PA |
| JOHNSON, GEORGE MILTON | PFC | 04 JAN 48 | 09 OCT 68 | CLARKSTON, GA |
| JONES, BENNIE RAY | PVT | 20 SEP 48 | 17 MAY 68* | JACKSON, TN |
| JONES, RAYMOND PARKER | L/CPL | 03 APR 48 | 05 JAN 69 | ARLINGTON, VA |
| JUAREZ, OSCAR REINA | PFC | 14 SEP 49 | 28 JUN 68 | SAN ANGELO, TX |

# Every Marine-414

**INDIA COMPANY (continued)**

| | | | | |
|---|---|---|---|---|
| KINSWORTHY, LOYD E. | CPL | 12 NOV 48 | 27 APR 68 | SAN JOSE, CA |
| LEE, NATE FRANCS | SGT | 31 DEC 38 | 17 MAY 68* | HAZLETON, PA |
| LEWIS, DONNIE GORDON | L/CPL | 29 MAR 48 | 14 MAY 68* | STIGLER, OK |
| LYONS, JAMES ANDREW | CPL | 20 SEP 47 | 13 AUG 68 | WAYLAND, MI |
| MADDUX, ROY R., JR | PFC | 04 MAY 49 | 28 FEB 68 | INDEPENDENCE, CA |
| MARSHALL, CHARLES RAY | PFC | 05 DEC 47 | 15 MAY 68* | OAKLAND, CA |
| MILLER, PHILLIP DENNIS | PFC | 08 JUL 49 | 17 MAY 68* | GRANDJUNCTION, CO |
| MILLS, THOMAS WAYNE | CPL | 01 MAR 49 | 28 MAY 68* | CINCINNATI, OH |
| NOWAK, LEONARD M. | PFC | 13 JUL 49 | 28 MAY 68* | LUXEMBURG, WI |
| OROZCO, TONY SALAZAR JR | PFC | 05 MAR 47 | 05 AUG 68 | WINSLOW, AZ |
| POOLE, RONALD DEAN | L/CPL | 30 MAY 48 | 13 JUN 68 | DELAWARE, OH |
| RODRIGUEZ, GEORGE | L/CPL | 14 AUG 48 | 23 MAY 70 | WESTRICHLAND, WA |
| SCHETTL, DAVID LEROY | L/CPL | 04 MAR 47 | 17 MAY 68* | MANITOWAC, WI |
| SCHWEIG, VICTOR JOHN | PVT | 23 DEC 49 | 17 MAY 68* | CHICAGO, IL |
| SEAMSTER, WILLIE P. | L/CPL | 08 JAN 49 | 15 JUN 68 | MINDEN, LA |
| SPENSKO, LOUIS PAUL | SGT | 20 N0V 45 | 13 MAY 68 | HELPER,UT |
| SULLIVAN, STEPHAN T. | L/CPL | 20 DEC 47 | 28 MAY 68* | MELROSE, MA |
| THIBODEAUX, EDWARD J. | L/CPL | 15 MAR 47 | 19 OCT 68 | GREENWELL SPNGS, LA |
| TURNER, RICHARD | CPL | 29 MAY 44 | 17 MAY 68* | WASHINGTON, D.C. |
| TYLER, SYLVESTER G. | PFC | 30 AUG 48 | 17 MAY 68* | WASHINGTON, D.C. |
| VINGE, RICHARD LONNIE | PVT | 05 APR 47 | 05 JUN 68 | SEATTLE, WA |
| WEST, LARRY JOE | L/CPL | 17 SEP 48 | 17 MAY 68* | MORENCI,. AZ |
| WHISNAN, JAMES CARL | PFC | 22 JUL 48 | 14 MAR 68 | MEDFORD, OR |
| WHITE, JACK L | CPL | 25 JUL 44 | 17 MAY 68* | TACOMA, WA |
| WHYTE, CHARLES JAMES | SGT | 24 JUN 43 | 28 MAY 68* | OLYMPIA, WA |
| WILLIAMS, DEWAYNE T. | PFC | 18 SEP 49 | 18 SEP 68 | ST CLAIR, MI |
| WYANT, ALFRED LEROY | CPL | 14 DEC 48 | 02 AUG 68 | TITUSVILLE, PA |
| WYATT, PHILLIP EDGAR | PFC | 13 NOV 45 | 28 MAY 68* | ST. PETERSBURG, FL |
| YAZZIE, LEONARD LEE | PFC | 10 FEB 45 | 28 MAY 68* | PINION, AZ |
| ZUCROFF, STEVEN DALE | CPL | 15 NOV 46 | 13 MAY 68* | PANORAMA CITY, CA |

**KILO COMPANY**

| | | | | |
|---|---|---|---|---|
| AGUILAR, ARNOLD | PVT | 10 JUL 45 | 21 APR 68 | AUSTIN, TX |
| ALLEN, DONALD RAY | L/CPL | 12 OCT 48 | 19 APR 68 | SAN BENITO, TX |
| ALMAGUER, BENJAMIN F. | PFC | 30 NOV 49 | 10 MAR 68 | MONMOUTH, IL |
| ATKINSON, JERRY DOYLE | CPL | 16 AUT 46 | 30 MAR 68 | LAWNDALE, CA |
| BARCA, JOHN JR. | L/CPL | 15 APR 49 | 22 MAR 69 | NEW YORK, NY |
| BLALOCK, GHERALD E. | PFC | 16 MAY 49 | 17 MAY 68* | HOUSTON, TX |
| BLANDIN, RAYMOND W. | L/CPL | 14 JUN 48 | 04 JAN 69 | N. CHARLESTON, SC |
| BROWN, ROGER THOMAS | L/CPL | 05 MAY 47 | 30 MAR 68 | KITTANNING, PA |
| CHAPMAN, JERRY JUNIOR | SGT | 25 JAN 46 | 20 APR 68 | ALBION, IL |
| CURETON, RONNIE C. | L/CPL | 11 AUG 48 | 23 MAR 68 | KANSAS CITY, MO |
| EDNEY, DONALD WAYNE | CPL | 04 MAY 48 | 04 FEB 69 | MONTICELLO, AZ |
| FIALKO, DAVID ANDREW JR | PFC | 04 DEC 49 | 14 NOV 68 | BRIDGEPORT, CT |
| FINA, RICHARD C. | HN | 08 JUN 47 | 24 MAY 68 | HUDSON, WI |
| FOSTER, JOHN MICHAEL | CPL | 05 AUG 45 | 24 MAR 69 | GARDEN GROVE, CA |
| GARRETT, ROBERT LEE | PFC | 10 NOV 48 | 22 OCT 68 | ZANESVILLE, OH |
| HAWKINS, PHILIP III | SGT | 09 OCT 45 | 15 MAY 68 | HOUSTON, TX |
| HILBERT, JERRY LEE | PFC | 22 AUG 49 | 24 MAY 68* | LOUISVILLE, KY |
| JARONIK, ROBERT W. | SGT | 24 APR 36 | 29 JUN 68 | SOUTH BEND, IN |
| JERSTAD, LESLIE ARTHUR | PFC | 04 AUG 48 | 03 FEB 69 | JACKSON, TN |
| JIMINEZ, ANASTACIO | L/CPL | 08 JUL 50 | 09 JUL 69 | NEW YORK, NY |
| KALKA, CHARLES CLINTON | SGT | 22 MAR 45 | 01 JUL 68 | BANDERA, TX |
| KAMINSKI, JOSEPH M. JR | PFC | 23 SEP 48 | 24 MAY 68* | WILMINGTON, DE |
| KUHSE, MICHAEL DARRELL | L/CPL | 05 AUG 46 | 17 MAY 68* | HUNTSVILLE, AL |
| KUYKENDALL, HENRY J. | PFC | 16 DEC 47 | 12 OCT 68 | LOS ANGELES, CA |
| LESTAGE, WILLIAM FRED | L/CPL | 28 JAN 49 | 03 FEB 69 | ST. ALBANS, VT |
| LEWIS, PAUL | L/CPL | 17 JUN 48 | 24 MAY 68* | SAUGERTIES, NY |
| McGEE, GEORGE WILLIAM | PFC | 03 FEB 50 | 11 SEP 68 | OKLAHOMA CITY,OK |

Every Marine-415

## KILO COMPANY (continued)

| | | | | |
|---|---|---|---|---|
| METZGER, FRANKLIN H. | PVT | 29 JAN 48 | 17 MAY 68* | HILLSIDE, MD |
| MILOT, LARRY JOSEPH | L/CPL | 25 SEP 47 | 02 APR 68 | MANCHESTER, NH |
| NORVELL, JEFFREY W. | L/CPL | 04 MAR 50 | 06 SEP 68 | MEMPHIS, TN |
| O'CONNOR, WILLIAM J., JR. | PFC | 21 OCT 49 | 12 MAY 68 | CHICAGO, IL |
| OLIVER, ROMMIE | PFC | 26 DEC 49 | 29 JUN 68 | ORLANDO, FL |
| PETERSON, DILLARD ERIC | L/CPL | 16 MAY 47 | 19 APR 68 | PHILADELPHIA, PA |
| PURCELL, GARY WILLIAM | PFC | 27 OCT 48 | 24 MAY 68* | TORRANCE, CA |
| RILEY, RICKY VAUGHN | PFC | 15 JUN 49 | 29 JUN 68 | COMPTON, CA |
| ROSE, DANIEL PARICK | L/CPL | 15 DEC 47 | 28 JAN 69 | LOS ANGELES, CA |
| SHERLOCK, ROBERT E. | L/CPL | 24 NOV 48 | 03 FEB 69 | PITTSFIELD, PA |
| SHEWMAN, RONALD JAMES | L/CPL | 09 AUG 46 | 24 MAY 68* | LOS ANGELES, CA |
| SINCLAIR, PATRICK EUGENE | L/CPL | 11 DEC 46 | 06 SEP 68 | NEW ORLEANS, FL |
| STANLEY, DON SCOTT | PVT | 20 AUG 48 | 01 JUL 68 | ALBUGUERQUE, NM |
| STAVINOHA, ROBERT J. | PFC | 01 AUG 49 | 21 APR 68 | LA GRANGE, TX |
| THOMAS, GEORGE JR. | PFC | 28 JAN 48 | 17 MAY 68* | CINCINNATI, OH |
| VALLONE, FRANK | PFC | 04 APR 49 | 11 SEP 68 | NEW YORK, NY |
| WALKER, GARY LAYNE | PVT | 22 DEC 46 | 17 MAY 68* | CUDAHY, CA |
| YOUNG, STEPHEN ROGERS | PVT | 12 JUN 48 | 17 MAY 68* | KENNEWICK, WA |

## LIMA COMPANY

| | | | | |
|---|---|---|---|---|
| ACOSTA, JAMES A., JR. | L/CPL | 14 OCT 46 | 15 JUL 68 | NEW ORLEANS, LA |
| BAYLOR, HAROLD B.T. | L/CPL | 25 JUN 46 | 18 MAY 68* | COLUMBUS, OH |
| BOTES, GEORGE | PFC | 12 AUG 49 | 19 MAY 68* | LA GRANGE, IL |
| BOWEN, CLIFTON LEE | PVT | 29 DEC 48 | 14 SEP 68 | BELL BUCKLE, TN |
| BROOKS, STEVEN RANDALL | L/CPL | 03 FEB 50 | 13 SEP 68 | LAFAYETTE, IN |
| BROWN, VERNON JR | PFC | 14 FEB 45 | 18 JUN 68 | NASHVILLE, AK |
| BRYANT, CREED LORENZIO | L/CPL | 06 MAY 49 | 11 SEP 68 | NEW HAVEN, CT |
| BURTON, JOHN THOMAS | SGT | 03 JUN 46 | 18 MAY 68* | MT JULIET, TN |
| CHUTE, STEPHEN FORREST | PFC | 03 SEP 49 | 18 MAY 68* | CARMICHAEL, CA |
| DAVIS, GARY RAY | PFC | 12 JUN 48 | 18 MAY 68* | WARREN, OH |
| DAVIS, ROBERT | L/CPL | 24 JAN 48 | 11 MAR 68 | SWANTON, OH |
| EVANS, PAUL RAYMOND | CPL | 04 JUN 46 | 05 MAY 68 | IRON CITY, GA |
| GORTON, JACK BURT | SGT | 19 SEP 46 | 17 MAY 68* | CULVER CITY, CA |
| HETRICK, GERALD EVERETT | L/CPL | 21 AUG 49 | 12 JUL 68 | NEWBERRY, MI |
| LEACH, JAMES ANDREW | PFC | 26 JUN 50 | 24 APR 69 | ARCADIA, CA |
| LEJEUNE, HORACE J., JR | PFC | 05 JAN 50 | 04 SEP 68 | CROWLEY, LA |
| MELTON, RODNEY WAYNE | PFC | 01 JAN 47 | 05 MAY 68 | WYOMISSING, PA |
| MOON, THOMAS HENRY | CPL | 23 DEC 47 | 02 SEP 68 | TOLEDO, OH |
| MORALES, ANGELO R. | SGT | 27 OCT 49 | 26 MAR 70 | SAN JOSE, CA |
| MULLEN JR., JOSEPH | L/CPL | 15 AUG 46 | 17 APR 68 | TORRANCE, CA |
| MUNCY, GILBERT HOWARD | L/CPL | 31 MAY 46 | 18 MAY 68* | LONG BEACH, CA |
| NELSON, LOUIS HOWARD | PFC | 01 AUG 49 | 05 MAY 68 | HARLOETON, MT |
| NORA, RAYMOND VERNON | PVT | 20 JUL 44 | 18 MAY 68* | ALBANY, CA |
| O'NEAL, HAROLD JR. | L/CPL | 15 MAR 48 | 15 SEP 68 | SHREVEPORT, LA |
| SHANE, WALLACE WILLIAM | PFC | 21 APR 46 | 05 MAY 68 | BADEN, PA |
| SHARPE, THOMAS EDWARD | PFC | 12 APR 49 | 18 MAY 68* | EMMET, MI |
| SMITH, ROBERT JOSEPH | PFC | 04 AUG 48 | 26 AUG 68 | COLUMBUS, GA |
| SWANKER, NELSON C. | L/CPL | 13 NOV 47 | 09 MAY 68 | FT. JOHNSON, NY |
| TIFFANY, JOHN MICHAEL | PFC | 08 JUL 49 | 05 MAY 68 | NORMAN, OK |
| TOADVINE, DENNIS | CPL | 09 JUL 47 | 11 MAR 68 | AURORA, IL |
| WILEY, JAMES JOSEPH | PVT | 27 MAY 48 | 21 JAN 69 | CHICKAMAUGA, GA |
| WILSON, WILLIAM LARRY | CPL | 01 MAR 47 | 05 MAY 68 | COQUILLE, OR |

## MIKE COMPANY

| | | | | |
|---|---|---|---|---|
| TUTTLE, ROBERT ERVIN | 2NDLT | 21 JUL 45 | 08 MAY 68 | MEMPHIS, TN |
| WEISS, THOMAS JOSEPH | 2NDLT | 25 MAR 45 | 18 MAY 68* | HAVERTOWN, PA |
| ABBATE, RICHARD CLARK | CPL | 28 MAY 47 | 18 MAY 68* | ELMWOOD PK, IL |

# Every Marine-416

| | | | | | |
|---|---|---|---|---|---|
| ADKINS, TERRY LEE | CPL | 07 JUL 49 | 11 MAY 69 | DUPO, IL |
| BLANCHARD, DAVID M. | PFC | 12 JAN 50 | 18 MAY 68* | GLENDALE, OR |
| BOWLING, JAMES WISDOM | PFC | 24 APR 48 | 07 DEC 68 | EVANSVILLE, IN |
| BROWN, LARRY LEE | SGT | 27 APR 48 | 08 APR 70 | SAND SPRINGS, OK |
| BRYANT, CHARLIE PAUL | L/CPL | 23 AUG 49 | 20 APR 69 | DETROIT, MI |
| CHAPMAN, CLINTON | CPL | 14 NOV 46 | 24 MAY 68* | NEWTON, MS |
| CLARK, GEORGE WILLIAM | CPL | 13 JAN 50 | 24 MAY 68* | LAKEVILLE, CT |
| GEORGE, JOHN WESLEY | PFC | 13 AUG 49 | 17 SEP 68 | WASHINGTON, DC |
| GREEN, WALTER JR | PVT | 31 JUL 48 | 22 MAR 69 | BALTIMORE, MD |
| HUBBARD, THOMAS LEE | PFC | 23 FEB 47 | 18 MAY 68* | FORTWHITE, FL |
| HUNT, JAMES ANTHONY | CPL | 08 JUL 48 | 01 OCT 68 | LA PUENTE, CA |
| JONES, DONALD BYRON | L/CPL | 27 JAN 49 | 18 MAY 68* | LYNWOOD, CA |
| LUPE, EUGENE KENNETH | PFC | 08 OCT 49 | 18 MAY 68* | GREENBAY, WI |
| MACK, JOSEPH DEAN | L/CPL | 31 JAN 48 | 24 MAY 68* | PRARIE POINT, MS |
| MILLER, JOHN M. | PFC | 2 MAY 50 | 11 APR 68 | PERU, IN |
| NOBLE, GARY PAUL | PFC | 19 OCT 45 | 19 MAY 68* | BREMERTON, WA |
| POUSSON, MICHAEL W. | CPL | 02 MAR 47 | 17 SEP 68 | IOTA, LA |
| ROWLAND, ROGER LEE | L/CPL | 18 DEC 48 | 06 MAY 68 | MONTICELLO, MN |
| STEPHENSON, FREDERICK D. | CPL | 15 MAY 47 | 22 JUL 68* | CALUMET CITY, IL |
| THERIAULT, PAUL R. | CPL | 27 AUG 45 | 24 MAY 68* | CAMBRIDGE, MA |
| VINSON, ALBERT GAMALIEL | CPL | 02 JUL 49 | 24 DEC 68 | TOLEDO, OH |
| WALKER, JOHN WESLEY | PFC | 08 AUG 49 | 17 SEP 69 | ORANGE, CA |

\* INDICATES KIA ON OPERATION ALLEN BROOK

Every Marine-417

## ROLL CALL 2004

The below listed Marines are the known 3/27 survivors.

They are now teachers, truck drivers, pharmacists, loggers, accountants, fire chiefs, farmers, police officers, and electricians. Some are retired from the Marine Corps or other jobs. Some have never worked since their Vietnam experience. Many are still disabled from wounds, while others suffer from deep psychological problems. They are all survivors and <u>EVERY MARINE</u> is a brother.

# H&S

Al Alvarez, Bill Boyd, Larry Cazier, Chip Chaffey, Harold Chamberlain, Rick Cooper, Bill Crawford, Joe DeCorte, Ray Delgado, Bruce Dillingham, Robert Dyer Jr., Ramon Estrada, Ernie Fitzgerald, Thomas Fuleky, Alton Graves, Bradford Hall, George Hight, Brian Jackson, Brian Kerr, Jerry Kline, Michael Lipari, Richard Marron, John Martin, Ted Mendenhall, Andres Mendoza, Kenneth Mercer, Paul Michael, Lupe Montalvo, Don Moye, Bill Munson, Charles Murphy, R. Vernon Nickel, Gary Null, Father Michael O'Neil, Mike Petri, Paul Richards, Richard Reynolds, Richard Risner, David Scarano, Kurt Schinze, Wally Singleton, Richard Sneltzer, Bill Steed, Frank Steiner, Bob Stelli, William Stern, Fred Steube, Jerry Styck, Michael Szekely, Joe Van Eeteen, Ermilo Villarreal, John Walker, Tom Watson, Fred Wesche, John Williams, Tullis Woodham Jr., John Zalipski

## India

Francisco Albert, Ray Allison, Eugene Anselmi, Thomas Barletta, Terry Beasley, Mike Berjans, John Best, Dave Boden, Andy Boyko, Paul Brannon, Wayne Bridges, Dale Camp, Denny Christy, Al Ciezki, James Colella, John Croteau, Tim Davis, Mingo de Leon, Bob Detty, Steve Easton, Ray Fisher, Raul Fonseca, John George, Juan 'Speedy' Gonzalez, Leroy Gonzales, Tom Hanson, Gary Harlan, John Huber, Art Kibat Jr., Brian Long, Mike Lutz, Shelby Monk, Bob Neilson, Claude Oden, Jon Pahl, William Prieto, Bill Prish, Dave Roehm, Walter Rosales, Bob Simonsen, Mark Smith, Tom Smith, Mike Vanderhoef

## Kilo

Bob Banks, Dennis Bier, Scott Campbell, Michael Court, Mike Cunningham, Leroy Driffill, Tim Galvin, Tony Garcia, Herbert Gilbert, Lloyd Goff, Jerry Graymire, Ron Griffin, Dana Harper, Joseph Hecht, Johnny Johnson, Bill Jung, Jim Kent, Mark Killinski, G.J. Kroepjl Jr., Wes Love, Gary May, Lonnie Miller, Larry Mitchell, Geno (Moe) Moroz, Dan O'Connor, Tim Origer, Wayne Plut, Clois Reppond, Randy Richardson, Terry Sawyer, Robert Schultz, Garland Sisco, David Smith, Chris Stirling, Andre Tabayoyon, Foster Wood, Tom Wursthorn, Charles Yordy

## Lima

Don Andrews, Roy Barnett, Jerry Breseman, David Burns, Charlie Butler, Gary Colpas, Carl Cotton, Richard Cousins, Bill Dahl, Steve Dewitt, Daniel Dregger, John Ernest, Bill Gostlin, John Halsey, Fred Harden, Charles Hayman, Evale Hill, Doug Holzhuaer, Jerry Home, Pat Ibanez, Don Inchek,

Joe Jackson, Dave Jenkins, Wayne Kassel, John Kobberman, Mike Little, Edward Mathis, Gary Much, H. Richard Neal, Frank Neihart, Nick Nichols, Karl Ostberg, George Pettyjohn, Matt Raible, Joseph Renaghan, Mike Ricci, Paul Rickson, Art Riordan, Robert Siler, John Skelnar, C.J. Spencer, Jess Spencer, Everett Stone, Henry Stringer, Mel Thane, Dave Thompson, Del Westover, Al Wilson, James Yockey.

# Mike

Claude Bailey, Edward Benavidez, Glen Brewer, Paul Brewer, Richard Buchanan, Robert Callan, John Campbell, Ronald Campora, Frank Cortez, Juan Diaz, Robert Fontana, Larry Frye, Jack Gleason, W. Ray Green, Al Guhl, Bill Hartmann, Marlin Jackson, E.M. Keefe Jr., Richard Lewerenz, Gerald Mallon, William Morrissey, Rudy Pierce, Duane Pounder, Richard Richards, Ben Sanchez, Dick Schmidt, Mike Skotarczak, Michael Stoppa, Charles Swagerty, Blake Thomas, Richard Vannatta, Edwin Velez, Ray Watkins, David Watson.

# Unit and Individual Citations

The following citations are a representation of awards earned by both 3/27 and its members. These are in no way the total number of citations achieved by this Battalion.

## Presidential Unit Citation

First Marine Division

## Meritorious Unit Commendations

- Third Battalion, 27th Marines
- India Company, 3/27

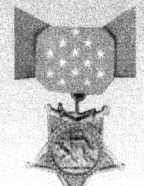

### Medal of Honor
Burke, Robert C.

### Navy Cross
Buchanan, Richard W.
Yordy, Charles R.

### Silver Star
Belser, Joseph H.
Bower, Burton K.
Burton, John T.
Butler, Charles R.
Chiofolo, Vincent N.
Hazelwood, John Edward
Jester, Herbert A.
Jackson, Marlin Winslow
Neal, Hiawhahnah R.
Much, Gary W.
Sharpe, Thomas E.
Stoppa, Michael D.
Thuesen, Thomas R.
Woodham, Tullis J.
Whyte, Charles

### Legion of Merit
Woodham, Tullis J.

### Bronze Star
Benavidez, Edward
Dyer, Robert A.
Fina, Richard
Jung, William C.
May, Gary E.
Prish, William A.
Smith, Mark F.
Swagerty, Charles M.
Thompson, Stephen
Zalipski, John M.

### Navy Commendation Medal
Casteel, Roy J.
Hight, G.E.
Jenkins, Craig
Pelkey, Richard
Raible, Matthew H.
Watkins, Ray C.

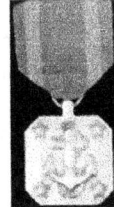

### Navy Achievement Medal
Fontana, Robert
Hight, G. E.
Schultz, Robert

Every Marine-422

The Secretary of the Navy takes pleasure in presenting the MERITORIOUS UNIT COMMENDATION TO

THIRD BATTALION, TWENTY-SEVENTH MARINES
FIRST MARINE DIVISION (REINFORCED)

for service as set forth in the following

CITATION:

    For valorous achievement in action against enemy North Vietnamese Army forces during engagements on Go Noi Island, Quang Nam Province, Republic of Vietnam, from 17 to 28 May 1968. Ordered to insert two companies and a command group into an area in the southern portion of Go Noi to relieve one of its own companies which had been inserted two days before, and which was engaged in heavy fighting with an estimated enemy battalion, the Third Battalion, Twenty-Seventh Marines, commenced a heliborne assault at 1500 on 17 May 1968. Immediately upon landing, the battalion was taken under heavy enemy mortar fire and, despite numerous friendly casualties, launched a series of assaults to reach the besieged company. Intensive enemy mortar, small-arms, and automatic weapons fire was encountered as the battalion aggressively moved forward in an attempt to link up with friendly forces. Only after fierce fighting, which lasted well into the night, did the enemy withdraw, allowing elements of the two forces to join. Relentlessly pursuing the enemy, the battalion continued to sweep the island, engaging North Vietnamese Army units on three more occasions and defeating them each time after fierce fighting and intensive use of tanks, artillery, and close air support, resulting in the death of 225 of the enemy. Supported by Marines, were materially instrumental in the clearing of the island of organized resistance, relieved the pressure on friendly units, and set an inspiring example for our own and allied forces. Through their effective teamwork, aggressive fighting spirit, and the many individual acts of bravery, the men of the Third Battalion, Twenty-Seventh Marines, together with supporting Marine units, dealt the enemy a severe blow and in so doing demonstrated those qualities of valor and professional skill which were in keeping with the highest traditions of the Marine Corps and the United States Naval Service.

Every Marine-423

The Secretary of the Navy takes pleasure in presenting the MERITORIOUS UNIT COMMENDATION to

SEVENTH MARINE REGIMENT (REINFORCED)
FIRST MARINE DIVISION (REINFORCED)
FLEET MARINE FORCE, PACIFIC

for service as set forth in the following

CITATION:

For meritorious service in action against North Vietnamese Army and insurgent Viet Cong forces during Operations ALLEN BROOK and MAMELUKE THRUST in Quang Nam Province, Republic of Vietnam, from 4 May to 6 July 1968. Displaying aggressive, tenacious tactics, the Seventh Marine Regiment (Reinforced) found, fixed, and severely mauled the 36th Regiment, 308th Division of the North Vietnamese Army, and various Viet Gong Force units preparing to initiate offensive operations in the Danang and Thuong Duc areas of Quang Nam Province. The demoralizing losses inflicted on the enemy included 1080 killed in action, 14 prisoners of war, significant quantities of weapons and supplies captured, and numerous prepared positions destroyed. By their effective teamwork, aggressive fighting spirit, determination, and individual acts of valor and courage, the gallant officers and men of the Seventh Marine Regiment (Reinforced) not only preempted the enemy offensive against Danang and the Special Forces camp at Thuong Duc, but also decimated a fresh, combat-ready North Vietnamese Army regiment with the concomitant destruction of irreplaceable Viet Gong Main Force units in Quang Nam Province. As a direct result of the achievements of the Seventh Marine Regiment (Reinforced), the enemy was unable to seriously threaten Free World Military Assistance Forces units or installations for the remainder of 1965. The Seventh Marines' exemplary courage, devotion to duty, and performance in the face of a determined enemy resistance were in keeping with the highest traditions of the Marine Corps and the United States Naval Service.

ATTACHED AND SUPPORTING UNIT

COMPANY "I", THIRD BATTALION, 27th MARINE REGIMENT   13 May 68 - 17 May 68

Every Marine-424

By virtue of the authority vested in me as President of the United States and as Commander-in-Chief of the Armed Forces of the United States, I have today awarded

THE PRESIDENTIAL UNIT CITATION (NAVY)
FOR EXTRAORDINARY HEROISM TO
FIRST MARINE DIVISION (REINFORCED),
FLEET MARINE FORCE

For extraordinary heroism and outstanding performance of duty in action against enemy forces in the Republic of Vietnam from 16 September 1967 to 31 October 1968. Operating primarily in Quang Nam Province, the First Marine Division (Reinforced) superbly executed its threefold mission of searching for and destroying the enemy, defending key airfields and lines of communication, and conducting a pacification and revolutionary development program unparalleled in the annals of warfare. With the Division responsible for over 1,000 square miles of territory, it extended protection and pacification to more than one million Vietnamese. The countless examples of courage, resourcefulness, and dedication demonstrated by the officers and men of the First Marine Division attest to their professionalism and esprit de corps. Their combat activities were skillfully carried out in the face of adverse weather and difficult terrain such as canopied jungles, rugged mountains, swampy lowlands, and hot, sandy beaches. During the enemy Tet-offensive in late January of 1968, the First Marine Division dealt a devastating blow to enemy forces attempting to attack Da Nang. AGAIN, IN MAY 1968, THE DIVISION TOTALLY CRUSHED AN ENEMY DRIVE DIRECTED AGAINST THE DA NANG AREA THROUGH THE GO NOI ISLAND REGION SOUTHWEST OF DA NANG. THE DIVISION ACHIEVED THIS RESOUNDING VICTORY THROUGH THE SKILLFUL COORDINATION OF GROUND FORCES, SUPPORTING ARMS, AND AIRCRAFT SUPPORT. Most action in the I Corps Tactical Zone during August of 1968 was centered in the First Marine Division's tactical area of responsibility. The enemy, now looking for a victory which would achieve some measure of psychological or propaganda value, again mounted an attack of major proportions against Da Nang but were thoroughly repulsed, sustaining heavy casualties. The valiant fighting spirit, perseverance, and teamwork displayed by First Marine Division's tactical area of responsibility. The enemy, now looking for a victory which would achieve some measure of psychological or propaganda value, again mounted an attack of major proportions against Da Nang but were thoroughly repulsed,

# Every Marine-425

sustaining heavy casualties. The valiant fighting spirit, perseverance, and teamwork displayed by First Marine Division personnel throughout this period reflected great credit upon themselves and the Marine Corps, and were in keeping with the highest traditions of the United States Naval Service.

Every Marine-426

The President of the United States in the name of The Congress takes pride in presenting the MEDAL OF HONOR posthumously to

PRIVATE FIRST CLASS ROBERT C. BURKE
UNITED STATES MARINE CORPS

for service as set forth in the following

CITATION:

For conspicuous gallantry and intrepidity at the risk of his life above and beyond the call of duty for service as a Machine Gunner with Company I, Third Battalion, Twenty-Seventh Marines, First Marine Division in the Republic of Vietnam on 17 May 1968. While on Operation ALLEN BROOK, Company I was approaching a dry river bed with a heavily wooded tree line that bordered the hamlet of Le Nam (1), when they suddenly came under intense mortar, rocket propelled grenade, automatic weapons and small arms fire from a large, well-concealed enemy force which halted the company's advance and wounded several Marines. Realizing that key points of resistance had to be eliminated to allow the units to advance and casualties to be evacuated, Private Burke, without hesitation, seized his machine gun and launched a series of one man assaults against the fortified emplacements. As he aggressively maneuvered to the edge of the steep river bank, he delivered accurate suppressive fire upon several enemy bunkers, which enabled his comrades to advance and move the wounded Marines to positions of relative safety. As he continued his combative actions, he located an opposing automatic weapons emplacement and poured intense fire into the position, killing three North Vietnamese soldiers as they attempted to flee. Private Burke then fearlessly moved from one position to another, quelling the hostile fire until his weapon malfunctioned. Obtaining a casualty's rifle and hand grenades, he advanced further into the midst of the enemy. Observing that a fellow Marine had cleared his malfunctioning machine gun he grasped his weapon and moved into a dangerously exposed area and saturated the hostile fire until he fell mortally wounded. Private Burke's gallant actions upheld the highest traditions of the Marine Corps and the United States Naval Service. He gallantly gave his life for his country.

Every Marine-427

The President of the United States takes pleasure in presenting the NAVY CROSS MEDAL to

CORPORAL RICHARD W. BUCHANAN
UNITED STATES MARINE CORPS
for service as set forth in the following

CITATION:

For extraordinary heroism while serving as an Automatic Rifleman with company M, Third Battalion, Twenty-seventh Marines, First Marine Division (Reinforced) in the Republic of Vietnam on 24 May 1968. While participating in Operation ALLEN BROOK in Quang Nam Province, Corporal Buchanan's company was serving as battalion reserve, following in trace of company K, as the unit moved against well-entrenched North Vietnamese forces in the village of Le Bac (1). Advancing into the objective area, Company K was ambushed by an enemy force in a tree line and two platoons were separated from the remainder of the company. As Corporal Buchanan's platoon quickly maneuvered toward the beleaguered Marines, it suddenly came under intense small-arms and automatic weapons fire from a North Vietnamese Army unit entrenched in a series of bunkers and spider holes. In the initial burst of fire, several Marines were killed or seriously wounded, including the platoon commander, platoon sergeant, all the squad leaders and the radio operator. Observing a well-hidden enemy bunker, he fearlessly assaulted the position and directed accurate rifle fire into the emplacement. Then, retrieving the platoon radio and shouting to his comrades to follow, he led the Marines to the relative safety of a nearby pagoda where he established a hasty defense. Unable to establish radio communication with his company and upon observing several medical evacuation helicopters in the vicinity, he relayed a request for armed helicopter support. As he directed numerous air strikes on the enemy positions often within ten feet of his position, he courageously rushed into the fire-swept area to move the casualties to better protected positions. Upon discovering an adjacent bunker occupied by several North Vietnamese Army soldiers, Corporal Buchanan boldly assaulted it single-handedly, silencing the hostile fire. Throughout the intense three-hour battle, his superb command ability and calm presence of mind in hazardous situations undoubtedly saved numerous Marine lives and inspired all who observed him. By his outstanding leadership, intrepid fighting spirit and selfless devotion to duty, Corporal Buchanan upheld the highest traditions of the Marine Corps and the United States Naval Service.

Every Marine-428

The President of the United States takes pleasure in presenting the NAVY CROSS MEDAL to

CHARLES R. YORDY
UNITED STATES MARINE CORPS
for service as set forth in the following

CITATION:

For extraordinary heroism while serving with Company K, Third Battalion, Twenty-Seventh Marines, First Marine Division (Reinforced), in connection with operations against the enemy in the Republic of Vietnam. On 24 May 1968 during Operation ALLEN BROOK in Quang Nam Province, Private Yordy's platoon was assigned the mission of enveloping an enemy village in order to relieve the pressure on an adjacent platoon which was pinned down by the heavy volume of fire from well fortified hostile positions. As the Marines moved up on the flank of the enemy, the unit came under intense automatic weapons fire from several North Vietnamese bunkers and spider holes, pinning down the platoon and inflicting numerous casualties, including the platoon commander who fell directly in front of the enemy machine-gun emplacement. Unhesitatingly and with complete disregard for his personal safety, Private Yordy rushed across the hazardous area firing his M-16 rifle from the hip and succeeded in reaching the side of the injured officer. Picking up the wounded man's M-79 grenade launcher and ignoring the enemy rounds striking around him, he fired directly into the aperture of the bunker silencing the hostile fire. Observing another enemy bunker nearby which had pined down his companions, he crawled to the emplacement and destroyed it with several hand grenades. As the platoon began to withdraw, Private Yordy selflessly remained behind and covered the withdrawal of his unit by throwing hand grenades and firing his grenade launcher at the hostile position, abandoning his precarious position only when he was assured that his fellow Marines had reached relative safety. Throughout the battle, his heroic actions and presence of mind were an inspiration to all who observed him and were responsible for the successful extraction of his unit, undoubtedly saving the lives of many of his comrades. By his courage, aggressive fighting spirit, and selfless devotion to duty in the face of great personal danger, Private Yordy upheld the highest traditions of the Marine Corps and the United States Naval Service.

Every Marine-429

The President of the United States takes pleasure in presenting the
SILVER STAR MEDAL to

CORPORAL MARLIN WINSLOW JACKSON
UNITED STATES MARINE CORPS

for service as set forth in the following

CITATION:

For conspicuous gallantry and intrepidity in action while serving as a Radio Operator with the Second Battalion, Thirteenth Marines, First Marine Division in connection with operations against the enemy in the Republic of Vietnam. On 18 May 1968, Corporal JACKSON was assigned to an artillery forward observer team supporting Company M, Third Battalion, Twenty-Seventh Marines during Operation Allen Brook. Upon being helicopter lifted into an area south of Da Nang, the Marines came under intense hostile fire as they debarked from the aircraft and sustained numerous casualties. Realizing the seriousness of the situation, Corporal JACKSON unhesitatingly organized several Marines to evacuate the injured men. Undaunted by the enemy fire, he repeatedly led the Marines about the fire-swept area and supervised the expeditious evacuation of the casualties. Although two of his men were seriously wounded, he continued his resolute efforts ensuring that all of the wounded were moved to covered positions. On 24 May, Company M established contact with a large North Vietnamese Army force. Fearlessly maneuvering across the fire-swept terrain, Corporal JACKSON delivered water and ammunition to the forward positions and evacuated casualties to positions of relative safety. Disregarding his own safety, he removed his protective vest and discarded his weapon in order to carry the maximum amount of supplies. On 26 May, Company M was again heavily engaged with the enemy. Alertly observing a hostile soldier occupying a bunker, Corporal JACKSON immediately delivered a heavy volume of fire and pinned down the North Vietnamese soldier. Assisted by another Marine, he maneuvered forward to the position and captured the enemy, seizing an antitank rocket launcher, an automatic rifle and a large amount of ammunition. By his courage, bold initiative and unwavering devotion to duty in the face of great personal danger, Corporal JACKSON contributed significantly to the accomplishment of his unit's mission and upheld the highest traditions of the Marine Corps and of the United States Naval Service.

Every Marine-430

The President of the United States takes pleasure in presenting the SILVER STAR MEDAL to

LIEUTENANT COLONEL TULLIS J. WOODHAM, JR.
UNITED STATES MARINE CORPS

for the service as set forth in the following

CITATION:
For conspicuous gallantry and intrepidity in action while serving as Commanding Officer of the Third Battalion, Twenty-Seventh Marines, First Marine Division in connection with operations against the enemy in the Republic of Vietnam. On 13 May 1968, the Third Battalion launched Operation Allen Brook against a numerically superior North Vietnamese Army force occupying well prepared defensive positions on Go Noi Island in Quang Nam Province. When the advance company became heavily engaged with the enemy on 17 May, Lieutenant Colonel WOODHAM unhesitatingly led the remainder of his battalion in a heliborne attack to assist the besieged unit. Undaunted by a heavy volume of automatic weapons and mortar fire, he repeatedly advanced to dangerously exposed positions as he aggressively deployed his companies and engaged the hostile force. Displaying outstanding professional knowledge and superior tactical ability, he ably planned and directed supporting arms fire and air strikes, which inflicted heavy losses on the enemy and enabled his battalion to accomplish its mission with a minimum number of friendly casualties. His bold initiative and exceptional tactical ability were instrumental in his battalion accounting for over 200 North Vietnamese soldiers confirmed killed and the seizure of a large number of weapons. By his courage, superb leadership and steadfast devotion to duty in the face of great personal danger, Lieutenant Colonel WOODHAM upheld the highest traditions of the Marine Corps and of the United States Naval Service.

Every Marine-431

The President of the United States takes pride in presenting the SILVER STAR Medal posthumously to

CORPORAL JOHN EDWARD HAZELWOOD
UNITED STATES MARINE CORPS

for service as set forth in the following

CITATION:

For conspicuous gallantry and intrepidity in action while serving as a Squad Leader with Company I, Third Battalion, Twenty-Seventh Marines, First Marine Division in connection with operations against the enemy in the Republic of Vietnam. On the morning of 28 May 1968 during Operation ALLEN BROOK, Corporal HAZELWOOD's platoon was advancing across an open area toward a tree line near the village of Cu Ban (4), when the Marines came under heavy automatic weapons, small arms and rocket fire and were pinned down by a well entrenched enemy force. As supporting tanks moved into the area to aid the besieged unit, one vehicle was immediately disabled by an enemy rocket propelled grenade. Alertly detecting the source of the enemy fire, Corporal HAZELWOOD fearlessly exposed himself to hostile fire as he ran thirty-five meters to the nearest tank and utilizing the vehicle's tank-infantry phone, directed accurate 90mm fire into the enemy position, destroying it. Returning across the fire-swept area to his squad and realizing the importance of gaining fire superiority, Corporal HAZELWOOD again exposed himself to hostile fire as he organized his men and led an aggressive assault against the enemy-held tree line. Throughout the ensuing battle, he moved from one man to another, offering words of encouragement and directing accurate fire at enemy positions until he was mortally wounded. His dynamic leadership and determined actions inspired all who observed him and were instrumental in the accomplishment of his unit's mission. By his extraordinary courage, bold initiative and selfless devotion to duty, Corporal HAZELWOOD upheld the highest traditions of the Marine Corps and of the United States Naval Service. He gallantly gave his life in the service of his country.

Every Marine-432

The President of the United States takes pleasure in presenting the SILVER STAR MEDAL to

CORPORAL HIAHWAHANH R. NEAL
UNITED STATES MARINE CORPS

for service as set forth in the following

CITATION:

For conspicuous gallantry and intrepidity in action while serving as a Machine Gunner with Company M, Third Battalion, Twenty-Seventh Marines, First Marine Division in connection with operations against the enemy in the Republic of Vietnam. On 24 May 1968 while participating in Operation Allen Brook in Quang Nam Province, Corporal NEAL's squad was directed to relieve a squad from Company K which had been ambushed by North Vietnamese Army forces and was pinned down near the hamlet of Le Bac (1). As his squad approached the beleaguered unit's position, it immediately came under a heavy volume of automatic weapons and small arms fire from numerous well concealed enemy bunkers within a tree line. Realizing the seriousness of the situation, Corporal NEAL obtained a supply of ammunition, seized his machine gun and ran to the top of a deserted enemy bunker. Exposed to the enemy fire, he manned his weapon and began delivering a heavy volume of suppressive fire into enemy positions until his machine gun malfunctioned. Observing an unmanned machine gun, Corporal NEAL ran fifty meters to the position, seized the weapon and an ammunition resupply and returned to his position. Immediately bringing accurate fire to bear against the enemy, he quickly gained fire superiority. Subsequently, after expending all his ammunition, he ran across the fire-swept area to the side of a wounded ammunition carrier, seized the resupplies and returned to his bunker. Although constantly exposed to enemy fire, he ignored the rounds striking around him as he steadfastly sustained his position and continued to deliver effective machine gun fire against the enemy. Observing several casualties awaiting evacuation, he assisted in expediting their movement from the hazardous area. By his extraordinary courage, bold initiative and selfless devotion to duty, Corporal NEAL inspired all who observed him and upheld the highest traditions of the Marine Corps and of the United States Naval Service.

Every Marine-433

The President of the United States takes pride in presenting the SILVER STAR MEDAL posthumously to

SERGEANT CHARLES JAMES WHYTE
UNITED STATES MARINE CORPS

for service as set forth in the following

CITATION:

    For conspicuous gallantry and intrepidity in action while serving as a Platoon Guide with Company I, Third Battalion, Twenty-Seventh Marines, First Marine Division in connection with operations against the enemy in the Republic of Vietnam. On the morning of 28 May 1968 during Operation Allen Brook, Sergeant WHYTE's platoon was advancing across an open area toward a tree line near the village of Cu Ban (4), when the Marines came under heavy automatic weapons, small arms and rocket fire, and were pinned down by a well entrenched enemy force. Realizing the seriousness of the situation and the importance of gaining fire superiority, Sergeant WHYTE, fearlessly exposed himself to hostile fire as he moved from one squad to another, encouraging the Marines and directing their fire. Assisting one squad leader in quickly organizing the members of his squad in preparation for an assault against enemy positions in a nearby tree ring, he subsequently joined the unit as it aggressively engaged the hostile force. During the ensuing battle, he maintained the momentum of the assault by remaining in the forefront of the squad, delivering accurate rifle fire and encouraging the men until he was mortally wounded. His dynamic leadership and determined actions inspired all who observed him and were instrumental in the accomplishment of his unit's mission. By his extraordinary courage, bold initiation and selfless determination to duty, Sergeant WHYTE upheld the highest traditions of the Marine Corps and of the United States Navel Service. He gallantly gave his life in the service of his country.

Every Marine-434

The President of the United States takes pleasure in presenting the SILVER STAR MEDAL to

PRIVATE FIRST CLASS VINCENT N. CHIOFOLO
UNITED STATES MARINE CORPS

for service as set forth in the following

CITATION:

For conspicuous gallantry and intrepidity in action while serving with, Company K, Third Battalion, Twenty-Seventh Marines, First Marine Division in connection with operations against the enemy in the Republic of Vietnam. On 17 May 1968, during Operation Allen Brook, Company K launched an attack on a well entrenched North Vietnamese Army force near Le Bac in Quang Nam Province and immediately came under intense small arms and automatic weapons fire. Realizing the seriousness of the situation, Private First Class CHIOFOLO immediately commenced delivering a heavy volume of rifle fire into the fortified emplacements, which enabled a machine gun team to move forward and engage the enemy. In the ensuing fire fight, the team became pinned down, and when the M-60 machine gun malfunctioned, Private First Class CHIOFOLO fearlessly maneuvered across the fire-swept terrain in an attempt to draw the fire and attention of the enemy away from his comrades. Delivering accurate fire into the hostile emplacements, he succeeded in diverting the enemy fire, enabling the Marines to maneuver to positions of relative safety. Alertly observing three North Vietnamese soldiers launching a determined assault upon his comrades, he boldly exposed himself to the intense hostile fire and aggressively engaged the enemy soldiers, killing two of them. Although seriously wounded by a hostile sniper, he ignored his painful injury and steadfastly remained in his hazardous position, until forcibly restrained and moved to a covered position by fellow Marines. His resolute determination and heroic actions inspired all who observed him and contributed significantly to the accomplishment of his unit's mission. By his courage, aggressive fighting spirit and unfaltering devotion to duty in the face of great personal danger, Private First Class CHIOFOLO upheld the highest traditions of the Marine Corps and of the United States Navel Service.

The President of the United States takes pleasure in presenting the
SILVER STAR MEDAL to

PRIVATE FIRST CLASS BURTON K. BOWER
UNITED STATES MARINE CORPS

for service as set forth in the following

CITATION:

    For conspicuous gallantry and intrepidity in action while serving as a Rifleman with Company L, Third Battalion, Twenty-Seventh Marines, First Marine Division in connection with operations against the enemy in the Republic of Vietnam. On 18 May 1968 during Operation Allen Brook, Companies L and M became heavily engaged with North Vietnamese Army forces in well concealed, fortified and mutually supporting positions in a tree line. In the ensuing battle, friendly casualties from enemy machine gun, automatic weapons and small arms fire rapidly increased and Company L was pinned down while evacuating the wounded. Realizing the seriousness of the situation, Private First Class BOWER picked up twelve Light Antitank Assault Weapons and his rifle and unhesitatingly moved to the point of heaviest contact. Completely disregarding his own safety, he stood in the open, exposed to hostile fire and began delivering accurate rocket fire into the enemy positions. Although the North Vietnamese concentrated their fire against him, he steadfastly maintained his position in the hazardous area and was painfully wounded in the shoulder. Undaunted, he continued to deliver rocket fire into the hostile emplacements until he had expended his ordnance. He then began delivering a heavy volume of accurate rifle fire and received a second wound and was medically evacuated. By his courage, bold initiative and selfless devotion to duty at great personal risk, Private First Class BOWER contributed materially to the subsequent defeat of the enemy and upheld the highest traditions of the Marine Corps and of the United States Naval Service.

# Every Marine-436

The President of the United States takes pleasure in presenting the SILVER STAR MEDAL to

LANCE CORPORAL GARY W. MUCH
United STATES MARINE CORPS

for service as set forth in the following

CITATION:

For conspicuous gallantry and intrepidity in action while serving as an Antitank Assault Squad Leader with Company L, Third Battalion, Twenty-Seventh Marines, First Marine Division in connection with operations against the enemy in the Republic of Vietnam. On 18 May 1968 during Operation Allen Brook, elements of Companies L and M were pinned down by machine gun, automatic weapons and small arms fire from well concealed, fortified and mutually supporting North Vietnamese Army positions in a tree line. Realizing the seriousness of the situation, Lance Corporal MUCH quickly moved to the point of heaviest contact and, standing in the open exposed to hostile fire, began delivering 3.5 inch rockets into the enemy positions. Ignoring the enemy fire all around him, he steadfastly maintained his position in the hazardous area until he had expended all of his ammunition. Obtaining a resupply, he then continued to deliver a heavy volume of accurate fire on the enemy fortifications, sufficiently suppressing hostile fire to enable the beleaguered Marines to move to positions of safety. By his courage, bold initiative and selfless devotion to duty at great personal risk, Lance Corporal MUCH was instrumental in the subsequent defeat of the enemy and upheld the highest traditions of the Marine Corps and of the United States Naval Service.

The President of the United States takes pleasure in presenting the
SILVER STAR MEDAL to

FIRST LIEUTENANT JOSEPH HENRY BELSER, JR.
UNITED STATES MARINE CORPS

for service as set forth in the following
CITATION:

For conspicuous gallantry and intrepidity in action while serving as a Platoon Commander with Company K, Third Battalion, Twenty-Seventh Marines, First Marine Division in connection with operations against the enemy in the Republic of Vietnam. On 24 May 1968 during Operation Allen Brook in Quang Nam Province, Company K was attacking the village of Le Bac (1) which was well fortified and occupied by a large North Vietnamese Army force. As the company approached the area it came under intense automatic weapons fire and two platoons were separated from the remainder of the company. Assigned to assist the besieged units and in an attempt to envelop the enemy, First Lieutenant BELSER moved his reserve platoon to within 300 meters of the hostile positions when the Marines encountered heavy fire which inflicted several casualties, including First Lieutenant BELSER. Calmly informing his men of the situation, and although seriously wounded in the arm, he courageously moved across the fire-swept area from one position to another, encouraging his men and directing their fire while simultaneously keeping his commanding officer appraised of the situation. Under his courageous leadership, his men successfully repulsed repeated attempts by the enemy to overrun their position. Assisted by a platoon from Company M, First Lieutenant BELSER utilized supporting arms fire, hand grenades and a smoke screen to withdraw his platoon along with their casualties to the company perimeter. Informed that Company M was heavily engaged with the enemy and had sustained numerous casualties, he refused to be evacuated for treatment of his injury and organized a group of Marines to retrieve the casualties. With complete disregard for his own safety, he made several trips into the fire-swept area until he was wounded in the leg by the intense enemy fire and subsequently evacuated. By his courage, dynamic leadership and selfless devotion to duty in the face of grave personal risk, First Lieutenant BELSER inspired all who observed him and upheld the highest traditions of the Marine Corps and of the United States Naval Service.

Every Marine-438

The President of the United States takes pleasure in presenting the SILVER STAR MEDAL to

PRIVATE FIRST CLASS HERBERT A. JESTER
UNITED STATES MARINE CORPS

for service as set forth in the following

CITATION:

For conspicuous gallantry and intrepidity in action while serving as a Rifleman with Company K, Third Battalion, Twenty-Seventh Marines, First Marine Division in connection with operations against the enemy in the Republic of Vietnam. On 24 May 1968 during Operation Allen Brook in Quang Nam Province, Company K was ambushed near the village of Le Bac (1) by a large North Vietnamese Army force and two platoons were pinned down and separated from the remainder of the company. Although fully realizing the danger involved and that previous attempts to reach several seriously wounded Marines had resulted in additional casualties, Private First Class JESTER disregarded his own safety as he made three trips into the fire-swept area to move his injured comrades to safety. During one of these trips, he observed an enemy machine gun position. Crawling to within ten feet of the bunker, he killed two enemy soldiers with hand grenades. Observing another North Vietnamese soldier firing from a nearby spider hole, he aggressively attacked the position and killed the enemy with accurate rifle fire. Although hampered by the tropical heat, he continued his selfless efforts, resupplying his companions with water and ammunition on each return trip from the rear area. When the forward units were ordered to withdraw to facilitate the employment of supporting arms, Private First Class JESTER voluntarily remained with the last group to leave in order to provide covering fire for the movement of his comrades. Throughout the fire fight, his heroic efforts and presence of mind were an inspiration to all who served with him and contributed significantly to the accomplishment of his unit's mission. By his courage, bold initiative and unswerving devotion to duty at great personal risk, Private First Class JESTER upheld the highest traditions of the Marine Corps and of the United States Naval Service.

Every Marine-439

The President of the United States takes pleasure in presenting the SILVER STAR MEDAL to

CORPORAL MICHAEL D. STOPPA
UNITED STATES MARINE CORPS

for service as set forth in the following

CITATION:

    For conspicuous gallantry and intrepidity in action while serving as a Rifleman with Company M, Third Battalion, Twenty-Seventh Marines, First Marine Division in connection with operations against the enemy in the Republic of Vietnam. On the afternoon of 24 May 1968, during Operation Allen Brook, Company M was assigned to assist a friendly unit which was pinned down by intense small arms and automatic weapons fire from a large North Vietnamese Army force near the village of Le Bac (1) in Quang Nam Province. As the Marines neared the besieged unit, they were suddenly halted by a heavy volume of fire from concealed enemy positions which inflicted numerous casualties. Alertly observing a hostile automatic weapon emplacement, Corporal STOPPA seized a satchel charge and, with complete disregard for his own safety, began maneuvering across the fire-swept terrain toward the enemy position. Ignoring the intense fire impacting around him, he fearlessly crawled next to the fortified emplacement and hurled the explosive charge inside, killing several North Vietnamese soldiers and silencing their automatic weapon. Upon returning to his unit's position, he boldly moved about the hazardous area administering first aid to his wounded comrades and evacuating them to positions of relative safety, until he was seriously wounded by the hostile fire. His bold initiative and sincere concern for the welfare of his comrades inspired all who observed him and were instrumental in the accomplishment of his unit's mission. By his courage, aggressive fighting spirit and selfless devotion to duty in the face of great personal danger, Corporal STOPPA upheld the highest traditions of the Marine Corps and of the United States Naval Service.

Every Marine-440

The President of the United States takes pleasure in presenting the
SILVER STAR MEDAL to

LANCE CORPORAL THOMAS R. THUESEN
UNITED STATES MARINE CORPS

for service as set forth in the following

CITATION:

For conspicuous gallantry and intrepidity in action while serving as a Machine Gunner with Company M, Third Battalion, Twenty-Seventh Marines, First Marine Division in connection with operations against the enemy in the Republic of Vietnam. On 18 May 1968 during Operation Allen Brook, Lance Corporal THUESEN's platoon was moving to reinforce other units operating in the vicinity of Le Bac (2) in Quang Nam Province when the platoon came under intense small arms and automatic weapons fire from a well camouflaged, entrenched North Vietnamese Army force, wounding several Marines. Rapidly assessing the situation, Lance Corporal THUESEN moved to a position where he began delivering a heavy volume of suppressive fire, enabling several of the casualties to be treated and evacuated from the hazardous area. When his ammunition was expended, he ignored the hostile fire and moved to another position where ammunition was located and then resumed firing until his resupply of ammunition was expended. Realizing the serious condition of the wounded and their urgent need for medical care, he crawled across the fire-swept area, obtained a medical kit and additional personnel and ammunition and guided a small relief force back to his position. Repeatedly exposing himself to the North Vietnamese fire, he completely disregarded his own safety as he moved to positions to delivering more effective fire. When his weapon malfunctioned, he remained exposed to hostile fire as he dismantled the machine gun, cleared the malfunction, reassembled the weapon and resumed firing. After a second malfunction, he ran across the fire-swept area where he obtained another weapon and continued to bring accurate fire to bear against the enemy. Although he had been moving constantly in the intense heat throughout the five hour battle, he refused to withdraw until all the casualties had been evacuated. When his platoon was ordered to break contact, he provided covering fire until the withdrawal was completed. By his courage, aggressive fighting spirit and selfless devotion to duty in the face of great personal risk, Lance Corporal THUESEN inspired all who observed him and upheld the highest traditions of the Marine Corps and of the United States Naval Service.

Every Marine-441

The President of the United States takes pleasure in presenting the BRONZE STAR MEDAL to

FIRST LIEUTENANT JOHN M. ZALIPSKI
UNITED STATES MARINE CORPS

for service as set forth in the following

CITATION:

For heroic achievement in connection with operations against the enemy in the Republic of Vietnam while serving as Executive Officer of Company M, Third Battalion, Twenty-Seventh Marines, First Marine Division. On the afternoon of 18 May 1968, Company M was moving to assist a friendly unit which was heavily engaged with a large North Vietnamese Army force near the village of Le Bac (2) in Quang Nam Province. Upon being informed that a squad from another unit had become pinned down by intense automatic weapons fire and sustained numerous causalities, First Lieutenant ZALIPSKI unhesitatingly led six other Marines across the fire-swept terrain to the besieged unit's location. Disregarding his own safety, he boldly moved about the hazardous area, shouting words of encouragement to the men and skillfully directing their withdrawal to positions of relative safety. Alertly observing a wounded Marine lying in a position dangerously exposed to the intense fire, First Lieutenant ZALIPSKI quickly directed the delivery of suppressive fire on the hostile emplacements and, fearlessly moving forward, evacuated the casualty to a covered position. His bold leadership and sincere concern for the welfare of his men inspired all who served with him and were instrumental in saving the lives of several Marines. First Lieutenant ZALIPSKI's courage, aggressive fighting spirit and selfless devotion to duty in the face of great personal danger were in keeping with the highest traditions of the Marine Corps and of the United States Naval Service.

First Lieutenant ZALIPSKI is authorized to wear the Combat "V."

Every Marine-442

The President of the United States takes pleasure in presenting the BRONZE STAR MEDAL to

CORPORAL MARK F. SMITH
UNITED STATES MARINE CORPS

for service as set forth in the following

CITATION:

For meritorious service in connection with operations against the enemy in the Republic of Vietnam while serving as a Rifleman and subsequently as a Radio Operator with Company I, Third Battalion, Twenty-Seventh Marines, First Marine Division. Throughout this period, Corporal SMITH, then a Lance Corporal, performed his duties with exemplary professional skill and resourcefulness. As a Rifleman, he participated in numerous combat patrols, frequently volunteering to serve in the dangerous position as Point Man. On 17 May 1968 during Operation Allen Brook, when the platoon came under attack by an entrenched enemy force, the primary radio operator was wounded and subsequently evacuated. Although Corporal SMITH was not a trained radio operator, he unhesitatingly assumed his companion's duties and, despite intense enemy fire, maintained reliable communications with the command post throughout the day. When the platoon commander was mortally wounded, Corporal SMITH, displaying exceptional composure under fire, calmly relayed vital communications, contributing significantly to the accomplishment of his unit's mission. On the afternoon of 24 June, when his platoon was ambushed by a North Vietnamese Army force, Corporal SMITH was seriously wounded by fragments from an exploding rocket round. Despite the severity of his wounds, he calmly assisted in treating his own injuries, inspiring all who observed him. Corporal SMITH's courage, superior professionalism and selfless devotion to duty throughout were in keeping with the highest traditions of the Marine Corps and of the United States Naval Service.

Corporal SMITH is authorized to wear the Combat "V."

Every Marine-443

The President of the United States takes pleasure in presenting the
BRONZE STAR MEDAL to

CORPORAL WILLIAM C. JUNG
UNITED STATES MARINE CORPS

for service as set forth in the following

CITATION:

For heroic achievement in connection with operations against the enemy in the Republic of Vietnam while serving as a Squad Leader with Company K, Third Battalion, Twenty-Seventh Marines, First Marine Division. On the afternoon of 24 May 1968, during Operation Allen Brook southwest of Da Nang, elements of Company K suddenly came under a heavy volume of small arms and automatic weapons fire from a numerically superior North Vietnamese Army force. Realizing the seriousness of the situation, Corporal JUNG unhesitatingly commenced maneuvering his squad forward in order to assist the lead elements of his unit. Undaunted by the hostile rounds impacting near him, he skillfully maneuvered his squad through dense foliage, shouting words of encouragement to his men and directing their fire upon the enemy emplacements. Although painfully wounded, he fearlessly continued moving forward, boldly exposing himself to the enemy fire while throwing hand grenades. Upon reaching the besieged unit, he ably supervised the evacuation of casualties and skillfully deployed his men to cover the withdrawal of the other Marines. His bold initiative and resolute determination were an inspiration to all who observed him and contributed significantly to the accomplishment of his unit's mission. Corporal JUNG's courage, aggressive fighting spirit and steadfast devotion to duty at great personal risk were in keeping with the highest traditions of the Marine Corps and of the United States Naval Service.

Corporal JUNG is authorized to wear the Combat "V."

Every Marine-444

The President of the United States takes pleasure in presenting the BRONZE STAR MEDAL to

SECOND LIEUTENANT WILLIAM A. PRISH
UNITED STATES MARINE CORPS RESERVE

for service as set forth in the following

CITATION:

For meritorious service in connection with operations against the enemy in the Republic of Vietnam while serving as a Platoon Commander with Company I, Third Battalion, Twenty-Seventh Marines, First Marine Division from 23 May to 2 August 1968. Throughout this period, Second Lieutenant PRISH performed his duties in an exemplary and highly professional manner. Demonstrating exceptional resourcefulness and initiative, he expeditiously accomplished all assigned tasks and consistently provided his command with outstanding support. Despite a critical shortage of personnel, he skillfully trained and reorganized his platoon into an effective fighting unit which successfully engaged the enemy during numerous combat operations. On 28 May 1968, while participating in Operation Allen Brook south of DaNang, Second Lieutenant PRISH's platoon suddenly came under intense small arms and automatic weapons fire from a large, well entrenched North Vietnamese Army force and sustained several casualties. Reacting instantly, Second Lieutenant PRISH unhesitantly maneuvered across the fire-swept terrain to a position from which he could effectively direct his unit. Disregarding his own safety, he fearlessly moved about the hazardous area, shouting words of encouragement to his men and directing their fire upon the hostile emplacements. Continuing his determined efforts, he ably directed supporting tanks in delivering a heavy volume of suppressive fire, enabling other units to advance and assist his platoon in evacuating the wounded. On 15 June, when Second Lieutenant PRISH's platoon was suddenly ambushed by a large enemy force utilizing automatic weapons and hand grenades, he quickly deployed his men and boldly led them in an aggressive assault through the hostile positions forcing the enemy to flee in panic and confusion. On 2 August, while conducting a combat patrol in heavily mined territory, the lead elements of Second Lieutenant PRISH's platoon alertly observed hostile activity. Immediately deploying his platoon to pursue the enemy force, he commenced maneuvering forward when he was suddenly wounded by an enemy explosive device. Ignoring his painful injuries, he continued to encourage and inspire his men until he was medically evacuated. Second Lieutenant PRISH's initiative, aggressive fighting spirit and unwavering devotion to duty throughout inspired all who served with him and were in keeping with the highest traditions of the Marine Corps and of the United States Naval Service.

Second Lieutenant PRISH is authorized to wear the Combat "V."

Every Marine-446

The President of the United States takes pleasure in presenting the BRONZE STAR MEDAL to

LANCE CORPORAL ROBERT A. DYER, JR.
UNITED STATES MARINE CORPS

for service as set forth in the following

CITATION:

"For heroic achievement in connection with operations against the enemy in the Republic of Vietnam while serving as a Radio Operator with Company K, Third Battalion, Twenty-Seventh Marines, First Marine Division. On 24 May 1968 during Operation Allen Brook in Quang Nam Province, Company K was attacking the village of Le Bac (1) which was well fortified and occupied by a large North Vietnamese Army force. As the company approached the area, the Marines encountered heavy enemy automatic weapons, mortar and sniper fire and sustained numerous casualties. As a member of the Tactical Air Control Party, Lance Corporal DYER skillfully coordinated the fire from armed helicopters against the enemy positions. Realizing that the numerous casualties lying exposed to the enemy fire required prompt medical attention and evacuation, he ran across the fire-swept area to a pagoda where he established a temporary aid station. Without regard for his own safety, he returned to the besieged area three times to assist wounded Marines to the covered position while continuing to coordinate friendly small arms fire and direct air strikes by armed helicopters to within ten meters of friendly positions. When the forward units were ordered to withdraw to facilitate the employment of supporting arms, he assisted in the evacuation of numerous casualties and was among the last to leave the area. Throughout the fire fight, his heroic efforts and calm presence of mind were an inspiration to al who served with him and contributed significantly to the accomplishment of his unit's mission. Lance Corporal DYER's courage, outstanding professional skill and unswerving devotion to duty throughout were in keeping with the highest traditions of the Marine Corps and of the United States Naval Service."

Lance Corporal DYER is authorized to wear the Combat "V".

The President of the United States takes pleasure in presenting the BRONZE STAR MEDAL posthumously to

HOSPITAL CORPSMAN THIRD CLASS RICHARD C. FINA
UNITED STATES NAVY

for service as set forth in the following

CITATION:

For heroic achievement in connection with combat operations while serving as a Corpsman with the First Platoon, Company K, THIRD Battalion, TWENTY-SEVENTH Marines during Operation ALLEN BROOK, Go Noi Island, Republic of Vietnam from 17 to 24 May 1968. On 17 May 1968, Petty Officer Fina demonstrated extreme bravery while under heavy enemy automatic weapons and sniper fire by advancing himself to the lead elements of Company K, to render medical aid to fallen Marines. His actions continued into the night resulting in saving many Marines from possible death. On 24 May 1968, while maneuvering across a dry riverbed several Marines fell wounded from enemy small arms and automatic weapons fire, and helplessly laid in the open area. During the heavy engagement with enemy forces, Petty Officer Fina unhesitatingly and with total disregard for his own safety, crawled approximately seventy-five yards to the fallen Marines. With no protection from the hostile fire, Petty Officer Fina administered medical attention to the fallen Marines and his actions continued until he was fatally wounded by an enemy sniper. Petty Officer Fina consistently demonstrated extraordinary heroism and devotion to the Marines with whom he so proudly served and made the ultimate sacrifice. Petty Officer Fina's bravery, personal initiative, and total dedication to duty reflected great credit upon him and were in keeping with the highest traditions of the United States Naval Service.

The Combat Distinguishing Device is authorized.

Every Marine-448

The President of the United States takes pleasure in presenting the BRONZE STAR MEDAL to

PRIVATE FIRST CLASS GARY EUGENE MAY
UNITED STATES MARINE CORPS

for service as set forth in the following

CITATION:

For meritorious service while serving as a Rifleman with the 1st Platoon, Company "K", 3d Battalion, 27th Marines, 1st Marine Division (Rein), in connection with operations against insurgent communist (Viet Gong and North Vietnamese Army) forces in the Republic of Vietnam from 20 February 1968 to 12 April 1968. Throughout this period Private First Class MAY displayed exceptional professional skill and resourcefulness in the performance or his demanding duties. Upon joining his unit, he quickly established a reputation for initiative and courage while performing his duties as a Rifleman. Participating in numerous combat patrols and daytime sweeps, he fearlessly exposed himself to enemy fire on countless occasions while aggressively closing with the enemy. This dynamic Marine's continuous efforts to improve himself and his squad reflected in his initiative and personal dedication in striving to maintain perfection whether it be in the care of weapons and equipment or his own personal performance of duty. By his willingness to place himself in the forefront of the action and through alertness and keen perception, he contributed immeasurably to the accomplishment of his platoon's mission. When on patrol, Private First Class MAY carefully observed potential ambush sites and located many hidden enemy explosive devices before they were detonated. On 23 February 1968, while aggressively closing with the enemy, he was wounded by an enemy grenade. After receiving treatment at the Battalion Aid Station, he demonstrated selfless devotion to duty by volunteering to rejoin his platoon despite the fact that he was still convalescing from his wound. In the early morning hours of 12 April 1968, while serving as the pointman for a reinforced squad patrol moving to ambush positions near a hamlet, Private First Class MAY was seriously wounded when a hidden enemy explosive device was detonated. Disregarding his own serious wounds, he displayed outstanding courage as he directed the efforts of his fellow Marines, offering words of encouragement. By his bold initiative, sustained courage, outstanding professionalism and selfless devotion to duty throughout, Private First Class

Every Marine-449

MAY upheld the highest traditions of the Marine Corps and the United States Naval Service.

Private First Class MAY is authorized to wear the Combat "V."

Every Marine-450

The President of the United States takes pleasure in presenting the BRONZE STAR MEDAL to

SERGEANT EDWARD BENAVIDEZ
UNITED STATES MARINE CORPS

for service as set forth in the following

CITATION:

For heroic achievement in connection with operations against the enemy in the Republic of Vietnam while serving as a Squad Leader with Company M, Third Battalion, Twenty-Seventh Marines, First Marine Division. On 18 May 1968 during Operation Allen Brook, the lead platoon of Company M was moving to reinforce other units operating in the vicinity of Le Bac (2) in Quang Nam Province when the platoon came under intense small arms and automatic weapons fire from a well-camouflaged, entrenched North Vietnamese Army force, temporarily pinning down the unit and wounding several Marines. Rapidly assessing the situation, Sergeant BENAVIDEZ deployed his squad and maneuvered them to relieve the pressure on the platoon. Although painfully wounded he ignored the heavy volume of hostile fire and his own injury in order to direct his squad in providing effective suppressive fire and assisting in the evacuation of casualties from the fire-swept area. Subsequently, on 24 May when a squad from an adjacent company was pinned down near a pagoda in Le Bac (1) and unable to move because of heavy casualties, Sergeant BENAVIDEZ directed his squad to remove all of their excess equipment and carry only their individual weapons and as many fragmentation and smoke grenades as possible. After maneuvering his squad across the fire-swept area to the beleaguered Marines' position, he organized the evacuation of the wounded. Moving forward, he exposed himself to hostile fire as he threw hand grenades at enemy spider holes twenty meters away and utilized smoke grenades to form a screen between his position and the North Vietnamese, facilitating the evacuation of the wounded from the hazardous area. After ensuring that all the casualties had been evacuated and the remainder of the Marines had withdrawn to safety, he ignored the danger from hostile fire as he withdrew from his exposed position under sniper fire. Sergeant BENAVIDEZ' courage, aggressive fighting spirit and selfless devotion to duty at great personal risk inspired all who observed him and were in keeping with the highest traditions of the Marine Corps and of the United States Naval Service.

Sergeant BENAVIDEZ is authorized to wear the Combat "V."

Every Marine-451

The President of the United States takes pleasure in presenting the
BRONZE STAR MEDAL to

LANCE CORPORAL CHARLES M. SWAGERTY
UNITED STATES MARINE CORPS

for service as set forth in the following

CITATION:

For heroic achievement in connection with operations against the enemy in the Republic of Vietnam while serving as a Rifleman with Company M, Third Battalion, Twenty-Seventh Marines, First Marine Division. On the afternoon of 24 May 1968 during Operation Allen Brook, Company M was assigned to assist a friendly unit which was pinned down by intense automatic weapons fire from a large North Vietnamese Army force near the village of Le Bac (1) in Quang Nam Province. As Lance Corporal SWAGERTY'S squad neared the besieged unit's position, the Marines suddenly came under a heavy volume of sniper fire and were unable to evacuate several casualties who lay in positions dangerously exposed to the hostile fire. Although his rifle was struck by the enemy fire and rendered inoperative, Lance Corporal SWAGERTY boldly advanced across the fire-swept terrain and located the source of hostile fire. Disregarding his own safety, he fearlessly exposed himself to the accurate fire and skillfully hurled numerous hand grenades at the camouflaged emplacement, silencing the enemy fire and allowing his comrades to evacuate the wounded. His bold initiative and resolute determination inspired all who observed him and contributed significantly to the accomplishment of his unit's mission. Lance Corporal SWAGERTY'S courage, aggressive fighting spirit and steadfast devotion to duty in the face of great personal danger were in keeping with the highest traditions of the Marine Corps and of the United States Naval Service.

Lance Corporal SWAGERTY is authorized to wear the Combat "V."

Every Marine-452

The President of the United States takes pleasure in presenting the LEGION OF MERIT to

LIEUTENANT COLONEL TULLIS JOSEPH WOODHAM, JR.
UNITED STATES MARINE CORPS

for service as set forth in the following

CITATION:

  For exceptionally meritorious conduct in the performance of outstanding service as the Commanding Officer of the Third Battalion, Twenty-Seventh Marines, First Marine Division in connection with operations against the enemy in the Republic of Vietnam from 17 February to 5 September 1968. Throughout this period, Lieutenant Colonel Woodham performed his demanding duties in an exemplary and highly professional manner. Expeditiously displacing his battalion from the United States to the combat zone, and assuming responsibility for a large sector of the Da Nang Tactical area, he skillfully organized his unit into an effective fighting force, established a firm defensive perimeter and conducted continuous patrolling activities which countered repeated attempts by the enemy to penetrate the area. Participating in numerous major combat operations, Lieutenant Colonel Woodham frequently disregarded his own safety while coordinating supporting fires and maneuvering his unit into advantageous fighting positions. In July 1968, he led his battalion to the Go Noi Island area and conducted operations which destroyed a large enemy staging area and thwarted the North Vietnamese Army's plans for a major assault against the Da Nang complex. He resolute determination and indomitable fighting spirit inspired all who observed him and contributed immeasurable to the accomplishment of his unit's mission. By his professionalism, dynamic leadership and unwavering devotion to duty, Lieutenant Colonel Woodham rendered distinguished service to his country and thereby upheld the highest traditions of the Marine Corps and of the United States Naval Service.

Lieutenant Colonel Woodham is authorized to wear the Combat "V".

Every Marine-453

The Secretary of the Navy takes pleasure in presenting the NAVY COMMENDATION MEDAL to

SERGEANT RICHARD A. PELKEY
UNITED STATES MARINE CORPS

for service as set forth in the following

CITATION:

For meritorious service while serving as a Squad Leader with Company M, Third Battalion, Twenty-Seventh Marines, First Marine Division in connection with operations against the enemy in the Republic of Vietnam from 15 July 1967 to 18 May 1968. During this period, Sergeant PELKEY performed his duties in an exemplary and highly professional manner. Upon learning of the battalion's proposed deployment to the Republic of Vietnam, he demonstrated superior leadership and loyalty by waiving his overseas control date in order to assist his company at a time when experienced personnel were critically needed. Because his unit consisted mostly of inexperienced personnel, he devoted many hours to the training of his men, molding them into an efficient, combat ready unit. Arriving in the Republic of Vietnam on 19 February 1968, he led over fifty patrols through heavily mined areas and participated in numerous company size operations. On 18 May during Operation Allen Brook, Company M became heavily engaged with a large North Vietnamese Army force in the village of Le Bac (2). Aggressively deploying his men, Sergeant PELKEY was seriously wounded by the intense enemy fire and subsequently medically evacuated. By his outstanding leadership, superb professionalism and unwavering devotion to duty throughout, Sergeant PELKEY upheld the finest traditions of the marine Corps and of the United States Naval Service.

Sergeant Pelkey is authorized to wear the Combat "V."

Every Marine-454

The Secretary of the Navy takes pleasure in presenting the NAVY COMMENDATION MEDAL to

CORPORAL MATTHEW H. RAIBLE
UNITED STATES MARINE CORPS

for service as set forth in the following

CITATION:

"For meritorious achievement while serving as a Radio Operator with Company L, Third Battalion, Twenty-Seventh Marines, First Marine Division in connection with operations against the enemy in the Republic of Vietnam from 18 to 27 May 1968. On 18 may during Operation Allen Brook, Company L was heavily engaged with an enemy force entrenched in fortified positions and sustained heavy casualties. For approximately five hours during intense heat of the day, Corporal RAIBLE moved from one position to another with the executive officer and displayed exceptional composure under fire as he maintained reliable communications and assisted in the evacuation of casualties. As a result of the oppressive tropical heat and the weight of his radio, he became a heat casualty. Realizing his unit was short of radio operators, he refused medical evacuation and remained in the field to provide reliable communications for his unit, despite sickness and recurring dizzy spells. While standing watch on the night of 27 May 1968, Corporal RAIBLE was severely wounded by mortar fragments and was medically evacuated. By his courage, unfaltering determination and steadfast devotion to duty throughout, Corporal RAIBLE inspired all who observed him and upheld the finest traditions of the Marine Corps and of the United States Naval Service."

Corporal RAIBLE is authorized to wear the Combat "V."

Every Marine-455

The Secretary of the Navy takes pleasure in presenting the NAVY COMMENDATION MEDAL to

SERGEANT G.E. HIGHT, JR.
UNITED STATES MARINE CORPS

for service as set forth in the following

CITATION:

"For heroic achievement while serving as a Field Operator with the Tactical Air Control Party, Third Battalion, Twenty-Seventh Marines, First Marine Division in connection with operations against the enemy in the Republic of Vietnam. On 18 May 1968 during Operation Allen Brook, the lead elements of two companies from the Third Battalion sustained heavy casualties and were pinned down by an enemy force entrenched in fortified positions. Realizing the critical situation, Sergeant HIGHT voluntarily left his relatively safe position with the command group to aid the casualties. With complete disregard for his own safety, he fearlessly ran across the fire-swept area with a medical kit and moved from one casualty to another, using his own body to shield his comrades as he administered first aid treatment. Working with seemingly tireless energy for almost two hours, Sergeant HIGHT expended an entire medical kit and twice rendered mouth-to-mouth resuscitation before he collapsed from heat exhaustion. After being revived, he steadfastly returned to the hazardous area and continued to aid his fellow Marines. By his courage, bold initiative and selfless devotion to duty in the face of intense enemy fire, Sergeant HIGHT inspired all who observed him and upheld the finest traditions of the Marine Corps and of the United States Naval Service."

Sergeant HIGHT is authorized to wear the Combat "V."

Every Marine-456

The Secretary of the Navy takes pleasure in presenting the NAVY COMMENDATION MEDAL to

SERGEANT RAY C. WATKINS
UNITED STATES MARINE CORPS

for service as set forth in the following

CITATION:

For meritorious service while serving in various capacities with the First Marine Division in connection with operations against the enemy in the Republic of Vietnam from 12 February 1968 to 19 March 1969. Throughout this period, Sergeant Watkins performed his duties in an exemplary and highly professional manner. Initially assigned as a Squad Leader with Company M, Third Battalion, Twenty-Seventh Marines, he led forty-seven patrols and repeatedly disregarded his own safety to maneuver his men into advantageous positions from which to direct accurate fire against the enemy. During Operation Allen Brook, when elements of his platoon sustained several casualties and were temporarily pinned down in an area dangerously exposed to hostile fire, Sergeant WATKINS unhesitatingly moved his squad forward and provided covering fire while the wounded were treated and evacuated. Subsequently reassigned as a Squad Leader with Company E, Second Battalion, Fifth Marines, he participated in six major combat operations, including Operation Maui Peak, and continued to distinguish himself by his composure in the face of the enemy. Reassigned as the Battalion Indoctrination Noncommissioned Officer in November 1968, he ensured that all newly arrived enlisted personnel were briefed concerning the current tactical situation, the battalion's mission, and pertinent factors concerning Vietnamese culture. By his leadership, tireless initiative and steadfast devotion to duty, Sergeant WATKINS contributed significantly to the accomplishment of his unit's mission and upheld the finest traditions of the Marine Corps and of the United States Naval Service.

The Combat Distinguishing Device is authorized.

Every Marine-457

The Secretary of the Navy takes pleasure in presenting the NAVY COMMENDATION MEDAL to

        FIRST LIEUTENANT ROY J. CASTEEL
        UNITED STATES MARINE CORPS

for service as set forth in the following

CITATION:

        For meritorious service while serving as the 81mm Mortar Platoon Commander of the Third Battalion, Twenty-Seventh Marines, First Marine Division in connection with operations against the enemy in the Republic of Vietnam from 18 February to 13 September 1968. Throughout this period, First Lieutenant Casteel performed his demanding duties in an exemplary and highly professional manner. Displaying exceptional initiative and resourcefulness, he quickly molded inexperienced personnel into an effective, motivated fighting force, capable of accomplishing all assigned tasks under the most adverse conditions. Through a continuous training program, he enabled his men to achieve maximum proficiency which greatly enhance the operational effectiveness of his unit. Under his inspiring leadership, his platoon provided a high level of support to battalion units during numerous combat operations. On one occasion, during Operation Allen Brook, when his men were unable to fire their mortars because of the enemy's proximity to friendly lines, he skillfully directed them in employing their rifles and inflicting numerous casualties upon the enemy. By his professionalism, superb leadership and steadfast devotion to duty, First Lieutenant Casteel contributed significantly to the accomplishment of his unit's mission and upheld the finest traditions of the Marine Corps and of the United States Naval Service.

First Lieutenant Casteel is authorized to wear the Combat "V."

Every Marine-458

The Secretary of the Navy takes pleasure in presenting the NAVY ACHIEVEMENT MEDAL to

SERGEANT GEORGE E. HIGHT, JR.
UNITED STATES MARINE CORPS

for outstanding achievement in the superior performance of his duties in the field of leadership achievement as set forth in the following

CITATION:

While serving with the Third Battalion, Twenty-Seventh Marines, First Marine Division in connection with operations against the enemy in the Republic of Vietnam from 20 February to 13 September 1968, Sergeant HIGHT performed his duties in an exemplary and highly competent manner. As Tactical Air Control Party Chief, he displayed outstanding leadership and initiative despite extremely adverse conditions and the difficulties of a combat environment. Distinguishing himself by his consistently high level of efficiency, he materially enhanced the operational effectiveness and combat readiness of his unit. Prior to his unit's deployment to the Republic of Vietnam, he instituted a comprehensive training program for his inexperienced personnel which greatly enhanced their proficiency and enabled his section to provide outstanding tactical air control support to the battalion during numerous combat operations. As a result of his diligence and seemingly unlimited resourcefulness, he gained the respect and admiration of all who observed him and contributed significantly to the accomplishment of his unit's mission. Sergeant HIGHT's outstanding professional ability, untiring determination and steadfast devotion to duty throughout reflect great credit upon himself, the Marine Corps and the Naval Service.

Sergeant HIGHT is authorized to wear the Combat "V."

Every Marine-459

The Secretary of the Navy takes pleasure in presenting the NAVY ACHIEVEMENT MEDAL to

CORPORAL ROBERT M. SCHULTZ
UNITED STATES MARINE CORPS

for outstanding achievement in the superior performance of his duties in the field of professional achievement as set forth in the following

CITATION:

While serving with the First Marine Division in connection with operations against the enemy in the Republic of Vietnam from 21 February 1968 to 15 March 1969, Corporal Schultz performed his duties in an exemplary manner. Initially assigned as an Infantryman with Company K, Third Battalion, Twenty-Seventh Marines, he displayed outstanding professionalism and initiative despite extremely adverse conditions and the difficulties of a combat environment. Distinguishing himself by his consistently high level of efficiency, he materially enhanced the operational effectiveness and combat readiness of his unit. Reassigned as a Tank Crewman with Company C, First Tank Battalion, he participated in the defense of the Song Cau Do Bridge. During the night of 22 August 1968 when the bridge was attached by a large enemy force, Corporal Schultz was temporarily stunned by the impact of an antitank rocket on his vehicle. Regaining consciousness, he skillfully maneuvered the tank into an advantageous firing position to deliver effective machine gun and cannon fire onto the advancing enemy, breaking the momentum of the attack and forcing the enemy to withdraw. Subsequently reassigned on 15 October 1968 as a Battalion Operations Clerk, he continued to distinguish himself in the performance of his duties. As a result of his diligence and seemingly unlimited resourcefulness, he gained the respect and admiration of all who observed him and contributed significantly to the accomplishment of his unit's mission. Corporal Schultz' outstanding professional ability, untiring determination and steadfast devotion to duty reflect great credit upon himself, the Marine Corps and the Naval Service.

Corporal Schultz is authorized to wear the Combat "V."

Every Marine-460

The Secretary of the Navy takes pleasure in presenting the NAVY ACHIEVEMENT MEDAL to

CORPORAL ROBERT F. FONTANA
UNITED STATES MARINE CORPS

for outstanding achievement in the superior performance of his duties in the field of professional achievement as set forth in the following

CITATION:

While serving as a Mortar Man with Company M, Third Battalion, Twenty-Seventh marines, First Marine Division in connection with operations against the enemy in the Republic of Vietnam on 18 May 1968 during Operation Allen Brook, Lance Corporal FONTANA performed his duties in an exemplary and highly professional manner. The lead platoon of Company M was moving to reinforce units operating in the vicinity of Le Bac (2) in Quang Nam Province when the platoon came under intense small arms and automatic weapons fire from a well-camouflaged, entrenched North Vietnamese Army force, wounding several Marines and temporarily pinning down the remainder of the unit. When the extremely close range of fighting precluded the employment of mortars, Lance Corporal FONTANA ignored the heavy volume of hostile fire as he moved to positions along the front lines to encourage his comrades and administer first aid to the casualties. Although physically exhausted due to the intense heat during the five hour battle, he refused treatment for himself and continued to assist in the evacuation and care of the wounded. Lance Corporal FONTANA's courage, bold initiative and selfless devotion to duty at great personal risk reflect great credit upon himself, the Marine Corps and the Naval Service.

Lance Corporal FONTANA is authorized to wear the Combat "V."

Every Marine-461

## ABBREVIATIONS

The following abbreviations were used in this text and should be helpful to the non-military reader.

## UNITS

| | |
|---|---|
| 3/27 | 3rd Battalion, 27th Marine Regiment |
| 2/27 | 2nd Battalion, 27th Marine Regiment |
| 1/27 | 1st Battalion, 27th Marine Regiment |
| 1/7 | 1st Battalion, 7th Marine Regiment |
| 2/7 | 2nd Battalion, 7th Marine Regiment |
| 3/7 | 3rd Battalion, 7th Marine Regiment |
| 2/1 | 2nd Battalion, 1st Marine Regiment |
| 2/3 | 2nd Battalion, 3rd Marine Regiment |
| 3/5 | 3rd Battalion, 5th Marine Regiment |
| Co I | India Company |
| Co K | Kilo Company |
| Co L | Lima Company |
| Co M | Mike Company |
| H&S Co | Headquarters and Service Company |
| Co | Company |
| Bn | Battalion |
| Reg | Regiment |
| Div | Division |
| (-) | Under Strengthed Unit |
| (+) | Reinforced Unit |

## MILITARY RANKS / POSITIONS

| | |
|---|---|
| PVT | Private |
| PFC | Private First Class |
| L/CPL | Lance Corporal |
| CPL | Corporal |
| SGT | Sergeant |

Every Marine-462

| | |
|---|---|
| S/SGT | Staff Sergeant |
| GY/SGT | Gunnery Sergeant (Gunny) |
| SGT/MAJ | Sergeant Major |
| LT | Lieutenant |
| CAPT | Captain |
| MAJ | Major |
| LT COL | Lieutenant Colonel |
| COL | Colonel |
| GEN | General |
| BGEN | Brigadier General |
| CO | Commanding Officer |
| NCO | Non-Commissioned Officer |
| XO | Executive Officer |

## WEAPONS

| | |
|---|---|
| AK-47 | Soviet automatic/semi-automatic rifle |
| B-40 | Enemy rocket |
| Beehive | USA flechette (small steel darts) - loaded fragmentation, anti personnel shell |
| CBU | Cluster Bomb Unit |
| C-4 | Plastic explosive |
| Chicom | Chinese Communist grenade |
| HEAT | High explosive anti-tank |
| LAW | USA light anti-tank weapon |
| RPG | Soviet enemy rocket launcher |
| RPK | Soviet machine gun |
| SKS | Chinese semi-automatic rifle |
| M-14 | USA semi-automatic rifle |
| M-16 | USA automatic/semi auto rifle |
| M-60 | USA assault machine gun |
| M-79 | USA grenade launcher |
| .45 | USA semi-automatic pistol |

| | |
|---|---|
| 60mm | Mortar round sizes in millimeters |
| 81mm | Mortar round sizes in millimeters |
| 82 mm | Mortar round sizes in millimeters |
| | |
| 106 RR | 106 millimeter recoilless rifle |
| | |
| 105mm | Artillery round sizes in millimeters |
| 155mm | Artillery round sizes in millimeters |
| 175mm | Artillery round sizes in millimeters |
| | |
| 8" | Naval gun round size in inches |
| | |
| WP | White Phosphorous (Willy Peter) |

## CASUALTY STATUS

| | |
|---|---|
| DOW | Died of wounds |
| KIA | Killed in action |
| MIA | Missing in action |
| NBC | Non-battle casualty |
| POW | Prisoner of War |
| WIA | Wounded in action |
| WIANE | Wounded in action - not evacuated |

## MISCELLANEOUS

| | |
|---|---|
| ARVN | Army Republic of Vietnam |
| NVA | North Vietnamese Army |
| USA | United States Army |
| USAF | United States Air Force |
| USMC | United States Marine Corps |
| USN | United States Navy |
| VC | Viet Cong - Communist Irregular soldier in South Vietnam |

| | |
|---|---|
| ALO | Air Liaison Officer |
| BAS | Battalion Aid Station |
| CAP | Combined Action Platoon |
| CP | Command Post |
| COC | Combat Operations Center |
| CONUS | Continental United States |
| EOD | Explosive Ordnance Disposal |
| FO | Forward Observer (Artillery) |
| FSC | Fire Support Coordinator |
| FSCC | Fire Support Coordination Center |
| G2 | Intelligence Section (Division) |
| H&I | Harassment & Interdiction |
| HQ | Headquarters |
| LP | Listening Post |
| LZ | Landing Zone |
| MAB | Marine Amphibious Brigade |
| MAF | Marine Amphibious Force |
| MEB | Marine Expeditionary Brigade |
| MED | Medical |
| MOS | Military Occupation Specialties |
| MP | Military Police |
| NSA | Naval Support Activities |
| OA | Operational Area |
| OCS | Officer Candidate School |
| OP | Observation Post |
| OP CON | Operational Control |
| PPB | Platoon Patrol Base |
| PTSD | Post Traumatic Stress Disorder |
| S1 | Administration |
| S2 | Intelligence Section (Battalion/Regiment) |
| S3 | Operations Section (Battalion/Regiment) |
| S4 | Transportation and Supplies |
| SOG | Special Operations Group |
| TAD | Temporary Assigned Duty |
| TAOR | Tactical Area of Responsibility |

| | |
|---|---|
| T/O | Table of Organization |
| 782 gear | Miscellaneous field gear (packs, canteens, etc.) |
| 6Xs | Military trucks |

## SOURCES

### PERSONAL ACCOUNTS:

The majority of the personal accounts which make up the bulk of this book were taken from in-person interviews, oral tapes, telephone calls, letters, questionnaires, e-mails and stories written by the quoted sources. Some of this information has been edited for both clarity and accuracy. All other material was taken from the below listed sources.

### BOOKS:

Dougan, Clark. <u>Vietnam Experience 1968</u>. Boston, MA: Boston Publishing, 1983.

Drew, Paul. <u>The Navy Cross</u>. Forest Ranch, CA: Stevens, Sharp and Dunnigan, 1987.

Lewy, Guenter <u>America in Vietnam</u>. New York, NY: Oxford University Press, 1978.

Puller, Lewis B. Jr. <u>Fortunate Son</u>. New York, NY: Grove Weidenfeld 1991.

Spector, Ronald H. <u>After Tet</u>. New York, NY: The Free Press, MacMillian, Inc., 1993.

<u>The Marines in Vietnam, 1954-1973: An Anthology and Annotated Bibliography</u>. Washington, DC: US Marine Corps, History and Museums Division, 1985.

<u>The Marines in Vietnam, 1968</u>. Washington D.C.: U.S. Marine Corps, History and Museums Division, 1995.

Every Marine-468

Books (continued)

Vietnam Veteran Memorial - Directory of Names. Washington, D.C.: Public Vietnam Veterans Memorial Fund, Washington DC, 1991.

MAPS:

Buchanan, Richard. Placerville, CA.
Jung, William C. Onalaska, WI
Simonsen, Robert A. Riverside, CA

MAGAZINES:
Abbott, Bill. Vietnam Magazine, June 1993.
Davis, CPL Tim. Leatherneck, April 1994.
Johnson, Lt Col Maxwell. Marine Corps Gazette, July 1987.
Hemingway, Al. Vietnam Magazine, April 1991.
Kibat, L/CPL Art. Leatherneck, December 1968.

MANUSCRIPTS (Unpublished):

Jung, William C. - Onalaska, WI
Boyko, Andrew - Riverside, CA
Harland, Gary - Brighton, MO

MILITARY DOCUMENTS:

3/27 Command Chronology - February 1968, March 1968, May 1968, July 1968, August 1968 and September 1968.

27th Marines Regimental Combat After Action Report - 17 May - 06 June 1968.

3/27 Combat After Action Reports - May 1968, July 1968.

Every Marine-469

Military Documents (continued)

3/27 Company Personnel Rosters - February thru August 1968.

3/27 History 1966-69 - Marine Corps Historical Center, Washington, D.C.

3/7 Command Chronology - May 1968.

Marine Corps Oral History Tapes (#2871, 2873, 2874, 2875, 2876) - Marine Corps Historical Center.

Press Release - 9 September 1968, 9:00 AM; Command Information Bureau, Marine Corps Recruit Depot, San Diego, CA.

27th Marine History, by James S. Santelli - August 1968.

3/27 Unit and Individual Awards - Marine Corps Historical Center and Marine Headquarters, Quantico, VA.

NEWSPAPERS:

Chevron. 13 September 1968, MCRD, San Diego, California.
Gypsum Advocate. 20 June 1968, Gypsum, Kansas.
Navy Times. Various dates 1968.
News Leader. 20 February 1994, Missouri.
News Gazette. 17 May 1998, Illinois.
Press Enterprise. 18 May 1994, Riverside, California.
Pendleton Scout. 29 August 1969, Camp Pendleton, California.
San Diego Union. 29 August 1969, San Diego, California.
Sea Tiger. Various dates 1968.

Every Marine-470

<u>Newspapers</u> (continued)

Stars & Stripes. Various dates 1968.
Star Ledger Wire Service.
Times - Union and Journal. 14 July 1968, Jacksonville, Florida.
Washington Post. 12 November 1993, Washington, D.C.

Every Marine-471

# NAME INDEX

ABBATE, Richard, 415
ACOSTA, Clovis, 22, 55, 92, 93, 94, 114
ACOSTA, James, 415
ADKINS, Terry, 416
AGHAMALIAN, Richard, 257, 258
AGUILAR, Arnold, 414
ALBERT, Francisco, 418
ALLEN, Donald, 414
ALLISON, Ray, 63, 190, 195, 202, 330, 331 332, 335, 366, 367, 418
ALMAGUER, Benajamin, 414
ALVAREZ, Al, 417
ANDERSON, Robert, 72, 117, 252, 253, 317, 342, 391
ANDERSON, L/Cpl, 324
ANDREWS, Don, 418
ANDREWS, William, 413
ANSELMI, Eugene, 418
ATKINSON, Jerry, 414
BACH, William, 12, 104, 123
BAILEY, Claude, 419
BANKS, Bob, 418
BARCA, John, 414
BARCROFT, Robert, 257
BARLETTA, Thomas, 58, 418
BARNARD, Lt Col Roger, 152, 154, 167, 169, 173, 178, 184, 202, 221
BARNETT, Roy, 418
BAUER, Bob, 143, 148, 214, 413
BAYLOR, Harold, 415
BEAN, Jerry, 325
BEASLEY, Terry, 418
BELSER, Jimmy, 119
BELSER, Joseph, 171, 227, 277, 284, 285, 291, 292, 293, 437
BENAVIDEZ, Edward, 101, 102, 103, 105, 220, 236, 239, 247, 266, 305, 306, 312, 315, 325, 419, 450
BENECH, 'Doc' Paul, 67, 212
BENNETT, Richard, 257
BENOIT, Kenneth, 31, 255
BERJANS, Mike, 418
BEST, John, 418
BIER, Dennis, 418
BILBERRY, Dwain, 325
BILLS, Lyle, 413
BLACK, Isiah, 146, 193
BLALOCK, Gherald, 414
BLANCHARD, David, 254, 416
BLANDIN, Raymond, 414
BLAZER, John, 30, 32, 38
BLEY, Bruce, 341
BLONDI, James, 357
BOCANEGRA, Felix, 413
BODEN, Dave, 418
BOTES, George, 228 229, 415
BOWEN, Clifton, 415
BOWER, Burton, 259, 435
BOWLING, James, 416

BOYD, Bill, 279, 417
BOYKO, Andrew, 23, 41, 43, 73, 77, 79, 85, 88, 343, 396, 397, 402, 418
BRADY, James, 270
BRANNON, Paul, 313, 418
BRESEMAN, Jerry, 418
BRETTMAN, Orville, 223, 268, 286, 323
BREWER, Glen, 419
BREWER, Paul, 419
BRIDGES, R.B., 413
BRIDGES, Wayne, 418
BROOKS, Steven, 230, 415
BROWN, Larry, 416
BROWN, Rodney, 54, 69, 72
BROWN, Roger, 414
BROWN, Vernon, 415
BRYANT, Charles, 175
BRYANT, Charlie, 416
BRYANT, Creed, 415
BUCHANAN, Richard, 124, 239, 293, 295, 299, 300, 302, 303, 306, 320, 419, 427
BURKE, Marilyn, 380
BURKE, Robert, 120, 166, 194, 195, 196, 379, 380, 381, 413, 426
BURNS, David, 355, 418
BURTON, John 415
BUTLER, Charlie, 116, 418
BYRD, Dale, 323
CALLAN, Robert, 419
CAMP, Dale, 18, 43, 54, 81, 107, 114, 126, 141, 146, 150, 153, 157, 158, 160, 174, 176, 177, 183, 184, 195, 198, 212, 213, 223, 226, 261, 322, 418
CAMPBELL, John, 419
CAMPBELL, Scott, 418
CAMPORA, Ronald, 59, 237, 363, 419
CARPENTER, Lewis, 173
CASEY, Robert, 166
CASTEEL, Roy, 8, 32, 222, 224, 240, 266, 268, 408, 457
CAZIER, Larry, 417
CHAFFEY, Chip, 417
CHAMBERLAIN, Harold, 417
CHAPMAN, Clinton, 298, 320, 416
CHAPMAN, Jerry, 414
CHAPMAN, Gen Leonard, 401
CHIOLOLO, Vincent, 210, 211, 434
CHRISTY, Denny, 97, 98, 418
CHUTE, Stephen, 415
CIEZKI, Allen, 27, 30, 114, 115, 165, 174, 177, 183, 198, 199, 202, 215, 418
CLARK, George, 293, 294, 298, 416
COBB, Paul, 166
COCKER, Joe, 406
COLES, Vincent, 159, 160, 169, 262, 413
COLLECA, James, 380, 418
COLPAS, Gary, 125, 418
COMPTON, Don, 98
COOPER, Rick, 417

# Every Marine-472

CORTEZ, Frank, 11, 12, 35, 62, 104, 419
COTTON, Carl, 418
COURT, Michael, 418
COUSINS, Richard, 230, 418
COX, Melvin 'Senator Mudflap', 114, 139, 198, 218
CRAFT, Ezra, 413
CRAIG, Harry, 413
CRAMM, Eddy, 237
CRAWFORD, Bill, 417
CROOK, Thomas, 413
CROTEAU, John, 418
CUMMINS, Lanny, 189, 190, 413
CUNNINGHAM, Michael, 284, 418
CURETON, Ronnie, 67, 414
CURTIS, Bruce, 156, 182, 193
DAHL, Bill, 109, 418
DAVIDSON, Ronald, 413
DAVIS, Gary, 415
DAVIS, Robert, 415
DAVIS, Tim, 22, 42, 54, 96, 98, 143, 144, 148, 403, 418
DAWSON, Stephen, 9
DECORTE, Joe, 417
DEEDS, Leland, 413
DELACERNA, Pedro, 8
DELEON, Domingo, 151, 163, 418
DELGADO, Ray, 417
DETTY, Bob, 418
DEVITT, Doc, 28, 32, 40, 47
DEWITT, Steve, 418
DIAZ, Juan, 106, 419
DICKEY, Robert, 304
DILLINGHAM, Bruce, 257, 417
DREGGER, Daniel, 418
DRIFFILL, Leroy, 67, 79, 83, 127, 128, 204, 235, 269, 282, 287, 307, 418
DULACKI, B Gen Leo, 400
DUPARD, Ronnie, 371
DWYER, B Gen Ross, 407
DYER, Robert, 298, 300, 303, 305, 306, 383, 417, 446
DYRDAHL, Vernon, 193, 194, 226, 261, 262
EASTON, Steve, 15, 42, 143, 148, 166, 182, 185, 338, 373, 418
EDNEY, Donald, 404, 414
EDWARDS, Daniel, 413
EGGERS, Michael, 343
ELDRIDGE, Daniel, 413
ENGLISH, Maj Gen Lowell, 401
ERNEST, John, 8, 33, 120, 209, 243, 257, 270, 281, 309, 323, 326, 342, 380, 388, 400, 406, 418
ESTRADA, Ramon, 417
EUBANKS, George, 391
EVANS, Paul, 95, 415
FELICIANO, Steven, 372
FIALKO, David, 414
FIEBLEKORN, Marcus, 9, 190, 191, 413
FINA, 'Doc' Richard, 307, 414, 447
FINCH, 'Doc' M, 166
FISHER, Ray, 328, 331, 336, 339, 345, 418

FITZGERALD, Ernest, 8, 51, 138, 233, 241, 270, 279, 352, 391, 417
FONES, LARRY, 290
FONSECA, Raul, 12, 57, 106, 149, 169, 174, 181, 200, 338, 368, 418
FONTANA, Robert, 419, 460
FOSTER, James, 347
FOSTER, John 414
FRANCIS, Charles, 393
FRYE, Larry, 59, 81, 254, 287, 354, 365, 370, 384, 389, 419
FULEKY, Thomas, 22, 54, 70, 72, 96, 105, 241, 272, 274, 278, 323, 342, 388, 417
GAFFNEY, Edward, 277
GALVIN, Tim, 418
GARCIA, Tony, 418
GARRETT, Robert, 414
GEORGE, John, 201, 418
GEORGE, John W., 416
GIBSON, Guy, 279
GIBSON, John, 186, 187, 188, 413
GILBERT, Herbert, 418
GIVENS, Duane, 330, 332
GLEASON, Jack, 419
GLICK, 'Doc' M., 158, 159, 163, 165, 194
GOFF, Lloyd, 418
GONZALEZ, Juan, 159, 162, 163, 166, 170, 418
GONZALEZ, Leroy, 9, 121
GORTON, Jack, 415
GOSTLIN, Bill, 94, 95, 96, 144, 145, 418
GRAHAM, Col Paul, 51
GRAVES, Alton, 417
GRAYMIRE, Jerry, 78, 307, 418
GREEN, Allen, 413
GREEN, Ray, 419
GREEN, Walter Jr., 416
GRIFFIN, Ron, 418
GRUPPA, Paul, 30
GUHL, Al, 101, 102, 103, 104, 105, 293, 419
GUSTI, Dante, 93
HAGE, Mark, 413
HALL, Bradford, 417
HALL, Col Reverdy, 139, 153, 167, 168, 204, 209
HALSEY, John, 418
HAMILTON, L, 363
HANSON, Tom, 58, 68, 117, 143, 148, 150, 168, 181, 185, 188, 213, 418
HARLAND, Gary, 8, 10, 37, 64, 121, 122, 191, 406, 418
HARLEY, Charles, 193
HARPER, Dana, 220, 418
HARDEN, Fred, 418
HARTMANN, Bill, 399, 419
HAUGEN, Thomas, 9, 121, 191
HAWKINS, Albert, 413
HAWKINS, Phillip III, 414
HAYES, John, 124, 125, 239, 294, 298
HAYMAN, Charles, 418
HAZELWOOD, John, 122, 123, 235, 330, 332, 334, 335, 337, 339, 413, 431
HECHT, Joseph, 418
HEIN, David, 101, 103, 304, 312, 325

# Every Marine-473

HENDERSON, Jack Jr, 159, 165, 166, 413
HENRY, William, 31
HERRERA, Cpl, 344
HETRICK, Gerald, 96, 415
HIGHT, George, 10, 242, 417, 455, 458
HILBERT, Jerry, 284, 414
HILL, Donald, 204, 227, 266
HILL, Evale, 418
HIMES, Bernard, 413
HINDEN, Carleton, 158, 163
HOAGLAND, William, 119, 120
HOFFMAN, Cpl, 156, 182, 193, 194
HOLZHUAER, Doug, 418
HOME, Jerry, 418
HOPKINS, William, 314
HOWARD, Jim, 330, 331
HUBER, John, 418
HUBBARD, Thomas, 416
HUKABY, Charles, 228, 270, 283, 313, 318, 323
HUNT, James, 416
HUNT, Lt Col R.G., 407
IBENEZ, Pat, 418
IGNATIUS, Paul, 401
INCHEK, Don, 418
JACKSON, Brian, 417
JACKSON, Joe, 419
JACKSON, Marlin, 10, 44, 223, 237, 251, 259, 268,
    275, 286, 290, 308, 311, 314, 317, 323,
    324, 352, 356, 358, 361, 362, 369, 374,
    375, 384, 397, 419, 429
JANKE, Theodore, 413
JARONIK, Robert, 414
JENKINS, David, 271, 419
JERSTAD, Leslie, 414
JESTER, Herbert, 291, 438
JIMINEZ, Anastacio, 414
JOHNSON, George, 413
JOHNSON, Johnny, 217, 231, 267, 274, 418
JOHNSON, President Lyndon, 7, 13, 15, 35, 37, 39,
    40, 41, 262, 387
JONES, Bennie, 413
JONES, Donald, 254, 416
JONES, Raymond, 413
JUAREZ, Oscar, 413
JUNG, Bill, 15, 27, 30, 38, 40, 46, 171, 172, 193, 208,
    210, 216, 220, 231, 234, 255, 263, 265,
    266, 268, 269, 272, 274, 275, 277, 279,
    281, 284, 285, 350, 353, 355, 357, 359,
    364, 365, 367, 370, 372, 374, 375, 392,
    394, 395, 403, 418, 443
KALKA, Charles, 210, 285, 319, 414
KAMINSKI, Joseph, 414
KASSEL, Wayne, 419
KEEFE, E. Miles Jr., 8, 12, 64, 72, 81, 109, 110, 376,
    419
KELLER, Lt Co A.W., 382
KELLEY, 'Doc' Raul, 218, 225
KENT, James, 8, 14, 15, 17, 257, 303, 304, 306, 391,
    418
KERR, Brian, 417
KIBALT, Art, 382, 418
KILLINSKI, Mark, 418

KINCAD, Limey, 279
KINSWORTHY, Loyd, 121, 414
KINYON, Rodney, 413
KIRKPATRICK-HOLMES, Sandy 'Miss K', 144,
    145, 404
KLASEN, David, 279
KLINE, Jerry, 10, 417
KOBBERMAN, John, 419
KROEPJL, G.J. Jr, 418
KUHSE, Michael, 208, 414
KUYKENDALL, Henry, 414
LAWERENZ, Rich, 263
LEACH, James, 415
LEE, Nate, 9, 62, 122, 191, 414
LEE, Tony, 191
LEFFEW, Larry, 331
LEJEUNE, Horrace, 415
LESTAGE, William, 231, 285, 414
LEWERENZ, Rich, 255, 419
LEWIS, Donne, 414
LEWIS, Douglas, 204, 227
LEWIS, Michael, 413
LEWIS, Paul, 414
LEYTEM, John, 30
LIPARI, Michael, 417
LIPPS, Marvin, 230
LITTLE, Michael, 360, 419
LONG, Brian, 418
LOVE, Wes, 19, 68, 78, 90, 192, 204, 211, 216, 217,
    227, 418
LOWERY, Thomas, 31
LOZANO, Justo, 325
LUPE, Eugene, 416
LUTZ, 'Doc' Mike, 18, 55, 67, 90, 113, 115, 120,
    139, 148, 149, 150, 168, 175, 183, 197,
    213, 418
LYONS, James, 414
MACK, Joseph, 416
MADDUX, Roy, 63, 414
MALLON, Gerald, 419
MARRON, Richard, 417
MARSHALL, Charles, 414
MARTIN, Arthur, 413
MARTIN, John, 8, 417
MARTINEZ, Oscar, 331
MASSEY, Gary, 67, 176, 177, 183, 197
MATHIS, Edward, 419
MAXWELL, Keith, 175
MAY, Gary, 66, 418, 448
McADAMS, William, 102
McCARVILLE, Ron, 264
McGEE, George, 414
MELTON, Rodney, 95, 415
MENDENHALL, Ted, 417
MENDEZ, Jessie, 30
MENDOZA, Andres, 417
MERCER, Kenneth, 417
METZGER, Franklin, 210, 415
MEYER, Lt Col Edward, 402
MICHAEL, Paul, 417
MILLER, John, 101, 102, 103, 416
MILLER, Lonnie, 14, 78, 390, 418

# Every Marine-474

MILLER, Phillip, 199, 262, 414
MILLS, Thomas 335, 414
MILOT, Larry, 415
MINH, Ho Chi, 126, 163
MINTON, David, 151, 152, 185
MITCHELL, Larry, 418
MITCHNER, Jan, 96, 113, 157, 158, 159, 163, 213
MONK, Shelby, 157, 169, 174, 188, 373, 418
MONTALVO, Lupe, 188, 417
MOON, Thomas 415
MORALES, Angelo, 415
MOROZ, Geno, 418
MORRISON, Michael, 106
MORRISSEY, William, 419
MOYE, Don, 417
MUCH, Gary, 258, 259, 260, 419, 436
MUELLER, Lt Col Charles, 138
MULLEN, Joseph, 415
MUNCY, Gilbert, 415
MUNSON, Bill, 417
MURPHY, Charles, 417
MURPHY, William, 30
MURRAY, Richard, 408
MYERS, George, 413
NAJEWSKI, James, 93, 125
NEAL, Hiahwahnah Richard, 11, 29, 57, 73, 304, 305, 419, 432
NEIHART, Frank, 124, 305, 419
NEILSON, Bob, 96, 157, 418
NELSON, Louis, 95, 415
NICHOLS, Nick, 419
NICKEL, R. Vernon, 417
NOBLE, Gary, 239, 416
NOEL, Chris, 87
NOONAN, Ken, 98
NORA, Raymond, 415
NORVELL, Jefrey, 415
NOWAK, Leonard, 414
NOWAK, Marty, 354
NOWLIN, _____, 221
NULL, Gary, 417
O'CONNER, Daniel, 128, 211, 418
O'CONNER, William Jr, 415
ODEN, Claude, 418
O'HARA, William, 216, 226, 408
OLIVER, Rommie, 415
O'NEAL, Harold Jr, 322, 415
O'NEILL, Bob, 154
O'NEILL, Father Michael, 341, 381, 417
ORIGER, Tim, 418
OROZCO, Tony, 414
OSTBERG, Karl, 419
OSTER, William, 338, 339
PAHL, Jon, 16, 66, 128, 145, 155, 158, 163, 170, 176, 182, 189, 190, 193, 218, 384, 418
PARKER, Lynn, 204, 228
PARKS, Joel, 203, 209, 216, 221, 224, 225, 235, 255, 265, 278, 283, 306, 364
PARRISH, Julian, 8, 32, 312, 329, 381, 391
PARSONS, Jack, 152, 184
PATERSON, H.D. Jr, 382
PELKY, Richard, 11, 51, 90, 247, 249, 453

PEREZ, Rodolfo, 413
PETERSON, Dillard, 90, 91, 415
PETRI, Mike, 417
PETTYJOHN, George, 419
PHILLIPS, Marron, 143, 182, 185, 188
PIERCE, Rudy, 419
PINNICK, James, 8
PLUT, Wayne, 418
POKRZYWA, Walter, 16
POOLE, Ronald, 414
POTKALITSKY, Robert, 306
POUNDER, Duane, 267, 419
POUSSON, Michael, 416
PRICE, 'Doc' D., 144, 182
PRIETO, William, 390, 418
PRISH, Bill, 293, 309, 329, 331, 332, 366, 418, 444
PRITCHETT, Gregory, 413
PULLER, Gen Louis B. 'Chesty', 293, 392
PULLER, Louis B. Jr, 293, 391, 393
PURCELL, Gary, 284, 285, 415
RAHN, 'Doc' Donald, 255, 413
RAIBLE, Matthew, 326, 419, 454
RALPH, Thomas, 8, 66, 140, 143, 154, 155, 158, 169, 175, 176, 177, 181, 185, 186, 187, 188, 189, 190, 192, 384, 413
RAY, Jerry, 323
REISNER, Lt Col Pierre, 4
RENAGHAN, Joseph, 60, 118, 119, 419
REPPOND, Clois, 418
REXROAD, Lt Col, 221
REYNOLDS, Richard, 417
RICCI, Mike, 419
RICHARDS, Paul, 417
RICHARDS, Richard, 105, 419
RICHARDSON, Bruce, 289, 290
RICHARDSON, Randy, 307, 418
RICKSON, Paul, 419
RIDDLE, L/Cpl, 156, 193
RILEY, Ricky, 415
RIORDAN, Art, 46, 86, 89, 91, 94, 107, 111, 114, 116, 118, 125, 208, 228, 232, 258, 266, 273, 315, 393, 398, 406, 419
RISNER, Richard, 417
ROACH, Fred, 204, 227, 413
ROBB, Charles, 262
ROBERTS, Tony, 194
ROBERTSON, Maj Gen Donn, 137, 138
RODRIGUEZ, George, 414
ROEHM, Dave, 418
ROLL, Bill, 154
ROSALES, Walter, 418
ROSE, Daniel, 415
ROSENFELT, S/Sgt, 104
ROWLAND, Roger, 416
SAMBAS, Ted, 54, 69, 70
SANCHEZ, Ben, 419
SAWYER, Terry, 279, 284, 418
SCARANO, David, 417
SCHALER, Joseph, 284
SCHETTL, David, 414
SCHINZE, Kurt, 417
SCHMIDT, 'Doc' Richard, 239, 247, 267, 371, 372

# Every Marine-475

419
SCHULTZ, Robert, 418, 459
SCHWEIG, Victor, 414
SCHWENK, Col Adolph, 4, 7, 138, 179, 191, 192, 249, 270, 342, 382, 383, 400
SEAMSTER, Willie, 414
SHANE, Wallace, 95, 415
SHARPE, Thomas, 415
SHAW, James, 123, 125
SHAW, Joe, 239
SHERLOCK, Robert, 415
SHEWMAN, Ronald, 415
SILER, Robert, 419
SIMONSEN, Robert, 15, 16, 17, 19, 29, 33, 35, 77, 111, 126, 139, 140, 146, 152, 157, 158, 159, 161, 162, 163, 166, 176, 234, 312, 320, 340, 343, 354, 358, 359, 365, 366, 394, 395, 418
SINCLAIR, Patrick, 415
SINGLETON, Wally, 417
SISCO, Garland, 15, 57, 67, 91, 204, 207, 211, 230, 232, 257, 277, 283, 307, 418
SKELNAR, Jon, 419
SKOTARCZAK, Mike, 419
SMITH, David, 418
SMITH, Frank, 329
SMITH, Mark, 45, 100, 111, 145, 189, 190, 404, 418, 442
SMITH, Robert, 415
SMITH, R.D., 407
SMITH, Tom, 418
SNELTZER, Richard 215, 222, 345, 417
SPENCER, Chuck, 21, 55, 108, 388
SNYDER, Sgt Maj Robert, 8, 51, 54, 110, 113, 229, 238, 241, 273, 322, 349, 357
SPENCER, C. J., 419
SPENCER, Jess, 419
SPENSKO, Louis, 414
STANLEY, Don, 415
STAVINOHA, Robert, 415
STEED, Billy, 8, 13, 32, 45, 55, 170, 240, 317, 319, 327, 345, 356, 380, 391, 417
STEFFENSEN, David, 18, 206, 208
STEPHENSON, Frederick Dale, 362, 416
STEINER, Frank, 417
STELLI, Bob, 417
STERN, William, 417
STEWART, 'Doc' Michael, 100
STEIR, Dave, 405
STIRLING, Chris, 98, 418
STOPPA, Michael, 294, 419, 439
STONE, Everett, 419
STRINGER, Henry, 419
STUEBE, Fred, 143, 169, 175, 188, 224, 263, 266, 267, 417
STYCK, Jerry, 417
SULLIVAN, Steve, 328, 332, 334, 335, 414
SUTHERLAND, Grant, 228
SWAGGERTY, Charles, 98, 101, 127, 238, 244, 265, 288, 312, 388, 419, 451
SWANKER, Nelson, 96, 415
SZEKELY, Michael, 417

TABAYOYON, Andre, 418
THANE, Mel, 118, 419
THERIAULT, Paul, 416
THIBODEUX, Edward, 414
THOMAS, Blake, 8, 220, 236, 237 242, 258, 261, 274, 277, 286, 293, 300, 302, 303, 307, 316, 318, 319, 324, 391, 419
THOMAS, George Jr, 415
THOMAS, Joe, 146
THOMPSON, Dave, 46, 92, 93, 419
THOMPSON, Steven, 147, 157, 158, 162, 188, 193, 194, 213, 310
THUC, Col Truong Tan, 172
THUESEN, Thomas, 242, 243, 289, 440
TIFFANY, John, 415
TILGHMAN, Richard, 221, 237, 286, 305
TOADVINE, Dennis, 415
TRA, Le Van, 122
TRENTHAN, Russell, 42, 43
TURNER, Richard, 414
TUTTLE, Bob, 104, 105, 106, 415
TWILLING, 'Cpl', 204, 282
TYLER, Sylvester, 414
VALLONE, Frank, 415
VANDERHOEF, Mike, 418
VAN EETEEN, Joe, 417
VANNATTA, Richard, 419
VELEZ, Edwin, 103, 237, 267, 419
VILLAREAL, Ermilo, 417
VILLEGAS, Eli, 338, 339
VINGE, Richard, 414
VINSON, Albert, 416
VIRGIL, _____, 357
WALKER, Gary, 415
WALKER, James, 413
WALKER, John, 417
WALKER, John W., 416
WALT, Lt Gen Lewis, 40
WALTERS, 'Doc' K., 242, 300, 303, 304, 305
WASHINGTON, Luther, 293, 296
WATKINS, Caesar, 99
WATKINS, Ray, 103, 252, 419, 456
WATSON, David, 58, 103, 113, 353, 354, 355, 360, 361, 362, 369, 371, 419
WATSON, Jack, 146
WATSON, Tom, 417
WEBB, James 383
WEBBER, James, 31
WEISS, Thomas, 236, 252, 415
WELCH, Danny 'Chief', 30, 285, 302, 303, 305, 357
WESCHE, Fred, 417
WEST, Larry 201, 414
WESTMORELAND, Gen William, 7
WESTOVER, Del, 109, 419
WHALEY, Carl, 384
WHEELER, Gen Earle, 7
WHISNAN, James, 414
WHITE, Jack, 414
WHYTE, Charles, 165, 175, 330, 332, 336, 337, 338, 414, 433
WILEY, James, 415
WILKIE, Arlyn, 330, 331

WILLIAMS, Dewayne 354, 414
WILLIAMS, Fredrick, 316, 317
WILLIAMS, Hank, 143
WILLIAMS, John 417
WILLIAMSON, John, 223, 358
WILSON, Al, 419
WILSON, William, 415
WINGARD, David, 31
WOOD, Foster, 418
WOODHAM, Lt Col Tullis, 4, 7, 14, 27, 51, 56, 60,
       61, 72, 73, 75, 76, 110, 113, 117, 138,
       139, 140, 171, 172, 179, 191, 192, 203,
       209, 222, 224, 231, 234, 239, 240, 241,
       249, 250, 251, 263, 264, 267, 268, 269,
       276, 278, 308, 311, 312, 316, 320, 322,
       329, 342, 345, 347, 349, 356, 363, 368,
       375, 376, 390, 391, 417, 430, 452
WOODS, Paul, 335
WURSTHORN, Tom, 418
WYANT, Alfred, 414
WYATT, Phillip, 328, 332, 334, 414
YAZZIE, Leonard, 166, 328, 332, 334, 338, 414
YOCKEY, James, 419
YORDY, Charles, 292, 296, 418, 428
YOUNG, Steve, 207, 208, 415
ZALIPSKI, John, 243, 244, 417, 441
ZUCROFF, Steven, 146, 147, 150, 414

www.ingramcontent.com/pod-product-compliance
Lightning Source LLC
Chambersburg PA
CBHW071432300426
44114CB00013B/1403